A Dictionary Of The Targumim, The Talmud Babli And Yerushalmi, And The Midrashic Literature

ed. Lag. (some ed. יְתִרְדּוּן, corr. acc.; ed. Wil. וְתִשְׁתַּהֲאוּן).—3) *to throw, pitch.* B. Kam. 98ª, a. e. אַדְּיֵיהּ אַדּוּיֵי, v. אֲדֵי.

נְדִידַיָּא* m. pl. (נְדַד) *fugitives.* Y. Sabb. IV, 7ª חרי נ׳ דאשקלון (ed. Krot. נדירי׳) is there not against thee the case of the fugitives of Ashkelon? (Koh. R. to I, 15 והלא יורדי אשקלון שקעוה וכ׳;—the case cited is unknown).

נַדְיָין m. (נָדָה) *nadyan,* a species of edible locusts, v. כַּהוֹנָא. Sifra Sh'mini, Par. 3, ch. V, expl. חגב (Lev. XI, 22); Ḥull. 65ª גדיאן, read נַדְיָאן.

נַדְיָין, נַדְ׳ m. (v. נְדֵי II) *wash-pond.* B. Bath. 19ª חנדי׳ (Ms. M. חניד׳, Ms. H. המנדיאן, ed. Pes. הנידאן, v. Rabb. D. S. a. l. note 5), contrad. to מחמצן.

נדוריא, v. נְדִידַיָּא.

נַדָּל m. (v. Syr. נדנדא, דנדלא, P. Sm. 2290, 925) *polyp, centipede.* Sifra Sh'mini, Par. 10, ch. XII, expl. מרבה רגלים (Lev. XI, 42); Ḥull. 67ᵇ.—Mikv. V, 3 מעין שהוא משוך כנ׳ a well the waters of which are conducted in channels radiating like the feet of a centipede. Erub. 8ᵇ, v. מָבוֹי.

נַדַּל ch. same. Targ. Y. Lev. XI, 42.—Y. Sabb. I, 3ᵇ bot. בר.. אתעביד נ׳ the skeleton of a fish changes into a centipede.

נָדַן (Assyr. nadanu, v. Fried. Del. Proleg. p. 139; v. נדונייא) *to give; to place;* (neut. verb) *to be given.* Y. Snh. X, 29ᵇ bot. (ref. to לא ידון, Gen. VI, 3) לא יָדוֹן... שאיני נותן רוחי וכ׳ my spirit shall not be given to him, (which means) I shall not put my spirit into them &c. (at the time of the resurrection); Bab. ib. 108ª; Gen. R. s. 26; v. next w.

נָדָן m. (b. h.; preced.) [*place where a thing is put,*] *sheath, case.* Snh. 108ª (ref. to יָדוֹן, v. preced.) שלא.. תחזרה לִנְדָנָהּ their souls shall not return to their cases (bodies); Y. ib. X, 29ᵇ bot.; Gen. R. s. 26.—*Pl.* נְדָנִים. Ib. ... איני מחזיר לִנְדָנֵיהֶן I shall not return their spirits to their cases.

נְדָנָא ch. same. Targ. Ez. XXI, 35 (ed. Lag. לדנ׳), v. לְדָנָא.

נִדְנֵד (*Pilp.* of נָדַד) 1) *to make restless, shake, weaken.* Lev. R. s. 18 (ref. to נֵד, Is. XVII, 11) נִדְנַדְתֶּם עליכם קצירן וכ׳ (or קצירין; Ar. נִדַּדְתֶּם, fr. נָדַד) (through your willing acceptance of the Law) you had made powerless over you the harvest (harvests, destructive forces) of the governments &c.; Yalk. Is. 287 נדית עלי (corr. acc.).—2) (neut. verb) *to be rocked.* Gen. R. s. 53 לא נִדְנְדָה עריסה וכ׳ never was a cradle rocked before it was rocked in the house of Abraham, i. e. never before was there such a festival at the weaning of a child.

Nithpa. נִתְנַדְנֵד *to be moved, stirred up.* Ex. R. s. 20, end נ׳ הארון Joseph's coffin (sunk in the Nile) was stirred up (and came to the surface; Tanḥ. Ekeb 6 נזדעזע; Tanḥ. B'shall. 2, a. e. צָף). Cant. R. to VI, 10 (play on כַּנִּדְגָּלוֹת, ib.) כדור שנתנדנד לגלות like the generation (of Hezekiah) that was stirred up for its exile; ib. כדור שנ׳ לגלות ולא גולה (read: שֶׁיִּתְנַדְנֵד... ולא יגלה) like the generation (of the Messiah) which shall be moved about as if to go into exile, but shall not go. Ib. מִתְנַדְנְדִים ממסע וכ׳ moving from journey to journey; a. e.

נִדְנוּד, נִד׳ m. (preced.) *moving about, exile.* Gen. R. s. 39 (expl. נֹדִד, Ps. LV, 9) נ׳ טלטול וכ׳ *n'dod* means moving about, exile after exile.—2) (sub. ראש) *head-shaking;* נ׳ עבירה an act at which people shake their heads as being wrong. Tosef. Yeb. IV, 8; Pes. 50ᵇ (Ar. נד׳ לעברה).

נדע, יִנְדַּע, מִנְדַּע, v. יְדַע.

נָדַף (b. h.; cmp. הָדַף) [*to drive, scatter,*] (neut. verb) *to spread* (of odors). Gen. R. s. 39, beg. הדיה ריחו נוֹדֵף its perfume went forth. Ber. 51ª מי שאכל שום וריחו נודף.. נודף יותר Ms. M., shall he who has eaten garlic so that his breath smells, eat again, that his breath may smell still more?, i. e. having done one wrong, shall one do another wrong?; a. fr.

נְדַף ch. same; part. נְדִיף. Targ. Cant. IV, 10. Targ. Y. Ex. XL, 5 (ed. Vien. נָדִיף).

**Ithpe.* אִינְדִּיף *it blows.* Ab. Zar. 55ª כי מִנְדִּיף בעלמא ולא אתי מיטרא Ms. M., when a wind blows in the world and no rain comes, (v. נוּף).

נָדַר (b. h.; cmp. נָדָה) [*to keep off,*] *to vow* (abstinence). Ned. V, 1 שֶׁנָּדְרוּ זה מזה who vowed not to receive benefits from one another. Ib. III, 6 הנּוֹדֵר מיורדי הים he who vows to forbid himself benefits from seafarers. Ib. VI, 1 הנודר מן המבושל who vows to abstain from whatever is cooked. Ib. 77ᵇ כל הנודר אע״פ וכ׳ whoever vows, even if he fulfills his vow, is called a sinner. Ib. I, 1 .. נ׳ בנזיר ובקרבן his is a valid vow implying nazariteship and sacrifice. Naz. IV, 4 שֶׁנָּדְרָה בנזיר who vowed to be a Nazarite; a. fr.—Imperative: הִדּוֹר. Snh. III, 2 הדור לי בחיי ראשך vow (swear) to me by anything concerning thy person (and I will accept it as a legal oath). Kidd. 41ª דור הנאה ממנו renounce all benefit from him.—Ned. III, 4 נוֹדְרִין להרגין וכ׳ (Tosef. ib. II, 2 חולין) you are not bound by a vow made to escape robbery by highway-men &c. Arakh. I, 1, a. e. נודרים may vow to dedicate the value of a certain person to the sanctuary, contrad. to עָרַךְ q. v.—*Part. pass.* נָדוּר *being under the obligation of a vow; being the legitimate subject of a vow.* Shebu. 20ª והוא שנ׳ ובא מאותו היום provided he was bound by a vow to fast on that day; Ned. 12ª והוא שנ׳ באותו היום (v. Rashi a. l.). Ib. שנ׳ ובא מאותו היום ואילך that he has vowed to fast regularly on that day (every week). Ib. 13ª דבר הנ׳ a thing which can be made forbidden by a vow (not otherwise forbidden by law). Ib. 46ª תני מודר ונ׳ הנאה וכ׳ interpret מודר as meaning, and he through his own vow is forbidden any benefit &c. Naz. 9ᵇ נ׳ ונזיר he is under the influence of a vow (of abstention from dried figs) and is also a Nazarite; a. e.

Nif. נִידַּר 1) *to be made the subject of a vow; to have one's personal value dedicated to the sanctuary.* Arakh. I, 1 נודרים וְנִידָּרִים are entitled to dedicate (v. supra) and to be dedicated. Ib. 3 לא נ׳ cannot be dedicated (has no value); a. fr.—2) *to be vowed for a sacrifice.* Meg. I, 10 כל שהוא נִידָּר, v. נָדַב; a. e.

Hif. הִדִּיר *to put a person under the influence of a vow; to prohibit, forbid.* Keth. VII, 1 הַמַּדִּיר את אשתו מליהנות לו if one vows that his wife shall derive no benefit from him. Ib. המדיר .. שלא תטעום וכ׳ if a man (by confirming her vow) subjects his wife to a restriction from tasting &c. Y. ib. 31^b ויש אדם שמדיר את אשתו מחיים (not חבירו) can a man forbid his wife that which belongs to the necessaries of life? Ib. bot. הִדִּירָהּ שלא לתשאיל וכ׳ if he, by means of a vow, forbade her to lend to her neighbors a winnow or a sieve. Ned. III, 3 הִדִּירוֹ חבירו וכ׳ if his friend urged him under a vow to dine with him. Naz. IV, 6 מַדִּיר את בנו בנזיר has power to make his (minor) son a Nazarite; a. fr.—Trnsf. *to make inaccessible.* B. Bath. 22^a בַּמַּדִּיר את כותלו, v. מְדַר.

Hof. הוּדַּר *to be forbidden by a vow; to be subjected to the influence of a vow.* Gitt. 35^b נדר שה׳ ברבים a votary prohibition imposed on a person in public; ib. 36^a; a. e. Ned. IV, 1 המּוּדָּר הנאה מחבירו he who is forbidden, by his neighbor's vow, to derive any benefit &c. Ib. 46^a היה אחד מהם מודר וכ׳ if one was forbidden &c., expl. 'forbidden through his own vow', v. supra. Ib. V, 4 המודר אסור he against whom the vow was directed is forbidden (all benefits). Ib. I, 1 מוּדְּרַנִי ממך I will be (as if) subjected to a vow of thine forbidding me any benefit at thy hands. Ib. 5^a מודר אני ממך לא משתעינא וכ׳ 'I will be *muddar* (kept distant) from thee' may mean, I will not talk to thee; a. fr.

נְדַר I ch. same. Targ. Num. XXX, 3; a. fr.—Ned. 22^a אילו הוה ידעת .. מי נְדַרְתְּ if thou hadst known …, wouldst thou have vowed? Ib.^{b} נדרת אדעתא דהכי wouldst thou have made the vow, if thou hadst known this. Ib. לא נְדְרִי I should not have vowed. Ib. 9^a לא יָדַרְנָא I will not vow; a. v. fr.

Af. אַדַּר as preced. *Hif.* Ib. 21^b דאַדַּרְתַּהּ לברתה who forbade her daughter all benefits from her. Ib. 24^a אַדְּרֵיה אדריה מזמנא וכ׳ the host urged the guest with a vow; זמינא וכ׳ the guest caused the host to invite him with a vow. Ib. 22^a מי אדרתה wouldst thou have forbidden her? Gitt. 36^a דאַדְּרֵיה ר׳ אחא whom R. A. forbade to teach. Keth. 70^b אַדַּרְתַּן thou hast put me under restrictions; a fr.

נְדַר II (transpos. of נרד, cmp. מְדַר) *to run down* (v. Peshit. Mic. I, 4).

Pa. נַדֵּר *to roll down.* Targ. O. Gen. XXIX, 3; a. e., v. גַּנְהַר I.

Af. אַנְדַּר same. Targ. I Kings XIV, 10 Var. ed. Lag., v. גַּנְהַר I.—V. מְדִרְאָ, מְדִרוֹן.

נֶדֶר m. (b. h.; נָדַר) *vow.* Kinn. I, 1, v. נְדָבָה. Ned. II, 3 יש נ׳ בתוך נ׳ there is a vow within a vow, i. e. if one repeats the vow to be a Nazarite, it is a double vow. Ib. 8^a נ׳ גדול נָדַר וכ׳ (by saying so) he has made a great vow to the God of Israel; a. v. fr.—Y. Sabb. II, 5^b bot. הותר הנ׳ the vow is annulled, i. e. the ban is rescinded.—*Pl.* נְדָרִים, constr. נִדְרֵי. Ned. I, 1, v. כִּינּוּי. Ib. III, 1 ארבע נ׳ וכ׳ four sorts of vows have the scholars declared not to be binding; נדרי זרוזין וכ׳, v. זֵירוּז, הֶבַאי &c. Ib. XI, 1, a. fr. נדרי עינוי נפש vows referring to privation of the necessaries of life; a. fr.—*N'darim*, name of a treatise, of the Order of Nashim, of Mishnah, Tosefta, Talmud Babli a. Y'rushalmi.

נְדַר III, **נִדְרָא**, נִדְ׳ ch. same. Targ. Jud. XI, 36. Targ. Num. XXX, 3; a. fr.—Ned. 8^b, v. יָאלֵי. Ib. רבינא הוה לה נ׳ וכ׳ the wife of R. had made a vow. Snh. 109^b נ׳ נְדְרִי I have vowed; a. fr.—*Pl.* נִדְרִין, נִדְ׳. Targ. Ps. LXXVI, 12. Targ. Num. XXX, 12; a. fr.

נַדָּרָא m. (preced.) *he who vowed.* Targ. O. Lev. XXVII, 8 ed. Lisb. (ed. Berl. a. oth. נִדְרָא, corr. acc.; ed. Amst. נַדְּרָא; Y. נוֹדְרָא).

נַדְּרִיוֹת, v. next w.

נוֹדְרָן, **נַדְּרָן** m. (preced. wds.) *one wont to make vows.* Yalk. Sam. 143; Midr. Sam. ch. XXVI נו׳.—*Fem.* נַדְּרָנִית. Keth. 71^a, a. e. אי אפשי באשה נ׳ I will not live with a woman in the habit of vowing; Y. ib. VII, 31^b bot. נדרית (v. אֶפְשׁ).

נדרשיר, v. נַרְהַשְׁיר.

נָה, v. נָא I.

נָהָא, v. נְהֵי.

נָהַג (b. h.) [*to drive* an animal,] *to lead, conduct; to demean one's self; to be guided by, be wont to; to apply, be practiced.* Keth. 103^b נְהוֹג, v. הָמִים. Hull. VII, 1 נוֹהֵג, v. גִּיד. Sifra Tsav, Par. 11, ch. XVIII שיִנְהוֹג הדבר לדורות which intimates that this order should be preserved at all times. Pes. IV, 1 מקום שנָהֲגוּ וכ׳ where it is a local usage to &c. Meg. 6^b כל מצות שנוֹהֲגוֹת בשני וכ׳ all laws that apply to the second (Adar) apply also to the first. Ib. 5^b, a. e. דברים … ואחרים נָהֲגוּ בהן איסור things which are permitted, but which some treat as forbidden; a. v. fr.—נ׳ כבוד, v. כָּבוֹד.—נ׳ קלות (ראש), v. קַלּוּת.—Ab. Zar. 54^b נוהג .. עולם, v. מִנְהָג.—Yalk. Num. 764 נ׳ שמנים וכ׳ he applied oils and baths.

Hif. הִנְהִיג same, esp. 1) *to drive, direct; to take possession of an animal by driving.* Kil. VIII, 2 לְהַנְהִיג, v. מָשַׁךְ. Ib. 3 הַמַּנְהִיג the driver of heterogeneous animals. B. Mets. I, 2 אחד רוכב ואחד מנהיג one rode (the animal that was found), and the other directed it (by leading). Ib. 8^b רכוב במקום מנהיג the rights of the driver as against those of the leader. Ib. במנהיג ברגליו when the rider drives by means of his heels. Ib. תרי גווני מנהיג there are two ways of driving; a. fr.—B. Bath. V, 1 ואת כל הַמַּנְהִיגִין אותה and all the implements needed for directing the ship; a. e., v. מַנְהִיג.—2) *to lead, conduct.* Ber. 35^b הַנְהֵג בהן דרך ארץ combine with the study of the Law a secular occupation; Yalk. Deut. 863 הַנְהוֹג. Snh. 92^a כל פרנס שמנהיג .. ומַנְהִיגָם וכ׳ a manager that leads a community with gentleness, will be privileged to lead it in the days to come (of resurrection); a. fr.—Tosef. Bets. II, 15 ה׳ את בני רומי וכ׳ made it a custom among the Jews in Rome &c.—ה׳ עצמו ברבנות to assume airs of superiority. Sot. 13^b; a. fr.

Hithpa. מִתְנַהֵג 1) *to conduct one's self.* Sifré Deut. 323 הִתְנַהֲגוּ זה את זה וכ׳ conduct yourselves towards one another in charity; a. fr.—2) *to be conducted.* Y. B. Kam. VI, 5^c top רוח שהעולם מִתְנַהֵג בו a wind by which the world is maintained, i. e. an ordinary wind, opp. של אונסים a calamitous wind (Bab. ib. 60[a] רוח מצויה, v. מְצָא).—3) *to move.* Gen. R. s. 68 מתנהג בה וכ׳ moves with her (Israel) from tent to tent.—V. נוּהַג.

נְהַג, נְהִיג ch. same. Targ. Lam. I, 8. Ruth IV, 7. Targ. Koh. X, 4.—Part. pass. נְהִיג; *pl.* נְהִיגִין. Targ. Y. Ex. XXXIX, 37.—Ber. 22[a]; Ḥull. 136[b] נָהוּג עלמא כהני וכ׳ the world follows in practice the opinion of these three elders &c. Gen. R. s. 83 שרי נָהֵיג ביה יקרא he began to do him honor (= h. נהג כבוד).—Part. pass. as ab. *accustomed.* Y. Pes. IV, 30[c] sq. נשייא דנְהִיגָן ... אינו מנהג (not דנהיגין) that custom of the women not to do ...., is no binding custom; ib.[d] top דנַהֲגָן. Y. R. Hash. II, 58[b] top חכין אהין נ׳ גבריכון וכ׳ is that your custom, to annoy your superiors?; a. fr.

נְהוּג, v. נִיהוּג.

נְהַוַנְדְּ pr. n. pl. *Nahăwand*, a Median town south of Ecbatana (v. Neub. Géogr. p. 377, a. Sm. Dict. Geogr. II, 495[a] s. v. Orontes). Kidd. 72[a] 'the cities of Maday' (II Kings XVIII, 12) זו נ׳ וחברותיה וכ׳ that means N. and her neighbors; ... the forts of the Moschi &c.; Yeb. 17[a] ניהר (corr. acc.). Kidd. l. c. חלזון נידתונד, v. חָלְזוֹן (v. Neub. Géogr. p. 372, sq.).—[Our art. מוֹשְׁכִי needs correction; כרך מ׳ must be sought in Media.]

נְהוּם, constr. of נַהֲמָא.

נְהוֹר, נְהוֹרָא c. (נְהַר) *light; eye-sight.* Targ. Job. XVIII, 6. Targ. Prov. IV, 18. Ib. ed. Lag. נוֹהֲרֵיה (oth. ed. נַהֲרֵ׳). Targ. Ps. XVIII, 29 (ed. Lag. נידהור). Targ. Prov. VI, 23 נוֹהָ׳; a. fr.—Pes. 2[a] (expl. Gen. I, 5) קרייה רחמנא לנ׳ וכ׳ the Lord called the light and appointed it over the service of the day. Ib. 7[b] נ׳ דאבוקה torch-light; נ׳ דשרגא candle-light; דנפיש נ׳ טובא whose light is very strong; דזוטר נ׳ טפי whose light is very small (of limited range). Ib. 8[a]; Hor. 12[a] משיך נְהוֹרֵיה, v. מְשַׁךְ I. Lam. R. to I, 1 זיתא נ׳ וכ׳ (1 חד כות׳) רבתי the olive tree (in thy dream) means light &c. Ber. 52[b] חדא נ׳ איכא בנורא fire contains only one sort of light. B. Kam. 83[b] דילמא נ׳ שקיל מיניה וכ׳ perhaps the law says (Ex. XXI, 24), he deprived him of his eye-sight, let him be deprived of his eye-sight?—Kidd. 24[b] נ׳ בריא good (normal) eye-sight, נ׳ כחישא defective sight; a. fr.—[Y. Orl. II, 62[c] top נהור אתית, v. נְהַר I.]—סגי נ׳ rich of light, euphem. for *blind.* Ber. 58[a]. Lev. R. s. 34. Y. Peah VIII, end, 21[b], v. infra; a. e.—*Pl.* נְהוֹרִין, נְהוֹרַיָּא, נְהוֹרֵי. Targ. Gen. I, 14; 16; a. fr.—Ber. l. c. טובא נ׳ איכא בנורא there is a combination of lights in fire, v. מְאוֹר. Pesik. R. s. 21 הא בריתי לך תרין נְהוֹרִים וכ׳ I created two lights for thee, thy father and thy mother; a. fr.—סגי(א) נהוריא, v. supra. Y. Peah V, end, 19[a] (ref. to Prov. XXIII, 10, quot. in Mish. ib. V, 6 עוֹלִים, Ms. M. a. Y. ed. עולם) סַגָּיָא נ׳ .. אלו שירדו מנכסיהן by 'those going up' are meant those who went down from their estates (reduced to poverty), as the blind are euphemistically called rich of light. Y. Keth. I, 25[a] bot. [read:] כאינשי דצווחין לסמייה סגיא נ׳. Y. Peah VIII, end, 21[b] חד דס׳ נ׳ one of the blind men (whom the charitable honored by inviting them to their tables).

נְהוֹרַאי, נְהוֹרַיי pr. n. m. *N'horay*, name or title of several persons. Sabb. 147[b]; Erub. 13[b] לא (ר׳) נ׳ שמו וכ׳ his name was not N., but ...., and he was named N., because he enlightened &c. Naz. IX, 5; a. fr.—[Y. Ber. III, 6[a] bot. נ׳ אחתיה וכ׳ N., sister of &c., v. יְהוּדִינַיי.]

נְהוֹרִיתָא I f. (נְהַר) *affection of the eye-sight occasioned by lightning*, prob. *Gutta Serena.* B. Mets. 78[b], expl. חבריקה, v. בְּרַק (Rashi נחורייתא, Ms. R. 2 נַהֲרִיתָא).

נְהוֹרִיתָא II pr. n. f. *N'horitha*, legendary name of one of queen Esther's maids, attending on Wednesdays (v. Gen. I, 14). Targ. Esth. II, 9.

נְהֵי I (b. h. נָהָה; cmp. נהם) *to move; to be in commotion* (cmp. Syr. אתנהי, P. Sm. 2295).

Ithpe. אִתְנְהִי *to follow eagerly.* Targ. I Sam. VII, 2. Targ. Jer. III, 17 ויִתְנְהוֹן (some ed. ויִתְהַנְהוֹן; h. text ונקוו). Ib. XXX, 21 (h. text ונגש). Targ. Hos. II, 18; ib. III, 3; a. e.—Targ. Is. LIII, 5 ובדנִיתְנְהִי וכ׳ ed. Lag. (ed. Wil. וכד צָוֵית) and when he pursues (is eager for) &c.

נְהִי II m. (b. h.; v. preced.) *commotion; lamentation, elegy.* Lam. R. to IV, 11, v. קִינָה. Y. Pes. VIII, 36[b]; Y. M. Kat. I, 80[d] top, v. קִינָה; a. e.

נְהֵי or **נְהִי** II (= נהוי; v. הֲוֵי) *let it be, granted, admitted.* Yoma 64[a] נ׳ נמי די even if I admit that. B. Kam. 76[a] נ׳ דסבר וכ׳ granted that R. S. holds &c.; a. fr.

נְהִילָא, v. נְהַל.

נְהִילַאי pl. n. m. *N'hilay.* Taan. 6[a] (Ms. M. חֲנִילַאי; v. Rabb. D. S. a. l. note).

נְהֵים, v. נְהַם.

נְהִימָה f. (נְהַם) *cooing, expression of love.* Pesik. R. s. 21 (play on מנחמכם, Is. LI, 12) [מאותה] הנ׳ שנהמתם לפני וכ׳ for the sake of that love to which you gave expression &c.; Yalk. Is. 336; Pesik. Anokhi, p. 140[a] הנהמה שנהמתם (corr. acc.; v. Bub. a. l. note).

נְהִיקָא f. (נְהַק) *braying.* Targ. Y. Gen. XXX, 16.

נְהִיר, v. נְהַר I.

נְהִירָא pr. n. m. *N'hira (Light)*, allegorical name of the Messiah. Lam. R. to I, 16 (ref. to Dan. II, 22).

נָהַל (b. h.), *Pi.* נֵיהַל *to quiet, support, lead* (v. Del. Proleg., p. 17 sq.). Num. R. s. 12 (interpret. Ex. XV, 13) נֵיהֲלָם בזכות התורה וכ׳ he supported them for the sake of the Law which they accepted, until the sanctuary was erected.

נְהַל (Syr. נהל, P. Sm. 2336; cmp. נְהֵי I) *to shake, sift* (cmp. Am. IX, 9). Bets. 29[b] דביתהו .. נַהֲלָא וכ׳ the wife of R. J. sifted flour (on the Holy Day) on the back of &c., v. מְהוּלְתָא I; a. e.—Part. pass. נְהִיל, נְהִילָא. Ḥull. 51[b]. קטמא נ׳ sifted ashes (which bake and harden when piled up). Ber. 6[a]. Taan. 9[b] (עיבא) נ׳ 'a sifted cloud', a form of light and scattered clouds.

נָהַם (b. h.; v. נָהַר I) *to be agitated; to make a noise.* Ber. 32ª אין ארי נוהם וכ׳ the lion does not get excited over a heap of straw but over a heap of flesh, i. e. plenty produces haughtiness. Yalk. Jer. 277 (play on בן הִנֹּם, Jer. XIX, 2) שקולו של תינוק נוֹהֵם וכ׳ for the voice of the child shrieked under the fire; a. fr.

Pi. נִיהֵם same, esp. *to coo* (in love, longing &c.). Ber. 3ª מְנַהֶמֶת כיונה cooing (in mourning) like a dove. Pesik. R. s. 21, a. e., v. נְהוּסָה.—Midr. Till. to Ps. CVI, 9 מְנַהֵם עליהם כנהמת ים (adapted fr. Is. V, 30) he roared over them &c.; Yalk. Ps. 864 וַיְנַהֵם.

נְהַם, נְהִים ch. same. Targ. Prov. V, 11. Targ. Is. XXXVIII, 13. Ib. 14; a. e.—Hull. 59ᵇ נהים חד קלא (not נירהם) he roared once; Yalk. Am. 541.

נַהֲמָא m. (dialect. for לחמא) *bread.* Bets. 16ª דאכלי נ׳ בנ׳ who eat bread with bread i. e. use farinaceous food to go with bread, instead of herbs &c.; (Ned. 49ᵇ לחמא בלחמא). Ber. 35ᵇ (Ms. F. לחמא); a. fr.—Constr. נְהַם. B. Kam. 97ª; Gitt. 12ª נ׳ כריסיה (Ar. נְהַם), v. פַּרְסָא.—Trnsf. (with ref. to הלחם, Gen. XXXIX, 6; v. Gen. R. s. 86, end, quot. s. v. לָשׁוֹן) *marital intercourse.* Nidd. 17ª.

נְהָמָה f. (b. h.; נָהַם) *excitement, shrieking, roaring.* Lam. R. to I, 19 נְהָמַת בניהן the shrieking of their children (passed through the fire). Midr. Till. to Ps. CVI, 9; Yalk. Ps. 864, v. נָהַם. Yalk. Prov. 959 (ref. to Prov. XX, 2) נַהֲמָתוֹ של הקב״ה the roaring (anger) of the Lord.

נַהֲמוּתָא ch. same. Targ. Ps. XXXII, 3 (h. text שאגה).

נַהֲפְכָנוּתָא f. (הֶפֶךְ) *perversity.* Targ. Prov. I, 32 (ed. Lag. מהפ׳; Ms. הפכ׳).

נָהַק (b. h.; cmp. נָהַם) *to shout,* esp. *to bray.* Cant. R. to I, 1 חמור נוֹהֵק והוא וכ׳ when the ass brayed, he (Solomon) knew what his braying meant; Koh. R. to I, 1; Yalk. Kings 175.

נְהַק ch. same, *to cry, groan* (for hunger). Targ. Job XXIV, 12 (h. text נאק). Ib. XXX, 7 (Ms. נאק).

Pa. נַהֵק *to bray.* Y. Dem. I, 21ᵈ bot. שריית מְנַהֲקָה (the ass) began to bray.

נָהַר (b. h.; v. נור) *to break forth, shine* (v. אוֹר I).

Hif. הִנְהִיר *to enlighten.* Erub. 13ᵇ; Sabb. 147ᵇ שמַנְהִיר וכ׳, he enlightened the eyes &c., v. נְהוֹרַאי.

נְהַר I ch. same, *to shine.* Targ. O. Gen. XLIV, 3 (Y. נְהַר). Targ. Job XVIII, 5; a. fr.—Taan. 10ª נְהוֹר ענני וכ׳ when the clouds are bright, their waters are little. Pesik. Ekha, p. 123ª יִנְהוֹר דינא וכ׳ let justice shine before thee like this lamp; Yalk. Is. 258 יִנְהַר דיני וכ׳ let my case shine &c.; Sabb. 116ᵇ נְהוֹר נהורך וכ׳ let thy light (wisdom) shine (prob. to be read: ינהור); a. fr.—*Part. pass.* נְהִיר; f. נְהִירָא; pl. נְהִירִין; נְהִירָן a) *bright, clear.* Lev. R. s. 19 אולפני מה נ׳ באפי how my learning shines on my face (makes me look well); Yalk. Prov. 964 נהיר באפיי (corr. acc.). Y. Sabb. VIII, beg. 11ª אפוי נהירין (נהירן) his looks were bright.—Ber. 58ᵇ נ׳ לי שבילי וכ׳ the paths of the heavens (the courses of the heavenly bodies) are as clear (well-known) to me as the streets &c.; a. fr.—b) *knowing clearly, remembering.* Y. Taan. I, 64ª bot. נ׳ את כד הוינן וכ׳ dost thou remember when we were standing &c.?; Y. Meg. III, 74ᵇ bot. Y. Keth. V, 30ª top נ׳ דהוייתון וכ׳ (insert את) dost thou remember that thou &c.? Y. Orl. II, 62ᶜ top [read:] נ׳ את דאמריתון את וכ׳ dost thou remember that you, thyself and R. J., said &c. Y. Naz. V, end, 54ᵇ נ׳ הויינן וכ׳ we remember that an old man was here &c.; Y. Ber. VIII, 11ᵇ bot. נ׳ אנן; Gen. R. s. 91 נהירין אנן (corr. acc.); Koh. R. to VII, 11. Hull. 54ª ולא נְהִירַת ליה וכ׳ dost thou not remember (recognize) that student &c.? Ib. 93ª נְהִירְנָא I remember. B. Bath. 91ᵇ; a. fr.—[R. Hash. 34ᵇ כי נהורנא לך, v. נְהַר.].

Af. אַנְהַר, *Pa.* נַהַר 1) *to give light, shine; to illumine, brighten, make shine.* Targ. O. Gen. I, 15 (Y. לְמַנְהָרָא). Targ. Num. VI, 25; a. fr.—Y. Yoma III, beg. 40ᵇ א׳ מַנְהָרָא, v. בְּרַק I; Y. R. Hash. II, beg. 57ᵈ. Y. Taan. III, 66ᵈ bot. שמענן ... והוה מְנַהֲרָה we hear that when he entered the Temple court, it used to shine; עאל ואַנְהַרַת he entered, and it shone. Cant. R. to V, 11 הוה מנהרא לי וכ׳ it (the Law) brightened my countenance by night. Sot. 6ª וא׳ לן עיינין וכ׳ and he enlightened our eyes (by evidence) from our Mishnah; a. fr.—2) *to recall to memory, remember.* Y. Peah III, 17ᵈ bot. וא׳ ר׳ אימי וכ׳ whereupon R. I. recalled (that he had heard the same tradition), and rescinded his decision. Y. Kidd. I, 61ª bot. א׳ ונפיק וכ׳ it struck him (that he had forgotten to hear his grandson's lesson), and he left the bath house &c.; a. e.—Part. pass. מְנַהַר; pl. מְנַהֲרִין. Gen. R. s. 33 אתון .. מְנַהֲרִין אנא מְנַהַר ליה you do not remember that poor man, I will remember him.

Ithpe. אִתְנְהַר 1) *to be brightened, enlightened.* Targ. Y. Gen. III, 7. Targ. Ps. XXXIV, 6.—2) *to come forth.* Cant. R. to IV, 1 טורא דאִתְנַהֲרִיתוּן וכ׳, v. פְּלַשׁ.

נָהָר m. (b. h.; v. נָהַר) *river, stream, canal.* Ex. R. s. 15 נְהַר אש, נ׳ של אש a river of fire (v. דִּינוּר). Gen. R. s. 16 עד מקום שהנ׳ מהלך וכ׳ as far as the river (Euphrates) goes, goes the border of the land of Israel. Shebi. VI, 1 מכזיב ועד הנ׳ from Kezib to the river (N'har Mitsrayim); a. fr.—*Pl.* נְהָרוֹת, נְהָרִים. Gen. R. l. c. (ref. to Gen. II, 10) והיה לארבעה נ׳ אין וכ׳ it does not say, 'and it divided into four rivers' but 'into four heads'. Ib. אוחנטין של נ׳, v. אֲיוּחַנְטִי. Bekh. 55ª כל הנ׳ למטה וכ׳ all other rivers are lower than the three (mentioned Gen. II, 11, sq.), and these three are lower than the Euphrates; a. fr.—נְהַר in pr. n. of rivers, e. g. נ׳ פקוד, v. respective determinants.

נְהַר II, **נַהֲרָא** I, **נַהֲרָה** ch. same. Targ. Jon. II, 4. Targ. Gen. II, 10; a. fr.—Gen. R. s. 16 אעבריה נ׳ בְּנֵה build (me a house) on the (western) banks of the river. Gitt. 60ᵇ קא מתקיל לְנַהֲרִין he spoils our portion of the canal. Ib. נ׳ כפשטיה ליזיל let the canal run its natural course (and those above have no right to dam it before those below have used it for irrigation). Hull. 18ᵇ (prov.) נ׳ נ׳ ופשטיה every river has its own course, i. e. each place has its own usages; ib. 57ª; a. fr.—*Pl.* נַהֲרִין, נַהֲרַיָּא. Targ. Gen. l. c. Targ. Ex. VIII, 1.—Y. Sabb. VII, 9ª top, a. e., v.

בְּרִי I; a. fr.—Fem. forms: נַהֲרְוָר, נַהֲרְוָתָא, נַ֗הֲרָן. Targ. Is. XLIII, 19. Targ. Ps. XXIV, 2; a. e.—Taan. 25ª תליסרי נ׳ וכ׳ thirteen rivers of balsam oil; a. e.—נְהַר in pr. n. of canals or places, e. g. נ׳ אבא *N'har Abba*, Sabb. 140ᵇ; v. respective determinants (v. Berl. Beitr. Geogr. p. 47).

נַהֲרָא II, pr. n. *Nahăra* (v. preced.) 1) בָּב נ׳ *Bab Nahăra* (River Gate), name of a canal or bay containing salt water. Succ. 18ª; Ab. Zar. 39ª.—2) פּוּם נ׳ *Pum Nahăra* (River Mouth), name of a town. Kidd. 72ᵇ, a. e., v. הוּמַנְיָא. Yeb. 17ª; a. fr.

נַהֲרָא III m. *brightness*, v. נְהוֹרָא.

נַהֲרְבִּיל pr. n. pl. *N'harbel*, in Babylonia (v. Neub. Géogr. p. 395). Ḥull. 87ᵇ; 136ª ר׳ אשי (יוסי) מנ׳.—Denom.

נַהַרְבְּלָאֵי m. pl. *of N'harbel.* B. Mets. 104ᵇ. Snh. 17ᵇ נ׳ מתנו וכ׳ wherever it is said, 'those (scholars) of N'harbel taught', it alludes to &c. Bets. 8ᵇ.

נְהַרְדְּעָא pr. n. pl. *N'hard'ʿa, Nehardea* (Wood-River), 1) a place in the Arabian desert. Targ. Y. Deut. II, 26.—2) a town in Babylonia, renowned as the seat of a college founded by Samuel. Ber. 58ᵇ. Snh. 17ᵇ דייני דנ׳ וכ׳ by 'the judges of N.' is meant &c.; אמוראי דנ׳ וכ׳ by 'the Amoraim of N.' is meant &c.; a. fr.—Denom.

נְהַרְדְּעִי, נְהַרְדְּעָאִי m. *of Nehardea.* Y. Pes. V, 32ª bot.—*Pl.* נְהַרְדְּעִים. Bab. ib. 62ᵇ.—Chald. נְהַרְדְּעֵי. B. Mets. 104ᵇ (Ms. M. נְהַרְדְּעָאֵי); B. Bath. 70ᵇ; a. e.

נַהֲרַת, v. נַהֲרָא.

נוּ (=נִיהוּ) *itself, it indeed.* Y. Kil. IX, end, 32ᵈ והחנן נו נשוך (=וְהַהִיא) this, indeed, is 'interlaced' (v. נָשַׁךְ). Y. Naz. III, end, 52ᵈ, v. חֲיִירָהּנוּ. Y. Yeb. X, 11ª bot. והחנן נו קל (not נוקל) is this the lighter case?

נוֹא I (b. h. נֹא) pr. n. pl. No (Thebes), in Egypt. Pesik. Vayhi, p. 63ᵇ נ׳ זה אלכסנדריא No is Alexandria; Pesik. R. s. 17 נוון אלכסנדרי (corr. acc.); v. Targ. Nahum III, 8.—V. אָמוֹן II.

נוֹא II, **נוֹאר** *beauty*, v. נוֹי.

נְוַאי pr. n. pl. *N'vay.* Tosef. Shebi. IV, 8 תחום נ׳ ed. Zuck. (Var. גיתו, נְוַיִי) the district of N. in northern Palestine; Y. Dem. II, 22ᵈ top נכי (prob. נְוַי).—Sabb. 30ª ר׳ תנחום דמן נְוַי (Ms. M. נווה) R. Tanḥum of N. (?).

נוּב (b. h.; cmp. נבע) *to spring forth, flow.*—V. נִיב.

Hif. הֵנִיב *to cause to flow, be fluent.* Lev. R. s. 16, end (ref. to Is. LVII, 19) אם הֲנִיבוּ וכ׳ if one's lips are fluent in prayer &c. (Y. Ber. V, end, 9ᵈ עשאו... תנובה).

נוֹב I m. (preced.) *growth, bud.* Targ. Hos. VIII, 7; IX, 16.

נוֹב II (b. h. נֹב) pr. n. pl. *Nob,* 1) a town in Benjamin. Snh. 95ª עֲוֹנָהּ של נ׳ the (unexpiated) sin committed at Nob (I Sam. XXII, 19). Ib. על ידך נהרג נ׳ וכ׳ on thy account were the inhabitants of Nob, the sacerdotal city, massacred; a. e.—2) a place in the district of Tyre (v. Hildesh. Beitr., p. 22, note 167). Y. Dem. II, 22ᵈ top.

נוּבְדִיקוֹס m. (Numidicus) *a Numidian ass.* Y. Kil. VIII, 31ᶜ נִיבְד׳ Ar. (some ed. ניבר׳; corr. acc.); Y. Sabb. V, beg. 7ᵇ לנדקס (corr. acc.); v. לִיבְדִּקוֹס.

נוֹבֶלֶת f. (נָבַל) *unripe fruit,* esp. *date, fruit falling off unripe.* Y. Maasr. I, 48ᵈ bot. נ׳ היא it is unripe fruit (and not yet subject to tithes).—*Pl.* נוֹבְלוֹת. Midr. Till. to Ps. XIV עתיד... להשירו כנ׳ וכ׳ the Lord will cause him (Esau-Rome) to drop like unripe fruit which drops from the tree—Esp. *nob'loth* a) *an inferior quality of dates* (which generally fall off unripe). Dem. I, 1 נ׳ התמרה. Ber. VI, 8, expl. ib. 40ᵇ בושלי כמרא (v. בּוּשְׁלָא), and תמרי דזיקא (v. זִיקָא I). Y. ib. VI, 10ᶜ top ראה נ׳ שנשרו וכ׳ when one sees *nob'loth* which fell off, one says, 'blessed be the faithful Judge'. Tosef. Dem. I, 1 הנ׳.. התמרה the unripe dates which are sold with the palm; Y. ib. I, 21ᶜ bot. Tanḥ. B'midb. 15 מה התמרה הזו עושה תמרים ועושה נ׳ as the palm bears good dates and inferior ones &c.; Num. R. s. 3, beg. תמרים רטובין ניקלווסין נ׳ (read ונ׳); a. e.—b) (trnsf.) *an inferior variety.* Gen. R. s. 17 נ׳ מיתה וכ׳ a variety of death is sleep, of prophecy, dream &c.; ib. s. 44; Yalk. ib. 23; 77; Yalk. Sam. 139. Ib. נ׳ אורה של מעלה וכ׳ a variety of the upper (divine) light is the globe of the sun, of the upper wisdom, the Law.

נוּבָר, v. נבר.

נוּגְבָא m. (נְגַב) *dryness.* Targ. Job XXX, 30. Targ. Y. Lev. XI, 37.

נוּגְדָא, v. נִגְדָּא I, II, a. נוּגְרָא.

נוֹגַהּ m. (b. h. נֹגַהּ; נָגַהּ) *splendor, light*; esp. (sub. כּוֹכָב) *the planet Venus.* Num. R. s. 21; Tanḥ. Pinḥ. 14.—Pesik. R. s. 20 כוכב חנ׳.

נוֹגַהּ, נוֹגְהָא ch. same, כוכב נ׳ *the planet Venus*; v. כּוֹכְבָא.

נוֹגְחָן, v. נַגְחָן.

נוּגְרָא m. (נְגַר) *prolongation.* Targ. Prov. III, 2; 16 ed. Lag. (oth. ed. נוּגְדָא); v. נִגְדָּא.

נוֹגֵשׂ, v. נָגַשׂ.

נוּד (b. h.; cmp. נדד) *to move, be unsteady; to escape.* Sabb. 63ᵇ נַד; v. וָלָד.

Hof. הוּנַד *to be removed.* Part. מוּנָד. Yalk. Esth. 1059 (adapted from II Sam. XXIII, 6) נטלו קוץ מ׳ משם they took a chip (of a pillar) removed from there (the palace).

נוּד ch. same, 1) *to move, be unsteady.* Targ. Is. XXIV, 19; a. e.—Part. נָד, נָאִיד, נָיֵיד; f. נָיְדָא; *pl.* נָיְדִין, נָיְדֵי, נָיְדָן. Targ. I Kings XIV, 15. Targ. I Sam. I, 13.—Erub. 46ª מיא.. מִינַד נוידי the waters in the cloud are constantly in motion. Keth. 15ª הנך נוידי these (the caravans) are unsteady, opp. קביעי stationary (v. דיר ch.). Zeb. 73ᵇ דנוידי, v. infra.—Ber. 59ᵇ והאי דנוידי עינייהו and the reason why their eyes are unsteady. Kidd. 72ª כי חזה ... חיוא רוכב דנוידא when he saw a Persian on horseback, he said, this is a restless bear. B. Bath. 25ᵇ חזה נוידא אפדניה his cottage shook; a. e.—2) (with ל־) *to shake the head, sympathize.* Targ. Job II, 11. Ib. XLII, 11 ונָדוּ.

Af. אָנֵיד 1) *to scare.* Targ. O. Lev. XXVI, 6 מָנִיד (Y. מָנִיט); a. fr.—2) *to shake,* (with רישא or ברישא) *to shake the head; to nod.* Targ. Zeph. II, 15. Targ. II Esth. I, 2. Targ. II Kings XIX, 21; a. e.—Snh. 95ª ומניד ברישיה and shook his head (in derision).

Ithpa. אִינַּדֵּד *to be chased, scattered.* Zeb. 73ᵇ ניכבשינהו דלִיתְנַיְידוּ Rashi (Ms. M. דניניידן, ed. דנוידד; corr. acc.) let us force them to scatter.

נוֹד c. (b. h. נֹאד; preced., v. Ges. Thes. s. v. נָאַד) *leather bottle, skin.* Gen. R. s. 53 (ref. to Ps. LVI, 9) כאותה בעלת נ׳ as (thou didst to) that woman carrying the water bottle (Hagar); Yalk. Ps. 774 נאד; Yalk. Gen. 94. Ḥull. 14ᵇ, v. בָּקַע. Lev. R. s. 6 משביעין האדם .... אתמול היה הנ׳ הזה וכ׳ they administer an oath to a person by the book of the Law and bring before him blown-up (empty) hides, to intimate, yesterday this hide was filled with sinews and bones and now it is empty, so will he who wantonly causes his neighbor to swear become empty &c. Mekh. B'shall., Shir, s. 6 (ref. to נֵד Ex. XV, 8) כזה נוד צרור וכ׳ as a tied-up skin stands and neither lets (air) escape nor receives any &c.; Yalk. Ex. 248 כנוד; a. e.—*Pl.* נוֹדוֹת. Lev. R. l. c. נ׳ נפוחים, v. supra. Y. Taan. IV, 69ᵇ top נ׳ נפוחות; Lam. R. to II, 2 נ׳ מנופחות blown-up bottles (having the appearance of being filled with water). Ab. Zar. II, 4; a. e.

נוֹדָא ch. same. Targ. I Sam. XIX, 13; 16 נ׳ דעיזא a cushion of kid-skin (h. text כביר העזים).

נוֹדִיִין m. pl. (perh. from their shape, v. preced.) *Nodiin,* name of a superior variety of *olives.* Y. Peah VII, 20ª זיתי נ׳ (not זית). Ib. דרכן ליבחן בנ׳ (not כנ׳) they are usually examined to see whether there are Nodiin among them.

נוֹדֵירָא, (נוֹדִי׳) v. נְדֵרָא.

נוֹדְרָן, v. נַדְרָן.

נָוָה *to be pleasing,* v. נוי.

נָוֶה I m., (=נָאֶה) *becoming, handsome.* Arakh. III, 1 הנ׳ שבישראל Ar. (ed. הנָאֶה) the handsomest in Israel, v. כָּאוּר. Naz. I, 1 אהא נ׳ Mish. (Bab. ed. נאה; Y. ed. נָאוֶה) I will be handsome (like the Nazarite).

נָוֶה II m., **נָוָה** f. (b. h.; =נאוה, v. אָוָה II) *marked-off place, circle, dwelling.* Y. Ber. IX, 13ᶜ bot. (ref. to Jer. XXV, 30) בשביל נְוֵיהוּ on account of his (destroyed) dwelling (the Temple); Midr. Till. to Ps. XVIII. Mekh. B'shall., Shir., s. 3 (ref. to ואנוהו, Ex. XV, 2) ואין נ׳ אלא וכ׳ (not נאה) *naveh* means the Temple (ref. to Ps. LXXIX, 7, a. e.). Sot. 9ª (ref. to Ps. XXXIII, 1) אל תקרי נאוה אלא נְוֵה תהלה read not *nâvah* (becoming) but *n'veh* of glory, i. e. a dwelling of glory is that of the righteous (which no human hand is permitted to destroy). Ib. 47ᵇ (ref. to Hab. II, 5) לא יִנְוֶה אפי׳ בנ׳ שלו he will not be pleasing (popular) even in his own household; B. Bath. 98ª; Yalk. Hab. 562. Keth. XIII, 9 כמוציאין מנ׳ הרעה נ׳ היפה וכ׳ a husband may compel his wife to move with him from a worse to a better house (and style of living). Ib. הנ׳ היפה בודק, v. בָּדַק. Ib. 110ᵇ לאיתויי.. לנ׳ הרע including even a change from a better to a worse household; Arakh. 3ᵇ.—Trnsf. *climate; health.* Gen. R. s. 64 [read:] מפני מה לא גזרו על הנ׳ .... שנָוָה רע why did they not forbid (as unclean) the air of Gerariké? Because its climate is bad; Y. Shebi. VI, 36ᶜ bot. מפני מה לא גזרו על הרוח .. שנְוָוָתָהּ וכ׳. Ib. והרי עזה נוויה יפה but there is Gaza whose climate is healthy. Y. B. Bath. II, 13ᶜ top נְוָאוֹ רע (prob. to be read: נְיָוְיוֹ) a tree makes the neighborhood unhealthy; v. נוי 2.

נָוֶה, נָוֶוה III pr. n. pl. *Naveh,* east of Gadara in Galilee (v. Neub. Géogr. p. 245). Lev. R. s. 23, a. e., v. חַלָּמִיש.—Ruth R. to II, 19 ר׳ שילא דנווה; Lev. R. s. 34 דנָוְתָא.—Y. Shebi. VI, 36ᶜ bot. חוטא דנ׳ the line passing N. [prob. Neveh in Peraea].

נוֹהַג m. (נָהַג) *custom;* כנ׳ שבעולם according to the custom of the world, *ordinarily, naturally.* Y. Ber. I, 2ᵈ top, v. אֲנַנְקֵי. Gen. R. s. 70, end; a. fr.

נוֹהֲרָא, v. נְהוֹר.

נָוֶוה, נָוְוה, v. נָוֶה, נָוָה.

נַוְוטָא m. (nauta, ναύτης) *seaman, sailor.*—*Pl.* נַוְוטִים, נַוְוטִין. Gen. R. s. 12 ואח״כ הוא מעמיד עליה נ׳ and finally (when the ship is finished) he places sailors upon her; ונוטיהם ונַוְוטֵיהֶם כתיב *v'noṭehem* (Is. XLII, 5) allows the reading *v'navṭehem* (and their (the heavens') sailors); Yalk. Is. 314 חכוטי׳ (corr. acc.).—Chald. *pl.* נַוְוטַיָּא. Koh. R. to III, 6.

נַוְוטִי m. (v. נַבְטָיָא) *Nabatean.* Gen. R. s. 48; Yalk. ib. 82.—V. נְיוֹתִי.

נָוֶול m. (next w.) *contemptibility, degeneracy.* Tanḥ. Vayesheb 1 להודיע נְוולָם (נִוּולָן) to make their meanness known.—*Pl.* נִוּוּלִים. Ib. להודיע לבריות עקריהן ונִוּולֵיהֶם to let people know their origins and their degeneration.

נָוַל, נָוֵול (cmp. נָבֵל) *to be disfigured, look repulsive; to degenerate.* Tosef. Sot. XIV, 7 אזלה ונָוְלָה (Var. ונִבְלָה) becomes more and more corrupt.

Pi. נִוֵּל *to disfigure; to disgrace.* B. Bath. 154ª אי.. לנַוְּולוֹ you are not permitted to disgrace him (to search a corpse for tokens of maturity). Sot. I, 6 מעבירים ממנה כדי לנַוְּולָהּ we divest her (of all jewelry) in order to disgrace her. Ned. 66ª בנות ישראל.. שהעניות מְנַוַּולְתָּן Israel's daughters are handsome, it is only poverty that makes them appear homely. Sifré Deut. 240 (ref. to נבלה, Deut. XXII, 21) לא עצמה בלבד נִוְּולָה וכ׳ she has disgraced not only herself but all virgins of Israel; a. e.—Part. pass. מְנוּוָּל; f. מְנוּוֶּלֶת; *pl.* מְנוּוָּלִין, מְנוּוָּלוֹת. Y. Pes. VI, 33ª, sq. זבח מ׳ (not מזבח) a repulsive (putrid) sacrifice (Sabb. 116ᵇ מוטלין כנבלה).

Naz. IV, 5, a. e., v. אֲמַשׁ. Tosef. Sot. II, 8 הרי היא בדוקה ומנ׳ she (by refusing to drink the searching waters) is already searched and disgraced, i. e. has admitted her guilt. Y. M. Kat. III, beg. 81^c. שלא.. מנ׳ that they may not enter the Sabbath with neglected hair; a. e.—Kidd. 80^b אם פגע בך מנ׳ זה וכ׳ if that ugly one (the tempter) meets thee, drag him to the house of learning, i. e. overcome evil inclinations by study.

נְוַל, נְוָול I ch. same. Sot. 47^b ומלכותא אזלא וְנָוְלָא, v. preced.

Pa. נַוֵּל as preced. *Pi.* Ib. 8^b הואיל וניוולה מְנַוְולֵי לה וכ׳ since the law requires her disgrace (by stripping her upper body), can there be any question as to these (jewels)? Ḥull. 11^b נִינַוְּולֵיה we may dishonor his body (by a post-mortem examination); a. e.

Ithpa. אִיתְנַוֵּל *to be disfigured, disgraced.* Ib. הא קא מִיתְנַוֵּול he would be disgraced (by autopsy, v. supra). B. Bath. 8^b האי קא מינוול וכ׳ the one (put to death by the sword) is disfigured &c. Ib. 154^b לִיתְנַוֵּל ולינוול let him be disgraced (by autopsy, v. supra); a. e.—V. מְנַוְּולְתָּא.

נְוַל, נְוָול II (denom. of next w.) *to weave.* Snh. 95^a דהות נָוְולָא (Ms. M. קא טויא; early ed. קא נוזלא; Ms. F. קא עזלא, v. Rabb. D. S. a. l. note) was weaving. Gitt. 34^a יתבא וְנָוְולָה she was sitting and weaving.

נַוְולָא, נְוַל III, נְוָול I m. (v. נְבֶל ch. 2) *loom,* also *the web on the loom.* Targ. Is. XXXVIII, 12 מנול גרדאין Var. ed. Lag. (read: כְּמִנְּוָול; ed. נחל, corr. acc.; oth. ed. כְּנְוַל) as from the loom (as the web) of the weavers.—Y. B. Bath. II, 13^b bot. מיתן חד נוול וכ׳ to place one loom in the space between two neighboring walls. Bab. ib. 13^b ידעא פילכא ונ׳ (v. Rabb. D. S. a. l. note 8) understands the spindle and the loom (spinning and weaving).—*Pl.* נַוְלַיָּה. Y. l. c. (ed. Krot. דנו ליה, corr. acc.), v. מַסְמְרָא.

נַוְולָא II pr. n. f. *Navla.* B. Mets. 67^a את ונ׳ אחי (Rashi וְנַוְולָה) thou and N. are relatives (and she will surely restore the field to thee whenever thou art able to redeem it). Ib. כל את ונ׳ אחי סמכא דעתיה וכ׳ Ms. M. (v. Rabb. D. S. a. l. note 80) in every case when such an expression as 'thou and N. are relatives' is used, the seller relies on it &c. [Oth. opin. נ׳, a colloquial expression for 'a certain person', as our 'N. N.', both male and female; v. Koh. Ar. Compl. I, p. XXI].

נַוְולָה f. h. (a Chaldaism)=נַוְולָא I. Meïl. 18^a שבן עומד לנ׳ for it (a small piece of cloth) may be used to tie around the weaver's frame (Rashi: to tie around the weaver's finger when he puts up the frame; Var. לטולא, v. טוּלָא).

נוון, Pesik. R. s. 17, v. נוֹא I.

נוונא, Gitt. 69^b bot. צימרא נ׳ some ed., read: גוונא, v. צִימְרָא.

נַוְנָא, נִוְנֶת, v. נוני.

***נַוְסִין** m. pl. (ναῦς) *ships, ship-building.* Gen. R. s. 16 Ar., ed. בנימוסין, v. נִימוֹס II.

נוורתוק, v. נַרְתֵּיק.

נְוְותִּי, v. נַיְותִּי.

נוז (cmp. לוז) *to twist, twine; to weave.* Part. pass. נוז. Kil. IX, 8 (expl. שעטנז) דבר שהוא שוע טווי ונוז a substance (of wool and linen) which is hackled and fulled, or spun, or twined (R. S. *woven*); Sifré Deut. 232; Yeb. 5^b; a. e.—Nidd. 61^b עד שיהא שוע טווי ונ׳ until it is fulled *and* spun *and* twisted (or woven).—Y. Kil. IX, end, 32^d הוון אמרינן הא לָנוּז מותר we might have thought, but to twist (wool and linen) is permitted.

נוז ch. same; part. pass. נְיז. Targ. Y. Deut. XXII, 11 (ed. Vien. גיז, corr, acc.).

נוזלא, Snh. 95^a early ed., v. נְוַל II.

נוּזְלַיָּא, נוּזְלִים, v. נָזַל, נְזַל.

נוּחַ (b. h.) *to rest, lie; to be at ease, rest satisfied.*—Sabb. 7^b זרק.. והלכה וְנָחָה וכ׳ if one threw an object higher than ten handbreadths, and in its course it came to rest in a little hole. Ib. וזרק ונָח על גביו and he threw an object and it came to rest on it. Gen. R. s. 25 כיון שעמד נֹחַ נָחוּ when Noah rose, they rested (submitted to man's rulership; Yalk. Chr. 1072 נִיתְנוּחוּ; Yalk. Gen. 42 נִחֲמָן he appeased them); ib. וכיון שעמד נֹחַ נחו and when Noah rose, they remained undisturbed in their graves; Yalk. Chr. l. c. נִינוחו.—Meg. 25^b, a. fr. יָנוּחוּ לו ברכות וכ׳ blessings rest upon his head. Sabb. 152^b, a. e. תָּנוּחַ.. שהנחת וכ׳ let thy mind be at rest, for thou hast set my mind at rest; a. fr.—Part. נָח, נוֹחַ, f. נוֹחָה; *pl.* נוֹחִים, נוֹחִין; נוֹחוֹת a) *resting.* Gen. R. s. 11 אתם נוחין you rest. Y. Erub. III, end, 21^c, a. fr. נוחי נפש whose souls are at rest; a. fr.—b) *pleased.* Ab. III, 10 כל שרוח הבריות נ׳ הימנו וכ׳ in whom the mind of man finds pleasure, the mind of God finds pleasure. Shebi. X, 9; a. fr.—V. נוֹחַ.

Hif. הֵנִיחַ, הִנִּיחַ (fr. יָנַח) 1) *to set at rest; to set down, place.* Gen. R. l. c. (ref. to Gen. V, 29) או נח זה יְנִיחֵנוּ וכ׳ either let him be called Noaḥ, then it ought to read, 'he shall set us at rest', or Naḥman &c. Sabb. l. c. שהִנַּחְתָּ, v. supra; (Snh. 30^b שהתמתה, v. תָּנַח; v. Rabb. D. S. a. l. note 20). Ḥull. 91^b עלי יַנִּיחַ צדיק וכ׳ let this righteous man rest his head on me.—B. Kam. III, 1. B. Mets. VI, 6 הַנַּח לפני put it down before me (I will take charge of it). Sabb. 21^b לְהַנִּיחָהּ על פתחו וכ׳ to place it over the entrance &c.; a. fr.—2) *to leave; to leave alone; to allow.* B. Bath. IX, 1 מי שמת והנ׳ בנים וכ׳ if a person died and left sons and daughters. Ib. 3 ראו מה שהנ׳ לנו וכ׳ see what our father left us. Snh. 30^a מעות שהנ׳ לו אביו money which his father had left him (without telling him where it was deposited). Pesik. R. s. 26; Yalk. Ps. 884 אבינו ירמיה הדין אתה מַנִּיחֵנוּ שם J., our father, wilt thou leave us there (in Babylonia, without a prophet)?—Bets. 30^a, a. fr. הַנַּח להם לישראל leave Israel alone (let them do as they please). Yoma I, 4 לא היו מַנִּיחִים אותו וכ׳ they did not let him eat much. Ab. Zar. 10^b יַנִּיחֶנָּה, v. נוֹמִי. Ib. 17^a לא הנ׳ זונה וכ׳ he did not forego a single prostitute &c. Ex. R. s. 30 לא הנ׳ שלא היה מצעיר he allowed no opportunity to pass without tormenting him; a. v. fr.—3) *to relieve, remit.* Ab.Zar. 13[a] יום שע״א מֵנִיחַ בו וכ׳ a day on which the idol grants a remission of duties. Ib. כל מי ... וְיַנִּיחַ .. יָנִיחַ וכ׳ to him who will take a wreath and place it on his head (in honor of the deity), he will allow a remission &c.; a. fr.—4) *to wish rest* (to a deceased); *to bless the memory of.* Yalk. Ex. 411 מזכירין ומניחין there are those who are mentioned and blessed (opp. משחקין); Ex. R. s. 48 מדכרין ומניחין; (Tanḥ. Vayakh. 4 מזכירין ומשבחים;) [Midr. Sam. ch. I מדכרין ומניחין we mention and *let alone*, neither praising nor blaming by mentioning the ancestry].—5) *to give pleasure.* Gen. R. s. 16 לְהַנִיחוֹ וכ׳ to give him pleasure, to protect him &c.

Hof. הוּנַח *to be put down, rested.* Sabb. 4[a], a. fr. קלוטה כמי שהוּנְחָה דמיא an object intercepted in the air (crossing an area, v. רְשׁוּת) is considered as having rested there, v. הֲנָחָה. B. Mets. III, 4, a. e. יהא מוּנָח וכ׳, v. אֵלִיָּהוּ. Yoma 72[b] עדיין מונח הוא וכ׳ still lies (undisposed of), whosoever desires to obtain it &c. Kidd. 66[a] הרי כרוכה ומוּנַחַת וכ׳ it (the Law) is wrapped up and lies in the corner, whosoever wishes to study &c.; a. fr.

Nif. נִינּוֹחַ *to be released; to be rested.* Cant. R. to VII, 5 והגליות באות ונִינּוֹחוֹת וכ׳ and the exiles will come and rest under it; (Yalk. Is. 334 ונוחות; Yalk. Zech. 575 ונְחוֹת). Y. Ber. V, end, 9[d] בטוח אני שב׳ בנו וכ׳ I am confident that the son of ... will recover from his illness. Gen. R. s. 13 נִינּוֹחוּ they are relieved (out of danger). Yalk. Chr. 1072, v. supra; a. e.

נוּחַ ch. same. Targ. Gen. II, 2 וּנָח. Targ. II Sam. XXI, 10 לְמִנַח; a. fr.—Part. נָיַח, נָיְחָ. Targ. Y. Num. XXIII, 24. Targ. Job III, 25 נְיָיחִית (Ms. נְחִית); a. fr.—B. Mets. 86[a] נָח זעפא the storm subsided. Ib. כי הוה נָיְחָא נפשיה when his soul was at rest (when he was dead). Ib. תֵּינַח נפשיה וכ׳ let me rather die, than be delivered &c. Ib. ההוא יומא דנח נפשיה on the day when he died. Keth. 104[a], a. fr. נח נפשיה ד׳—is dead. Yoma 20[b] נְיַנַח מר leave it alone, sir (be no longer my interpreter). Sabb. 3[a] bot. גופו מִינַח נָיֵיח Ms. M. (v. Rabb. D. S. a. l. note) his body had been resting (and he lifted it from the ground in moving). Ib. 5[b] מים מי עבידי דנָיְיחִי is it possible that water (running down an incline) is at rest at any time?; a. v. fr.

Af. אַנַּח, אַנִּיחַ, אָנִיחַ 1) *to give rest, to assuage.* Targ. O. Deut. III, 20 דִּיְנִיחַ (ed. Vien. דִּי יְנִיחַ); Y. דִּיְנִיחַ. Targ. Ezek. XXIV, 13; a. fr.—Targ. II Chr. XV, 15; XX, 30 אַנְיָיח (ed. Lag. אניח; fr. נְיָיח, v. supra).—Ber. 28[b] לְאַנּוּחֵי דעתיה וכ׳ to quiet the mind of &c.—[Lev. R. s. 32, a. e. מדכרין ומניחין, v. preced.]—2) *to rest, put down; to leave alone.* Targ. Ex. XXXII, 10 אַנַּח (O. ed. Vien. הַנַּח; ed. Berl. אַ׳). Targ. Jud. VI, 18; a. fr.—Sabb. 6[a] כי מַנַּח ליה when he sets it down. Keth. 47[b] אַנּוּחֵי נַנְחִינְהוּ he must let them lie (store them); a. fr.—Part. pass. מַנַּח; f. מַנְּחָא; *pl.* מַנְּחֵי. Hull. 46[a] bot. דמ׳ בית וכ׳, v. נְוָקָא. Keth. 84[b] דמנחי היכא where were they placed (at the time of death)?; a. fr.

Ithpa. אִתְנַיַּיח *to be relieved, recover.* Targ. Y. Lev. XXVI, 35.

Ithpe. אִתְנַח 1) *to be laid down, placed.* B. Bath. 14[b] דמִיתְנַח ליה וכ׳ (Rashi דמַנַּח, v. supra) it was placed by the side; a. e.—2) (v. נִיחָא) *to be satisfactory.* Kidd. 45[b] אִיתְנוּחֵי אִיתְנָחָא ליה it was agreeable to him. B. Bath. 129[a] אִיתְנָחַת לן חדא Ms. R. (v. Rabb. D. S. a. l. note 60; ed. אנחתת, v. נְחַת) one of thy arguments has been satisfactorily disposed of for us.—Contr. תֵּינַח.—אִינַח, תֵּיתְנַח (a dialectical term) *this might be right, acceptable, might do well.* Sabb. 5[a] תינ׳ ברשות היחיד וכ׳ this might be acceptable with regard to a covered private ground, but &c. Ib. 132[b] ת׳ גדול וכ׳ this may apply to an adult, but &c.; a. fr.

נוֹחַ m. (b. h.; preced.) *rest; satisfaction.* Tosef. Sot. XIV, 10 ואין נ׳ בעולם לישראל and there is no rest in the world for Israel; Sot. 47[b] אין נ׳ בעולם there is no satisfaction (to the Lord) in the world.

נוֹחַ II m., נוֹחָה f. (preced. wds.) 1) *pleasing, kind.* Ab. III, 12 הוי קל לראש ונ׳ לתשחורת be quick (to serve) to thy superior, and kind to youth; Y. Taan. II, 65[b] bot. ונ׳ תשח׳ (corr. acc.).—2) *easy.* Gen. R. s. 17 מפני מה האיש נ׳ להתפתות וכ׳ why is man easily pacified, and woman not? Ab. V, 11 נ׳ לכעוס ונ׳ וכ׳ easily angered and easily reconciled, opp. קשה. Yalk. Deut. 845 נֹחַ לקנות שונא וכ׳ it is easy to acquire an enemy, but hard to acquire a friend; נח לעלות לבימה וכ׳ it is easy to be brought up to the platform of the court, but hard to come down (be acquitted); a. fr.—*Pl.* נוֹחִים, נוֹחוֹת, נוח׳. Gen. R. s. 90 ונוח׳; Yalk. ib. 148 ונוח׳, v. יָפֶה.—3) נ׳ לו *it is good* (*better*) *for.* Erub. 13[b] נ׳ לו לאדם שלא נברא יותר וכ׳ it would have been better for man not to have been born at all than &c. Sabb. 56[b] נ׳ לו לאותו ... ואל וכ׳ it would have been better for that pious man, had he been a slave in an idolatrous temple, only that it might not be written about him &c.; a. fr.

נוֹחַ III pr. n. m., v. נֹחַ.

נוֹחֵשׁ, pl. נוֹחֲשִׁים, v. נָחַשׁ.

נוּט ch. (b. h.; cmp. מוט a. נוד) *to shake.*
Af. אָנֵיט *to scare.* Targ. Y. Lev. XXVI, 6, v. נוד ch.

נוטומי, Y. Maas. Sh. II, 53[c] א״ר יונה והן נוטי נ׳, a corruption, prob. a corrupt tautography of א״ר יונה והוא שליקט מיכן ומוכן ib.

נוטי, v. preced.

נוטירין, v. next w.

נוֹטָרִין m. pl. 1) (notaria) *indictments.* Ex. R. s. 31 כיון שקרא נ׳ שלו וכ׳ and when he read the indictments against him, he said, And he lives yet?—2) (notarius, -ii) *clerks.* Sot. 35[b] שיגרו נ׳ שלהם וכ׳ (not נוטירין) they sent their clerks who peeled off the lime and copied the inscription; Y. ib. VIII, 21[d] משלחין נוֹטָרַיָּהן, Tosef. ib. VIII, 6 ושלחו נוטירין ed. Zuck. (Var. נטורין, corr. acc.).—[Sifré Num. 157 נוטרים, v. נָטַר].

נוֹטָרִיקוֹן m. (νοταρικόν, sub. μεθόδιον, S.) *stenographer's method, abbreviation.* Sabb. XII, 5 כתב אות אחת נ׳ if one wrote (on the Sabbath) one letter as an abbreviation (e. g. ק׳ for קרבן). Ib. 105ª לשון נ׳ the acrostic method of speech (ref. to אַב הֲמוֹן, Gen. XVII, 5, בחור, אב, חביב, מלך, ותיק, נאמן). Ib. אנכי נ׳, v. אָנֹכִי; a. fr.—Trnsf. לשון נ׳ by a mere hint. Deut. R. s. 2, v. קידוש.

נָוָה, נוי I (b. h.) *to be becoming, pleasing.* Sot. 47ᵇ, a. e. נָוֶה, יִנְוֶה, v. נָוֶה II.

Hif. הִנְוָה 1) *to beautify, adorn.* Y. Peah I, 15ᵇ (ref. to Ex. XV, 2) וכי ... לְנַוּוֹת את בוראו is it possible for man to beautify his Maker? Mekh. B'shall., Shir., s. 3 לְהַנְווֹת קונו; (Yalk. Ex. 244 לחשוות לקונו, v. infra).—2) *to equal, adapt one's self to.* Sabb. 133ᵇ (expl. ואנוהו, Ex. l. c.) הוי דומה לו be like Him; Mekh. l. c. נדמה לו let us be like Him. Yalk. l. c. וכי .. לחשוות לקונו is it possible for man to equal his Creator?

Nif. הִנָּוָה *to adorn one's self.* Mekh. l. c. אֶנָּוֶה לפניו, v. נָאָה.

Nithpa. נִתְנַוָּה *to make one's self handsome, to be vain.* Sot. I, 8 אבשלום נ׳ בשערו Y. ed. (Mish. a. Bab. ed. 9ᵇ נתגאה) Absalom was vain of his hair.

Pi. נַיֵּיה *to beautify.* Mekh. l. c. (ref. to ואנוהו, v. supra) נַיֵּיהוּ וְשַׁבְּחוּ לְהקב״ה וכ׳ beautify Him, and praise the Lord before all nations (Yalk. l. c. אגיד נאותיו וְשִׁבְחוֹ וכ׳, v. נָאָה).

נָוָה, נוי II, *Hithpa.* הִתְנַוָּה *to fall away,* v. נָיָה.

נוֹי, נוֹא m. (נָוָה, נָאָה) 1) *beauty, ornament.* Kel. XIV, 2 כשאן לנוי (ed. Dehr. לנואי) he attached them for ornamentation. Yeb. 39ᵇ הכונס את יבמתו .. לשם נ׳ he who married his deceased brother's wife (v. יְבָמָה) for her beauty (not with the intention of perpetuating his brother's name). Y. Maasr. III, end, 51ª לנויה של חצר to embellish the court. Zeb. 54ᵇ (play on בנוית, I Sam. XIX, 18) עוסקין בנויו של וכ׳ engaged in the embellishment of the world (consulting about building the Temple). Koh. R. to II, 12 והוא נ׳ או and this (the nose) is man's beauty; Gen. R. s. 12 נאה (corr. acc.). Pesik. R. s. 31 בעלת נ׳ a handsome woman; a. fr.—*Pl.* נוֹיוֹת. Yalk. Cant. 988 בנוֹיוֹתָיו (not בנויותיו), v. נָאָה.—2) נוֹי or נְוִיר (=נָוָה II) *dwelling, climate.* B. Bath. 24ᵇ משום נויי העיר because of the health of the town (which suffers from trees; Rashi: because of *the beauty* of the town which requires an open space all around); Y. ib. II, 13ᶜ top שנויא רע; Y. Shebi. VI, 36ᶜ bot. נְוִיָּיתָהּ, v. נָוֶה II.

נְוַי, pr. n. pl., v. נְוַאר.

נְוָיָה, v. נְבָיָיה.

נוּךְ m. (נָכָה) *diminution, lesser portion.* Sifra M'tsor'a, Neg., Par. 3, ch. III (expl. תְּנוּךְ, Lev. XIV, 14) תוך נ׳ וכ׳ inside of the lesser helix, which is the anti-helix, v. אֲוִירָא.

נוּכְזְרִיא, v. נִכְזְרָיָא.

נוּכְרָא, נוּכְרָאָה, נוּכְרָי, נוּכְרָיָא m. ch. = h. נָכְרִי, *strange; stranger; gentile.* Targ. Prov. VI, 1. Targ. O. Deut. XVII, 15; a. fr.—[Targ. Prov. XI, 17; XVII, 11 נוכריא some ed., v. נִכְזְרָיָא.]—Sabb. 65ᵇ גופא נוכראה another person's body, v. גּוּפָא.—*Pl.* נוּכְרָאִין. Targ. Lam. V, 2; a. e.—*Fem.* נוּכְרָאָה, נוּכְרִיָּא, נוּכְרֵיתָא. Targ. Ex. II, 22. Targ. Job XIX, 17; a. e.—Esp. נוּכְרֵיתָא *a gentile woman.* Targ. Prov. V, 20; a. fr.—[Ib. XXVII, 4 נוכריתא Ms. *abomination* (Pesh. מְרַחַקְתָּא), ed. נִכְזְרִיּוּתָא.]—*Pl.* נוּכְרָיָיתָא, נוּכְרָאָן. Targ. Gen. XXXI, 15 (not נוּכְרִיתָא).

נוּכְרֵיתָא, v. preced.

נוּכְתָּא f. (נְכַת)=h. נֶשֶׁךְ, *usury.* Targ. Prov. XXVIII, 8.

נָוֶל, נוֹל, נוֹלָא &c., v. sub נוי.

נוֹלַד, v. יָלַד.

נְוָלוּ, נְוָלִי f. (נְוַל) I) *offensiveness; dunghill, cesspool.* Ezra VI, 11. Dan. II, 5.

נוּם I (denom. of נְאוּם, נָאַם, as נָאַם, Jer. XXIII, 31) *to speak, say.* Cant. R. to I, 1 שָׁנַם, v. לְמוּאֵל. Tosef. Ohol. IV, 14 נם לי הן said he to me, Yes. Ib. נַמְתִּי said I; a. fr.—Part. נוֹמָה (fr. נוֹמָה), fr. which (as in Chald.) נוֹמֵינוּ, נוֹמֵיתִי &c. Yeb. XVI, 7 (122ª) ונומיתי לו (Y. ed. וְנִיַּמְתִּי, *Pi.*) and I said to him. Ib. נוֹמֵיה Bab. ed. (Y. ed. נוֹמַת; Mish. אמרה) said she. Gitt. VI, 7 נומינו לשליח (Ar. נַמְינוּ) we said to the messenger; a. e.—Y. Yeb. XII, 12ᶜ top תומה לי (ed. Krot. וְנוֹמָה); Y. Naz. II, end, 51ᶜ נִימָא (fr. נמא); Tosef. ib. IV, 7 נם; Sifré Num. 22 נָאַם, נָאַמְתִּי.—Treat. Der. Er. ch. II הַמְנַמְּיִן והמספקין בידיהם who make motions with their hands when speaking.—[Tosef. Ohol. V, 12 נמיתי ed. Zuck., oth. ed. נמתי, read: נעניתי, v. עָנָה II.]

נוּם II (b. h.) *to slumber.*

Hithpalp. הִתְנַמְנֵם, *Nithpalp.* נִתְנַמְנֵם *to be drowsy; to nap.* Meg. II, 2 וּמִתְנַמְנֵם or (he read the Book of Esther) while he was half asleep. Pes. X, 8 נִתְנַמְנְמוּ if they napped (at the table), opp. נרדמו. Ib. 120ᵇ; Meg. 18ᵇ היכי דמי נתנמנם what condition is meant by *nithnamnem*?, v. נִים. Yoma I, 7 בקש לְהִתְנַמְנֵם if he showed a disposition to fall asleep; a. fr.—Koh. R. to V, 11 (in Chald. dict.) נתנ׳ עבדא ודמך ליה the slave was overcome with drowsiness and fell asleep.

נוּם ch. same. Targ. Is. V, 27; a. e.—Part. נָאֵים, נָיֵים, נָיֵם. Targ. Ps. CXXI, 3, sq. ינום Ms. (ed. נָיֵם, נאים).—Erub. 65ª לא בעי מר מינם פורתא would you not take a little nap? Ib. השתא ... וניניים זוטא soon will come the days which are long and yet short (of deeds), when we shall have a long sleep. Pes. 120ᵇ מר מינם קא נאים were you asleep?, v. infra. Yeb. 24ᵇ, a. fr. כי ניים ושכיב וכ׳ Rab must have said so when he was sleepy and going to bed; B. Kam. 47ᵇ; 65ª (Ms. M. גאני, v. גְּנֵי). Snh. 7ª חיא נָיְימָא, v. הִיקְלָא.

Palp. נַמְנֵם *to be drowsy; to doze.* Pes. l. c. אין נַמְנוּמֵי Ms. O. (ed. incorr., v. Rabb. D. S. a. l. note 90) מְנַמְנְמִי קא no, I was dozing. Kidd. 17ᵇ, v. הִינוּמָא.—Esp. *to be in a comatose condition, be dying.* M. Kat. 28ª דהוה קא מְנַמְנֵם that he was dying. Kidd. 72ª bot. כי הוה קא מנ׳ רבי Ar. (ed. נייחא נפשיה) when Rabbi was dying.

Ithpalp. אִיתְנַמְנֵם, אִינְ׳ *to be drowsy.* Targ. Ps. LXXVI, 6. —Y. Yeb. I, 3ª bot. שריין מִתְנַמְנְמִין they began to be drowsy. Y. Meg. II, 73ª bot.; a. fr.

נוֹמָא, v. נוֹמִי.

נוֹמֶה, v. נוּם I.

נוֹמוֹרוֹן, v. נוּמִירוֹן.

נוֹמוֹס m. (νόμος) *law, custom*. Y. R. Hash. I, 57^{a} bot., v. אַגְרָפוֹס. Lev. R. s. 7, end נ׳ הוּא וקילוסין הוא Ar. ed. Koh. (ed. נימוס קלוסים; corr. acc.) it is a law and a command.—Mostly נִימוֹס.

נוֹמִי f. (νομή, nome, *pl.* nomae) *corroding sore, ulcer*. Ab. Zar. 10^{b} מי שעלתה לו נ׳ וכ׳ Ar. ed. Koh. (ed. שעלה .. נימא, corr. acc.) if one has an ulcer on his foot, shall he have it cut and live, or let it go and die?—Gen. R. s. 46 עלתה נ׳ בבשרם וכ׳ (some ed. נמי) they have an ulcerating sore ..., and the physicians advice circumcision. Ib. (play on ונמלתם, Gen. XVII, 11) כנומי היא תלויה בגוף it (the prepuce) is like an eating sore hanging from the body. Sifré Deut. 45 ואם .. הרי אתה מעלה נימי (corr. acc.) but if thou removest it (the plaster), thou wilt cause ulceration; Kidd. 30^{b}; a. e.

נוּמִירוֹן, v. next w.

נוּמִירוֹן, נוּמִירָן f. (numerus, νούμερος, -ον, S.) *a division of troops*. Mekh. B'shall., s. 1 שאין נ׳ אחת בטילה (not ואין) not one division (of the Roman empire) is unemployed; Yalk. Ex. 230 נומרון, נמירון (corr. acc.).

נוּמִיתָא, v. נוּמְתָא.

נוֹמָס, v. נוֹמוֹס.

נוּמְתָא f. (נוּם II) *slumber*. Targ. Prov. VI, 10 (some ed. נוּמִיתָא).

נו״ן the letter *Nun*. Ned. 54^{b}, v. next w. Sabb. 104^{a}; a. e.—Pl. נוּנִין. Ib. 103^{b}.

נוּן, נוּנָא m. (contr. of נענע, v. letter נ; cmp. זִיז = זיזו) *fish*. Targ. Jon. II, 1; a. e.—Targ. Lev. XI, 17; Deut. XIV, 17 שלי נונא, v. שְׁלֵינוּנָא.—Ned. 54^{b} נו״ן סמ״ך עי״ן נ׳ סמא לעינים the succession of the letters *Nun, Samekh, 'Ayin* serves as an intimation, 'fish is a remedy for the eyes'. Gen. R. s. 11; a. fr.—Ab. Zar. 39^{a} שפר נ׳ (καλλίχθος) *sh'far nuna*, name of a fish of the genus *anthias*; קדש נ׳ (ἱερὸς ἰχθύς) *K'dash nuna*, a name for *anthias*, called by some קבר נ׳ (Ar. קברנונא, in one w.) *K'bar nuna* (Grave-fish); [for corr. vers., v. Rabb. D. S. a. l. note 70, a. Tosaf. a. l.]. Ib. לשפרנונא (Ms. M. in two words).—*Pl.* נוּנִין, נוּנַיָּא, נוּנַיָּיתָה, נוּנֵי Targ. Deut. IV, 18; a. fr.—Y. Naz. IX, 57^{d}, v. צְלִי I.—Y. Ned. IV, beg. 39^{c}, v. חַל; a. fr.

נוּנֵי, נִינֵּה (=נענע=נונו, v. preced.; cmp. צִיצֵּר, s. v. צִיַּיץ) *to be tender, delicate*.

Hithpalp. הִתְנַיְנֵה, *Nithpa.* נִתְנַיְּנֵה *to become delicate, be failing, to fall away*. B. Kam. 91^{a} אמדוהו והיה מִתְנַוְנֵה והולך (Ms. M. מִתְנַוְונֶה; ed. Sonc. מִתְנַוֶּה) if the experts declared his injuries as curable (and the court assessed the damages accordingly), but he continues to be falling away. Hull. 57^{b} מִתְנַוְונָה והולכת (Tosef. ib. III, 9 מכחשת) if the animal loses flesh, opp. משבחת. Sot. III, 5; ib. 6^{a} מתנוונא (corr. acc.). Ib. 26^{a} במתנונה דרך איברים when she is ailing all over the body (not suffering locally as predicted for the faithless woman, Num. V, 27); Y. ib. III, 19^{a} bot. המִתְנַוָּוה.

נוּנֵי ch., *Ithpalp.* אִתְנַוְנֵי same. Sot. 6^{a} הוא מִתְנַוְונָא she was falling away (before witnesses arose against her).

נוּס (b. h.) *to flee*. Ex. R. s. 3 למה נָס why did he flee (before the serpent)? Yalk. Ex. 237 בכל מקום שהיה מצרי נס וכ׳ withersoever an Egyptian fled, the sea ran against him; Mekh. B'shall. 6 מצרים נָסִים; a. fr.

נוּס ch., v. נְסַס.

נוּעַ (b. h.) *to shake, move; to be tender*.

Pilp. נִעְנַע, נִי׳ 1) *to shake; to stir up, scare*. Tosef. Bets. I, 8 עד שיְנַעְנֵעַ unless he stirred the bird up (the day before, by which act he made it his property and designated it for slaughtering); Y. ib. I, 60^{c} top. אלא אם כן נו׳ מבעוד יום. Succ. III, 1 כדי לְנַעְנֵעַ בו large enough to (hold it in his hand and) shake. Ib. 9 והיכן היו מְנַעְנְעִים and at what passages of the Hallel did they shake (the Lulab)? Sabb. XX, 5 (141^{a}) חקש .. לא יְנַעְנְעוֹ וכ׳ (Bab. a. Y. ed. יְנַעְנְעֶנּוּ) must not stir up with his hand the straw &c.; a. fr.—נ׳ (ב)ראש *to (shake) bow the head*. Ber. 28^{b} כיון שנ׳ ראשו וכ׳ if he only bows his head (in prayer), it is sufficient. Yeb. 121^{a} וכל גל ... נִעְנַעְתִּי לו ראשי and as each wave came, I dipped my head under (to let it pass over me). Ib. אם ... יְנַעְנֵעַ לו ראשו if wicked people come over man, let him bow his head. Pesik. R. s. 37 ומנענעים בראשיהם and shook their heads (in derision, ref. to Ps. XXII, 8).—Yalk. Prov. 953 ומנענע בו בקולו and sings it with a tremulous voice; Snh. 101^{a} מנענע בקולו Ms. K. (v. Rabb. D. S. a. l. note 2); Tosef. ib. XII, 10 מנ׳ קולו.—Part. pass. מְנוּעְנָע, *pl.* מְנוּעְנָעִין. Bets. 25^{a} המקושרים והמ׳ the birds designated a day before the Holy Day by being tied or by being stirred up; ib. והמקושרין והמ׳ בכ״מ אסורין birds found anywhere tied or stirred up are forbidden to be taken up (because somebody has taken possession of them); Tosef. ib. I, 10 והמְנוּעְנָעִין (Var. והמנענעין, corr. acc.).—2) *to move in different directions, to introduce a surgical instrument*. Nidd. 25^{b}, v. סִכְסֵךְ I.

נוּעַ ch. same, *to totter*. Targ. Ps. CVII, 27.

Palp. נַעְנַע *to shake*. Gen. R. s. 75, beg. דמְנַעְנְעָה (=דמנענעה), v. נְעַר.

נוֹעֲרָן, נוֹעֲדָן, v. נַעֲרָן.

נוּף (b. h.) *to move in the air, to soar*. [Yalk. Ps. 676 שהוא נפח, read: שהיא צפח, v. צוּף.]

Hif. הֵנִיף 1) *to swing, wave*. Men. 61^{b} כהן מניח .. ומֵנִיף the priest places his hand under those of the owner of the offering and waves. Ib. אין העכ״ום מְנִיפִין gentiles are not permitted to wave their offerings; אין הנשים מְנִיפוֹת women are not permitted &c. Ib.^{a} וכול יָנִיף ויחזור ויניף I might think that he must wave twice. Snh. VI, 1

מֵנִיף בסודרין gave the signal by waving a cloth; Succ. 51[b]. Pesik. R. s. 41 (ref. to יפה נוף, Ps. XLVIII, 3) היפה שהיא עתידה לְהָנִיף את וכ׳ the beautiful one (Israel) who is destined to swing (rule) the nations; Yalk. Ps. 755; Yalk. Ex. 417 שהיא מְנִיפָה לאו״ה (ref. to Is. XXX, 28); a. fr.—2) *to fan.* B. Mets. 86[a] הֲנִיפִי עלי, v. מְנִיפָא. Y. Yoma I, 38[c] ומניפין לרבוניהם and fan their masters. Pesik. R. l. c.; Yalk. Ps. l. c. והכל מניפין עליה and all fan her (are subservient to her); a. e.

Pilp. נִפְנֵף *to swing, fan.* Y. Ber. I, 2[d] ורוחת רוח.. וּמְנַפְנֶפֶת בו and the northern wind blew and set the harp swinging. Yalk. Ps. l. c. שיוצא ומְנַפְנֵף את רגנרה (not רגלירה) (the dew) which goes forth and makes her grain in the ear wave (bend with its weight); Pesik. R. l. c. וּמְנַפֵּף את הדגנים. Ohol. VIII, 5 טליה הַמְנַפְנֶפֶת a sheet suspended as a banner (cmp. מַפָּה).

Hithpol. הִתְנוֹפֵף 1) *to be winnowed.* Yeb. 63[a] (addressing the ears in the field, in Chald. dict.) אַי במנפה תִּתְנוֹפְפִי Ar., eh! thou desirest to be winnowed with the fan; [oth. vers. in Ar.: כמנפה תתנופפי (not במנ׳) thou swingest thyself like a swing, v. infra]; ed. v. next w.—2) *to swing one's self; to soar; to be proud.* Ab. Zar. 24[b] הִתְנוֹפְפִי וכ׳ rise (O Ark) in the &c., v. הָדָר; Gen. R. s. 54. Yeb. l. c., v. supra.

נוּף ch. same; part. נָיֵיף. Yeb. 63[a] חזנהו דקא נָיְיפָן he saw them (the ears in the field) waving.

Af. אָנֵיף *to swing, wave, winnow.* Targ. Is. XIII, 2. Targ. Y. II Lev. VII, 30.—M. Kat. 16[b] מְנִיפְתָּא, v. הוּשְׁלָא.

Ithpol. אִתְנוֹפַף, *Ithp.* אִתְנִיף, אִתְּנִיף *to swing one's self; to be proud.* Yeb. l. c. (addressing the standing grain) אַתְנִיפָא אִיתְנוֹפְפִי וכ׳ Ar. (not הניפא) swing thyself (be as proud as thou wilt): trading in business brings more profit than thou dost; ed. אי נַיְיפַת אִיתְנוֹפִי how thou wavest! swing thyself &c.; (Rashi אי תנפיפי, read: אִיתְנוֹפִי or אִיתְנִיפִי).

נוֹף I (b. h. נֹף) pr. n. pl. *Nof, Memphis* in Egypt. Pesik. R. s. 17; Pesik. Vayhi, p. 63[b], v. מֶמְפִּים.

נוֹף II m. (b. h.; נוף) *boughs of a tree, swinging branches, summit.* Y. Ber. I, 2[c] bot. לא סוף דבר נופו וכ׳ (not נטפו) after all, not only its boughs in swinging, but even its main branches (extended over an area of &c.). Macc. II, 7 אילן ... ונופו נוטה וכ׳ a tree which stands within the limits (of the place of refuge), but whose branches spread beyond &c. Ib.; Maasr. III, 10 הכל הולך אחר הנ׳ the location of the branches decides the nature of the territory; Tosef. Arakh. V, 14 הנוף. Kidd. 40[b]; a. e.—*Pl.* נוֹפִים, נוֹפִין, נוֹפוֹת. Num. R. s. 20 מי שאינו בקי קוצץ את הנ׳ וכ׳ he who is no expert (in felling trees) lops off the branches, each branch separately, and gets tired. Yalk. Ps. 755 (ref. to יפה נוף, Ps. XLVIII, 3) [read:] יפה בנ׳ שלה בהקפת וכ׳ she (Israel) is beautiful with her waving boughs when marching around the altar (on the Feast of Booths); Pesik. R. s. 41 יפה שלה (corr. acc.; Friedm. emends יָפָה נוֹף שלה).

נוֹפָא ch. 1) same. Targ. II Kings XIX, 30 (h. text פרי). Targ. Ez. XIX, 10; a. e.—2) = נַפְיָא, q. v.

נוּפִי, Tanḥ. Ki Thissa 18, v. נִיקְנֵפִי.

נוֹפֶךְ I *a jewel,* v. נֹפֶךְ.

נוֹפֶךְ II m. (חָפַךְ; cmp. אַפּוּכֵי) *exchange, consideration.* B. Kam. 99[b]; Kidd. 48[b] אם הוסיף לה נ׳ משלו if he gave her in addition a consideration (a small coin) out of his own.

נוּפָר, v. נִיפָר.

נוֹפֶת f. (b. h. נֹפֶת; denom. of נָפָה) 1) *sifted flour, flour-dust;* 2) *the net-like honey, honey-comb.* Sot. IX, 12 בטל ... וכ׳ צופים the *shamir* ceased and the *nofeth tsufim;* ib. 48[b] מאי נ׳ צ׳ סולת שצפה ע״ג נפה what is meant by *n. ts.?* Fine flour which floats on (sticks to) the top of the sieve; (anoth. explan.) שתי ככרות וכ׳ two loaves stuck to opposite walls of the oven, which rise so that they touch each other; (anoth. explan.) דבש הבא מן הצופים Rashi (ed. מן הצפיא) honey which comes from Tzofim (v. צוֹפִים); Y. ib. IX, 24[b] bot. דבש הבא בצפייה, v. צִיפְיָא.—Gen. R. s. 71 (play on נפתלי) נֹפֶת כצמח לא שלי היא (not עצמו) is not mine the honey-comb itself? (allud. to Ps. XIX, 11); Yalk. ib. 127. Tanḥ. Ekeb I .... שאין בכל מיני שהיא צפה בנפה וכ׳ (not בפה) for among all kinds of grain flour there is none more precious than the fine wheat flour which sticks to the sieve, but the words of the Law are more precious than it, for we read (Ps. l. c.), 'sweeter than honey and flour-dust;' Yalk. Ps. 676.—[Gen. R. l. c. נופתי פירותיו some ed., v. יָפַת.]

נוּץ h., v. נָצַץ.

נוּץ ch., v. נְיץ.

נוֹצָה f. (b. h.; = נוֹצְאָה; יָצָא) 1) [*growth,*] *feathers, down.* Ḥull. III, 4 אם נטלה הנ׳ if the down is lost, contrad. to כָּנָף; Tosef. ib. III (IV), 18 נוֹצָא. Ib. VI, 11. Zeb. VI, 5 והסיר את המוראה ואת הנ׳ וכ׳ he must remove the crop and the down-covered skin with the entrails that go along with it; ib. 65[a] בנוצתה נוטל את הנ׳ עמה 'with its plumage' (Lev. I, 16), he must take the plumage that covers it with the crop; Sifra Vayikra, N'dab., ch. VIII, Par. 7 יטלנה עם הנ׳; a. fr.—Sabb. 28[b] נ׳ של עזים *goats-hair.*—2) cmp. צוֹאָה) *maw containing the faeces* (= קורקבן). Zeb. l. c. (expl. בנצתה, Lev. l. c.) נוטלה ונוטל וכ׳ he takes it (the crop) and takes the maw with it; Sifra l. c.

נוצחוּרִיא, v. צוֹתָא.

נוֹצָיָא, v. נָצָא II.

נוֹצִיצְיָא* f. (v. נוֹצָה) *feathers, pinion.* Targ. Job XXXIX, 13 נוֹצִיצְיָיתָא (ed. Lag. נוֹצְצָיָתָא; Ms. נִיצוֹצְיָתָא); [ed. Wil. נוֹצִיצְיָתָא *pelican* (?)].

נוֹצְרִי m. *Nazarene, of Nazareth* (in southern Galilaea).—יֵשׁוּ הנ׳ Jesus of N. Snh. 43[a] Ms. M.; a. fr., v. יֵשׁוּ.—Ab. Zar. 7[b] יום נ׳ Ms. M. (v. Rabb. D. S. a. l. note; ed. יום א׳) the day of the Nazarene (Sunday).—*Pl.* נוֹצְרִים *Christians.* Taan. 27[b] מפני הנ׳ Ms. M. (ed. הצב״ום; in some ed. the entire passage omitted) on account of (in order not to be identified with) the Christians (v. Treat. Sof'rim ch. XVII, 5).

נוֹצְרִין, Tosef. Toh. XI, 16, v. נֵצֶר III.

נוּקְבָא, נוּקְבָא I *hole*, v. נִקְבָא.

נוּקְבָא II נוּקְבָה, נוּקְבְתָא f. ch.=h. נְקֵבָה, *female*. Targ. Gen. I, 27. Targ. Lev. XXVII, 4; a. fr.—Y. Taan. IV, 69ª bot. Gen. R. s. 33, v. דְּכַר II; a. fr.—*Pl.* נוּקְבִין, נוּקְבָתָא, נוּקְבָן. Keth. IV, 11, v. בַּר II. Y. Kil. IX, 32ᵇ; Y. Keth. XII, 35ª bot.; Gen. R. l. c., v. דְּכַר II, a. e.

נוּקְבְתָא pr. n. pl., v. נְקִיפְתָא.

נוֹקֵד m. (b. h. נֹקֵד; נָקַד I) [*marker, accountant*,] *shepherd*. Pesik. Shek., p. 12ᵇ; ib. Eth Korb., p. 60ª; Pesik. R. s. 16; Tanḥ. Ki Thissa 5 מהו נ׳ רועה what is *noked* (II Kings III, 4)? A shepherd.

נוּקְד m. (נָקַד I; cmp. Arab. *nakd* probus et justi ponderi nummus) *a stamped coin*. Par. I, 3 בן עזאי קורהו נ׳ וכ׳ Ben ʿAzzai called it (the sheep between one and two years of age, when it is neither כֶּבֶשׂ nor אַיִל) 'a distinct coin;' R. Yishm. called it 'counterfeit;' v. פַּרְכְּרִגְמָא.

נוֹקְדָן, נוֹקְדָנָא, v. sub נַקְדָּן.

נוּקל, Y. Yeb. X, 11ª bot., v. נִגּ.

נוּקְנִיקָה m. (lucanica) a sort of *sausages*. Y. Shek. VII, 50ᶜ bot. (Bab. ed. VII, 2 נקניקה, Var. נקא כי קא, נקוניא כי קא, Ms. M. נקאני קא, read: נוּקָאנִיקָא).

נוֹקְרָן, v. נַקְרָן.

נוֹקְרָנָא, v. נַקְדָּנָא.

נוּקְשָׁה m. (קָשָׁה) *old, spoiled*, esp. נ׳ (חמץ) *a leavened substance unfit for food*. Pes. 48ª נ׳ בעיניה spoiled leavened substance in its natural condition, opp. ע״י תערובת in a mixture. Men. 54ª; a. fr.—[Ar.: נוּקְשָׁא.]

נוּר as a verb, v. נִיר I.

נוּר, נוּרָא m. (v. נְהַר; cmp. מול a. מְהַל) *fire*. Targ. Job XVIII, 5; a. fr.—Ḥag. 13ᵇ, a. e. דינור, v. דִּינוּר. M. Kat. 12ᵇ, v. מַדְבּוּרָא. Ned. 62ᵇ עבדא דנ׳ a fire-worshipper (gheber). Ib. בי נ׳ fire temple, gheber-service; a. fr.—[Lev. R. s. 27, a. e. בנור ובזפת, v. מַרְזוֹבוֹת.]

נוֹרָא, נוֹרָאוֹת, v. יָרֵא.

נורה, Tosef. B. Kam. VII, 8, some ed., v. גָּרָה II.

נוּרִי pr. n. m. *Nuri*, father of R. Johanan. Erub. IV, 5; a. fr., v. יוֹחָנָן.

נוּרִיתָא f. (Syr. נורתא, Löw Pfl., p. 258) *Crow-foot* (Ranunculus). Ḥull. 59ª top Ar. (ed. מרידתא), v. מְרָדִיתָא.

נורתוק, נורתק, v. נַרְתִּיק.

נוּשְׁקְתָא f. (נְשַׁק) *kiss*.—*Pl.* נוּשְׁקָאתָא. Targ. Prov. XXVII, 6 (ed. Wil. נוּשְׁקָתָא).

נוֹתָר, v. יָתַר.

נִיזְבָּא, נִיזְ׳ m. *nizba*, supposed to be a *measure of length*, the height of a fist with the thumb. Men. 69ᵇ רום נ׳ חיטי Ms. M. (ed. כיזבא, v. Rabb. D. S. a. l. note) a layer of wheat of the height of a *nizba*; [for oth. vers., v. רוּזִינְקָא].

נָזָה, v. נזי.

נְזַה (Syr. נזה, P. Sm. 2295; cmp. זוח II) *to be agitated; to roar, low* &c. Targ. Job VI, 5 יִנְזַח Ms. (Bxt. יַנְזֶה *Af.*; ed. Lag. יגיח, ed. Wil. יגעי).

Pa. נַזַּה *to chide, rebuke*. Sabb. 48ª נַזְהֵיה רבא Ms. M. (ed. רבה) R. chid him.

נִיזְ׳, נִזְהָא m. (preced.) *chiding off, stirring on, cry*. Pes. 112ᵇ נ׳ דתורא (Ms. M. נהום, corrected into נזהא, v. Rabb. D. S. a. l. note) the cry with which to chase an ox away (or goad him on); נ׳ דארייה the lion-hunter's cry; נ׳ דארבא the sailor's cry, v. חַיָּיא.

נְזוּפָא, constr. נְזוּף m. (נְזַף) *rebuke*. Targ. Koh. VII, 5.

***נָזַז** (cmp. זוז I) *to be unsteady*. Lev. R. s. 10 שנ׳ לבו עליו Ar. (ed. נתגאה; Ex. R. s. 37, v. זוּחַ I) whose heart within him was unsteady (whose mind was unbalanced, who was wanton).

Hif. הֵזִיז *to make unsteady*. Part. pass. מוּזָז, *pl.* מוּזָזִין *staggering, reeling*. Pesik. Zutr. Haäz., ed. Bub. p. 115 (expl. מזי רעב, Deut. XXXII, 24) שיהו מ׳ ... מפני הרעב they shall be reeling and shall fall on the dunghill from hunger; Sifré Deut. 321 מאווים ברעב (or מאוזים, read: מוּזָזִים) staggering in starvation; Yalk. ib. 945 מוּזָחִין, v. נָזַח.

נְזַז ch. same. Part. נָזֵיז, *pl.* נָזִיזֵי. Yoma 78ᵇ מאני נ׳ Ar. shaky vessels (that cannot stand, and are used as toys), v. גָּזַז.

נָזַח (b. h.; cmp. זוח II) *to be unsteady, shift*. Yoma 72ª כדי שלא יִזַּח that it (the breast plate) may not slip.

Hif. הִזִּיחַ *to move, loosen; to remove*. Ib. ויסתירה, v. הוּשַׁן. Keth. 10ᵇ מַזִּיחַ (or מֵזִיחַ); Ḥull. 7ª מַזִּיחִין (or מְזִיחִין), v. זוח II.—*Part. pass.* מוּזָח, *pl.* מוּזָחִין *unsteady, reeling*. Yalk. Deut. 945, v. נָזַז. [Ib. (ref. to זוחלי, Deut. XXXII, 24) שיהו מ׳ בעפר, read with Sifré ib. 321 מוּזְחָלִין *dragged along* in the dust, v. זָחַל.]

נָזָה, נזי (b. h.; cmp. זוע, a. נָדָה, נְזִי II) *to move, shake; to drip*.

Hif. הִזָּה *to sprinkle*. Yoma V, 3 והזה ממנו וכ׳ and sprinkled from it once upward &c. Ib. ולא היה מתכוין להזות and he did not aim at definite points in sprinkling. Tosef. Toh. VIII, 12 שבא להזות who comes asking to be sprinkled upon; אין מַזִּין עליו וכ׳ we do not sprinkle upon him &c. Par. XII, 8 לא יַזֶּה וכ׳ he must not sprinkle upon the spindle and the whorl separately; a. fr.—Trnsf. *to have a cleansing influence.* Tosef. Dem. I, 14; Tosef. Makhsh. III, 15 טהור אחד מַזֶּה על וכ׳ one clean person has a cleansing influence on one hundred unclean persons; Y. Dem. III, 23[c] bot.

Hof. הוּזָּה *to be sprinkled.* Par. l. c. ואם הזה מוּזָּה but if he has sprinkled (on each separately), it is sprinkled (the lustration is valid).

נְזִיאֲתָא, v. נְזִירְתָא.

נָזִיד m. (b. h.; זוד) *dish, pottage.* Toh. II, 3 נְזִיד תרומה a pottage containing T'rumah. Ib. 4 נְ׳ הקודש a pottage containing sacrificial matter.

נְזִיהוּתָא f. (נְזַח) *chiding, railing.* Snh. 41[b] מטיבותיה דמר אמרינן ... מנְזִיהוּתֵיה וכ׳ (v. Rabb. D. S. a. l. note; Ms. M. מנזיותיה) as you speak kindly, we have said many things about it (which we will tell you), but when you rail at us &c.

נזיות, Targ. Y. Num. V, 28, v. זִיוָה.

נזיותא, v. נְזִיהוּתָא.

נָזִיחַ *naziah*, a substitute for נָזִיר (v. כִּינּוּי). Ned. I, 2.

נְזִיֵּי m. pl. (v. next w.) *seeds to be pressed for their oil.* M. Kat. 12[b] חזו לנ׳ דאית בהו (Ms. M. נְזִיֵּיתָא) they (the sesame plants) are fit (for immediate use) for the seeds which they contain.

נְזִיָּתָא f. pl. (cmp. זוּעַ, a. זִיתָא I, II) *beer in the process of brewing, brewage.* Ab. Zar. 31[b]. Pes. 20[a] וסימנך כ׳ and the mnemonical word (for remembering the order of the objects named) is the brewing process ('vessel', 'eatable' (dates), 'liquid'). Ib. 113[a] לבי כ׳ רהוט Ar. a. Ms. M. 2 (ed. סורנא) run to the brewery, v. חָלַט. Succ. 20[b] חזו לנְזִיָּאתָא they (the mats) are fit for covering up the brewing vat. Keth. 6[a], a. e., v. מְסוֹכְרַיָּא. B. Kam. 35[a] פתקיה (פסקיה) לנ׳ וכ׳ (=לבי נ׳) he burst the vat open and drank the beer, and was cured.

נְזִיפָה f. (נְזַף) *anger, rebuke,* esp. *n'zifah,* a lower degree of excommunication; v. נִידּוּי. Snh. 68[a] נזף בו ויצא בנ׳ he frowned at him, and he (the son) went away feeling the rebuke. Sabb. 31[a] והוציאו בנ׳ and made him go out in anger. Ib. 97[a] ההוא בנ׳ בעלמא this (בם, Num. XII, 9) refers only to the anger (of the Lord, not to leprosy). M. Kat. 16[a] אין נ׳ פחות וכ׳ the minor ban lasts no less than seven days. Ib.[b] נ׳ דידהו their (the Palestinian) *n'zifah*; נ׳ דידן our (the Babylonian) *n.*; a. fr.

נְזִיפוּתָא ch. same. Targ. Koh. X, 12.—M. Kat. 16[a] נהג נ׳ בנפשיה וכ׳ he considered himself under the minor ban for thirty days. Ib.[b]; a. e.

נָזִיק *nazik*, a substitute for נָזִיר, v. כִּינּוּי. Ned. I, 2.

נְזִיקִין, v. נֶזֶק.

נְזִיר, v. נֵזֶר.

נָזִיר m. (b. h.; v. נָזַר) 1) *abstinent.* Naz. II, 3 הריני נ׳ ממנו I will abstain from this (cup); a. e.—*Pl.* נְזִירִים, נְזִירִין. Lev. R. s. 24, end, opp. שכורים.—Esp. *nazir, Nazarite,* one bound by a vow to be set apart for the service of God, and as such to abstain from grapes and all productions of the vine and from intoxicating drinks, and to let his hair grow (Num. VI, 1—21). Naz. I, 1, a. fr. הרי זה נ׳ he is a Nazarite (his words mean the vow of nazaritism). Ib. 2 נ׳ שמשון a Nazarite like Samson; נ׳ עולם a nazarite for life; a. v. fr.—*Pl.* as ab. Ib. V, 5; a. fr.—Fem. נְזִירָה. Ib. III, 6. Ib. II, 2 אמר אמרה פרה זו הריני נ׳ וכ׳ if he said, this cow thinks I will be a *nazir*, if I stand up ... he is a Nazarite by implication (it being his meaning that he will be a Nazarite if the cow gets up); a. fr.—2) *guarded.* Sifra B'har ch. I; Y. Shebi. VIII, 38[b] top. (expl. נזירך, Lev. XXV, 5) מן השמור בארץ וכ׳ of that which is guarded in the ground &c. (v. Rashi to Lev. l. c.), opp. מובקר.—*Nazir,* name of a treatise, of the Order of Nashim, of Mishnah, Talmud Babli and Y'rushalmi (in Tosefta *N'ziroth*).

נְזִירָא, נְזִיר I ch. *same,* 1) *Nazarite.* Targ. Num. VI, 18; a. fr.—Num. R. s. 10 (ref. to the precautions prescribed for the Nazarite, Num. VI, 3) מתלא אמר לך לך אמרין (ל)נ׳ סחור וכ׳ the proverb says, go, go, they say (to the) Nazarite, go all around that thou mayest not come near the vineyard; Sabb. 13[a], a. fr. משום לך לך אמרי נ׳ וכ׳ as a measure of precaution; a. e.—*Pl.* נְזִירַיָּא, נְזִירִין. Y. Naz. V, end, 54[b]; Gen. R. s. 91; a. fr.—2) *crowned, nobleman. Pl.* as ab. Targ. Lam. IV, 7.

נְזִירָה I, נְזִירָא II pr. n. m. *N'zira.* Gen. R. s. 12 ר׳ לוי בשם ר׳ נ׳ (ib. s. 11 זעירא). Midr. Till. to Ps. XCII לוי בשם בר נזירה (ed. Bub. בשם ר׳ מרי) בר מרא; Pesik. R. s. 23 בשם ר׳ בזירה; Y. Ber. VIII, 12[b] בשם ר׳ בזירה (corr. acc.); Yalk. Ps. 843; 888. Y. Ber. II, 4[b] bot. לוי בר נ׳; Y. Shek. II, end, 47[a] בר נ׳; Y. M. Kat. III, 8 בר כירא׳ (corr. acc.); שמעון בן נ׳ Yeb. 97[a] שמעון נ׳ (v. however, Bekh. 31[b]). Y. Sabb. II, 5[a] top ר״ש נ׳; Pesik. Dibré, p. 111[a] שמשון בן נזירה.

נְזִירָה II f., v. נָזִיר, a. נְזִירוּת.

נְזִירוּ, v. נְזִירוּתָא.

נְזִירוּת, נְזִירָה f. (denom. of נָזִיר or נָזַר) *abstinence,* esp. *the Nazarite's vow, nazariteship.* Sifra Emor, ch. III, Par. 4 (ref. to Lev. XXII, 2 וינזרו) אין נזירה אלא הפרשה the verb *nazar* means to abstain (guard); Num. R. s. 10 אין נזירות .. אלא פרישות; Yalk. Lev. 632; Sifra l. c. הא אין נזירות וכ׳. Num. R. s. 10 אדם קובע עליו נזירות בתוך נְזִירָתוֹ a person may take the Nazarite's vow within the time of his vow. Naz. IV, 7 מגלח על נזירות אביו may cut his hair (and sacrifice at the expiration of his vow) on the nazariteship of his (deceased) father, i. e. use his father's money set apart for the purpose. Ib. הפריש ... לנְזִירָתוֹ (Rashi to ib. 30[a]; נְזִירוּת) he had set apart money for his nazaritic expenses without mentioning special items; Tosef. ib. III, 16; Tosef. Meïl. I, 9. Ned. 3[b] הנ׳ חל על הנ׳ (sub. נֶדֶר) one nazaritic vow may take effect on top of another, i. e. a vow taken within the term of another, takes effect when the first expires, v. supra; a. fr.—*Pl.* (of נְזִירָה) נְזִירוֹת, (of נְזִירוּת) נְזִירִיּוֹת. Ned. I, 1 כינויי נ׳ כנ׳ the substitutes for *nazir* are as effective as the word *nazir* itself. Tosef. Naz. l. c. לשאר נְזִירוּתָיו for his other nazaritic expenses. Naz. 14ᵇ שתי נ׳ two nazaritic vows. Y. ib. V, end, 54ᵇ וכולן ... נזירויות and all of them must observe nine nazaritic vows in succession; a. fr.

נְזִירוּ, נְזִירוּתָא ch. same. Targ. O. Num. VI, 2 ed. Berl. (oth. ed. a. Y. נזירא).—Naz. 14ᵇ חדא נ׳ one Nazarite vow. Ib. 3ᵃ למיעבר על נְזִירוּתֵיה to violate his vow; a. e.

נָזַל (b. h.; cmp. אזל) *to run, melt, be distilled.* Gen. R. s. 13 (ref. to Job XXXVI, 28) והיכן הם נוֹזְלִין בשחקים where are they (the salty waters of the Ocean) distilled? In the clouds; Yalk. Gen. 20 (corr. acc.); Koh. R. to I, 7 אירכן הם נעשים נוֹזְלִים בשחקים where are they made into distilled (sweet) waters? In the clouds; Yalk. Koh. 967.—Esp. נוֹזְלִין, נוֹזְלִים *running waters.* Mekh. B'shall., Shir., s. 6; a. e.

Pi. נִזֵּל, *Hif.* הִזִּיל *to cause to flow; to distill.* Sifré Deut. 306 (ref. to Deut. XXXII, 2) אם כנסת ... לסוף שאתה מְנַזֵּל ומשקה וכ׳ if thou gatherest the words of the Law after the manner of those who collect rain water in the cistern, thou shalt finally be able to make them flow and give drink to others. B. Bath. 25ᵃ (ref. to Deut. l. c.) זו רוח צפונית שמַזֶּלֶת וכ׳ that is the nothern wind which makes the gold run (increases commerce; Rashi: *makes* gold *cheap,* v. זול). Cant. R. to IV, 15 (ref. to ונזלים וכ׳, ib.) זה מַזִּיל מקצת דבר וזה מזיל וכ׳ the one lets flow (utters, cmp. נָבַע) one part of the argument, and the other another part, until the *halakhah* shines forth like the Lebanon.

נְזַל ch. same; *part.* (or *adj.*) *pl.* נוֹזְ׳, נָזְלַיָּא *running waters, rivers*; v. preced. Targ. Y. Ex. XV, 8 (O. אזליא). Targ. Ps. LXXVIII, 16; a. e.

נֶזֶם m. (b. h.; זָמַם II, cmp. זְמָמָא) *nose-ring, earring.* Kel. XI, 9; a. e.—*Pl.* נְזָמִים. Ib. 8 נ׳ earrings; נִזְמֵי האף nose-rings. Sabb. VI, 1 בנ׳, expl. ib. 54ᵇ נזמי האף. Ex. R. s. 48, end; a. fr.

נָזַף (cmp. זוּף II a. זעף) *to be angry, to rebuke, chide.* Gen. R. s. 12 נז׳ בעבדו who rebuked his servant. Num. R. s. 13 נ׳ בו משה Moses reprimanded him; a. e.—Part. pass. נָזוּף, *pl.* נְזוּפִים, נְזוּפִין *reprimanded, placed under the ban* (v. נְזִיפָה). Tanh. Ki Thissa 16 נ׳ הוא לפני וכ׳ he is banned in the sight of the Lord; Ex. R. s. 41 הרי זה נ׳ לחקב״ה; Ab. VI נקרא נ׳; a. fr.—Sabb. 115ᵃ יוחנן חנ׳ Joh. the excommunicated; Tosef. ib. XIII (XIV), 2 בן חנ׳ (Var. נִיזָּף *Nif.*), v. חֲלָו. Taan. I, 7 כבני אדם הנ׳ למקום like men excommunicated in the sight of God. Yeb. 72ᵃ; a. e.

נְזַף, נְזִיף ch. same. Targ. Gen. XXXVII, 10 (h. text גער). Targ. Ps. IX, 6. Targ. Num. XII, 14 מְיזַף ed. Berl. (Y. מְנַזְיִף, not כ׳); a. fr.—Part. pass. נְזִיף. Hull. 133ᵃ רבא נ׳ הוה (Rashi נְזוּף) Raba was under the ban.

Ithpe. אִיתְנְזִיף *to be chid, chastised.* Ab. Zar. 55ᵃ מִיתְנְזִף עלמא, v. גזה.

נָזַק *Hif.* הִזִּיק (denom. of נֶזֶק) *to hurt, injure, damage.* Ex. R. s. 20, beg. דלג ... ולא הִזִּיקוֹ stepped over the child and did not injure it. B. Kam. I, 1 לילך ולהַזִּיק to do injury in moving (be an active agency of damage); ib. וכשה׳ חב וכ׳ and when one of them caused damage, the offender (מַזִּיק) is responsible. Ib. III, 6 והִזִּיקוּ זה וכ׳ and hurt one another (by collision); a. fr.—V. מַזִּיק.

Hof. הוּזַּק *to be hurt, injured, damaged.* Ib. III, 1, sq. Ib. 31ᵇ שהוּזְקוּ כלים בכלים vessels (belonging to one person) were damaged by collision with (another person's) vessels; a. fr.

Nif. נִיזַּק same. Ex. R. l. c. end שלא יִנָּזְקוּ that they be not hurt (by the wolves). Deut. R. s. 7 ולא תִנָּזֵק צפורנו של אחד מהם rather than a nail of one of them be injured; a. e.—Usu. part. נִיזּוֹק, נִזּוֹק; *pl.* נִיזּוֹקִים, נִיזּוֹקִין. Ber. 9ᵇ אינו נ׳ כל וכ׳ has no evil to fear for the entire day. Ib. 40ᵃ ואי אתה נ׳ and thou shalt not get sick; a. fr.—Hull. 142ᵃ; Pes. 8ᵇ, a. e. שלוחי מצוה אינן נ׳ those going on a religious mission will not meet with evil; a. e.—V. נִיזָּק.

נְזַק ch. same. Targ. Ps. XCI, 7 יקרבון לְמִנְזַק (h. text יגש); a. e.

Pa. נַזֵּיק same. Targ. Jer. XII, 14 (h. text נגע); a. e.

Af. אַזִּיק (הַנְזֵק), אַנְזִק same. Targ. O. Gen. XXVI, 11. Targ. Ex. XI, 7 לא יַנְזֵק ... בלישניה ed. Berl. (ed. Vien. לישניה, corr. acc.; Y. יְחַךְ); a. e.—B. Kam. 27ᵇ הוא דא׳ אנפשיה it is he who hurt himself (through his own action); ib. 28ᵃ א׳ נפשיה. Ib. 13ᵇ אַזְקֵיה תורא דמשאיל וכ׳ the ox of the lender injured that of the borrower. Ib. אזקי ed. (read with Ms. M. אזקיה). B. Mets. 117ᵃ אולי ואַזְקֵי וכ׳ the water came down and damaged the property of those living below; a. fr.—Gitt. 53ᵃ לאזוקי קא מכוין (read: לְאַזּוּקֵיה or לְאַנְזוּקֵיה, Rashi לצעריה) he has the intention to harm him.

Ithpa. אִתְנַזַּק, *Ittaf.* אִיתַּזַּק; *Ithpe.* אִיתְנְזִיק, אִיתְנְזִיק *to be hurt, to meet with an accident.* Targ. II Chr. XXXII, 31. Targ. Job V, 24.—B. Kam. 13ᵇ אילו איתזק מעלמא if he had been hurt through any other cause. Ber. 9ᵇ ואִיתְּזַקִי and I met with evil; במאי אִיתְּזַקְתְּ what was the evil thou didst meet with?—Lev. R. s. 24 ולית אתון מִתְנַזְּקִין and you have never been injured. Kidd. 29ᵇ הוו מִיתַּזְּקֵי they used to be hurt (by a demon, v. מַזִּיק); a. fr.

נֶזֶק m. (b. h.; denom. of זקק) [*junction, touch*; cmp. נגע, ריע &c.,] *accident, evil, injury, damage*; תַּשְׁלוּמֵי נ׳ *indemnity.* Ab. Zar. I, 7 וכל דבר שיש בו נ׳ לרבים or anything through which the public may be injured. B. Kam. I, 1 ... חב לשלם תשלומי נ׳ וכ׳ the offender is bound to pay indemnity with the best of the land (out of his best lands, v. עִידִית). Ib. 2 הכשרתי במקצת נִזְקוֹ I have been partly instrumental in injuring him, v. הֶכְשֵׁר. Ib. II, 5, a. fr. חצי נ׳ indemnity up to half the damage, opp. נ׳ שלם full indemnity. Ib. VIII, 1 בנ׳ בצער וכ׳ (has to pay) damages (for the maimed limb), an indemnity for the pain inflicted &c.; a. fr.—*Pl.* נְזָקִים, נְזָקִין; constr. נִזְקֵי. Ib. 84ᵃ דנין נ׳ מנ׳ וכ׳ we may draw an analogy between different cases of mayhem, but not between mayhem and homicide. Ib. נ׳ שור בשור damages for an ox injured by an ox; a. fr.—נְזָקִין, נְזִיקִין (fr. נָזִיק) *cases of damages, laws concerning injuries; damages.* Ib. I, 1, v. אָב II. Mekh. Mishp. s. 14; a. fr., v. נִיזָּקִין.—Esp. *N'zikin,* (*Seder N'zikin*) name of the fourth Order of the Mishnah, Tosefta and Talmud, also of a section of M'khilta Mishpatim. Sabb. 31ᵃ. Lev. R. s. 19 נ׳ ל׳ פרקים *N.* which contains thirty chapters; a. e.—B. Kam 102ª מלח נ׳ חדא וכ׳ the entire *N'zikin* (*Baba Kamma, M'tsi'a and Bathra*) is one treatise.

נִיזְ׳, נִזְקָא, נֶזֶק ch. same. Targ. O. Ex. XXIV, 11. Targ. Y. ib. XXX, 12 נ׳ דמותא (h. text נגף). Ib. XXI, 19; a. e.—B. Kam. 84ª לבר מנזקא Ms. M. (ed. מנזק) except indemnity for loss of limb. Ib. שומו ליה נִיזְקֵיה assess the damages due him for the loss of his hand; a. fr.

נְזָקִין, v. נֵיזֶק.

נָזַר (b. h.; sec. r. of זור) 1) *to surround; to keep off; to set apart.* V. נֵזֶר, נָזִיר.—2) (denom. of נָזִיר) *to vow to be a Nazarite; to dedicate one's self to nazariteship.* Naz. III, 2 שנ׳ שתי וכ׳ who vows to be a Nazarite for two terms. Ib. 5 מי שנ׳ והוא וכ׳ if one makes the vow while in a burial ground. Ib. 17ª לא תִּינְזוֹר thou must not vow (while in a burial ground). Ib. I, 5 אחת גדולה נָזַרְתִּי I meant by my vow one nazaritic term which I consider a long one. Ned. 3ᵇ נימא קרא לִינְזוֹר the text (Num. VI, 2) ought to read *lizzor* (instead of *l'hazzir*). Y. Naz. I, beg. 51ª במתכוין לִינְזוֹר when he intended to vow nazariteship; a. fr.

Hif. הִזִּיר 1) (sub. נפשו) *to abstain.* Ned. 4ª עד שיַזִּיר מכולן (Naz. 3ᵇ שיִזּוֹר) unless he vows abstinence from all of them (mentioned Num. VI, 3).—2) *to impose the vow of abstinence.* Sifré Num. 22 לְהַזִּיר אף את אחרים *l'hazzir* (Num. VI, 2) includes also the imposition of nazariteship on others (one's son &c.). Ib. את עצמו מַזִּיר וכ׳ himself he may obligate, but he cannot obligate others; Num. R. s. 10; a. e.—3) *to be a Nazarite.* Naz. 19ª אע״פ שלא הביא ח׳ even if he did not bring the due sacrifice, he must resume his nazariteship. Ib. אימתי ח׳ וכ׳ when can he resume &c.? After he brought the sacrifice (Num. VI, 12).

Nif. נִזַּר 1) (with ל) *to dedicate one's self to.* Sifré l. c. המצוה לְהִנָּזֵר לשם the merit of nazariteship consists in the dedication of one's self to the Lord (in the sacred motive).—2) (with מ) *to abstain from; to renounce.* Ib. 131 הִנָּזֵר מתורתו .. והוא נִזּוֹר renounce the law of Moses, and he did renounce; Y. Snh. X, 28ᵈ הִינָּזֵר.

נְזִיר, נְזַר ch. same, *to abstain; to vow, observe nazariteship.* Targ. O. Num. VI, 3 יַזַּר (ed. Berl. יַזֵּר *Af.*; Y. II יִתְנְזַר *Ithpe.*). Targ. O. ib. 5 דִּנְזִיר ed. Berl. (Var. דִּנְזַר, דְּיִנְזַר, v. Berl. Targ. O. II, p. 40).

Af. אַזַּר, אַזִּיר, אַנְזַר same. Ib. 12; v. supra.

Ithpe. אִתְנְזַר *to abstain*, v. supra.

נֵזֶר m. (b. h.; preced.) 1) *crown,* esp. *the Nazarite's hair.* Num. R. s. 10 (ref. to Num. VI, 7) קראו הכתוב עטרה לראשו the text calls it (his long hair which defaces him) a crown on his head. Ib. נִזְרוֹ כקרבן his hair is as sacred as the sacrifice; a. fr.—2)=נְזִירוּת, *the Nazarite's vow.* Num. R. l. c.; Tosef. Naz. II, 6 (ref. to Num. VI, 21) ולא נ׳ על קרבנו but not the vow to follow the dedication of his sacrifice; Y. ib. II, 52ᵇ top שיקדים נזרו וכ׳ his vow must precede the dedication of his sacrifice &c. Ib. V, 54ª גילגל בנזרו he turned around (trifled with) his vow. Ned. 90ª נשאל על נזרו, v. שָׁאַל; a. fr.

נִי׳, נִזְרָא ch. same, *crown; vow.* Targ. Num. VI, 19. Ib. 5; a. fr.—V. נְזִירוּ.

נַחַ *easy,* v. נוֹחַ.

נֹחַ (b. h.) pr. n. m. *Noah.* Ab. V, 2. Snh. 108ᵇ; a. fr.—בֶּן נֹחַ, *pl.* בְּנֵי נֹחַ *Noahide, the human race;* מצוות ב׳ נ׳ laws obligatory upon all mankind, contrad. to such as bind Israelites alone, *universal laws.* Tosef. Ab. Zar. VIII (IX), 4 על ... נצטוו בני נ׳ the gentiles have been commanded seven laws, namely, concerning justice, idolatry &c.; Snh. 56ª; a. e.—Ib.ᵇ כל האמור ... בן נח וכ׳ the gentile stands forewarned concerning all that is said in the section on sorcery (Deut. XVIII, 10-12); Tosef. l. c. 6. Snh. 59ª כל מצוה שנאמרה לב׳ נ׳ וכ׳ whatever law has been published for the Noahides (prior to the Sinaitic legislation) and repeated at Sinai &c. Tosef. l. c. 8. Ab. Zar. 64ᵇ כל שקיבל .. ב׳ נ׳ (a gentile entitled to citizenship in Palestine) is he who obligates himself to observe the seven Noachidic laws, v. גֵּר; a. v. fr.

נַחְבִּי (b. h.) pr. n. m. *Nahbi,* one of the twelve spies. Sot. 34ᵇ; Tanh. Sh'lah 6. Ib. Haăz. 7, v. חָבָא.

נֶחְבָּל m. (חָבַל) *the complainant in a case of battery.* Shebu. VII, 1; a. fr.

נָחָה I, v. נחי.

***נָחָת** II f. (נוּחַ)=הֲנָחָה, *rest, relief.* Gen. R. s. 10, end כיון שנחו ... ניתן להם נ׳ when the hands of their Maker left off from (extending) them, they were given rest (permanency); Yalk. ib. 16 הנייה.

נָחוּם, v. נִיחוּם.

נַחוּם (b. h.) pr. n. m. *Nahum,* 1) N. the prophet. Pesik. Nah., p. 127ᵇ; a. e.—2) N., name of several Tannaim a. Amoraim. Peah II, 6; Naz. 56ᵇ נ׳ הלבלר.—Sabb. II, 1, a. fr. נ׳ המדי.—Taan. 21ª, a. fr. נ׳ איש גם זו, v. גַּמְזוֹ.—Y. Taan. I, 64ᵇ top נ׳; (Y. Ber. IX, 14ª top תנחום).—Ib. VIII, 12ᵇ bot., a. fr. נ׳ בר ר׳ סימאי; (Pes. 104ª; Ab. Zar. 50ª מנחם בר׳ סימאי;) Y. Meg. I, 72ᵇ bot., a. fr. נ׳ איש קודש קדשים.—Y. Bets. V, 63ᵇ R. N. brother of R. Ila; a. e.—V. Fr. M'bo, p. 116ª.

נְחוּמְיָה, Y. Ber. III, 6ª (ed. Krot. נְחֶמְיָה q. v.).

נְחוּנְיָה, נְחוּנְיָא pr. n. m. *N'hunia,* 1) son of one Joseph ben Pakhsas (Paskas). Sifra Emor, beg. (also חוניא); Y. Naz. I, beg. 55ᵈ; a. e.—2) name of several Tannaim. Eduy. VI, 2 נ׳ בן אלינתן.—Ib. VII, 9 נ׳ בן גודגדא (Gitt. V, 5 יוחנן).—Ab. III, 5; Ber. IV, 2, a. fr. נ׳ בן הקנה; Meg. 28ª. Ib. נ׳ הגדול (Ms. M. חנינא, v. Rabb. D. S. a. l. note).—3) Y. Shek. V, 48ᵈ; B. Kam. 50ª נ׳ חופר וכ׳ N. the well-digger. Cmp. חוֹנִי, חוּנְיָא.

נְחוּנְיוֹן pr. n. m. *N'hunion* (Onias, cmp. חוֹנְיו). Y. Ned. VI, end, 40ª; Y. Snh. I, 19ª top נִיחוּנְיוֹן.

נְחוּשׁ, v. נִיחוּשׁ.

נְחֹשֶׁת, נְחוֹשֶׁת f. (b. h.) 1) *copper.* Zeb. 22ª (ref. to Ex. XXX, 18) לנ׳ הקשתיו וכ׳ I compared it (the foot of the laver with the laver itself) with regard to its being of copper, but not with regard to anything else. Pesik. Ekhah, p. 122ᵇ מטבעות של נ׳ וכ׳ silver-plated copper coins. Keth.

VII, 10, v. צָרַת; a. fr.—2) *bronze*, v. next w.—3) *copper vessels*. Y. Keth. X, 33[d] bot. לחזות גובין מן חנ׳ וכ׳ to seize (for the widowhood) copper vessels and dining plates.—4) *the (copper) bottom* or *rim*. Sabb. 41[a] מפני שנְחוּשְׁתָּהּ מחממתה because its double bottom gives out heat to warm the water (even after the removal of the coals). Kel. VIII, 3; IX, 1; 3 נ׳ של תנור the (copper) rim of the stove. [Yoma 38[a], v. next w.]—5) *the polished, smooth side of skin* (קֶלֶף). Y. Meg. I, 71[d] top מקום נְחוּשְׁתּוֹ on its smooth side, opp. מקום שיער the hairy side.

נְחָשׁ׳, נְחוּשְׁתָּן I m. (preced.) *bronze*. Midd. II, 3; Tosef. Yoma II, 4; Y. ib. III, 41[a] מפני שנ׳ מצהיב because bronze has the appearance of gold; (Bab. ib. 38[a] מפני שנְחוּשְׁתָּן בצוהבת היתה (from נחושת, v. preced.) because the bronze of which they were made was goldlike). Tosef. l. c. נ׳ קלנתיא היה (Var. נְחוּשְׁתָּא) it was Corinthian bronze; Yoma l. c. נחושת קלוניתא היתה (Ms. M. קלניתא); Yalk. Cant. 985.

נְחָשׁ׳, נְחוּשְׁתָּן II m. (b. h.) *Nehushtan*, name of the copper serpent erected by Moses. Targ. II Kings XVIII, 4.

נְחוּתָה, נְחוּתָא, v. אַנְחוּתָה.

נָחוֹתָה, נָחוֹתָא m. (נְחַת) *one going* or *coming down*, esp. one coming from Palestine to Babylonia. Y. Shek. VIII, 51[a], a. e. אבדומא נ׳ (not אבודמא) A. who had been in Babylonia. Y. Kil. IX, 32[c] bot. עולא נ׳ הוה Ulla had gone to Babylonia; Y. Keth. XII, 35[b] bot. (not עללא).—*Pl.* constr. נָחוֹתֵי. Targ. Ps. CXV, 17 ed. Lag. (ed. נָחֲתֵי); a. fr.—נ׳ ימא *seafarers*. Ib. CVII, 23. Targ. Is. XLII, 10 נָחֲתֵי.—Sabb. 20[b]; 90[a] שאילתינהו לכל נ׳ ר׳, I inquired of all sea-farers. B. Mets. 85[a] (not נחיתי); a. fr.

נָחָה, נחי (b. h.; cmp. נוּחַ) *to bring to rest, to lead*. Ex. R. s. 20 (ref. to Ex. XIII, 17) לא נָחָם ממצרים וכ׳ he did not lead them from Egypt to Palestine by the route of eleven journeys; Tanh. B'shall. 1 נחם נהגם *naham* means, he led them; v. נִיחוּם.

נָחִיל m. (חֲלַל, חול; cmp. נַחַל) 1) *basket* for catching fish. Y. Sabb. XIII, end, 14[b] [read:] ולהעלות נ׳ של דגים וכ׳ and to bring up a basket of fish with the child; (Men. 64[a] מצודה).—2) *bee-hive*, also *the bees of a hive, swarm*. Y. Sabb. IV, 7[a] top נ׳ של דבורין (Bab. ib. 43[a] כוורת); Y. Bets. V, beg. 62[d]; a. e.—B. Kam. X, 2 מכאן יצא נ׳ זה this swarm came from here. Tosef. Bets. III, 4. Tosef. M. Kat. I, 6 נחיל דבורים שברח וכ׳ ed. Zuck. (Var. נחיל) a swarm of bees that flew away may be brought back (during the festive week); a. fr.—*Pl.* נְחִילִים, נְחִילִין. B. Bath. V, 3 פירות כוורת נוטל שלשה נ׳ וכ׳ he who buys the issue (bees) of a bee-hive takes three swarms of young bees &c., v. סָרַס.

נְחִיל ch. same, *swarm*. Targ. Y. Deut. XXI, 8 נ׳ דמורנין a swarm of worms, v. מוּרָנָא.

נְחִילָה f. (homilet.=נַחֲלָה) *inheritance*.—*Pl.* נְחִילוֹת. Midr. Till. to Ps. V, 1 (ref. to הנחילות ib.) על שתי חנ׳ שנחל דוד וכ׳ ed. Bub. (oth. ed. שני, corr. acc.) for the two inheritances, because David inherited royalty &c.; Yalk. ib. 629 על שני נְחָלוֹת. Midr. Till. l. c. בשתי נ׳ נחלנו וכ׳ two inheritances: we inherited thee and inherited the Torah.

נְחֵים, v. נְחַם.

נְחִיצָה f. (נָחַץ) *pressing, driving on*. Num. R. s. 10 (ref. to Jud. IV, 3) לפי שהיה מחרפם ומגדפם בנ׳ because he railed at them while driving them on to labor.

נָחִיר m., *pl.* נְחִירִין (b. h. נְחִירַיִם; נָחַר) *nostrils; trnsf. outlets*. Tosef. Mikv. V, 1.

נְחִירָא ch. same, *nostril*. Targ. Job XXXIX, 20; a. e.—Gitt. 69[a] לדמא דאתי מנ׳ for bleeding from the nose. Snh. 67[b] נפיץ ושדי ... מנְחִירֵיה blew his nose and threw bands of silk out of his nose (Rashi: מנְחִירָיו, v. preced.); a. fr.—*Pl.* נְחִירֵי, נְחִירִין. Targ. Ps. CXV, 6; a. e.—Y. Yeb. XVI, beg. 15[c] יהבין ... על נְחִירֵיהוֹן put plasters on their noses (to disguise themselves); Y. Sot. IX, 23[c] bot.; v. סִיפְלָנִי.

נְחִירָה f. (נָחַר) 1) *stabbing*. Hull. 17[a] נ׳ שלהן וכ׳ the stabbing of them is named *sh'hitah*. Ib. בשר נ׳ flesh of an animal killed by stabbing (instead of ritual cutting). Ker. V, 1 דם נ׳ blood of a stabbed animal; a. e.—2) *the mucous discharge of a healing wound*. Nidd. 64[b].

נְחֵית, v. נְחַת.

נְחִיתוּתָא, v. נַחֲתָא.

נ׳ ימא, נחיתי, v. נָחוֹתָא.

נְחִיתַת, v. נַחֲתָא.

נַחַל m. (b.h.; חלל, חול; cmp. מְחִילָּה) *wady, river-bed, ravine, stream*. Sabb. 56[b] (ref. to I Sam. XV, 5) על עסקי נ׳ (he was discussing) the subject of *nahal* (Deut. XXI, 4), i. e. the regard due to human lives. Cant. R. to I, 2 עד שנעשה כנ׳ נובע until he (through his erudition) becomes like a bubbling stream; a. e.—*Pl.* נְחָלִים, נְחָלִין. Ib. מה מים .. ונעשין נ׳ נ׳ as waters come down in drops and grow to be torrents; Midr. Till. to Ps. I. Ber. 16[a] (ref. to Num. XXIV, 6) מה נ׳ ... אף אהלים וכ׳ as the waters of streams raise man from uncleanness to cleanness, so do the tents (of learning) &c.; a. fr.

נַחֲלָא, נַחַל ch. same. Targ. Gen. XXVI, 19. Targ. Num. XIII, 24. Targ. Ps. LXXIV, 15; a. fr.—[Targ. Is. XXXVIII, 12 נַחַל, v. נְוַל III.]—*Pl.* נַחֲלִין, נַחֲלַיָּא, נַחֲלֵי. Targ. Deut. VIII, 7. Targ. Koh. I, 7. Targ. Prov. VIII, 26 (h. text חוצות); a. e.

נָחַל (b. h.; denom. of נַחֲלָה, q. v.) *to inherit*. B. Bath. VIII, 1 יש נוֹחֲלִין ומַנְחִילִין there are such relations as inherit from and eventually transmit to one another (e. g. father and son); ויש נוחלין ולא מנחילין and some inherit, but (when they die) do not transmit their estate to those whose natural heirs they would have been (e. g. son and mother). Kidd. I, 10 תוֹחֵל את הארץ and shall inherit the land (of life everlasting). Sifré Num. 133 יודע .. שהבנות נוֹחֲלוֹת Moses knew that daughters (in the absence of sons) are legal heirs. Midr. Till. to Ps. V, beg. (ref. to Num. XXI, 19) משנָחֲלוּ ע״ז בא עליהם וכ׳ when they adopted idolatry, the angel of death came upon them. Ib. נחלו

לחק״בה לאלוה והוא נ׳ וכ׳ they adopted the Lord as God, and he adopted them as a people; ib. ממתנה נַחֲלָתִי לאל through the gift (of the well in the desert) I adopted God; מתוך שנתן לי הקב״ה הבאר נחלתי אותו (ed. Bub.) because the Lord gave me the well as a gift, I adopted him; Erub. 54^a וכיון שניתנה לו במתנה נְחָלוֹ אל and since it (the Law) is given him as a gift, the Lord claims him as his own; a. fr.

Hif. הִנְחִיל *to transmit by legal succession; to give in possession.* B. Bath. l. c., v. supra. Tosef. B. Mets. XI, 32, a. fr. שעל מנת כן ה׳ וכ׳ for Joshua gave possession of the land with such provisions (restricting the rights of ownership). Ukts. III, 12 עתיד הקב״ה לְהַנְחִיל וכ׳ (Snh. 100^a ליתן) the Lord will in the hereafter give every righteous man possession of &c. B. Bath. 114^b אין הבן יורש את אמו בקבר להנחיל וכ׳ a son in the grave does not succeed his mother so as to transmit his estate to his paternal brothers; a. fr.

נַחֲלָא, v. נַחַל ch.

נַחֲלָה f. (b. h.; חזל) [*turn, lot,*] *inheritance, right of succession.* B. Bath. VIII, 4 אחד הבן ואחד הבת בנ׳ the same law of succession applies to sons and (eventually) to daughters (v. ib. 122^b). Bekh. VIII, 1, v. בְּכוֹר. Midr. Till. to Ps. V, 1 (play on נחילות ib.) על הנ׳ שנחלתם וכ׳ for the possession which you took from me, and for the possession which I took from you; a. fr.—Trnsf. *the central sanctuary at Shiloh* or *at Jerusalem.* Tosef. Zeb. XIII, 20; Zeb. 119^a, sq.; Meg. 10^a, contrad. to מְנוּחָה.—*Pl.* נַחֲלוֹת. B. Bath. VIII, 2 סדר נ׳ וכ׳ the following is the order of succession (among relatives). Ib. 117^a משונה נחלה זו מכל נ׳ שבעולם this division of inheritance (after the conquest of Canaan) is different from all other successions; a. fr.—Yalk. Ps. 629, v. נְחִילָה.

נָחַם (b. h.; cmp. נוּחַ) *to be at ease.* Ex. R. s. 20 (homiletic interpret. of נָחָם, Ex. XIII, 17) אמר הקב״ה איני מתנחם וכ׳ the Lord said, I shall not be contented, until &c., for we read ולא נָחַם (perhaps meant for נִחַם *Nif.*).

Pi. נִיחַם *to comfort, console.* Pesik. Naḥ., p. 128^a א״ל הקב״ה אני ואתם נלך וּנְנַחֲמֶנָּה the Lord said to them (the prophets), Myself and you, let us go and comfort her (Jerusalem); ib. נַחֲמוּהָ עמי וכ׳ comfort her, O my people; comfort her, you on high (angels) &c. Ib. הקב״ה שלחני אצלך לְנַחֲמֵךְ the Lord sent me to thee (Jerusalem) to comfort thee. Ib.[b] נַחֲמוּנִי נחמוני עמי comfort me, comfort me, O my people. Pesik. R. s. 30 ונכנסו חביריו לְנַחֲמוֹ and his friends came in to comfort him; אם על אשתו מְנַחֲמִים לו וכ׳ if it is for the loss of his wife that they seek to console him, and he refuses to be consoled &c. Midd. II, 2 השוכן בבית הזה יְנַחֶמְךָ may He who resides in this house console thee. Y. Gitt. V, 47^c top; Y. Dem. IV, 24^a bot. וּמְנַחֲמִין אבילי וכ׳ and you must comfort the gentile mourners (of your place) as well as the Jewish mourners; Y. Ab. Zar. I, 39^c bot. ניחמים (corr. acc.); Tosef. Gitt. V (III), 5; a. fr.—מְנַחֵם *the consoling friend of the mourner.* Yalk. Prov. 947 בבית האבל בחול פורס מנ׳ ויהיב לאבל ... יש לה מנ׳ פורס מנ׳ וכ׳ in the house of the mourner, on week days, the comforter breaks the bread and gives it to the mourner, as it is written (Lam. I, 17), 'Zion breaks (the bread) with her own hands, she has no comforter', but if she had a comforter, the comforter would break it &c.—*Pl.* מְנַחֲמִין, מְנַחֲמִים. M. Kat. 27^a בית המנ׳ the room where the comforters meet. Ib.[b] כיון שמינענע ... אין מנ׳ וכ׳ as soon as the mourner nods with his head (indicating that he accepts their consolations), the friends are no longer permitted to sit with him; a. fr.—Sabb. 152^a מת שאין לו מנ׳ a deceased person that leaves no direct relations to be comforted.

Nif. נִחַם, *Hithpa.* הִתְנַחֵם, *Nithpa.* נִתְנַחֵם 1) *to be comforted, accept consolation.* Pesik. l. c. מי צריך לְהִנָּחֵם which of them is in need of being comforted?; ib. לְהִתְנַחֵם. Snh. 19^a תִּתְנַחֲמוּ be comforted. Ib. מִתְנַחֵם מאחרים receiving consolations from others. Pesik. R. l. c. ואינו מתנחם, v. supra. Gen. R. s. 84 מִתְנַחֲמִים על המתים וכ׳ people accept consolation for dead persons but not for living ones (that have disappeared); a. fr.—Ib. s. 27 (expl. וינחם, Gen. VI, 6) מתנ׳ אני שבראתי וכ׳ I have that consolation that I created him (man) to live on earth below &c.—2) *to seek comfort; to be sorry, regret, reconsider.* Ib. מתנ׳ אני שעשיתי וכ׳ I regret that I made him, and that he was placed on earth. Ex. R. s. 45, beg. ואני מתנ׳ עליו and I am sorry for him (reconsider my judgment). Num. R. s. 23 (ref. to Num. XXIII, 19) לא בן עמרם עשה אותו לְהִנָּחֵם did not the son of Amram cause him (God) to reconsider (Ex. XXXII, 14); ib. לְהִתְנַחֵם; Y. Taan. I, 65^b bot. שעשה לאל שיִתְנֶחָם; a. fr.

נְחֵים, נַחֵם ch. same. [Targ. Y. II Gen. XXXV, 9 תְּחִימַת; some ed., read: נַחֵימַת *Pa.*; v. גְּרַם II.]

Pa. נַחֵים, נַחֵם *to comfort.* Targ. Gen. L, 21 נָחֵם ed. Berl. (v. Berl. Targ. O. II, p. 18). Targ. Is. LXI, 2; a. fr.—Targ. Job II, 11 לְנַחֲמוּתֵיה to comfort him.—Part. מְנַחֵם, pl. מְנַחֲמִין, v. preced. Targ. II Sam. X, 3.—Keth. 8^b אתא לְנַחוּמֵי צעוריי וכ׳ he came to console, and he grieved him? Y. Shek. V, 48^d bot., a. e. בעי מְנַחֲמְתֵיה desired to comfort him. Snh. 19^a כי מְנַחֲמֵי אחריני וכ׳ when others comfort him; a. fr.

Ithpa. אִתְנַחֵם as preced. *Nif.* Targ. Job XLII, 6; a. fr.—Y. l. c. ולא קביל עלוי מִתְנַחֲמָה and would not allow himself to be comforted; a. e.

נֶחָמָה f. (b. h.; preced.) *consolation, relief.* Taan. 11^b אל יראה בְּנֶחָמַת צבור (Yalk. Ex. 264 בנחמות, *pl.*) shall not live to see the relief of the community. Pes. 54^b (man does not know) יום הנ׳ what day his relief from trouble will come; a. fr.—Esp. הנ׳ *the comfort* (of Zion), *restoration of Israel.* Macc. 5^b, a. fr. (a euphemistic affirmation) אראה בנ׳ לא וכ׳ may I not live to see the consolation, if &c.—*Pl.* נֶחָמוֹת. Y. Ber. V, beg. 8^d the prophets שהיו חותמין ... ובדברי נ׳ who closed their books with words of praise and of consolation (predictions of relief; Bab. ib. 31^a תנחומים); a. e.

נַחֲמוּתָא, infin. *Pa.* of נְחֵם q. v.

נְחֶמְיָה (b. h.) *Nehemiah*, 1) N., son of Hacaliah, governor of Judea. Sabb. 123^b. Snh. 93^b; a. e.—2) name of several Tannaim and Amoraim. Yeb. XVI, 7 N. of Beth-Dŏli.—Ter. VIII, 6, a. fr. R. N.—Men. 68^b Judah ben N.—Pes. 22^b, a. fr. נ׳ העמסוני.—Y. Ber. III, 6^a (some ed.

(נחומיה).—Y. Peah I, 16ᶜ bot. ר׳ נ׳ בר עוקבן; Y. Yeb. XIV, beg. 14ᵇ ר׳ נ׳ בר מר ע׳.—Y. Shek. V, end, 49ᵇ; a. oth.—V. Fr. Darkhé p. 137; p. 176; M'bo p. 116ᵇ.

***נַחְמָם** m. (חָמַם; formed like נחתום) *attendant at hot baths, bather* (practicing medicine). Y. Ab. Zar. II, 40ᵈ top, opp. רופא אומן professional surgeon.

נַחֲמַן, *pl.* of נֶחָמְתָא.

נַחְמָן pr. n. m. *Naḥman.* Gen. R. s. 25, v. נוּחַ *Hif.*—Esp. name of several persons. Y. Dem. I, 22ᵃ; Y. Shek. V, 48ᵈ ר׳ שמואל בר נ׳. Y. Meg. I, 70ᵇ top; a. oth.—V. Fr. M'bo, p. 116ᵇ, sq.—Esp. R. N., the renowned Babylonian Amora. Keth. 94ᵃ; a. fr.

נַחְמָנִי pr. n. m. *Naḥmani.* Pes. 23ᵇ, a. fr. שמואל בר נ׳. Y. Sabb. I, 3ᵈ bot. נחמן בריה דר׳ שמואל בר נ׳; Y. Meg. I, 70ᵇ top נחמן בריה דר׳ ש׳ בר נחמן; v. preced.—R. Hash. 34ᵇ, a. fr. רבה בר נ׳.

נֶחָמְתָא f. ch.=h. נֶחָמָה.—*Pl.* נֶחָמָתָא, נַחֲמָן. Targ. Y. Gen. I, 21. Targ. Is. XVIII, 4 (ed. Lag. נִיחֲמַן); a. fr.—B. Kam. 38ᵃ מאי איח לי גבי נ׳ דבבלאי what do I care for the consolations of the Babylonians? B. Bath. 14ᵇ וסיפיה נ׳ and ends with consolations. Ib. סמכינן.. נ׳ לנ׳ we join ... the consolations at the end of one book to those at the beginning of the next, v. חוּרְבָּנָא.—Y. Snh. X, 28ᵇ bot. וכל טבן ונ׳ וכ׳ and all the good times and consolations (predicted) in the world have come true in my own days.

נַחְנָא, *pl.* of אֲנָא.

נָחַץ (cmp. חצץ I a. חוּץ I) *to squeeze in, strap. Part. pass.* נָחוּץ *closely corded.* Y. Meg. III, 74ᶜ bot. (not נחוח), v. קוֹנְטְרָא.

נָחַר (sec. r. of חור, חרר) 1) *to perforate,* esp. *to kill by stabbing.* Ḥull. V, 3 הנוחר if one stabs (instead of cutting according to ritual). Pes. 49ᵇ מותר לנוחרו you may stab him.—[Sifra Aḥăré, Par. 9, ch. XIII שלא תנחור, read: תְּנַחֵשׁ, v. נָחַשׁ; Rabad תנקור, v. נָקַר II.]—2) (denom. of נְחִירַיִם) *to discharge mucus, run.* Nidd. 64ᵇ כל זמן שנוחרת as long as the healing wound discharges matter. V. נְחִירָה.

Pi. נִיחֵר *to be stabbed.* Ḥull. 17ᵃ (ref. to ישחט, Num. XI, 22) יְנַחֵר להם מיבעיא ליה (not ינחר) if no ritual cutting was prescribed for the people in the desert, the text ought to have read, 'shall be stabbed for them'.

Pi. נִיחֵר (denom. of נחירים) *to snort.* Snh. 94ᵃ (play on סנחריב) שׂח וניחר וכ׳ he spoke and snorted forth words against heaven.

נְחַר ch. same, 1) *to stab.* Targ. Y. Num. XXII, 40.—Gitt. 69ᵃ ולִינְחְרֵיהּ לכלבא וכ׳ and let them stab the dog in the pupil of his eye.—2) *to blow the nose, sneeze, to give a sign by means of a nasal sound.* Ib. 68ᵃ נ׳ ליה רב וכ׳ R. Ḥ. uttered a sound of warning behind him. Sabb. 152ᵇ נ׳ בהו וכ׳ R. A. (who was buried there) snorted at them (warned them off; Ag. Hatt. נחם). R. Hash. 34ᵇ כי נְחִירְנָא לך (ed. נחירנא, v. Rabb. D. S. a. l. note 8) when I give thee a sign. Ber. 62ᵇ.

Pa. נַחַר *to rebuke.* Kidd. 81ᵇ נַחְרוּ ביה they rebuked him (for his misbehavior).

נַחְרְתָא f. (preced.) *wrath.* Gen. R. s. 67 (ref. to Am. I, 11) עברתיה ונַחְרְתֵּיה וכ׳ his anger and his wrath do not cease &c.; Yalk. ib. 116 וחרתיה (corr. acc.).

נָחַשׁ (b. h.; cmp. לחש) *to whisper.*

Pi. נִיחֵשׁ *to divine, to make action dependent on an omen, to augur.* Tosef. Sabb. VII (VIII), 13 איזהו מְנַחֵשׁ וכ׳ a diviner (under the law, Lev. XIX, 26) is he who says, 'my staff fell out of my hand' (it portends evil) &c.; Snh. 65ᵇ. Ib. 66ᵃ כגון אלו המְנַחֲשִׁים בחולדה וכ׳ like those who divine (evil or luck) from a weasel, birds &c. Y. Sabb. VI, end, 8ᵈ כל המנחש סופו לבוא עליו if one believes in omens, what he fears will finally befall him (with ref. to לא נחש Num. XXIII, 23, changed into לו נחש); Ned. 32ᵃ כל המנחש לו נחש for him who believes in omens, the omen exists (will be realized). Ib. כל אדם שאינו מנ׳ he who rejects divination. Mekh. B'shall. s. 2 שמא יְנַחֲשׁוּ ויחזרו וכ׳ lest they consider it a bad omen and go back. Ib. וזקני מדין נִחֲשׁוּ וכ׳ and the Midianite elders considered (Balaam's death) a bad omen and went home; a. fr.—Sifra Vayikra, Par. 9, ch. XIII (ref. to Lev. XVIII, 3) [read:] שלא תְּנַחֵשׁ thou must not augur (v. however, נָקַר II).

נְחַשׁ I, *Pa.* נַחֵישׁ, נַ׳ same. Targ. II Kings XXI, 6. Ib. XVII, 17 (ed. Wil. וּנְחִישׁוּ *Pe.*); a. fr.—Ḥull. 95ᵇ דְנַחֵישׁ because he had made his movements dependent on an omen. Yeb. 120ᵇ כיס.. מְנַחֲשֵׁי אינשי וכ׳ as to purse and bag people are superstitious and do not lend them; a. e.

נְחַשׁ II, *Af.* אַנְחֵשׁ, הַנְחֵשׁ (denom. of נְחָשׁ) *to use copper* and plate it with silver, *to plate.* Pesik. Ekhah, p. 122ᵇ הַנְחֵשׁ ליה make it plated for him (in place of solid silver); Yalk. Is. 258 אבחיש, read: אַנְ׳.

נַחַשׁ m. (b. h.; נָחַשׁ) *divination from omen, superstition.* Num. R. s. 20 בעל נ׳ a believer in omens. Ned. 32ᵃ, v. נָחַשׁ. Y. Sabb. VI, 8ᶜ bot. אע״פ שאין נ׳ יש סימן although you must not make them an omen, they are a sign (presage); Ḥull. 95ᵇ. Ib. כל נ׳ שאינו .. אינו נ׳ an omen which is not proposed in the manner of Eliezer ... (Gen. XXIV, 13, sq.) or of Jonathan (I Sam. XIV, 9, sq.) is not considered a divination (in the sense of Lev. XIX, 26); a. fr.—*Pl.* נְחָשִׁים. Tanḥ. Balak 4 בעל נ׳, v. supra.

נָחָשׁ m. (b. h.; נָחַשׁ) 1) [*the hissing,*] *serpent.* Gen. R. s. 22 נ׳ הקדמוני the original serpent (the seducer of Eve). Ib. s. 20 נ׳ זה רשע בעל תשובות that serpent is wicked and skilled in arguments. Bekh. 8ᵃ נ׳ לשבע שנים וכ׳ a serpent's pregnancy lasts seven years, and for that wicked animal I find no parallel (in the vegetable kingdom). Gen. R. s. 54 חנ׳ של בית the domestic serpent (harmless); a. fr.—*Pl.* נְחָשִׁים. Ib. s. 84 נ׳ ועקרבים snakes and scorpions; a. fr.—2) *a pungent (poisonous) fluid* in the leaves or in the stems of onions kept for a long time in the ground. Erub. 29ᵇ.—3) *a disease of the eye,* v. חִלָּזוֹן. Bekh. VI, 2 חלזון נ׳ וכ׳, expl. ib. 38ᵇ as identical with חלזון; Tosef. ib. IV, 2; Sifra Emor ch. II, Par. 3.

נְחַשׁ, נַחְשָׁא ch.=h. נָחָשׁ. Targ. Y. II Num. XXIII, 23.—

Snh. 19^a נ׳ קא רמי להו (by saying to his comforters, 'be comforted') does he not cast an evil omen on them (that they would suffer bereavement)? Gen.R.s.87, v. חָן; a.e.—*Pl.* נְחַד, נַחְשַׁיָּא, נַחְשִׁין. Targ. Num. l.c. (O. ed. Berl. נַחֲשַׁ׳). Targ. O. ib. XXIV, 1. Targ. Y. Lev. XIX, 26; a. fr.

נְחָשָׁא, (נְחַשׁ), נְחָשׁ m. ch.=h. נְחוֹשֶׁת. Targ. Jer. XV, 20. Targ. Num. XXI, 9; a. fr.—Y. Kidd. I, 58^d נ׳ יקיר נ׳ זליל copper rises and falls (silver being the standard), v. יַקִּירָא. Esth. R. to I, 22 (ר׳ עזריה) מה דהדין קיתונא דנ׳ וכ׳ what purpose this copper vessels serves, an earthen vessel may serve as well; Lev. R. s. 12 (not נחשת); a. e.

נַחְשׁוֹל m. (חָשַׁל; Syr. מחשולא, P.Sm. 1404) *a crushing wind* (cmp. I Kings XIX, 11); esp. (שבים) נ׳ *gale on high sea*, also *Nahshol*, a spirit. Tosef. Yoma II, 4; Yoma 38^a (Y. ib. III, 41^a סער גדול). Tosef. B. Mets. VII, 14; B. Kam. 116^b; Y. B. Mets. VI, end, 11^a ספינה שעמד עליה נ׳ והדיקל וכ׳ if a gale threatened the ship, and they lighted it. Pesik. R. s. 32 אחזו נחשולה (corr. acc.). Num. R. s. 13 (play on נחשון) על שם שירד תחלה לנ׳ שבים because he was the first to go down to the surf (or to Nahshol) in the sea. Gitt. 56^b עמד עליו נ׳ שבים וכ׳ a *nahshol* in the sea stood up against him to drown him; Yalk. Koh. 972 נ׳ של ים.

נַחְשׁוֹלָא, נַחְשׁוֹל ch. same. Targ. Jon. I, 4. Ib. 15; a. e.—Lev. R. s. 22 מחא נ׳ בימא a *nahshol* smote the sea; Gen. R. s. 10 מחאיה נחשלא בימא (corr. acc.); Koh. R. to V, 8 מחא נ׳ גו ימא.

נַחְשׁוֹן (b. h.) pr. n. m. *Nahshon*, prince of the tribe of Judah. Num. R. s. 13, v. נַחְשׁוֹל h. Snh. 12^a (in a secret letter) עמוסי ירכי נ׳ the burdened (the officers) of the offspring of N., i. e. of the Nasi of Palestine; a. fr.

נַחְשִׁירְכָן, נַחְשִׁר׳ (not נחשיד׳) m. (Pers., v. Nöld. Mand. Gramm. p. 63) ***hunter; a shrewd man.*** Targ. Gen. XXV, 27 (h. text ידע ציד; cmp. Gen. R. s. 63; Tanh. Tol'doth 8).

נחשלא, v. נַחְשׁוֹלָא.

נַחְשִׁרְכָן, v. נַחְשִׁירְכָן.

נְחָשֶׁת, נְחָשְׁתָּן, v. נְחוֹשֶׁת, נְחוּשְׁתָּן.

נַחַת f. (b. h.; נוּחַ) 1) *rest, tray, stand* (v. אַנְחוּתָה). Hag. 26^b; Men. 96^b, a. e. כלי עץ העשוי לנ׳ a wooden utensil intended for resting things on it (table &c.). Gen. R. s. 25; s. 33 לשם נ׳ התיבה נקרא Noah was named from the resting of the ark (Gen. VIII, 4). Yeb. 103^b סנדל של נ׳ ע״ז Ar. (in ed. our w. omitted) a sandal used as a rest for an idol.—2) *ease; gentleness; comfort.* Erub. 83^b שלזה תשמישו בנ׳ which one neighbor can make use of with ease, opp. בקשה with difficulty. Ber. 56^b בנ׳ at a slow trot, opp. בדהוק at full speed. Snh. 92^a, v. נָהַג; a. fr.—רוח נ׳ *gratification, pleasure.* Keth. 95^a תימא נ׳ ר׳ עשיתי לבעלי she may say, I did it only to gratify my husband (but did not mean to sell). Hag. 16^b כדי לעשות נ׳ ר׳ לנשים to let the (offering) women have the satisfaction (of putting their hands on the sacrifices). Ber. 17^a ועושה נ׳ ר׳ ליוצרו and acts so as to please his Creator; a. fr.

נָחַת (b. h.; sec. r. of נוּחַ) *to be put down, to go down.*

Nif. נִחַת same, *to be humbled, bow.* Y. Ber. IV, beg. 7^a (ref. to Mal. II, 5) קודם .... נ׳ הוא before he mentions the Name (in the benediction), he must bow.—V. חֲתָא.

נְחֵית, נְחַת ch. same, *to go down.* Impf. יֵחוֹת, inf. מֵיחַת, מֵיחוּת, imper. חוֹת. Targ. Ex. XV, 5. Targ. Y. Gen. XLIV, 26; a. fr.—[Targ. Y. II Gen. XLIX, 23 לְמִנְחָתָא, some ed. לְמִנְחֲתָא, read: לְמִנְחֲתָא *Pa.*]—Sabb. 41^a כי נָחֵית when one is going down (to bathe). Ib. כי קא נָחְתִי when they were going down. Meg. 25^a הההוא דנ׳ וכ׳ a man went down (to the praying desk) in the presence of &c. B. Kam. 39^a נ׳ לעומק וכ׳ goes down to the depth of the law; a. fr.—B. Bath. 133^a נָחְתָא לדיקלא she seizes the palm-tree for her widowhood, v. יָרַד.

Pa. נַחֵית 1) *to put down.* Yoma 47^a ונַחֲתֵית וכ׳ and let him put down the pan; v. חָתֵי I.—2) *to lower, remove.* Targ. Y. II Gen. XLIX, 23 (v. supra; Y. I לְמַחְתָא *Af.*).

Af. אַחֵית, אַנְחֵית *to put down, rest; to let come down.* Targ. O. Deut. XXVIII, 56 (h. text הַצֵּג). Targ. Y. I Gen. XLIX, 23, v. supra. Targ. O. ib. II, 5. Targ. Ez. XXIII, 15; a. fr.—*Part. pass.* מַחַת (מַחֵית); f. מַחֲתָא; *pl.* מַחֲתִין; מַחֲתָן *placed, resting, lying; inlaid.* Targ. O. Gen. VIII, 11 (ed. Vien. נְחִית; Y. מְחִית). Targ. Jer. XXIV, 1. Targ. Esth. VIII, 15; a. fr.—Pesik. B'shall., p. 91^a והוא מַחֵית לכון and he will take bread down out of the oven (cmp. רְדָה II). Taan. 21^b הוה מַחֵית גברי וכ׳ used to place men apart &c. Sabb. 101^a גוד אַחֵית וכ׳, v. נְגַד. Ned. 91^b הוו מַחֲתָן תחלי וכ׳ cress was deposited there. B. Bath. 69^a, a. fr.

Ithpe. אִיתְנְחַת, *Ithpa.* אִיתְּחַת 1) *to be brought down.* Targ. Gen. XXXIX, 1. Targ. Ez. XXXI, 17; a. fr.—Y. Peah XIII, 21^a bot. איתנחת בן ניכסוי became poor, v. יָרַד; Y. Keth XI, 34^b bot.—2) (of an argument) *to be settled.* B. Bath. 129^a אִנְּחַתָה לן חדא, v. נוּחַ *Ithpe.*

נַחְתָּא f., constr. נַחְתַּת (preced.) *layer.* Targ. O. Ex. XVI, 13 (Var. נְחִיתַת, נַחְתַּת; h. text שכבת). Targ. Ps. CX, 3 (Bxt. נְחִיתוּת).

נַחְתּוֹם, נחתּם m. (חָתַם; cmp. טָפוּס) *baker of bread in moulds, professional baker.* Tosef. Hall. I, 7 נ׳ אחד מארבעים וכ׳ the professional baker has to give one forty-eighth portion of his dough to the priest, opp. בעל הבית a private baker; Y. ib. II, end, 58^d. Hall. II, 7 נ׳ שהוא עושה למכור בשוק the baker that makes bread for sale in the market. Y. Dem. V, 24^d top נ׳ עושה טפוס אחד וכ׳ each baker makes his own peculiar form of bread, while the dealer (פלטר) deals with many bakers; ib. נ׳ עושה כמה טפוסין וכ׳ a baker makes several forms, while the dealer deals with one baker; a. fr.—ר׳ יהודה הנ׳ R. Judah, the baker, prob. identical with R. Judah ben Baba. Y. Hag. II, 77^b bot. Tosef. Ohol. XVIII, 13; a. e.—*Pl.* נַחְתּוֹמִים, נַחְתּוֹמִין. Y. Hall. l. c. Kel. XV, 2, v. אֲרוּבָה I; a. fr.

נַחְתּוֹם, נַחְתּוֹמָא, נַחְתּוֹ׳ ch. same. Targ. Gen. XL, 17; a. fr.—*Pl.* נַחְתּוֹמִין, נַחְתּוֹמַיָּא, נַחְתּוֹמֵי. Ib. 2. Y. ib. 1. Targ. Jer. XXXVII, 21; a. e.—B. Bath. 20^b בדנ׳ of the bakers' ovens.

נַחְתּוֹמַר m. (preced.; cmp. חֲלַיְטָר) *bread-shop-keeper.* Y. B. Bath. II, beg. 13[b].

נַחְתּוֹם, v. נַחְתּוֹם.

נְטָא, v. נְטַר.

בַּר נ׳, נְטוֹזָא pr. n. m. *Bar Natoza.* Y. Ter. VIII, 45[c] bot.; Y. Ab. Zar. II, 41[a].

נְטוּל m. (נְטַל) *heaviness, load.* Targ. Prov. XXVII, 3.

נְטוּל, v. נְטַל.

נְטוּלָא m. ch. = next w.—*Pl.* נְטוּלֵי. Hull. 54[b] דדמיא לנ׳ it may be classified with the cases of lost limbs.

נְטוּלֶת f. (נָטַל) *the case of an animal in whose body an organ is found to be absent* or *destroyed.* Hull. 43[a].—V. נָטַל.

נְטוּפָא pr. n. pl., v. נְטוֹפָה.

נְטוֹפָא m. ch. (נְטַף) = h. נָטָף, *balm.* Targ. O. Ex. XXX, 34 (ed. Vien. נְ׳). Targ. I Chr. II, 54 (Var. ed. Rahmer נטופתי). Targ. Ruth IV, 20.—Gitt. 69[b] וניגבול בנְטֹפָא let him knead it with balm.

נְטוֹפָה I pr. n. m. *Netofah.* Targ. Ruth IV, 20 (after I Chr. II, 54 נטופתי).

נְטוֹפָה II, נְטוֹפָא (b. h. נְטֹפָה) pr. n. pl. *Netofah,* near Bethlehem in Juda. Gen. R. s. 79 בקעתא דבית נ׳ the valley of Beth N.; Yalk. Koh. 972; (Gen. R. s. 10 טרפא); v. טוֹפָה.—(ח)נ׳ זית name of a species of olives, *Netofah olive.* Peah VII, 1 an olive which bore at one time a special name (אפי׳) כזית נ׳ בשעתו Ms. M. (ed. חנ׳) (even if it be) like the N. olive; Tosef. ib. III, 9. Y. ib. VII, beg. 20[a] היתה דהוו שניהן נ׳ if two of the trees were N. trees; כל שדהו נ׳ if all the trees of his field were N. Ib. (defining נ׳) נוטף שמן one dripping oil, contrad. to שפכוני (pouring), yielding large quantities of oil. Ib. ותהא נטופה (corr. acc.).—Denom.:

נְטוֹפָתִי m. (b. h.) *of Netofa.* Taan. 28[a] סלמאי הנטפתי Ms. M. (ed. סלמאי הנְתוֹפָתִי, v. Rabb. D. S. a. l. note; cmp. I Chr. II, 54); Tosef. ib. IV (III), 8 סלמאי הנט׳ Var. (ed. Zuck. הנתוצתי); Y. ib. IV, 68[b] bot. סלמיי הנתיצתי (ed. Krot. דנ׳; corr. acc.).

נְטוֹפְתָא, v. נְטוֹפְתָא.

נְטוֹרָא m. (נְטַר) *watchman, observer.* Yalk. Koh. 989 מה רשו... תציק האי נ׳ וכ׳ wherein lies the power of that sheep (Israel), that it can feed among seventy bears (nations)? Said he, strong is the watchman that guards it against all of them.—*Pl.* נְטוֹרַיָּא, נְטוֹרִין. Targ. Y. Deut. XVIII, 10 נְטוֹרֵי נחשין (ed. Amst. נט׳) observers of omens (h. text מנחש). Targ. Y. Gen. XLII, 6 (not נְטוֹ׳); a. e.—Y. Hag. I, 76[c] אייתון לן נְטוֹרֵי קרתא bring before us the guards of the town; Lam. R. introd. (R. Abba 2); Midr. Till. to Ps. CXXVII; Yalk. Ps. 881; ib. אילין נ׳ קרתא וכ׳ are these the guardians of the town? They are the destroyers &c. Lev. R. s. 12 צריו לי מן נ׳ I am afraid of the guards (to open the wine shop); Esth. R. to I, 22 (ר׳ עזירה); a. e.

נְטוּרָא m. (preced.) [*that which is reserved,*] *reward.* —*Pl.* נְטוּרִין. Gen. R. s. 11 דוגמא נ׳ some ed., v. הוּגְמַטְרִין.—[Tosef. Sot. VIII, 6 נטורים Var., v. גוֹעֲרִין.]

נְטוּשׁ m. (נָטַשׁ) *a fugitive whose estate is abandoned.* Y. Keth. IV, 29[a] bot. נ׳ זה שיצא לדעת a *natush* is he who left of his own accord (not carried away by force); Y. Yeb. XV, 15[a] top.—*Pl.* נְטוּשִׁים, נְטוּשִׁין. Ib.; Tosef. Keth. VIII, 3 אלו הן נכסי נ׳ וכ׳ this is (in a legal sense) the abandoned estate of *n'ṭushim*: if the heir took possession without a report of the absentee's death having arrived, contrad. to רטושים; B. Mets. 38[b]. Ib. שמעתי שהנ׳ כשבויין I heard a tradition that the estate of fugitives is of the same legal category as that of captured persons. Ib., sq. מאי שנא הנך.. נ׳ וכ׳ why are these called *n'ṭushim,* and the others *r'ṭushim?* נ׳ דבע״כ *n.* are those who emigrate against their will (fugitives from justice).

נָטָה, נטי (b. h.) 1) (cmp. נְטַע) *to stretch; to pitch* a tent. Yalk. Gen. 67 בתחלה נ׳ אהלה וכ׳ (Gen. R. s. 39 נטע) first he pitched Sarah's tent &c.—2) *to hang over, incline; to decline.* Macc. II, 7 ונופו נוֹטֶה, v. נוֹף II; Kidd. 40[b]. Ned. IV, 5, a. e. חנוטות overhanging fruit. Y. M. Kat. III, 82[a] בנוטות when one's mustache hangs over the mouth.—Snh. 6[b] להיכן הדין נוטה which way the judgment will incline (in whose favor the verdict will be). Ib. 3[b] (ref. to Ex. XXIII, 2) עשה לך בית דין נוטה arrange for thyself a court which can lean towards one side, i. e. of uneven numbers. Gen. R. s. 96, a. fr. נ׳ למות one inclines towards dying, feels death approaching; a. v. fr.—3) *to bend, pervert judgment.* Mekh. Mishp. s. 20 שמא תאמר.. ואיני נוטה את הדין lest you say, I will take a bribe but will not pervert the law.—*Part. pass.* נָטוּי; f. נְטוּיָה; *pl.* נְטוּיִים, נְטוּיִין; נְטוּיוֹת a) *hanging over, threatening, inclining.* Snh. 109[a] קיר נ׳ a threatening wall; R. Hash. 16[b]; a. e.—Gen. R. s. 49 נ׳ למות, v. supra.—b) *spread; pitched.* Ohol. VII, 2. Tosef. ib. VIII, 2; a. e.

Hif. הִיטָּה 1) (neut. verb) *to incline.* B. Mets. 59[b] הִיטּוּ כותלי וכ׳ the walls of the school-house bowed (threatening to fall). Ib. ועדיין מַטִּין ועומדין and so they still stand bending over. Ber. 11[a] הַטֵּהוּ, v. זָקַף. Keth. 84[b]; Erub. 46[b] מַטִּין one is inclined (in favor of R. Akiba's opinion), i. e. the presumption is in his favor, opp. הלכה definite decision for general practice. Y. Snh. I, 18[a] bot. (ref. to I Kings XXII, 19) אלו מטין לכף זכות וכ׳ these argued in favor, and those against. R. Hash. 17[a] ורב חסד מַטֶּה וכ׳ and He who is abundant in kindness inclines (the scales) towards the side of kindness; a. fr.—2) *to decline, move sideways.* Keth. 10[a] a man walking in the dark, הִ׳ מצאו פתוח if he moves sideways (towards the door), he finds it open, if he does not (but strikes against the door) &c.—Trnsf. *to perform coition without violently tearing the hymen.* Ib.—3) (act. verb) *to bend*; הִ׳ דין *to wrest judgment.* Mekh. l. c. שלא תאמר.. אַטֶּה עליו את הדין say not, because he is a wicked man, I will turn the verdict against him. Peah VIII, 9 כל דיין... ומַטֶּה את הדין a judge that takes a bribe and perverts judgment; a. fr.—4) (after Ex. XXIII, 2) *to decide by majority* (cmp. פְּרַע). Snh. IV, 1 דיני ממונות מטין וכ׳ in civil law a majority of one decides in favor or against (the claimant), ודיני נפשות מטין וכ׳ in criminal law a majority of one decides in favor of the defendant, but for a verdict against the defendant a majority of two is required, v. הַטָּיָה. Mekh. l. c. הרוג על פי מטין put to death on a majority vote; מה עדים.. אף מטין בשנים as incriminating witnesses must be two, so must the majority be two.—*Part. pass.* מוּטֶּה; f. מוּטָּה *reclining, bending over.* M. Kat. 21[a]; Yeb. 103[a] בין עומד.. בין מ׳ standing, sitting or reclining. Kel. IV, 3; Tosef. ib. B. Kam. III, 10 היתה מ׳ על צדה וכ׳ if the vessel was misshaped so as to bend sideways like a sedan chair. Ib.; ib. 5 מַטָּה על צדה.—V. מוּטָּה.

נְטֵי, נְטָא, נְטָה ch. same. Snh. 26[a] דילמא.. נַטְיָיה דעתיה וכ׳ perhaps the opinion of the Lord inclines after the majority. Y. B. Bath. II, end, 13[c] חד אילן נטה גו וכ׳ a tree the branches of which hung over that Roman's ground. Ib. זיל קוץ מה דנטה גו דידיה go and cut off what hangs over his ground; a. e.

Af. אַטֵּי *to bend.* Y. Ber. II, 4[b] top לית איפשר דלא יַטֵּי מילה it is not possible that he should not turn the discussion (so as to mention the exodus from Egypt; v. Bab. ib. 13[b]).

נְטִיָּיה, נְטִיָּה f. (preced.) *spreading.* Ohol. VII, 2 כִּנְטִיַּת האוהל as a tent is spread; Tosef. ib. VIII, 2.

נְטִיל m. (נְטַל) *heavy.* Y. Snh. VI, 23[d] bot., v. קְלַל.

נְטִילָא, v. נַטְלָא.

נְטִילָה f. (נָטַל) 1) *taking; lifting up; carrying.* Zeb. 34[a]; Macc. 14[b] נְטִילַת נשמה death penalty. Y. Sabb. VII, 10[c] נ׳ נשמה taking life (destroying vitality); Bab. ib. 75[a]; a. fr.—Meg. II, 5 נטילת לולב taking up the festive wreath.—Pesik. R. s. 10 נטילת ראש lifting up the head (with the ambiguous meaning of 'taking off the head' or 'promotion'). Lev. R. s. 17; Y. Ber. II, 5[c] bot. נטילת רשות, v. רְשׁוּת.—Y. M. Kat. III, 82[a] top, a. e. נטילת צפורנים cutting the nails; a. fr.—2) נטילת ידים, or נ׳ *washing the hands* before and after meals &c. Hull. 106[a], sq. Sot. 4[b]; a. fr.

נטילה, Targ. Ps. LV, 9, v. נְטַל.

נְטִילוּתָא ch. = h. נְטִילָה, esp. *washing the hands.* Ber. 22[a] בטלוה לנ׳ they abolished the washing of hands (before prayer or studying the Law).

נְטִיעָה f. (נָטַע) 1) *planting; plant.* Cant. R. to VI, 11 בשעת נְטִיעָתָן when you plant them. Ber. 35[a] בר נ׳ that which belongs to the vegetable Kingdom. Snh. 68[a] נְטִיעַת קישואין planting of cucumbers; a. fr.—Esp. *young tree, shoot.* Bets. 25[b] נ׳ מקטע וכ׳ the law concerning young trees (עָרְלָה) cuts off the feet of the butchers (ought to teach them patience, so as not to use meat before flaying and dissecting). Shebi. I, 8 נ׳ כשמה by 'a young plant' (with reference to the Sabbatical year law) we understand what its name indicates (during the first year). Y. ib. 33[b] bot. נ׳ מעין עשר as to young shoots the proportion of ten to a field of a S'ah's size is required, v. infra; a. fr.—*Pl.* נְטִיעוֹת. Cant. R. l. c. כחן של נ׳ וכ׳ the endurance of young plants and the beauty &c., v. זִיו. Shebi. I, 6 עשר נ׳ מפוזרות וכ׳ if ten young trees are scattered over a field of one S'ah's size, we may plough the entire field for their sake (on the eve of the Sabbatical year); Succ. 34[a], a. e. עשר נ׳ the law concerning young trees in a field &c. Taan. 5[b] bot. יהי רצון שכל נ׳ שנוטעין וכ׳ may all shoots taken from thee be like thyself. Y. Yeb. I, 2[b] חמש נ׳ נטע he planted five shoots, had five sons; a. fr.—Hag. 14[b], a. e. קיצץ בנ׳ he mutilated the shoots (of the garden of religion, v. פַּרְדֵּס), i. e. became irreligious, v. קָצַץ.—Mekh. B'shall., Shir. s. 10, v. נְתִיצָה.—2) *pitching a tent, putting up a temporary structure.* Meg. 5[b], a. e., v. אַכְוַרְנְקָא, a. נָטַע.

נטיפה, v. נְטוֹפָה II.

נְטֵיר, v. נְטַר.

נְטִיר m. 1) part. pass. of נְטַר.—2) (נְטַר) *observance, worth observing.* Targ. O. Ex. XII, 42.—3) בִּנ׳ *in secret.* Targ. Job IV, 12.

נָטֵיר, נָטֵר m. (preced.) 1) part. of נְטַר.—2) *guardsman.* Targ. Ps. CXXVII, 1. Ib. CXXI, 4; a. fr.

נְטִירָה f. (נָטַר) *guarding,* esp. (with ref. to Lev. XIX, 18) *bearing grudge.* Sifra K'dosh., Par. 2, ch. IV עד היכן כחה של נ׳ וכ׳ how far does the law forbidding to bear grudge extend? If you ask your neighbor for the loan of an axe, and he refuses, and the next day he asks thee …., say not, I am not like thee; Yoma 23[a].

נְטִירוּתָא ch. same, *watching, proper care.* B. Mets. 42[a], v. קְשִׁירוּתָא. B. Kam. 48[a] קביל עליה נ׳ he assumed the duty of guarding. Ib. עליה דידיה רמי נ׳ the duty of guarding rests upon him. B. Bath. 7[b], a. e. רבנן לא צריכי נ׳ scholars require no guard; a. fr.—Pesik. Hahod., p. 56[a], v. נַטְרוֹנָא.

נְטִישָׁה f. (נָטַשׁ) *renunciation, giving up.* Y. Peah VI, beg. 19[b] (ref. to Ex. XXIII, 11) יש לך נ׳ אחרת כזו there is another resignation like this (הֶפְקֵר). Ib. נ׳ מיעוט וכ׳ the superfluous ונטשתה (Ex. l. c.) intimates a limitation: *this* you must resign indiscriminately for the benefit of the poor or of the rich, but &c.

נָטַל (b. h.; cmp. טִלְטֵל) 1) *to move, carry off; to receive, take.* B. Mets. I, 1 זה נוטל וכ׳ the one (of the claimants) gets three shares &c. Y. Sot. I, 16[d] bot., a. e. ומה שכר נָטְלוּ על כך what reward did they get for it?—Sifra Sh'mini, beg. מסיני נטלו להם they got (their punishment) from Sinai. Sabb. 151[b] טול מה וכ׳ take away what thou hast put into me. Arakh. 16[b]; B. Bath. 15[b] טול קיסם מבין עיניך (Ag. Hatt. שיניך) remove the chip from between thy eyes (teeth); טול קורה וכ׳ remove the beam from &c. Gitt. VI, 1 אף האומרת טול לי גטי even if she says, get me my letter of divorce (instead of 'receive for me'). Ib. 78[a] טְלִי גיטיך וכ׳ take up thy letter of divorce from the ground. Pesik. R. s. 26, end נָטַלְתִּי עיני I lifted up my eyes. Ber. II, 8 לא כל הרוצה לִיטוֹל לו את השם יִטּוֹל Y. ed., not every one who desires to assume a name, may assume it, i. e. not every one has a right to consider himself superior to the masses (v. יוּהֲרָא); a. v. fr.—Part. pass. נָטוּל; f. נְטוּלָה *removed.* Ned. XI, 12 (if a woman says) נ׳ אני מן היהודים I will be removed from (keep no company with) Jews; ... יפר והוא נ׳ וכ׳ the husband may forbid the vow as far as it concerns himself, and (for the rest) let her be isolated &c.—Snh. 21ᵇ נְטוּלֵי טחול persons who had their milt cut out (to make them fast runners).—V. נְטוּלָה.—2) (sub. מים) *to pour water over one's hands* for purification; נ׳ לידים, (ellipt.) נ׳ ידים, or only נ׳ *to wash the hands* before and after meals, before prayer &c. Tosef. Yad. I, 1 מי רביעית נוֹטְלִין לידים וכ׳ (Var. ed. Zuck., a. Mish. ib. I, 1 נותנין) a quantity of one fourth of a Log of water may be used for pouring over the hands of one person &c. Ib. 13 הנוֹטֵל לידים הנוטל מתכוין והנותן וכ׳ if a person had his hands washed, himself having the intention (of purification), while he who poured it had not. Ib. 2; Mish. ib. II, 3 נ׳ את הראשונים if he began to use the water for washing before the meal (v. מַיִם). Ḥull. 107ᵃ נוטלין ממנו לידים you may use it for washing the hands; Tosef. l. c. 6. Ber. VIII, 2. Ib. 51ᵃ אל תִּטּוֹל ידיך ממי וכ׳ have not water poured over thy hands by one who has not washed his hands &c. Ḥull. 105ᵃ נוטלין .. בכלי you must wash over a vessel (receiving the water); ע״ג קרקע on the floor; a. v. fr.

Nif. נִיטַּל 1) *to be handled.* Sabb. XVII, 1 (122ᵇ) כל הכלים נִיטָּלִין בשבת all vessels (implements, utensils &c.) may be handled on the Sabbath. Ib. 43ᵃ, a. e. אין כלי נ׳ אלא לדבר הנ׳ בשבת a utensil must not be handled on the Sabbath except for the protection of a thing which may be used on the Sabbath. Par. V, 9 והן יכולות לְהִנָּטֵל וכ׳ and they can be handled simultaneously; a. fr.—2) *to be removed, be gone.* Ḥull. III, 1; 2, v. קָבַר III. Ohol. II, 3 כדי שֶׁיִּנָּטֵל מן כ׳ as much of it as, if cut out from the skull of a living being, would cause death; a. fr.—3) *to be used for washing hands.* Tosef. Yad. II, 7 לא נִטְּלוּ מן הכלי the water was not poured directly from the vessel; לא ניטלו מן הרביעית not poured from a vessel containing one fourth of a Log; a. fr.

Hif. הִטִּיל 1) *to throw; to put; to hang on, attach.* Gitt. V, 9 כשתַּטִּיל המים from the time she pours water on the flour. Yoma III, 2 המַטִּיל מים who urinates. Men. 40ᵇ ה׳ לבעלת וכ׳ if he attached the fringe (תְּכֵלֶת) to a three-cornered garment. Sabb. 42ᵇ לְהַטִּיל ביצתה to lay her eggs; a. fr.—2) (of plants) *to assume the shape of, to develop.* Maasr. I, 2 משיַּטִּילוּ שאור, v. שְׂאוֹר; ib. משיטילו גידין, v. גִּיד.

Hof. הוּטַל *to be thrown; to lie.* Part. מוּטָּל, f. מוּטֶּלֶת; pl. מוּטָּלִים, מוּטָּלִין; מוּטָּלוֹת a) *lying.* Kidd. 82ᵇ מ׳ ברעב lies prostrated from starvation. Ber. III, 1 מי שמתו מ׳ לפניו he whose dead relative lies before him; ib. 18ᵃ כיון שמ׳ עליו לקוברו כמ׳ וכ׳ since the duty of burying rests upon him, it is the same as if the body were lying before him. Yeb. 37ᵇ, a. fr. ממון המ׳ בספק, v. סָפֵק; a. fr.—b) מוּטֶּלֶת *a garment provided with show-fringes.* Men. l. c. הטיל למ׳ if he attached additional fringes to a garment provided &c.; a. fr.

נְטַל ch. same, 1) (corresp. to h. נָשָׂא) *to take, lift, move, carry.* Targ. Ex. X, 13. Targ. Ps. CXXXIV, 2 טולו (imperat.); a. fr.—2) (corresp. to h. נָסַע) *to move.* Targ. Gen. XX, 1. Targ. Ps. LV, 9 נָטְלָא (Bxt. נטילה; h. text סעה); a. fr.—3) *to wash the hands.* Y. Ber. VIII, 12ᵃ bot. הוה נ׳ ידיה is to be considered as if he had washed his hands.

Pa. נַטֵּיל *to lift, carry.* Targ. O. Deut. XXXII, 11. Targ. Is. LXIII, 9; a. e.—*Part. pass.* מְנַטַּל, מְנַטְּלָא; f. מְנַטְּלָא; *pl.* מְנַטְּלָתָא; מְנַטְּלַיָּא, מְנַטְּלִין *exalted, high.* Targ. Y. Deut. XXVIII, 13 (opp. מאיסין). Targ. Y. I ib. IV, 7. Targ. Is. LVII, 15. Targ. II Esth. I, 2. Targ. Prov. XXX, 13. Targ. Y. Ex. XV, 1 (not מְנַטְּלָ׳). Targ. Is. II, 14.

Af. אַטֵּיל, אַנְטֵיל 1) *to cause to move, to pass.* Targ. Ex. XV, 22. Targ. Ps. LXXVIII, 26. Targ. Y. Deut. XXVI, 9; a. fr.—2) *to throw;* א׳ (ב)אבנין *to stone* to death. Targ. Y. Deut. XIII, 11 תְּאַנְטְלוּן, תְּאַטְ׳ (!); a. fr.—[Targ. Y. II Ex. XXXIII, 22, v. טְלַל.]

Ithpa. אִתְנַטַּל, אִיטַּ׳; *Ithpe.* אִתְנְטֵיל, אִיטְ׳ 1) *to be lifted up; to be exalted.* Targ. Ps. XC, 2. Targ. Y. Ex. XV, 1; a. e.—2) *to lift one's self up, be overbearing.* Targ. Y. Num. XVII, 5.—3) *to be taken away, removed.* Targ. Job IV, 21. Targ. Esth. VIII, 10; a. e.—[Snh. 91ᵃ (quot. fr. Meg. Taan. ch. III) אתנטילו דימוסנאי, v. דִּימוֹסְנָאֵי.]

נַטְלָא c. (preced.) 1) *a ladle* or *small vessel* used for taking liquid out of a larger vessel, esp. for pouring over the hands before and after meals, before prayer &c. Targ. Y. Ex. XL, 31; a. e.—Ib. XXX, 21 נַטְלָא f.—2) (as a measure) *one fourth of a Log.* Ḥull. 107ᵃ אתקין ... נ׳ בת וכ׳ R. J. ordered that a *naṭla* (to be used for washing hands) must contain one fourth of a Log; (Rashi: had a standard *naṭla* made, containing &c.). Gitt. 69ᵃ bot. נ׳ בת מחוזא a Moḥazean *naṭla*.—Y. Sabb. III, 6ᵃ bot. [read:] הבא ע״י נ׳ והוא .. כלי שני get the hot water into the basin by means of a ladle, when it (the basin) becomes a 'secondary vessel' (v. שֵׁנִי; cmp. Bab. ib. 40ᵇ טול בכלי שני).—*Pl.* נַטְלֵי. Ber. 51ᵃ מעטר ליה בנ׳ surrounded the large cup (over which the benediction was said) with small cups (for distribution).

נטליתא, Targ. Prov. XIV, 30, v. מְלַטִּיתָא.

נָטַע (b. h.) [*to fix,*] 1) = נָטָה, *to pitch a tent; put up a temporary structure.* Meg. 5ᵇ נ׳ נטיעה של שמחה he put up a temporary structure for a festive religious occasion, v. אַבְוּרְנְקָא. Ib. היכי נ׳ נטיעה וכ׳ how dared he put up a temporary structure on Purim?—Snh. 111ᵃ ביקש מקום לִנְטוֹעַ אהלו (Ex. R. s. 6 לִנְטוֹת) he wanted a place to put up his tent; a. fr.—2) *to insert, to plant,* contrad. to זרע. *Kil.* II, 4 זרועה ונמלך לנוֹטְעָהּ if a field was sown, and he resolves to plant trees in it, לא יאמר אֶטַּע וכ׳ he must not say, I will first plant and then &c., v. אָסַךְ. Ib. I, 8 אין נוֹטְעִין ירקות וכ׳ you must not plant vegetables &c.; a. v. fr.—Part. pass. נָטוּעַ; f. נְטוּעָה; *pl.* נְטוּעִים, נְטוּעִין; נְטוּעוֹת. Ib. V, 1; 4; sq.; a. fr.—Trnsf. *to beget.* Y. Yeb. I, 2ᵇ, a. e., v. נְטִיעָה.

Nif. נִטַּע, נִיטַּע *to be planted* with trees. B. Bath. 24ᵇ; Erub. 23ᵇ נ׳ רובו if the larger portion of it was planted with trees, opp. נזרע. Ohol. XVIII, 3 אינה נִטַּעַת כל נטע must not be planted with any kind of trees; Tosef. ib. XVII, 10; a. fr.

נֶטַע m. (b. h.; preced.) *plant, plantation.* Koh. R. to IV, 6 כמה בית נ׳ וכ׳ how much land fit for plantation is in it?—נ׳ רבעי *the fourth year's fruits of a young tree* (Lev. XIX, 24). Maas. Sh. V, 4; a. fr.; v. רְבָעִי.

נָטַף (b. h.; cmp. טָפַף) *to drip, overflow.* Ker. 6^a שרף הנוֹטֵף וכ׳ the gum which exudes from balm-shrubs. Y. Peah VII, beg. 20^a, v. נְטוֹפָה II. Sabb. 30^b, a. e. שפתותיו נוֹטְפוֹת וכ׳, v. טַר II; a. fr.—נוֹטְפִין, נוֹטְפִים *dripping water, collected rain water.* Mikv. V, 5, v. זָחַל; a. fr.—Trnsf. (cmp. נָבַע) *to speak, prophesy.* Midr. Till. to Ps. LXXIII, end (ref. to Joel IV, 18) אין יִטְּפוּ אלא נבואה *yiṭṭ'fu* alludes to prophecy; v. הַטָּפָה.—2) (cmp. טְפֵי III) *to be too long, protrude, hang over.* Bekh. 43^b חוטמו נוטף one whose nose overhangs his lips; Tosef. ib. V, 3.—[Y. Ber. I, 3^c bot. שלא נטפו ed. Ven., v. חָשַׁף.]

Pi. נִיטֵּף *to drop.* Taan. 19^a התחילו גשמים מְנַטְּפִין the rain began to come down drop-wise. Ohol. III, 5 מת שדמו מְנַטֵּף a slain body whose blood flows in drops, opp. שותת. Y. M. Kat. I, 80^b top ועודה מְנַטֶּפֶת and when it is still overflowing; a. fr.

Nif. נִיטּוֹף, נִיטַּף 1) *to be fed by an overflow.* Tosef. M. Kat. I, 1 בריכה שנִיטוֹפֶת משדה וכ׳ (Var. ed. Zuck. נִיטְפָּה, נִיטְיַפְּה *Nithpa.* of טוּף) a pond formed by the overflow (of rain) from a field &c.—2) *to be inundated, to overflow.* Y. l. c. שדה .. שניטופת לתוך וכ׳ a field dependent on irrigation which discharged its overflow (from rain) into another field (and there formed a pond).

Hif. הִטִּיף *to cause to flow; to drop.* Y. Gitt. II, 44^b top וכתב לא (ה)כְּטִיף 'and he shall write' (Deut. XXIV, 1) but not form letters by dropping; Y. Sabb. XII, end, 13^d. Y. Pes. V, 32^c bot. ישפך לא יַטִּיף 'it shall be poured out' (Deut. XII, 27), but he must not let it fall in drops. Tosef. Sabb. XV (XVI), 9 צריך לְהַטִּיף וכ׳ he must cause a few drops of the blood of the covenant to flow; Gen. R. s. 46. Midr. Till to Ps. LXXIII, end; a. fr.

נְטַף ch. same, 1) *to drip.* Part. נָטֵף, נָטְיף. Targ. Prov. XXVII, 15. Targ. Ps. LXXII, 6 דְּנָטְפִין (ed. Wil. דְּנָטְפֵי).—B. Bath. 73^b לא נְטַפָא נימוחתא וכ׳ not a drop fell to the ground.—נָטְפֵי (=h. נוטפים, v. preced.) *dripping rain water,* contrad. to שפכי rain water collected in spouts (v. מַרְזֵב). Ib. 6^a אחזיק לנ׳ וכ׳ if one has the right to let the dripping water from his roof run into his neighbor's yard, he may make spouts and gutters &c.—*2) (cmp. טוּף) *to turn up, lift.* Keth. 60^a (to a woman who had her eyes cast down in order not to look at her child) נְטוֹף עיניך Rashi (ed. נטף) turn thy eyes up (look freely around).

Af. אַטִּיף *to drop.* Targ. Ps. LXVIII, 9; a. e.—V. טוּף.

נֶטֶף m. (נָטַף 2) *grapes hanging down directly from the trunk,* v. פֶּתַח. Peah VII, 4; a. e.

נִטְפָא, v. נְטוֹפָא.

נִטְפָא, *pl.* נָטְפֵי, v. נְטַף.

***נַטְפִּיק** f. (transpos. of נפטיק, corresp. to Pers. נפתיק, Fl. to Levy Talm. Dict. s. v.) *naphtha-salve.* Gitt. 86^a נ׳ חיורא a salve of white naphtha.

נָטַר (b. h.; cmp. נוּר I) *to guard, observe.* Sifré Num. 157 (expl. טירתם, Num. XXXI, 10) מקום שהיו נוֹטְרִים ע״ז וכ׳ the place where they guarded their idols; Yalk. ib. 785 שהיו נוטרין בית וכ׳ their idolatrous temple. Yalk. Prov. 964 כשם שהתרנגול .. ונוֹטֵר לבני אדם as the cock crows by night and holds guard for men; a. e.—Esp. (with ref. to Lev. XIX, 18) *to reserve anger, bear grudge.* Gen. R. s. 55 כתבת בתורתך .. ואת נוקם ונוטר thou hast written in thy Law (Lev. l. c.) thou shalt not &c., and thou takest revenge and reservest wrath (Nah. I, 2)?; Koh. R. to VIII, 4 לא אֶטּוֹר I will not reserve &c. Yoma 23^a; a. fr.—[Cant. R. to IV, 12 מנטרים, read: מנסכים, v. נָסַךְ.]

נְטַר, נְטֵיר ch. same, *to guard, wait; to observe; to reserve.* Targ. I Sam. XXX, 23, sq. Targ. Deut. V, 10. Targ. Ruth I, 13; a. fr.—Imper. טַר, *pl.* טְרוּ. Targ. O. Deut. V, 12. Ib. XXVII, 1 (Y. טורו); a. e.—Part. pass. נְטִיר, f. נְטִירָא; pl. נְטִירִין; נְטִירָן. Targ. I Sam. IX, 24; a. fr.—Targ. Y. Deut. V, 10 נְטִיר read: נָטֵיר.—B. Bath. 74^a נְטַר עד וכ׳ wait here until to-morrow. B. Meṭs. 63^b; 65^a, v. אַגְרָא I.—Ḥag. 5^a, v. infra.

Pa. נַטַּר same. Keth. 37^a מְנַטְּרָא נפשה (not מיל׳) she guarded herself (her purity).—[Yalk. Job 898 קטנטר תאני, read as Ḥag. l. c. מְנַקְּיט.]—Part. pass. מְנַטַּר, f. מְנַטְּרָא, v. infra.

Ithpa. אִתְנַטַּר, *Ithpe.* אִתְנְטֵיר, אִתְנְטַר, איני׳ 1) *to be guarded; to be reserved.* Targ. Hos. XII, 14. Targ. Y. Ex. XXIV, 11; a. fr.—Bets. 15^a מְנַטַּר מחמת כלבי ולא מִינְטַר וכ׳ (or מְנַטַּר) Ms. M. (ed. מְנַטְּרָא) it is safe from dogs, but not from thieves.—*2) *to keep watch.* Targ. Prov. VI, 22 (perh. to be read תְּנַטַּר *Pe.*).—3) *to be preserved.* Ḥag. 5^a הני מִינַּטְּרָן והני לא מִינַּטְּרָן Ms. M. a. Rashi (ed. נטרן, corr. acc.) these (the unripe figs) can be kept, but those (the ripe) cannot; Yalk. Job 898 מנטרן.

נָטֵר, v. נְטֵיר.

נָטְרָא m. (preced.) *guard.* Targ. I Sam. XXVIII, 2.—*Pl.* נָטְרַיָּא, נָטְרִין. Targ. Is. LXII, 6. Targ. Jer. LI, 12; a. fr.—[נָטְרָא f., part. of נְטַר.]

נִטְרוֹן m. (νίτρον) *nitrum,* (prob.) *native carbonate of soda* (v. Sm. Ant. s. v.). Y. Sabb. IX, end, 12^b (expl. נֶתֶר, ib. IX, 5).

נַטְרוֹנָה, נַטְרוֹנָא m. (נְטַר) *Natrona* (*Avenger*), a symbolical name. Pesik. R. s. 15 מי פורע לכם .. נ׳ who will avenge you on Rome? Naṭrona; Yalk. Ex. 191; Pesik. Hahod., p. 56^a נטירותא (corr. acc.).

נָטַשׁ I (b. h.; cmp. טוּשׁ I) *to polish, sharpen.* Snh. 95^b (כלום) מגלך נְטוּשָׁה is thy sickle (of death) polished? Sabb. 67^a (in an incantation) חרב שלופה וקלע נטושה the sword is drawn and (the stones of) the sling sharpened.

***נְטַשׁ** ch. same, esp. (cmp. מְרַק) *to dress* a dead animal. Snh. 100^b לא תִנְטוֹשׁ וכ׳ (Ms. M. תפשוט), v. גִּלְדְּנָא.—B. Bath. 110^a נְטוֹשׁ וכ׳ (Ms. M. פשוט; Ar. נשוט), v. נְבֵלְתָא; (Pes. 113^a פשוט, Ar. נשוט).

נָטַשׁ II (b. h.; cmp. טוּשׁ II) *to sink, drop* (cmp. Num. XI, 31); *to abandon, let alone*, v. infra. Gen. R. s. 75 אם רחקת ונְטַשְׁתָּה וכ׳ if thou wert to reject and abandon Jacob &c.; Yalk. Ps. 653.

Pi. נִטֵּשׁ same. Snh. 6ᵇ (ref. to Prov. XVII, 14) לְנַטְּשׁוֹ to drop it (the case, to compromise), v. בָּלַע; Tanh. Mishp. 6; Y. Snh. I, 18ᵇ לְנוֹטְשׁוֹ.

Pu. נוּטַּשׁ, *Nif.* נִיטַּשׁ *to be torn loose, be released.* Pesik. Bahod., p. 154ᵇ נר׳ מחורש וכ׳ (not מחודש) released from one thicket and caught &c.; ib. נר׳; Yalk. Num. 782 נר׳ וכ׳; (Y. Taan. II, 65ᵈ top ניתור, v. נָתַר I; Lev. R. s. 29, a. e. ניתש, v. נָתַשׁ).

נְטַשׁ ch. same. Targ. Ps. XCIV, 14.

Pa. נַטֵּשׁ same. Y. Shek. V, 48ᵈ top נטשנה דלא תימות נבן נטשת Ms. M. (v. Rabb. D. S. a. l. p. 42), read: נַטְשׁוּנָה.. נטשונה.. let her go, that she may not die while with us; they did let her go (ed. אפקונה).

נַטְשָׁא* m. (preced.) *dropping, excrements.* Targ. Y. II Lev. I, 16 (h. text נֹצָה).

נִיא* m. *climate.* Y. B. Bath. II, 13ᶜ top, v. נָוֶה II a. נוֹי.

נִיאוּב, נִיאָב* m. (נוב) *trough.* Y. Naz. I, end, 51ᶜ ניאב (ed. Amst. שאוב); Num. R. s. 10 ניאוב; (Y. Ned. I, 36ᵈ bot. שאוב).

נִיאוּף m. (b. h. נַאֲפִים; נָאַף) *lewdness, illicit intercourse.* Sifré Deut. 26 דבר נ׳ an unchastity; Deut. R. s. 2. Ned. 20ᵃ. Num. R. s. 9; a. fr.

נִיאוּץ m. (נָאַץ) *insult.* Gitt. 56ᵇ ניאוצו וגידופו וכ׳ this man's (Titus') insult and blasphemy.—*Pl.* נִיאוּצִים, נִיאוּצִין. Lam. R. introd. (R. Joh. 1) חן נ׳.. ניחומין these consolations ... are insults; Pesik. R. s. 28; Midr. Till. to Ps. CXXXVII; Yalk. Ps. 884 נאוצים.

נִיאוּצָא ch. same. Targ. II Kings XIX, 3; a. e.

נִיאוֹת, v. אות.

נִיאָקָא, v. נִירְקָא.

נִיאָר, *pl.* נִיָארוֹת, v. נִיָיר.

ניארת, Tosef. Kel. B. Kam. V, 8 ed. Zuck., v. כְּוֶורֶת.

נִיב *to flow*, v. נוב.

נִיב m. (b. h.; preced.) *flow, overflow; that which hangs over.*—נ׳ שפתים (borrowed fr. Is. LVII, 19; cmp. next w.) *upper lip.* Hull. 128ᵇ. Gitt. 56ᵃ.

נִיבָא I ch. same; (cmp. נטפי, a. נוֹטֵף s. v. נָטַף) *tusks, canine teeth;* also *pl.* נִיבֵי. Targ. Ps. LVIII, 7 (h. text מלתעות).—[Targ. Y. I Deut. XXXIV, 7 נ׳ לסתיה his *molar teeth;* (h. text לֵחֹה).]—B. Kam. 23ᵇ. Hull. 59ᵃ גמלא נ׳ אית ליה a camel has canine teeth. Sabb. 63ᵇ שקילי ניביה his (the dog's) tusks are gone. Gen. R. s. 86, פכרון ניביה break its tusks out; Yalk. ib. 145 תברון ניביה. Ib. מסתכל בניביה, v. סָכַל I.—Trnsf. *the sinews connecting the hip-bone with its socket.* Hull. 54ᵇ איפסוק ניביה (some ed. איפסיק) its sinews are severed.

נִיבָא II m. *sproutings*, v. נְבָיָיה.

ניבדקוס, v. נִקְבְּדִיקוֹס.

נִיבּוּל, נִבּ׳ m. (נָבַל) *disfigurement; disgrace, exposure.* Y. Ab. Zar. I, 39ᵇ bot., v. נִיוּוּל. Ib. III, end, 43ᶜ נִיבּוּלָהּ רע (an idol worshipped by an Israelite) is bad even when disfigured, i. e. its material can never be used even after its worshipper has abandoned and disfigured it. Gen. R. s. 87; Cant. R. beg., v. זִיבּוּל.—נ׳ פה *lascivious talk*, v. נָבַל. Lev. R. s. 24.

נִיבוּרְיָא, v. נִבוּרְיָא.

נִיבְזִין m. pl. (בזז; cmp. נְבָזִי; Samar. נבוזה) *lots.* Y. Snh. VI, beg. 23ᵇ אסקון נ׳ וכ׳ cast lots between you two, and one of you will at all events be caught.

נִיבְלָא, v. נִבְלָא.—[ניבלין, Targ. Is. LIII, 9 some ed., v. נִבְלָא.]

ניבלתא, Targ. Job V, 16 some ed., v. נְבֶלְתָּא.

ניבריות, Y. Erub. V, end, 23ᵃ וחוצה לה ע״ר נ׳, read: וחוצה לה אלפים אמה ע״ר עירובו.

ניברקוס, v. נִקְבְּדִיקוֹס.

נִיגְדָּא, v. נִגְדָּא.

נִיגּוּן, נִגּ׳ m. (נָגַן) 1) *playing on a musical instrument; use of the root* נגן. Pes. 117ᵃ; Y. Succ. III, 54ᵃ top; Y. Meg. I, 72ᵃ top; a. e.—2) *musical accent, melodiousness.* Cant. R. to IV, 11 בעירוגו ובניגונו, v. עִירוּג.

נִיגּוּנָא, נִגּ׳ ch. same, *music.* Targ. Is. XXXVIII, 20; a. e.

ניגמי, v. נגמי.

ניגני, v. תְּרִיגְנֵי.

נִיגְרָא, נִגְ׳ m. (נְגַר) 1) *gutter, dike.* B. Mets. 107ᵇ ד׳ אמות גרמידי דאג׳ לבני נ׳ Ar. (ed. דבני אג׳.. ד׳ אמות) four cubits on the shores of a dyke belong to the owners of the dyke. Pes. 113ᵃ לא תשוור נ׳ leap not over a dyke (oth. opin., v. infra). B. Bath. 12ᵇ תרתי אחד נ׳ two fields dependent on one dyke for irrigation; a. e.—*Pl.* נִיגְרֵי, נִגְ׳. Ib.—[V. also נִגְדָּא.]—2) *track, step.* Pes. l. c. לא תשוור נ׳ do not leap in place of walking (v. supra).—*Pl.* as ab. B. Kam. 57ᵃ נקטי להו נ׳ ברייתא Rashi (ed. sing.) they adopted the habit of running out into the fields; ib. 118ᵇ אנקטה נ׳ וכ׳ (not אנקטי) he taught her the way out of the fold; B. Bath. 88ᵃ אנקטינהו ניגרא וכ׳ he taught them &c.—Sabb. 51ᵇ נ׳ דחמרא שערי the gait of the ass is (in accordance with) the barley (which he feeds on). Ib. 66ᵇ קל נ׳ the sound of steps. Pes. 111ᵃ שתין נ׳ sixty steps. Ber. 41ᵇ נ׳ דפרולא iron run (unwearied walk).

נִידָא Targ. Cant. I, 12, v. נִרְדָּא.

נִידְבָא, v. נִדְבָא.

נִידָּה, v. נִדָּה.

נִידּוּי, נִדּ׳ m. (נָדָה) *banishment, isolation.* Num. R. s. 10 הוּא בנ׳ (Sabb. 64[b], a. e. בנדותה), v. נִדָּה.—Esp. *excommunication*, of a higher degree than נְזִיפָה and lesser than חֵרֶם. M. Kat. 16[a] אין נ׳ פחות וכ׳ *nidduy* lasts no less than thirty days. Ib. נִידּוּיוֹ נ׳ the excommunication pronounced by him is valid. Ber. 19[a] גוזרני עליך נ׳ I should have decreed the ban over; a. fr.

נִידּוּיָא ch. same. Ned. 7[b] (ref. to מנודה, v. נְדָה) לישנא דנ׳ הוא it has the meaning of excommunication (as if he had said מנדינא, v. נְדֵי I).

***נַיָּה** pr. n. pl. *Nayah* (prob. to be read נוה, v. נָוֶה III). Y. Snh. III, 21[b] רבנן דנ׳ the rabbis of N.

נִיהוּ m. = איהו (mostly after an open syllable to avoid a hiatus, or after ן) *he, himself; it, it is.* B. Kam. 114[b] דילמא .. והוא נ׳ קא מפיק שמא perhaps he sold them, and he himself spread the report (that they had been stolen). Ber. 58[b] לא ידענא מאי נ׳ I do not know what it is (its nature). Taan. 24[a] אנא נ׳ (differ. in Ms. M.) I am he (of whom you are speaking). Pes. 104[a], a. e. מאן נ׳ בנן וכ׳ (Ms. M. נינהו, v. Rabb. D. S. a. l. note) who is (are) meant by 'the son of saints'? a. fr.—*Fem.* נִיהִי. Ber. 44[a].—*Pl.* נִינְהוּ, נִנְהוּ. Hull. 38[a] מאי נ׳ דברים וכ׳ what are the movements indicating the agony of death? Ib. 79[a] כולהו חדא מינא נ׳ they all belong to the same species. B. Mets. 24[b] רובה ישראל נינהו the majority are Jews; a. fr.—With suffixes: נִיהֲלִי, נִיהֲלָךְ, נִיהֲלֵיהּ &c. (*to*) *myself, thyself, himself* &c. Hull. 59[b] בעינא דמחזית ליה ניהלי (Rashi דמחזית ניהליה) I want thee to show him to *me* (Rashi: to make him visible). Ib. 142[a] והדר לקנינהו נ׳ and then let him transfer them to thyself. Ber. 54[b] בריך רחמנא דיהבך נִיהֲלַן וכ׳ blessed be the Merciful who returned thee to *us* and not to the dust. Ned. 41[a]; Erub. 10[a], a. fr. את אמרת ניהלן וכ׳ thou didst cite it to ourselves &c. Keth. 92[a] מגבי להו נִיהֲלַיְיהוּ ארעא he will give land in payment to the very claimants, and then seize it from them; a. fr.

נִיהוּג, נִהוּג m. (נָהַג) *leading.* Mekh. B'shall. beg.; Yalk. Ex. 226, v. נִירוּם.

נִיהֲלִי, v. נִיהוּ.

נִיהוּר, Yeb. 17[a], v. נְהוּרָה.

נִיוּוּל m. (נָוַל) *ugliness; disgrace.* M. Kat. I, 7 מפני שנ׳ הוא לה because it defaces her (for the time being); Y. Ab. Zar. I, 39[b] bot. נִיבּוּל. Snh. VII, 3 (52[b]) נ׳ הוא זה this (the Roman way of decapitation with the sword) is a repulsive disfigurement. Y. Sot. III, end, 19[b] אבל אשה על ידי שנִיוּוּלָהּ מרובה וכ׳ but a woman, because her disgrace (feeling of shame) is greater, must not be executed naked. Ib. 18[d] bot. המקום .. תחת ניוולה the Lord will indemnify her for her (unmerited) exposure. Yalk. Prov. 943 חיים של נִוּוּל a hideous life (without enjoyment). Ned. 80[a] (in Chald. dict.) נ׳ דחד יומא לא שמיה נ׳ a neglected appearance for one day (by not bathing) is not considered self-neglect in the sense of the law; a. fr.

נִיוּוּלָא, נִוּוּ׳ ch. same. Targ. Lam. III, 51.—Ned. 80[a] אית לה נ׳ it would make her repulsive.

נִיוּמָאר, v. פִּיוּמָאר.

נִיוִיו, נִיוִיָּה, v. נוי.

***נִיוְוִיָּנָא** m. pl. (naeviana, sub. pira) *naeviana*, a species of *pears* (v. Sm. Ant. s. v. Pyrus). Y. Kil. I, 27[a] אֶת הנוגיני׳ (corr. acc.).

נִיוְלִי pr. n. m. *Nivli.* Hull. 45[b].

נִיוּמָא m. (נוּם) *slumber; idleness.* Targ. Prov. XXIII, 21.

נִיוּמְתָא, נִיוּ׳ f. same. Targ. Prov. VI, 4 ed. Lag. (ed. נִימְתָא; ed. Wil. נִימְתָא). Targ. Ps. CXXXII, 4.—*Pl.* נִיוּמָתָא, Targ. Job XXXIII, 15 Ms. (ed. sing.).

נִיוָתִי m. *Nabatean.* Sabb. 121[b] (Ms. M. נותי); Y. ib. XIV, beg. 14[b] נְפָתִי.

נִיזְבָא, נִיזְהָא, v. sub נִזְ׳.

נִיזָק, נִזָּק m. (v. נָזַק) *one who claims damages; pl.* נִזָּ׳, נִיזָּקִין *cases of damage claims.* Gitt. V, 1; v. עִידִּית. B. Kam. 83[b]; a. fr.; v. נֶזֶק.

נִיזְקָא, נִיזְרָא, v. sub נִזְ׳.

נִיחַ, v. נוּחַ.

נִיחַ, v. נִיחַ.

נִיחָא I m. (נוּחַ) *soft, gentle.* Targ. Job XXXVII, 13; Taan. 3[b] bot. מיטרא נ׳ a gentle rain, opp. רזיא. Ib. דאתא נ׳ when a gentle rain has fallen.—*Fem.* נִיחָתָא, נִיחָא. Targ. II Esth. VIII, 13.—Sabb. 7[b] נ׳ תשמישתיה it is convenient for use; a. fr.

נִיחָא II m. (preced.; v. נוּחַ) *ease, satisfaction.* Yeb. 118[b] נ׳ דגופא וכ׳ bodily comfort (even in an unhappy marriage) is preferable (to singleness). Snh. 45[a], v. בִּזְיוֹנָא. Sabb. 132[a] מעיקרא מאי קא נ׳ ליה וכ׳ what satisfactory reason had he at first (for his interpretation), and what was again the objection he attempted to meet?—נ׳ לי־ *one likes, prefers.* Targ. Y. Deut. XXXII, 50.—Meg. 28[a] לא נ׳ לי .. איתיקורי I do not want to be honored at the expense of thy disgrace. Ib. לא נ׳ לכו וכ׳ do you not want me to live? B. Bath. 172[a] מילתא דנ׳ ליה וכ׳ something which is satisfactory to the creditor and &c. Arakh. 30[b] נ׳ לאיניש דליזבן וכ׳ it is better for man to sell his daughter than to borrow on interest. Erub. 32[b]; a. fr.—נִ׳, הָנִ׳ (a dialectical term, v. נוּחַ *Ithpe.*) *it is right; it will do.* Y. Pes. I, 27[b] top נ׳ העליונים וכ׳ this is right as far as the uppermost and nethermost cavities are concerned. Y. Yoma III, 40[c], sq. אין תימר מיד נ׳ .. נ׳ של משה ... אין תימר וכ׳ if you say, sacred vessels are consecrated at once (as soon as finished), it is right; but if you say, they are not consecrated until they are used, it would be right as far as the Mosaic vessels are concerned, but &c.—Hull. 56[a]

הנ׳ למאן דאמר this would be right according to the opinion of &c.; a. fr.—Cant. R. to I, 6 נ׳ (an editorial gloss, as a punctuation mark) *as a positive assertion*, opp. אִתְמְהָא.—V. נְיָיח.

נִיחָא III pr. n. m. *Niḥa*, name of an Amora. Y. Kil. IX, beg. 31^d; Y. Yeb. VIII, end, 9^d; a. e.

נִיחוֹחַ m. (b. h.; נוּחַ) *pleasing.* Koh. R. to IX, 7 כריח נ׳ like the pleasing flavor (of a sacrifice); a. e.

נִיחוּם, נִח׳ m. (b. h.; נָחַם) *comfort, consolation.* Mekh. B'shall., beg. (ref. to נחם, Ex. XIII, 17) אין נ׳ זה אלא נהוג this (*naḥam*) does not mean comforting but leading (i. e. the מ is not radical); Yalk. Ex. 226 אין נו׳ בכ״מ וכ׳ (corr. acc.), v. נָחַם a. נָחָה.—*Pl.* נִיחוּמִין, נִיחוּמִים, נִוּד. Pesik. Shimʿu, p. 117^b דברי נ׳ comforting words, opp. קינטורין. Ib. Naḥămu, p. 124^a דברים טובים ונ׳; Yalk. Is. 307 דברים טובים דברי נ׳. Lam. R. introd. (R. Joḥ. 1), v. נִיאוּץ; a. e.—V. תַּנְחוּמִים.

נִיחוּנְיוֹן, v. נְחוּנְיוֹן.

נִיחוּתָא f. (נוּחַ) 1) *mildness, gentleness.* Targ. Job XXXI, 18 (v. תּוּנְחָתָא).—Taan. 4^a, v. אָלַף II. Arakh. 17^a לעניין תוקפא ונ׳ as regards ruling with rigor or with leniency. B. Bath. 25^b דאתיא מיטרא בנ׳ when the rain comes down gently, opp. בשפיכותא. Sabb. 34^a, a. e. צריך למימרינהו בנ׳ he must say them in a gentle way; a. e.—2) *submission, humility.* Gitt. 36^b, v. עוּלְבָּן.—3) *ease of mind, satisfaction.* Snh. 30^b; Pes. 32^b מאי נ׳ why this ease of mind (why does he say, Let thy mind be set at rest as thou didst mine)?

נִיחָתָא, v. נִיחָא I.

נִיטוּף m. (נְטַף) *overflow.* Y. M. Kat. I, 80^b top.

נִיטוּפְתָּא f. (נְטַף) *drop.* B. Bath. 73^b, v. נְטַף.—*Pl.* נִיטוּפְיָיתָא. Gitt. 69^b.

ניטליתא, v. מַלְטִיתָא.

נַיֵּיד, v. נוּד ch.

נַיֵּיח, *Pi.* of נָוַח.

נַיֵּיחַ I, v. נוּחַ ch.

נַיֵּיחַ II m. = h. נוֹחַ II, *kind, gentle, pleasing.* Targ. Y. Deut. XVII, 18.—נ׳ ל־ *it is good (better) for.* Koh. R. to X, 5 [read:] והוות נ׳ ליה דקברייתיה וכ׳ it would have been better for him that I should bury him than &c.; (Y. Sabb. XIV, 14^d bot. נוֹחַ הוה ליה אילו הוה מייית). Koh. R. l. c. נ׳ הוה דייתרים וכ׳ it would have been better that his head were taken off than to do this; a. e.

נְיָיח, נְיָיחָא, נִיחָא (נִיחָא) m. = h. נוֹחַ I, 1) *rest, satisfaction.* Targ. Ps. XCV, 11 ed. Lag. (ed. Wil. a. oth. נְיָיחַ). Ib. CXVI, 7 Ms. נִיחַיִיכִי (Regia נוחייכי; ed. מְנָחַיִיכִי). Targ. Job XXXVI, 16. Targ. Lam. I, 3; a. fr.—Y. Taan. I, 64^a (transl. Is. XXX, 15) בשׁוּבָה ונ׳ וכ׳ through Sabbath rest and repose you will be redeemed. Gen. R. s. 87 (ref. to Ps. CXXV, 3) אין לו נ׳ וכ׳ (the evil spirit) has no satisfaction in the company of the righteous; Midr. Till. to Ps. l. c.; Yalk. ib. 880; a. e.—2) *gentleness.* Snh. 94^b בנ׳ gently.—V. נִיחָא, a. next w.

נְיָיחָה, נְיָיחָה f. h. same. Gen. R. s. 30 (play on נח נח, Gen. VI, 9) נ׳ לו נ׳ וכ׳ (ed. Wil. נייחא) he was a comfort to himself, a comfort to the world &c.; Yalk. ib. 48; Yalk. Chr. 1072 נייחא. Gen. R. s. 25 (ref. to נח, Gen. V, 29, a. ינוח, Ex. XXIII, 12) נאמר כאן נ׳ .... נְיָיחַת שור וכ׳ here ease is mentioned, and so there: as there appeasement of the ox is meant, so here (the ox submitting again to man's control, v. נוּחַ); ib. נייחת קבר rest in the grave; Yalk. Chr. l. c.

נַיְימְתָא, v. נִימְתָא.

נִיאָקָא, נִיקָא pr. n. = אַנְיָאקָא; v. אַנְגְּרָא.

נְיָיר m. (נור) [*blank*,] *paper, parchment, papyrus &c.* Ab. IV, 20 דיו כתובה על נ׳ חדש ink on a new blank, opp. נ׳ מחוק palimpsest. Gitt. 9^b נ׳ חלק blank paper, v. קָרַע. Ib. 19^b נתן לה נ׳ חלק if he handed her a blank sheet. Tosef. Kel. B. Kam. VII, 11; Kel. X, 4. Sifré Deut. 160 לא על נ׳ not on a loose sheet, opp. מגילה; a. fr.—*Pl.* נְיָירוֹת. Pes. 42^b סופרים ... מדבקין בהו נְיָירוֹתֵיהֶן scribes .. glue their parchments with it (Ms. M. נַיְירוֹתַיְיהוּ ch. form). Kel. II, 5 כמוי ... נ׳ (Var. והנ׳) covers ... made of papyrus; Tosef. ib. B. Kam. II, 5 ניארות ed. Zuck. (Var. הנרות, corr. acc.).

ניכו׳, v. next w., end.

נִיכּוּשׁ, נִכּ׳ m. (נָכַשׁ) *weeding; lopping (trees).* Kel. XXIX, 7 קרדום של נכ׳ (perh. נָכוֹשׁ; ed. Dehr. נַפָּשׁ) the axe used for lopping trees (v. Maim. a. l. ed. Dehr.); Y. Meg. I, 71^b top ניכ׳; Y. Ned. IV, beg. 38^c מכוש (corr. acc.). Tosef. B. Mets. VII, 6 גמר נִיכּוּשׁוֹ (ed. Zuck. נִכּוּשׁוֹ) if he finished the weeding for which he was hired. Gen. R. s. 39 ראה אותן עסוקין בנ׳ בשעת הנ׳ וכ׳ when he saw them engaged in weeding (lopping) at the proper season &c.; a. fr.—[Pesik. R. s. 31 קטח כמין נ׳, ed. Fr. ניכו׳, read: כווי קטנה, v. פַּיָּור; Fr. emends: כווי קטנה כמין צינור.]

נִיכְלָא, נִיכְסָא, נִיכְסְתָא, v. sub נִכְ׳.

נִילוּס pr. n. (Νεῖλος) *the Nile*, also *the godhead Nilus.* Targ. Y. Gen. XLVII, 7; a. fr.—Sot. 13^a. Gen. R. s. 87; Pesik. R. s. 6, v. זִירְגּוּל; a. fr.

נִים *to slumber*, v. נוּם.

נִים m. (preced.) *slumber, sleep.* Pes. 120^b; Meg. 18^b, a. e. (expl. מתנמנם) נ׳ ולא נ׳ וכ׳ a sleep which is no sleep, a wakefulness which is no wakefulness.

נִימָּא, *Pi.* of נמא, v. נוּם I.

נֵימָא, v. אָמָא II.

נִימָה, נִימָא f. (נמא, cmp. נְבָיָה = נְמָיָה, also meanings of נִיב, נִיבָא) [*hanging over*,] 1) *fringe, cord, hair* (of the eye-brow); *bristle; fibre.* Bets. 14^b שמא תכרך נ׳ וכ׳ lest a fringe (shred of the garment used as mattress) wind itself around his body; Y. Kil. IX, 32ᵃ bot. Nidd. 67ᵃ, a. e. נ׳ אחת one single thread; Y. Sabb. VII, 7ᵈ top נמא (corr. acc.). Gen. R. s. 93 קשר חבל בחבל ונ׳ בנ׳ (Ar. נינייא) he tied rope to rope, string to string. Ib. נ׳ אחת הייתה לו בלבו he had one bristle on his chest; Yalk. ib. 150. Gen. R. s. 65, end קשר בה נ׳ וכ׳ (Ar. ניניא) he tied a string to it …., and hanged himself. Tosef. Sot. I, 2 כדי שיקשור הגרדי נ׳ as much time as the weaver needs to knot a fringe; Y. ib. I, 16ᶜ bot.—B. Bath. 16ᵃ (ref. to סערה, Job XXXVIII, 1) וכל נ׳ ונ׳ וכ׳ for each hair (of the eye-brow) &c., v. גּוּמָא. Sabb. 30ᵃ, a. fr. מלא נ׳ a thread's (or hair's) breadth. Erub. X, 13 קושרין נ׳ במקדש they were permitted to knot a broken string of a musical instrument in the Temple; ib. 102ᵇ נִימַת כינור; a. fr.—*Pl.* נִימִין. B. Bath. l. c. Shek. VIII, 5 ed. (Ms. M. נִירִין); a. fr.—2) (cmp. נִיב) *pl.* נִימִין *mustache*. Yoma 38ᵇ בין הנ׳ on the division line between the two parts of the mustache.—3) נ׳ של מים (cmp. תִּינָא III) *leech*. Ab. Zar. 12ᵇ. [Ib. 10ᵇ, v. נוֹמִי.].

נִימָא ch. same, *cord; string* &c. Targ. Ps. XI, 2 (h. text יתר); a. e.—*Pl.* נִימִין, נִימַיָּא. Targ. Koh. IV, 12. Targ. Y. Num. XV, 38. Targ. Ps. VI, 1; a. e.

נימאייק, v. עַמְקִי.

נִימָה, v. נִימָא h.

נִימוֹל, v. מוּל II.—[נימולין, Y. Yeb. VIII, 9ᵇ, v. נְמָלָה.]

נימום, נימוס, Tosef. Bekh. IV, 15; Tosef. Men. XIII, 6, read נָמוֹם, v. נָמַם.

נִימוֹס, v. מְסַס.

נִימוֹס I pr. n. m. *Nimos*, 1) נ׳ הגרדי, v. אַבְנִימוֹס.—2) N., brother of Joshua the grist-maker. Bekh. 10ᵇ; Tosef. Makhsh. III, 13 אונימים ed. Zuck. (oth. ed. אינ׳), read אַוְנִימוֹס, v. אַבְנִימוֹס.

נִימוֹס II m. (νόμος) *usage, law; religion* (v. נוֹמוֹס). Meg. 12ᵇ מוכתר בנִימוֹסוֹ, v. כָּתַר. Gitt. 65ᵇ עשו לה כנ׳ deal with her according to law. Ex. R. s. 15 כנ׳ המלכות in accordance with the royal usage of warfare; (Tanh. Bo 4, a. e. כְּטַקְסִין). Gitt. 43ᵇ כיון שעשה .. נִימוֹסוֹ Ar. (ed. נמוסו) as soon as the gentile did to him (the hypothecated slave) what the law requires (to take possession, v. נַשְׁקִי); Tosef. Ab. Zar. III (IV), 16 נימוסות (corr. acc.). Gitt. l. c. [read:] אע״פ שעשה לה נִימוֹסָהּ although he (the Jew) did what the law requires in regard to the field; a. fr.—*Pl.* נִימוֹסוֹת, נִימוֹסִין. Num. R. s. 18 בדרכי הגוים יש נ׳ וכ׳ it is the way of the nations to have many religious observances (for various deities) and many priests. Gen. R. s. 16 בשלשה .. בנ׳ (Ar. בנָוֹמִין) in three things is Greece in advance of Rome: in codes &c., v. פִּנַקְסִין. Ib. s. 67. Num. R. s. 8 בנ׳ שלנו in our (Roman) law; a. e.—[Ex. R. s. 15 הוציא הנמוסין read: הטוֹמוֹסִין, v. טוֹמוֹס.]

נִימוֹ׳, נִימוֹסָא ch. same. Targ. Ps. I, 2. Targ. I Sam. II, 13; a. fr.—Gen. R. s. 48 (prov.) עלת לקרתא הלך בנִימוֹסָהּ when you come to a place, follow its customs.—*Pl.* נִימוֹסִין, נִימוֹסַיָּא. Targ. Ez. XX, 25; a. fr.—Y. Ber. V, 9ᵃ בנ׳ דברייה וכ׳ (ed. Lehm. sing.) he is engaged in studying the laws of his Creator.

נִימוֹק, v. מָקַק.

נִימוּק, נְמ׳ m. (contr. of נעמוק; עָמֹק) *depth, penetration*. Ab. d'R. N. ch. XVIII; Gitt. 67ᵃ ר׳ יוסי נִימוּקוֹ עמו gave to R. Jose the surname, 'His depth is with him', i. e. he has deep reasons for whatever he says. Ib. אלמלא ראיתו נ׳ עמו if thou hadst seen him, (thou wouldst have seen) his depth was &c. Erub. 51ᵃ. Bekh. 37ᵃ מהו דתימא נ׳ עמו you might have thought, we must adopt R. Jose's opinion because he is known to have deep reasons.

נִימוֹרֶת* f. (מור; cmp. אֲמוּרְיָא) *a detachment of troops sent to take hostages* until a requisition be complied with. Y. Pes. IV, 31ᵇ bot., v. מַשְׁכּוֹנָא.

נִימְסַיִם* m. du. (מְסַס) *mashing mill*. Ab. d'R. N. ch. XXXI, end, contrad. to ריחים grinding mills (v. Ber. 61ᵇ top).

נִימְפִּי, v. נִינְפֵי.

נִימְפִּיוֹן, נְמְ׳ m. (νυμφεῖον, nympheum) *a fountain consecrated to the nymphs*, in gen. *fountain*. Tanh. Mishp. 8 (some ed. נמסינן, corr. acc.); Ex. R. s. 31 גיפרין (corr. acc.).

נִימְרָה, (נימרון), נִימְרִין, נִימְרִית, v. sub נְמַ׳.

נִין m. (b. h.; נִינֵי) [*tender*,] *child, offspring*. Mekh. B'shall., Amalek, s. 2 אם אניח נ׳ ונכד וכ׳ I will not leave over a son or son's son of Amalek; Yalk. Ex. 266).

נינגר, v. בְּנִירְגְּנֵי.

נִינְחוּ, pl. of נִיחוּ.

נִינְוֵה (b. h.) *Nineveh*, the capital of Assyria. Yoma 10ᵃ; Gen. R. s. 37. Sabb. 121ᵇ; Y. ib. XIV, beg 14ᵇ צירעה שבנ׳ the hornet of N.; a. e.

נִינְיָא*, נִנְ׳ I m. (contr. of נענע, cmp. נוני) (*slender*) *hemp-cord, line* (v. P. Sm. 2362; 2387). Gen. R. s. 65; s. 93 Ar. (ed. נִימָה).—[Lev. R. s. 22, beg. נינייא, read: נִינְיָא, v. סִינָא.]

נִינְיָא, נִנְ׳ II f. (v. preced.) *ammi, Bishop's-weed* (v. אַמִּיתָא). Ab. Zar. 29ᵃ (Rashi: *mint*). Sabb. 128ᵃ; 140ᵃ נִינְיָיא. Ib. הואי נ׳ מעליא וכ׳ *ninia* is good for seasoning cress. Gitt. 69ᵇ תלת ביעי נ׳ (Ar. בנ׳) three eggs' sizes of *n*.—V. נַכְנָא.

נינפה, v. next w.

נִינְפֵי, נִנְ׳ f. (νύμφη) *bride*. Targ. Cant. IV, 8, sq.—R. Hash. 26ᵃ הוו קורין לכלה נ׳ I heard them call a bride *nin'fe*. Gen. R. s. 71 (play on נַפְתּוּלֵי, Gen. XXX, 8) נ׳ הויה לי ליעשות וכ׳ (not פח …) I ought to have been made a bride before my sister; Yalk. Gen. 127 לינפה (corr. acc.). Ex. R. s. 36, beg. (ref. to יפה נוף, Ps. XLVIII, 3) לשון יוני .. נימפי (some ed. נִמְ׳) in Greek they call a bride *nymphe.* Ib. s. 52, end (ref. to Ps. l. c.) קלי ניני ed. Const. (missing in ed.) καλὴ νύμφη, the beautiful bride; Pesik. R. s. 41 קלוניפו (corr. acc.); Tanḥ. Ki Thissa 18 (ref. to נֹפֶת, Cant. IV, 11) כלה נופי; ed. Bub. ib. 9 קלונינפי, read קלי נ׳.—[Yoma 10ª, v. נִיפָר.]

נִים, *pl.* נִימִים, נִימִין, v. נֵם.

נִימָא, v. נִמָּא.

נִיסָא, נְסָא m. (an adapt. of νῆσος, as if fr. נסא=נסע *to emigrate*, or אנס *to subject*; cmp. אֲנִיסִין, Sam. ענוסוסי, Gen. X, 32, Mand. נסיסיא, v. Nöld. Mand. Gr. p. XXX) *settlement, colony*, esp. *island* (v. נַגְוָון). Targ. Is. XX, 6 (ed. Wil. נסא). Targ. Jer. XXV, 22; a. e.—*Pl.* constr. נִיסֵי, נִסֵּי. Targ. Is. XXIV, 15. Ib. II, 16 (ed. Wil. נסי; h. text אניות). Targ. Am. IX, 3 (h. text קרקע). Targ. Y. II Gen. X, 18 נ׳ אומיא (belonging to ib. 5, as quoted in Ar.); a. e.—Hebr. form, *pl.* (of נִיסוֹס) נִיסִים, נִיסִין, נִסִּין; v. אֲנִיסִין.—[Deut. R. s. 2 נֵס; Yalk. Is. 369; Yalk. Deut. 825 נֶסֶל.]

הַר נ׳, נִיסַאי pr. n. (v. נֵס) *Mount Nissay* (Miracle), a substitute for Sinai, introduced for argument. Sabb. 89ª (against one explaining הר סיני as הר שנעשו בו ניסים, the mount whereon miracles were wrought for Israel) הר נ׳ מיבעי ליה then its name ought to have been Har Nissay; v. סִימָנַאי.

נִיסָה f. (נוס) *flight.* Sot. VIII, 6 שתחלת נ׳ נפילה, corrected ib. 44ᵇ (as in Y. ed.) שתחלת נפילה נ׳ for the beginning of falling (in slaughter) is the rout; Y. ib. VIII, end, 23ª; Sifré Deut. 198 שתחלת נ׳ נפילה for the beginning of flight means falling.

נִיסּוּךְ, נִסּ׳ m. (נָסַךְ) 1) *libation.* Succ. IV, 1 נ׳ המים שבעה the water libation (on the Succoth festival) is continued for seven days. Y. ib. 54ᵈ top; Tosef. ib. III, 15 נִיסּוּכוֹ בקדושה at its libation the laws of sanctity must be observed; (Tosef. Meil. I, 16 נִסִּיכָתוֹ). Zeb. VI, 2. Snh. 62ª נ׳ libation to idols; a. fr.—*Pl.* נִיסּוּכִים, נִיסּוּכִין, נִסּ׳. Gen. R. s. 78, end כמה נ׳ ניסך יעקב how many libations Jacob performed. Taan. 2ᵇ, a. e. שני נ׳ two kinds of libations.—2) *the manipulation by an idolater* by which he causes wine to be forbidden to Jews as יֵין נֶסֶךְ (v. נָסַךְ). Ab. Zar. 56ᵇ (in Chald. dict.) נ׳ דרגל .. נ׳ operating with the foot is not called a ritual manipulation (does not affect the wine); a. e.

נִיסּוּךְ, נִיסּוּכָא, נִסּ׳ ch. same, *the act of libation*; (in Targ. Y. also) *the liquid used for libation.* Targ. Num. XXVIII, 7. Ib. IV, 7; a. fr.—*Pl.* נִיסּוּכִין, נִיסּוּכַיָּא, נִסּ׳. Ib. O. some ed. Targ. Y. ib. XV, 13 (not נְסוּכְיָיא); a. fr.—V. נִסְכָּא I.

נִיסְחָנָא m.; *pl.* נִיסְחָנֵי, נִסְ׳ (נְסַח, v. *Af.*) [*despaired of, given up,*] *palms which never mature their fruits, male palms*; ד׳ נ׳ *fruits of nishané, stunted dates* which cease growing early in the spring (נִיסָן). Pes. 53ª בדנ׳ קץ he selected for felling (in the Sabbatical year) palms whose fruits had reached their limited maturity. Erub. 28ᵇ התם בדנ׳ there it means fruits of the *nishané* (which having reached their maturity are considered as food). Ib. לאו בנ׳ (read בדנ׳, v. Rabb. D. S. a. l. note 60) it does not mean fruits of the *n.*—[Ms. M. נִסְחָנֵי, Var. נִיסָאנֵי, Ar. נִיסָנֵי, v. Rabb. D. S. to Erub. l. c.—The Var. ניסאני, dialect. for ניסחי (cmp. נסח a. נסע) gave rise to etymological derivation from נִיסָן.]

נִיסָיוֹן, נִיסְיוֹנָא, נִיסֵיתָא, v. sub נִס׳.

ניסיותא, v. נְשִׂיאוּתָא.

נִיסְכָּא, v. נִסְכָּא.

נִיסֵל or **נֶסֶל** m. (v. אַסְלָא II) *easy-chair, (royal) armchair.* Tosef. Snh. IV, 2 על נִיסְלוֹ ספסלו (strike out ספסלו, as a gloss; Var. כסאו); Y. ib. II, 20ᶜ bot. (Var. כסאו).

נִיסָן (b. h.; v. Fr. Del. Proleg., p. 138, note) *Nisan*, the first month of the Hebrew calendar, containing thirty days, varying between the sixteenth of March and the eighth of May. R. Hash. I, 1 באחד בנ׳ ראש וכ׳ on the first of Nisan begins the royal year. Ib. 2ᵇ מת בנ׳ .. בנ׳ וכ׳ if a king dies in N., and his successor ascends the throne in N., we count a year for the one, and one (the first year) for the other; a. v. fr.

נִיסַן ch. same. Targ. Y. Ex. XII, 8; 18; a. e.—Y. Maas. Sh. IV, end, 55ᶜ; Ber. 56ᵇ; Lam. R. to I, 1 רבתי (חד מתלמ׳), v. נִפָּא.

נִיסָנֵי, v. נִיסְחָנָא.

נִיסְקָא m. (transpos. of ניקסא), v. נִקְצָא.

נִיסְרָא, v. נִסְרָא.

ניסרדי, v. מִצְטַרְדֵי.

ניסרוי, Targ. II Esth. III, 8 בנ׳ ed. Lag. a. oth., read: בְּגוֹ סִדְרוֹי, v. סִדְרָא.

ניסרפו, v. לקת.

נִיסְתָּא, v. נִשְׁתָּא.

נִיעַ m. (נוּעַ) *the effort made to remove phlegm, hawking; the phlegm discharged by hawking*, contrad. to פִּיחַ. Nidd. VII, 1 הנ׳ והרוק the phlegm (of an unclean person) and the spittle. Ib. 55ᵇ וניעו; B. Kam. 3ᵇ, v. פִּיחַ; a. e.

נִיעָא, נִיְעָא m. (נוע) [*something hanging*, cmp. Syr. נִצָא *lobe of the liver*, P. Sm. 2403,] 1) *fat-tail, rump.* Targ. Y. II Lev. III, 9 (h. text אליה).—2) *breast of an animal.* Ib. VII, 30 (h. text חזה); [Ar. נִיבָא, v. Koh. Ar. Compl. s. v.].—Midr. Sam. ch. XIV שוקה וניעה the shoulder and the breast.

נִיעָה, v. preced.

נִיעוּר m. (נָעַר) *shaking* of a garment. B. Mets. 29ᵇ.

נִיעוֹר, v. עור.

נִיעוֹת, v. עות.

נִיעֲנֵעַ, נִיעֲנוּעַ, v. sub 'נִצְ.

נִיף, Tosef. Arakh. V, 14, v. נִיהַ II.

נִיפּוּחַ m. (נָפַח) *blowing into.* B. Bath. 79ª (play on נפח, Num. XXI, 30) אש שאינה צריכה נ׳ a fire which needs no fanning (hell); Yalk. Num. 765.

נִיפּוּל, נִפּ׳ m. (נָפַל) 1) *falling off*, esp. (with ref. to Lev. XI, 32) *of a limb detached from the body.* Ḥull. 74ª מיתה עושה נ׳ וכ׳ the natural death of an animal causes the hanging limb (דלדול) to be considered as if detached (in life-time, so that it does not come under the law of נְבֵלָה), but slaughtering does not &c. (and the dangling limb is considered as a part of the slaughtered animal. Ib. 129ª אי מיתה עושה נ׳ ליטמא וכ׳ if death causes the limb to be considered as detached, let it be susceptible of uncleanness as a limb cut off from a live animal, and if not &c.; a. fr.—*Pl.* פת נ׳ ניפולין *bread which falls apart, spoiled bread.* Tosef. B. Kam X, 9; B. Kam. 99ᵇ; B. Bath. 93ᵇ. Sifra B'ḥuck., Par. 2, ch. VI פת ניפולת (corr. acc.; Yalk. Lev. 675 נוֹפֶלֶת).—[V. ניפולין.]—2) *falling down* for prayer. Deut. R. s. 2, beg. (as one of the expressions for prayer, with ref. to Deut. IX, 25); Yalk. ib. 811; Sifré ib. 26.

נִיפּוּל, נִפּ׳ m. (preced.) 1) *young birds found near their nests.* B. Bath. II, 6 (23ᵇ) נ׳ הנמצא וכ׳ (Ms. O. נָפִיל; Ms. H. נָפֶל, v. Rabb. D. S. a. l. note 300) birds found within fifty cubits &c.—2) a species of *locusts, nippol.* Ḥull. 65ᵇ סלעם זה נ׳ (Ar. החרגל) *Sal'am* (Lev. XI, 22) is *nippol;* Sifra Sh'mini, Par. 3, ch. V חרגל זה נפול.

נִיפּוּלָא, נִיפּוֹלָא ch. as preced. 2. Targ. Y. Lev. XI, 22 (Ar. נפלא, corr. acc.; h. text חרגל).

נִיפּוּלֶת, Sifra B'ḥuck., Par. 2, ch. VI, v. נִיפּוּל.

נִיפּוּלִית, v. next w.

נִיפּוֹלִין pr. n. pl. *Neapolis* on the site of the ancient Shechem. Y. Ab. Zar. V, 44ᵈ ניפולית (corr. acc., or נִיפוֹלִים); Deut. R. s. 3 נ׳ של כותיים. Num. R. s. 23 (expl. שכם, Josh. XX, 7) 'נִפ.

נִיפְחָא, v. נִפְחָא.

נִיפּוֹרָא, v. נִיפְרָא.

נִיפֶל, v. נִפִילָה.

נִיפְלָא, נִפ׳ I m. (cmp. נְפִיל) [*giant,*] the constellation of *Orion* (h. כְּסִיל). Targ. Job IX, 9. Ib. XXXVIII, 31.—*Pl.* נְפִילִין, constr. נִפְלֵי, נְפִילֵי. Targ. Is. XIII, 10 (h. text וכסיליהם).—Snh. 96ᵇ בר נפלי *son of giants* (?), surname of the Messiah (with allus. to הנפלת, Am. IX, 11); Yalk. Am. 549 (some ed. נִפִילֵי).

נִיפְלָא II m. *untimely birth,* v. נִפְלָא II.

נִיפְקָא, v. נִפְקָא.

נִיפַּר pr. n. pl. (Assyr. Nipur, modern Niffer, v. Schr. KAT.², p. 572) *Nifar.* Yoma 10ª (identified with כלנה) נ׳ Ms. M. 2 (Ms. M. 1 נפגר for נפור, v. Rabb. D. S. a. l. note; ed. נופר נינפר, strike out the second w., as a corrupt gloss, induced by phonetic resemblance of כַּלְנֵה a. כַּלְחַ, v. נִינְפַּר).

***נִיפְרָא** m. (a mutilation of λυχνοφόρος, cmp. לוּפַר) *torch-bearer.* Ab. Zar. 11ª נ׳ Ar. (ed. נִיפְּרוֹרָא; Ag. Hatt. נוּפְרָא; Yalk. Ex. 229 ed. Salon. אנפירא, v. Rabb. D. S. a. l. note 200); v. פִּיפְּרוֹרָא.

נִיפַשׁ m. (נְפַשׁ) = h. רֶוַח, *vacant space.* Targ. Y. Gen. XXXII, 17.

נִיץ, נוּץ (נְיַץ) 1) *to sprout, blossom.* Targ. Ps. XC, 6 יְנִיץ. Ib. CXXIX, 6 יְנִיץ Ms. (ed. יציץ).—Snh. 18ᵇ יְנִיץ; Y. R. Hash. II, 58ᵇ top כְּיֵנֵץ, v. בְּצִיר; Y. Snh. I, 18ᶜ bot. נוּנֵץ (corr. acc.).—2) *to shine* (cmp. נְבַט). Targ. Ps. CXXXII, 18 (h. text יציץ).

Af. אֲנִיץ, אָנֵיץ *to bring forth blossoms.* Targ. Num. XVII, 23 (ed. Berl. אָנֵיץ).

נִיץ, נִיצָא, v. נֵץ.

נִיצְבָא, נִיצְבְתָא, v. sub 'נִצְ.

נִיצּוּחַ, נִצ׳ m. (נָצַח) *glory; use of the stem* נצח *for song.* Midr. Till. to Ps. IV (expl. למנצח) למי שנצחו נצח נצחים to him whose glory is everlasting. Ib. בני׳ וכ׳ with glorification (use of נצח) &c.; Pes. 117ª, a. e. נִיצּוּן.

נִיצּוֹחָא, v. נִצּוֹחָא.

נִיצּוּרֵי, נִצ׳ m. pl. constr. (נְצַר) *strife, rivalry.* Meg. 24ᵇ top, v. נְצַר.

נִיצוֹלִית, v. next w.

נִיצוֹלֶת, נִצ׳ f. (נָצַל) *remnants, refuse.* Gen. R. s. 67 (ref. to אצלת, Gen. XXVII, 36) מן הנ׳ ed. (Ar. הנִצוֹלוֹת) of the leavings (of the poorest kind). Ib. s. 74 (ref. to ויצל, Gen. XXXI, 9) כזה שהוא מציל מן הנ׳ (Ar. הנִצוֹלוֹת) like one that saves things from among the refuse.—*Pl.* נִיצוֹלוֹת, 'נִצ. Tosef. Ter. X, 3 הניצולית וכ׳ (corr. acc.; ed. Zuck. המצולות) the leavings and the rotten fruits &c.—V. נָצַל a. נְצוֹלָה.

נִיצוֹץ c. (נָצַץ) 1) (b. h.) *spark, sparkling light.* Tanh. Vayesheb 1 נ׳ אחד וכ׳ one spark from thy smithy.—*Pl.* נִיצוֹצִים, נִיצוֹצִין. Tosef. Yoma II, 3 היו נ׳ יוצאות מכנגה sparkling rays proceeded from it (the golden tablet); Yoma 37ᵇ נ׳ יוצאין; Y. ib. III, 41ª top הנ׳ מנחדין; Y. Sot. II, 18ª top הניצוצים וכ׳. Num. R. s. 5, beg. שני נ׳ של אש וכ׳ two sparks of fire &c. Ib. שני נצ׳ מקדמין וכ׳ two sparks preceded them. Y. Ab. Zar. V, end, 45ᵇ (v. לִיבּוּן) צריך שיהא נ׳ וכ׳ it must be so heated that sparks burst forth from it. Tosef. Sabb. VI (VII), 2 נפלו הימנו נ׳ ואמר וכ׳ if snuff falls off the candle, and he says, we shall have guests &c. (v. אֱמוֹרִי). Sabb. III, 6 לקבל נ׳ to receive the snuff; a. fr.—*2) *shivers scattering from the broken sledge-hammer.* Sabb. 88ᵇ; Snh. 34ª (ref. to Jer. XXIII, 29) מה פטיש זה מתחלק לכמה נ׳ as the sledge-hammer (when shattered by the harder rock) is divided into many shivers (differ. in commentaries).—3) *squirtings* (of boiling water &c.). Ab. Zar. 76ᵇ מה בולעו נ׳ וכ׳ as the rim of a caldron absorbs forbidden substances through squirtings, so does it emit them again through the squirtings (of the boiling cleansing water, v. גִּיעוּל). Nidd. 13ᵃ נ׳ נתוזין וכ׳ drippings (of urine) squirt upon his feet. Yoma 29ᵇ, sq.; a. e.—4) (cmp. Arab. *nuḍâḍah*) *residue*. Sabb. 139ᵇ והאיכא נ׳ but there is the residue (the last drops percolating through the dregs in emptying liquid from vessel to vessel); נ׳ לבי ר׳ וכ׳ that residue was not cared about in the house of &c.

נִיצוֹצָא ch. same, נִיצוֹץ נורא *spark*. Targ. Is. I, 31.

נִיצוֹצְיָא, v. נוֹצִיצְיָא.

נִיצוֹק, v. נִצּוֹק.

נִיצוֹר, בַּר נ׳ pr. n. m., v. נֵצֶר IV.

נִיצְחָנוּתָא, נִיצְחָנָא, נִיצָחוֹן, v. sub. נצח.

נִיצְיָיא, נִיצְיָרָא, v. נִצְיָיא.

נִיצֶל, v. נֵצֶל.

נִיצָנָא, נִצָּ׳ m. (נצץ) = b. h. נִצָּן, *blossom*.—*Pl.* נִיצָּנַיָּא, נִצָּ׳. Targ. I Kings VI, 1; 37.

נִיצְצָא, v. נִצְצָא.

נִיצְרָא, v. נִצְרָא.

נִיקְבָא, v. נִקְבָא.

נִיקּוּד, נִקּ׳ m. (נָקַד I) 1) *dot, point*.—*Pl.* נִיקּוּדִים, נִיקּוּדִין, נִקּ׳. Tosef. Sabb. XI (XII), 13 והכותב שני נ׳ וכ׳ if one writes (on the Sabbath) two dots, and another person finishes them up &c., v. נְקוּדָּה.—2) *pl.* (as ab.) *minute loaves, cakes* (of half the size of an egg). Ter. V, 1 (oth. opin. *crumbled pieces*; v. Josh. IX, 12); Bekh. 22ᵇ. Y. Ter. V, 43ᶜ top והדין נ׳ כחדא חצייר וכ׳ those *nikkadim* are half the size of eggs.—[Midr. Sam. ch. XXII ניקודים some ed., read: נִיקּוּרִים.]

נִיקּוּי, נִקּ׳ m. (נָקָה) *cleansing, clearing* from sin. Gen. R. s. 82, beg. עולמים אין לו נ׳ will never be cleared (forgiven).

נִיקוֹלוֹגוֹס m. (νεικολόγος, not found in Greek Dict.) *pleader in a law-suit*. Pesik. Baḥod., p. 153ᵇ מנה לך ניקלגיס וכ׳ (corr. acc.) retain for thyself such and such a man as pleader, and thou shalt be acquitted; Yalk. Num. 782; Yalk. Lev. 645 ניקולוג׳ (corr. acc.); Lev. R. s. 29 נקול׳; v. הִיקוֹלוֹגוֹס.

נִיקוֹמָכִי pr. n. m. (Νικομάχης) *Nicomaches*, an Amora. Y. M. Kat. I, 80ᵈ top; Y. Snh. II, 23ᵈ bot. (not ניקימ׳).

***נִיקוֹן** m. (Νίκων, v. Joseph. Bell. Jud. V, 7, 2) *an engine of war, iron ram*. Kel. XI, 8 (comment. *iron point of a javelin*, ref. to קינו II Sam. XXI, 16; R. Hai G. reads נקידן); [Tosef. Kel. B. Mets. III, 1 גירין].

נִיקּוּף, נִקּ׳ I m. (נָקַף I) *knock, bruise*. Ḥull. 7ᵇ דם נ׳ וכ׳ the blood of a bruise atones &c. Ib. נ׳ שני a second bruise (before the first one is healed).

נִיקּוּף, נִקּ׳ II m. (נָקַף II) *crown, rim*.—זיתי נ׳ (cmp. פֵּאָה; v. Is. XVII, 6) *the olives left on the tree for the poor, the poor man's share, gleaning*, opp. to זיתי מָסִיק. Ḥall. III, 9. Peah VIII, 3. Yib. 20ᵈ bot. מקום שנהגו .. ד׳ נ׳ וכ׳ where the custom prevails to take down the gleanings (instead of leaving them on the trees), the poor man may say, this oil is from gleanings; a. e.—[Comment. זיתי נ׳ olives which are *knocked down*, v. preced.]

נִיקּוּר, נִקּ׳ m. (נָקַר I) 1) *picking, biting; chiselling*.—נ׳ עינים *putting out the eyes*. Pesik. Aḥăré, p. 168ᵇ; Lev. R. s. 20; Tanḥ. Vaëthḥ. 1; Koh. R. to VIII, 17.—נ׳ אבנים *chiselling of stones*. Sot. 46ᵇ.—Esp. *the picking* or *biting* done by birds, snakes &c., *traces of biting*. Ab. Zar. 35ᵃ משום נ׳ (נחש) because a serpent may have touched it. Y. Ter. VIII, 46ᵃ top דג נ׳ a fish showing traces of bites; a. fr.—*Pl.* נִיקּוּרִים, נִיקּוּרִין, נִקּ׳. Ter. VIII, 6 נִיקּוּרֵי תאנים וכ׳ figs &c. which appear to have been bitten at (possibly by snakes); Tosef. ib. VII, 16 נ׳ תבשיל וכ׳ a dish &c. showing traces of bites. Kidd. 80ᵃ, sq. נמצאו נ׳ נ׳ וכ׳ the dough shows that it has been pecked at (by chickens); a. fr.—Esp. *nikkurin, laws concerning food suspected of having been touched by snakes*. Y. Ter. l. c.; v. אֶפֶק; a. fr.—2) *pl. worm-eaten cloth, shreds*. Midr. Sam. ch. XXII (some ed. ניקוד׳, corr. acc.); Yalk. ib. 129, v. בְּרוּקְלֵי.

נִיקּוּרָא ch. same.—*Pl.* נִיקּוּרִין, נִיקּוּרֵי. Ḥull. 59ᵃ לא חייש מר לנ׳ do you not apprehend that it may have been bitten by snakes?—Ab. Zar. 30ᵇ אי אית ביה נ׳ Ar. (ed. נְקִירֵי) if there are bites in it.—Ḥull. 57ᵃ צנא דנקורי Ar., v. אִינְקוּרָא.

נִיקּוּשָׁא, נִקּ׳ m. (נְקַשׁ) *knocking, rattling*. Targ. Jer. XLVI, 22. Targ. Nah. II, 11. Ib. III, 2; a. e.—V. נְקָשָׁא.

נִיקַטְמוֹן, נְקַ׳ m. (v. אַנְקְדִּיטְמִין) *a musical instrument resembling a wooden leg*. Kel. XV, 6.

נִיקָיוֹן, v. נִקָּיוֹן.—[Kel. XV, 8, R. H. G., v. נִיקוֹן.]

נִיקְלְבִים, נִיקְלְבוֹס, נִיקְלְבָס, v. נִיקְלָוְוס.

נִיקְלְגִים, נִיקְלוֹגוֹס, v. נִיקוֹלוֹגוֹס.

נִיקְלָוְוס, נִיקְלְבָס m. (Νικόλαος, S.) *a variety of the date*. Ab. Zar. I, 5 (13ᵇ) נקליבס (Bab. ed. נִקְלָב; Mish. Nap. ודנקלבס, v. Rabb. D. S. a. l. note 400; Y. ed. ניקלבים). Ib. 14ᵇ נקלס (Ms. M. נִקְלוּוס); Y. ib. I, 39ᵈ bot. נִקְלְבִי׳. Y. Sabb. XIV, 14ᵈ דניקלבס stones of *nicolaos* dates; Y. Ab. Zar. II, 40ᵈ דנִקְלְבִיסִין (*pl.*)—*Pl.* נִיקְלַוְוסַיָּא, נִיקְלַוְוסִין &c. Y. Ber. VI, 10ᶜ bot.—Num. R. s. 3, beg., v. נוֹבֶלֶת; Midr. Till. to Ps. XCII מקולסין (corr. acc.).

נִיקְלֵי, v. אוּנְקְלֵי II.

נִיקְלִיטִין, v. נְקָלִיטִין.

נִיקָנוֹר, נִקָּ׳ pr. n. m. (Νικάνωρ) *Nicanor*, 1) a general under Antioch Epiphanes and Demetrius I, defeated and slain by Judah Maccabi (I Macc. VII, 39; II Macc. XV, 30). Y. Taan. II, 66ª top (Meg. Taan. XII) יום נ׳ Nicanor-Day (a half-festival); Y. Meg. I, 70ᶜ bot.—2) N., who imported Corinthian bronze doors for a Temple gate. Yoma III, 10; Tosef. ib. II, 4; Y. ib. III, 41ª; Bab. ib. 38ª. Midd. II, 3, a. fr. שער נ׳ (שערי), v. נְחוּשְׁתָּן.

נִיקְרָא, נִיקְצָא, v. sub נִקְ׳.

נִיר I, נוּר (b. h.; v. Del. Proleg., p. 98, sq.) [*to conquer*,] *to break ground, clear*. Tosef. Men. IX, 3 נָרָהּ שנה ראשונה ושנייה חורשה וכ׳ he breaks the field the first year, the second year he ploughs it &c.; Men. 85ª. Arakh. IX, 1 (29ᵇ) נָרָהּ if he broke it (without planting). Tosef. B. Mets. IX, 7 לא ידוא נָר .. אלא נָאר וכ׳ (Var. נָר) he must not plough it over entirely one year and plant the next, but plough one half &c. Ib. 8 והיה נָרָהּ וכ׳ and he ploughed all of it one year &c. Ib. 26 נאר (Var. נָר, נָיִיר); a. fr.—Part. pass. נִיר; f. נִירָה. Ib. 29 מניחה לפניו נ׳ when he surrenders the field to him cleared, opp. שְׁלֵּחָה—[Men. 85ᵇ ניר חצירה, Ms. M. נָר.]

Pilp. נִרְנֵר *to plough over repeatedly*. Part. pass. מְנוֹנָר (=מְנוּרְנָר; cmp. מְטוּלְטֶלֶת a. מְטוֹטֶלֶת); f. מְנוֹנֶרֶת, *pl.* מְנוֹנָרוֹת. Men. 85ª שדות .. וחמ׳ לכך (Ms. M. הנונרות לבר, corr. acc. or חנִירָנָרוֹת *Nif.*) fields .. repeatedly ploughed over for that purpose; Tosef. ib. IX, 3 הגירנירות, Var. הניטרות, read חנִירָנוֹרוֹת or חנִירָנָרוֹת).

Nif. נִירְנַר, נִירְנוֹר (cmp. נִירְהוֹן fr. הִירְ) *to be broken*, v. supra.

נִיר ch. same. Targ. I Sam. VIII, 12 לְמֵירָנָר (ed. Wil. לְמֵירַנֵר).

נִיר II m. (b. h.; preced.) 1) *clearing, ploughing over*. Tosef. B. Mets. IX, 24 בשעת הנ׳ (read: בשנת) in the year during which he cleared the land.—2) *newly broken land*. Peah II, 1 הבור והנ׳ fallow land or newly broken land. Y. Naz. VII, 56ᵇ top; a. e.—*Pl.* נִירִין. Shebi IV, 3.

נִיר, נִירָא I ch. same. Targ. I Sam. VIII, 12.

נִיר III, נִירָא II m. ch. (preced. wds.; Assyr. *nîru*) *yoke; servitude*. Targ. Deut. XXI, 3. Targ. Num. XIX, 2.—Targ. Jer. XXVII, 8; a. fr.—Y. Sabb. V, end, 7ᶜ; Bab. ib. 54ᵇ, v. גִּרְמוֹן.—*Pl.* נִירִין. Targ. Jer. XXVII, 2. Ib. XXVIII, 13.

נִיר IV m. (v. preced.; cmp. jugum a. ζυγόν, v. Sm. Ant. s. v. Tela) *cross-beam of the loom*, also *the cross-rod* under the cross-beam (liciatorium) to which the ends of the leashes are fastened; trnsf (mostly *pl.*) נִירִין, נִירִים *the leashes* or *thrums* to which the threads of the warp are fastened; also *the warp*. Gen. R. s. 94, v. פְּתַל. B. Kam. 119ᵇ אין לוקחין .. ולא נ׳ you must not buy from the weaver remnants of woof or of warp threads. Kel. XXI, 1 הנוגע .. בנ׳ ... he who touches the upper beam ... or the rods, contrad. to קֵירוֹס.—בית נ׳ that portion of the web produced by passing the spool with the woof across the warp, *mesh, slip*. Sabb. XIII, 2 (105ª) העושה שני בתי נ׳ בנִירַיִים וכ׳ Ms. M. (ed. בנירין) he who starts a web by making two meshes, attaching them either to the cross-pieces or to the slips (קֵירוֹס). Ib. 105ª ברוחב ג׳ בתי נ׳ within a distance of three meshes; (Tosef. ib. XII (XIII), 1 על ג׳ בתים). Y. ib. VII, 10ᶜ שני נ׳ בחק ... בניר אחד two sets of warp threads fastened to one old border web (licium) or two borders fastened to one set of warp threads. Shek. VIII, 5 על ע״ב נ׳ וכ׳ Ms. M. a. Ar. (ed. נימין; v. Rabb. D. S. a. l., p. לד, note) the curtain was woven on seventy-two leashes, and each twist of the warp (נִימָה) contained twenty four threads; Ḥull. 90ᵇ; Tam. 29ᵇ נימין; Num. R. s. 4 נימין; Tanḥ. Vayakh. 7 נימין; ed. Bub. 10 נירים.

נִירָא III ch. same; בת נ׳ the *cross-rod* (liciatorium). Sabb. 105ª (expl. שני בתי נירין בנירין, v. preced.) תרתי בבת נ׳ וחדא בנ׳ Ms. M. a. Rashi (ed. בבתי, early ed. בבי; v. Rabb. D. S. a. l. note) he passes a thread twice around the cross-rod and once around the cross-beam (jugum). Ib. 67ª נ׳ ברקא a white twisted cord.—*Pl.* נִירַיָּא. Y. ib. XIII, beg. 14ª (expl. בנירין, v. supra) נ׳ the two cross-rods (the liciatorium and the jugum).

נִירְדָּא, v. נִרְדָּא.

נִירוֹן pr. n. m. *Nero*, the Roman emperor. Gitt. 56ª נ׳ קיסר. Lam. R. to I, 5 מיח נ׳ (Gitt. 56ᵇ קיסר).

נִירוֹנִית f. (preced.) *a Neronian coin*. B. Mets. 25ᵇ; Tosef. ib. II, 10. Kel. XVII, 12 כסלע הניר׳ ed. Dehr. (ed. הנר׳, corr. acc.) the size of the Neronian Sela; Bekh. 37ᵇ. Ib. 38ª.

נֵירוֹק, v. רקק.

נִישְׁבִּין, נִישְׁבִּים, נִישְׁבָּא, v. sub נִשְׁבּ׳.

נִישְׁדּוּר, נִשְׁ׳ m. (Pers. našâdur. v. Perl. Et. St. p. 48) *gum-ammoniac*. Gitt. 69ª bot.

נִישּׂוּאִין, נִשּׂ׳ m. pl. (נָשָׂא) *taking in marriage* (v. אֵירוּסִין); *married state*. Keth. I, 4 אלמנה ... מן הנ׳ a widow, a divorced woman ... after having been actually married, opp. to מן האירוסין. Ib. V, 1. Yeb. 23ª (ref. to Deut. XXI, 15) אהובה בנִישּׂוּאֶיהָ וכ׳ beloved for her (blameless) marriage, hated for her (illicit) marriage. Ib. 64ᵇ נ׳ ומלקיות as to marrying (a third time), and as to the treatment of one twice lashed; a. fr.

נִישּׂוּאִין ch. same. Targ. I Chr. VIII, 9 דאתחדתא בני שואת, read: דאתחדתא הלכה בנִישּׂוּאֶהָ for a novel interpretation of the law was established through her marriage; v. Y. Yeb. VIII, 9ᶜ top.

נִישִׁיוּתָה, v. נְשִׁיאוּתָא.

נִישׁוּבִים, v. נִשְׁבִּים.

נִישּׁוֹבֶת f. (נְשַׁב) *chaff*. B. Bath. 94ª (Ms. M. נִישׁוֹבוֹת *pl.*; Ms. R. נְשׁוֹפוֹת).

נִישְׁרָא, נִישְׁפָא, נִישְׁמָא, v. sub נִשְׁ׳.

נִישְׁתְּרוּפֵי m. pl. (denom. of שְׂרָף) *drippings*; קירא

רֹב *wax that runs through the beehive.* Sabb. 110b (Ms. M. נִטְ).

נִיתְבְּרָא, v. גְּדְבְּכָה.

נִיתּוּחַ, נִתּ׳ m. (נָתַח) *dissection.* Zeb. V, 4, v. הֶפְשֵׁט. Gen. R. s. 34; a. fr.

נִיתְקָא, נִיתְרָא, v. sub נִתְ׳.

נְכָא, v. נְכֵי.

נַכַּאי, v. נַכֵּי.

נְכָאלָא m. (נְכֵיל) *deceiver, hypocrite.* Targ. Prov. XI, 9 Ms. (ed. נִכְלָא).

נֶכֶד m. (b. h.) *offspring, grandson.* Mekh. B'shall., Amalek, s. 2, v. נִין.

נָכָה, v. נכי.

נֵכֶה m. (b. h.; נָכָה) *crippled,* נְכֵה רגלים *paralyzed, lame.* Yalk. Deut. 933. מֹשל לנ׳ ר׳ וכ׳ like a lame person that disturbed the peace of &c., opp. שָׁלֵם.—*Pl.* נֵכִים. Pesik. R. s. 13, v. צָלַע.

נְכֹה, פַּרְעֹה נ׳ (b. h.) pr. n. m. *Pharaoh Necho* (II), King of Egypt. Sot. 9a; a. e.

נָכוֹן m. (b. h.; כּוּן) 1) *firm, ready.* Ber. 60a; a. e.—2) pr. n. גּוֹרֶן נ׳, v. כִּידוֹן II.

נָכוֹסָא, נָכוֹסָה m. (נְכַס) *butcher.* Y. Yoma III, 40c top (expl. קֶרֶץ, Jer. XLVI, 20) חד אמר נ׳ one says, it means the butcher (with ref. to Yoma III, 4 קרצו).

נְכוּש, v. נִיכּוּש.

נָכוֹשׁ m. (נָכַשׁ) *he who lops trees,* v. נִיכּוּש.

נַכְזְרָיָא m. (v. אַכְזָר) *cruel.* Targ. Prov. XI, 17 (ed. Lag. נוכריא). Ib. XVII, 11 (ed. Wil. נוּכְרָ).

נַכְזְרְיוּתָא f. (preced.) *cruelty.* Targ. Prov. XII, 10 (ed. Wil. נַכְ׳). Ib. XXVII, 4 (v. נוּכְרָא).

נכי, נָכָה (b. h.) *to be lessened.*—[Lev. R. s. 33 אלא נכה, some ed., v. אָנָךְ.]

Pi. נִיכָּה, נִכָּה *to deduct.* Hull. X, 3 ואינו מְנַכֶּה לו וכ׳ and the seller is not bound to allow him a reduction for the priest's share. B. Bath. VII, 2, sq. יְנַכֶּה he must make an allowance for what there is less than specified in the contract. Num. R. s. 20 (ref. to נכה, ib. XXII, 6) כמי שמְנַכֶּה אחד מכ״ד לסאה as one (purchasing grain) is prepared for a deficiency of one twenty-fourth for each S'ah (allowance for chaff, v. טִינוּפֶת); Tanh. Balak 4 (not למאה); ed. Bub. 6; a. fr.—[Cant. R. to III, 4 שנכה מסנחריב some ed., read שֶׁנָּכַח, v. נְכִיחָה.]

Hif. הִיכָּה, הִכָּה 1) *to injure, knock, strike.* B. Kam. VIII, 1 הִכָּהוּ חייב וכ׳ if he hit him (created a sore), he must pay for curing him. Ib. 3 הַמַּכֶּה את וכ׳ if a person strikes his father &c. Snh. IX, 2 נתכוין להַכּוֹתוֹ וכ׳ if he intended to hit him on his loins. Y. Peah I, 16a bot. (ref. to Ps. CXX, 3, sq.) כל כלי זיין מַכִּין וכ׳ all weapons strike in their place, but this (calumny) strikes at a distance; a. v. fr.—Part. pass. מוּכֶּה; f. מוּכָּה; *pl.* מוּכִּים, מוּכִּין; מוּכּוֹת. Keth. VII, 10, a. fr. מוּכֵּה שחין afflicted with leprosy. Ib. I, 3, a. fr. מוּכַּת עץ one who lost her hymen through an accidental lesion. Par. VIII, 9; Mikv. I, 8, v. מַיִם.—2) (trnsf.) *to strike, produce sound, play.* Yoma I, 7 מַכִּין לפניו באצבע וכ׳ snap their middle-fingers. Arakh. II, 3, v. חָלִיל; a. fr.

נְכֵי, נְכָא ch. same.

Pa. נַכֵּי *to deduct.* Targ. Y. Lev. XXVII, 18.—Y. Sot. V, 20c bot.; Y. Ber. IX, 14b bot. אנא מְנַכֵּי, v. הַנְכָּיָה. Sabb. 140a מְנַכּוּ, v. זְכוּתָא. B. Kam. 97b, sq. אי מחמת ... מְנַכֵּינָן ליה וכ׳ if provisions have become cheaper in consequence of the increased weight of the coin, we impose upon the creditor a corresponding reduction of the debt &c.; a. fr.

Ithpe. אִינְּכֵי, אִתְנְכֵי *to be injured, suffer.* Y. Ab. Zar. II, 41d top אשתון .. ואִתְנְכוּן the first drank and did not die, but were sick; ib. ולא מייתין איתכון read ואִי׳; (Y. Ter. VIII, 45d bot. only מייתין). Y. Dem. I, 22a top ולא אנכון and they suffered no more (from mice). Ib. יעבור ולא מִתְנְכֵה let him cross, he shall not be injured. Y. Keth. XII, 35b top כל הן דהוא מית מִתְנְכֵי wherever he be buried, what does he lose (what difference does it make to him)?; Y. Kil. IX, 32c top מנכי (corr. acc.).

Af. אַנְכֵּי *to harm.* Y. Sabb. III, 6a bot. (in Hebr. dict.) ומַנְכֵּי הוא לה כלום can he harm her in any manner?; Y. Bets. II, 61c.

נַכַּאי, נַכֵּי m. (preced. wds.) *deduction.* B. Kam. 59a נכי חיה payment is made with a deduction of the expense for the midwife (which the husband now saves); נ׳ מזונות a deduction for nursing expenses (incident to a regular confinement). Y. ib. VIII, beg. 6b נותנין נכאי מזון the injured person must be fully indemnified, deducting what his ordinary alimentation would have cost; Tosef. ib. IX, 3 נכי מזון Var. (ed. Zuck. דמי ניזק, oth. var. זכי, זבי, corr. acc.).

נַכֵּי m. (preced.) 1) *deduction; less.* Gitt. 15b; B. Bath. 57a נ׳ ריבעא (the whole) less a quarter, i. e. *three fourths* (cmp. דַּל I).—2) *loss, harm.* Y. Kidd. IV, 66b bot. משם מה נַכְּיֵיה because of 'what is his loss?', i. e. because it makes no difference in the law.

נַכְיוּתָא, נַכְיָתָא f. (preced. wds.) *reduction of a debt against a landed security* (מַשְׁכַּנְתָּא) *by deducting a stipulated amount every year for usufruct.* B. Mets. 67b top האי משכנתא ... לא ניכול אלא בנ׳ where the usage prevails that a land pledge can be redeemed at any time, the creditor must not have the usufruct except for the consideration of a rent deductible from the debt, v. מַשְׁכַּנְתָּא. Ib. בלא נ׳ without paying any rent by deduction. Ib. 62a משכנתא בלא נכיתא (Rashi נכיי׳) in the case of usufruct from pledged land without consideration; a. fr.—Y. Ber. IX, 14b bot. מה נ׳ ed. Lehm., v. הַנְכָּיָה.

נְכֵיל, נְכַל *to be crafty; to contrive.* Targ. Ps. LXXXIII, 4.

Pa. נַכֵּיל same; (with accus.) *to deceive.* Targ. O. Num.

XXV, 18 ed. Berl. (oth. ed. *Pe.*). Targ. Ps. XII, 3 (ed. Wil. מנבל׳). Targ. I Chr. XII, 17.

נְבִיל m. (preced.) *craftiness, fraud.* Targ. Mal. I, 14 (ed. Lag. נכל).

נְבִיל, נְבִילָא m., **נְבִילָא, נְבִילְתָּא** f. (preced.) *crafty, deceitful.* Targ. Ps. XLIII, 1. Targ. Jer. IX, 2. Targ. Ps. CXX, 2; a. e.—Targ. Hos. VII, 16 (ed. Lag. נִיכְלָא).

נְבִילוּ, נְבִילוּתָא f.=נְכִיל. Targ. Ex. XXI, 14; a. e.—Targ. Ps. X, 2 נכילו׳ Ms. (ed. נִכְלְוָתָא; Regia נְכִילְתָא). Targ. Job V, 16 נְכֵלְתָא ed. Wil. (ed. Lag. נבילותא, h. text עלתה).

נְבִילְתָּא, v. נְבִיל, a. preced.

נְכֵיס *to slaughter*, v. נְכַס.

נְכִיס m., **נְכִיסָא, נְכִיסְתָּא** f. (preced.) *slaughtered.* Targ. Lev. XIV, 6 (O. ed. Amst. נְכֶסְתָּא). Ib. 51 (O. ed. Vien. נְכֵיסְתָּא); a. e.

נָכִישׁ m.=נִיתּוּשׁ q. v.

נְכֵית, v. נְכַת.

נְכִיתָה f. (נְכַת) *bite*; trnsf. *booty.* Cant. R. to III, 4 (play on נכתה, II Kings XX, 13) נ׳ שֶׁנָּכַת וכ׳ (some ed. נְכָיְתָה) he showed him the bite which he had bitten off from Sennacherib, the booty &c.

נְכֵל, v. נְכִיל.

נְכַל, נִכְלָא, נִ׳ m. (נְכִיל) 1)=b. h. נֵכֶל *deceit.* Targ. Ps. XXIV, 4; a. fr.—*Pl.* נִכְלִין, נִ׳. Targ. Is. LIII, 9 (not נכב׳). Targ. Mic. VI, 12. Targ. O. Num. XXV, 18; a. e.—2) *deceitful; hypocrite*, v. נְכָאלָא, a. נְכִיל.—*Pl.* נִכְלֵי, נִ׳. Gen. R. s. 49; Yalk. ib. 83, v. נִבְלָא II.

נִכְלוּתָא, נִכְלְתָא, v. נְכִילוּ.

נָכַס (cmp. כָּסַס) 1) *to cut; to slaughter.* Imper. כּוֹס. Pes. 61ª (expl. תכסו, Ex. XII, 4) לשון סורסי הוא ... כוס לי טלה זה it is an abbreviated form (v. סוּרְסִי), as one says to his neighbor, *kos* (for נְכוֹס) &c., cut this lamb for me; Y. ib. V, 32ª bot.; Mekh. Bo. s. 3.—Snh. 82ᵇ (play on כזבי, Num. XXV, 15) שאמרה לאביה כוס בי עם זה she said to her father, cut (ruin) this people through me. Ḥull. 37ᵇ בְּשַׂר כוס כוס meat of an animal about which one says, 'cut, cut', i. e. meat of an animal hurriedly cut, because it threatens to die; Treat. Kuthim (ed. Kirchh., p. 33, sq.) we must not sell to Samaritans כּוֹסְכּוֹס (sub. בשר) meat of an animal on the point of death.—2) *to mark, count*, v. נְכָסִים.

נְכַס, נְכֵיס ch. same; impf. יִכּוֹס. Targ. Gen. XXXI, 54. Ib. O. XXII, 10 לְמִיכַּס ed. Berl. (oth. ed. a. Y. לְמֵיכַס); a. fr.—Snh. 25ᵇ bot. והאידנא נ׳ אבא וכ׳ and presently he will slaughter the father for the son and the son for the father (he will exercise extortions). Y. Shebi. V, end, 36ª מִיכּוֹס תורא וכ׳ to slaughter an ox available for the plough; a. fr.

Ithpe. אִיתְנְכֵיס, אִתְנְכִיס, אִתְנְכֵס *to be slaughtered.* Targ. Lev. XIX, 6; a. fr.—Gen. R. s. 33 אזל לְמִתְנַכְסָה וכ׳ was going to be slaughtered, and it lowed, as if to say, save me; Y. Keth. XII, 35ª מִיתְנַכְּסִים; Y. Kil. IX, 32ᵇ מִתְנַכֵּס taken to be slaughtered.

נִכְסָא, נִכְסְתָּא, נִ׳ f. (preced.) *slaughter; slaughtering* (according to the ritual, שְׁחִיטָה); *sacrifice, feast* (=h. זֶבַח). Targ. Is. XXXIV, 6 (h. text טבח).—Targ. Y. Deut. XIV, 21. Targ. Y. Lev. XVII, 13 (ed. Vien. נִיכְסַתְּהּ). Targ. Gen. XXXI, 45; a. fr.—Targ. Y. Gen. XLIII, 16 בית נ׳ the place for ritual cutting (בית השחיטה), *ritually cut throat.*—B. Bath. 92ª אי גברא דזבין לנ׳ לנ׳ if it is a man that sells cattle for food, the purchase was made for slaughtering (and not for work); B. Kam. 46ª (not לנכסותא; v. Rabb. D. S. a. l.); a. fr.—*Pl.* נִכְסְתָא, נִכְסָן; constr. נִכְסַת, נִ׳; (also נִכְסִין, נִ׳). Targ. O. Ex. XXXII, 6 ניכסן ed. Berl. (oth. ed. a. Y. ניכסין). Ib. XVIII, 12; a. fr.—Targ. Ps. CVI, 28 נִכְסֵי (Ms. נכסת).

נכסותא, v. preced.

נִכְסַיָּא, v. נִכְסִין.

נְכָסִים m. pl. (b. h.; נָכַס or כָּסַס) [*counted things,*] *account; property, business.* Ber. 46ª ויצלח מאד בכל נְכָסָיו ויהיו נכסיו ונְכָסֵינוּ וכ׳ may he have great success in all his accounts (enterprises), and may his business and ours be successful and near a city. Ab. Zar. 19ᵇ, v. צָלַח. B. Bath. IX, 7, a. fr. נ׳ שיש להן אחריות, v. אַחֲרָיוּת. Ib. המחלק נכסיו וכ׳ if a person disposes of his belongings by word of mouth. Yeb. IV, 3 נ׳ הנכנסים וכ׳ property which the wife brings in and takes out again (v. מְלוֹג). B. Kam. I, 2 נ׳ של בני ברית Jewish property; נ׳ המיוחדין individual property; a. v. fr.

נִכְסִין, נִכְסַיָּא, נִכְסֵי, נִ׳ ch. same. Targ. Y. II Num. XXXII, 1 (h. text מקנה) *herds.* Targ. Josh. XXII, 8 (h. text נכסים). Targ. Deut. VIII, 17 (h. text חַיִל); a. fr.—B. Kam. 93ª (prov.) בתר מרא נ׳ וכ׳ behind a man of wealth chips are dragged along, i. e. in the company of a wealthy man you have an opportunity of making money. Bekh. 48ª נ׳ הא אשתעבד Rashi (read: אשתעבוד; ed. אשתעבדן להו לנ׳) has not the estate been made responsible for the debt (before the father's death)? Ib. מכדי נ׳ דבר וכ׳ does not a person's property merely take the place of a guarantor? B. Bath. 58ª כל נִכְסַי לחד ברא all my property shall go to one son (of mine). Ib. כולהו נִכְסֵי דהאי all the property (of the father) goes to this (son).

נִכְסְתָא, v. נִכְסָא.

נִכְפֶּת, v. כָּפַת.

נָכַר (b. h.) *to be unknown, strange.*

Hif. הִכִּיר 1) *to recognize, know; to favor.* Ruth. R. to II, 10 (ref. to להכירני, ib.) נתנבאה.. לְהַכִּירָהּ כדרך וכ׳ she prophesied that he would know her in the way of all people (as his wife, cmp. יָדַע). Ber. 10ᵇ האשה מַכֶּרֶת באורחין וכ׳ woman recognizes the character of guests better than man. R. Hash. II, 1 אם אינן מַכִּירִין אותו if the court does not know him personally. Y. Yeb. IV, 6ᵇ כנסה ולא הִכִּירָהּ he married her but did not touch her (v. supra). Snh. 7ᵇ (ref. to Deut. I, 17) לא תַכִּירוּ thou shalt not favor him (if he is thy friend); a. fr.—Num. R. s. 9 במקום שמכיר where he knows (the people), where he is acquainted; Sifré Num. 14 במקום שמכירין אותו.—2) *to make known, identify; to acknowledge, own.* R. Hash. l. c. מן המכירים on the declaration of those who identify (the witnesses; v. Rabb. D. S. a. l. note 2). Gen. R. s. 43 לא היה שמי ניכר .. והִכַּרְתָּ אותו וכ׳ my name was unknown .... and thou hast made me known among my creatures. Sifré Deut. 217; Kidd. 78[b], a. e. (ref. to יכיר, Deut. XXI, 17) יַכִּירֶנּוּ לאחרים he may identify him before others (as his first born son). Sifré Deut. 312 שאהיה מַכִּירוֹ that I may make it known as mine. Ib. מחיכן המקום מַכִּיר את חלקו beginning with whom does the Lord acknowledge his share (claim as his)? With Jacob; a. fr.

Hof. הוּכַּר *to be recognized; to be discernible.* Kidd. III, 5 ה׳ עוברה her pregnancy was certain, v. הַכָּרָה; ib. 62[b]. B. Mets. 93[b] ה׳ הגנב the thief was found out; a. e.

Nif. נִיכַּר same. Part. נִיכָּר. Ber. 28[a] מכותלי .. אתה נ׳ וכ׳ by the walls of thy house, one sees that thou art a smith. Kidd. 31[a] מסוף דברך נ׳ וכ׳ from thy last words (the fifth and following commandments of the decalogue) it is seen that thy first one is true. Ib. מבין ריסי עיניך נ׳, v. רִיס. Gitt. 53[a] שאינו נ׳, v. הֶיזֵּק. Sabb. 91[b] מקומו נ׳ its location is discernible. Sot. 9[b] נִיכָּרִין דברי אמת words of truth are easily recognized. Gen. R. s. 43, v. supra; a. fr.

Pi. נִכֵּר *to treat as a stranger, ignore; to discriminate against.* Snh. l. c. (ref. to Deut. I, 17) לא תְנַכְּרֵהוּ (if he is thy enemy) do not discriminate against him (v. supra). Sifré Deut. 322 בשעת ... מְנַכְּרִים וכ׳ when Israel is in trouble, the nations ignore them and act as though they did not know them; a. e.

נְכַר ch. same; *Af.* אַכַּר *to recognize, know.* Targ. Y. I Gen. XXXVIII, 25, sq.

Ithpa. אִיתְּנַכַּר *to be distinguishable.* B. Kam. 5[a] דמִיתְּנַכְּרָא, v. הֶיזֵּקָא. Ib. 97[a] מִיתְּנַכַּר היזיקה its reduction in value is distinguishable.

Pa. נַכֵּר *to make strange, remove.* Sabb. 82[b] (ref. to תזרם, Is. XXX, 22) נַכְּרִינְהוּ מינך כְּנָכָר (v. Rabb. D. S. a. l. note) remove them from thee like a strange (disgusting) thing.

נָכְרִי m. (b. h.; preced. wds.) *stranger, gentile.* [In editions published under the censor's supervision, our w. is frequently changed into עכו״ם, גוי, כּוּתִי, כּוּשִׁי &c.] Ab. Zar. IV, 4 (51[b]; 52[b]; Mish. ed. עכו״ם). Sabb. 31[a]; a. v. fr.—*Pl.* נָכְרִים. Ḥull. 13[b] נ׳ שבחוצה לארץ לאו עובדי ע״ז וכ׳ gentiles outside of Palestine are not to be considered as idolaters, they only continue their fathers' customs. Gitt. 61[a] מפרנסין עניי נ׳ וכ׳ we must support the poor of the gentiles &c.; (Tosef. ib. V (III), 4 גוים). Gitt. V, 9 (61[a]) מספידין מתי נ׳ וכ׳ (Mish. ed. עכו״ם) we must lament for the dead of the gentiles &c.; a. v. fr.—Fem. נָכְרִית. Yeb. 17[a]. Ib. III, 7 שלשה אחים ... ואחד נשוי נ׳ in the case of three brothers, two of whom married two sisters, and one a stranger; a. fr.

נָכַשׁ (cmp. כשכש, קשקש) *to come in near contact.*

Pi. נִיכֵּשׁ (denom. of מַכּוֹשׁ I) *to weed; to lop.* Kil. II, 5 אין מחייבין אותו לְנַכֵּשׁ the law does not bind him to pluck out (the plants which grow among the fenugrec). Ib. ואם נִכֵּשׁ (Y. ed. ני׳) but if he did &c. Tosef. ib. I, 15 והמְנַכֵּשׁ and he who does the weeding (in a field of mixed seeds); M. Kat. 2[b]; a. fr. [B. Bath. 54[a] Ms. R., v. מַכּוֹשׁ I.]

Hif. הִכִּישׁ 1) *to strike, wound, sting.* B. Mets. 30[b]; B. Bath. 88[a] הִכִּישָׁהּ if he struck the lost beast which he took in charge. Gen. R. s. 30, beg. הִכִּישׁוֹ ארי וכ׳ a lion struck and crippled him. B. Mets. 78[a] הִכִּישָׁהּ נחש a serpent bit her.—2) *to cause injury by contact.* B. Kam. 23[b] מַכִּישׁ (Ms. H. משיך) he who caused a neighbor's death by bringing the serpent's tooth in contact with his neighbor's body; Snh. 78[a]. Yalk. Deut. 944 שמַכִּישִׁין, v. קונטרינים; Sifré Deut. 317 שמכינים (corr. acc.).—3) (denom. of מַכּוֹשׁ I) *to insert the hoe* or *spade.* B. Bath. 54[a], v. מַכּוֹשׁ I.

Hithpa. הִתְנַכֵּשׁ, *Nif.* נִכּוֹשׁ *to be hoed for.* Gen. R. s. 45 הקוצים ... לא מִתְנַכְּשִׁין ולא נזרעין וכ׳ for thorns there is neither hoeing (digging over) nor sowing, but they grow of themselves, while wheat &c.; Yalk. ib. 79 לא נִכּוֹשִׁין ולא נחרשים וכ׳ neither digging, nor ploughing, nor sowing &c.

נְכַשׁ ch. same; *Pa.* נַכֵּישׁ *to bite.* Gen. R. s. 91 כן ... מְנַכְּשָׁא .... ואכלה וכ׳ so may this woman (I) take a bite of the flesh of this and eat; (Yalk. Gen. 148 only אכלה); v. נְכַת.

Af. אַנְכֵּישׁ *to weed.* B. Mets. 105[a] מַנְכִּישְׁנָא וכ׳ I shall weed as much as is required for thy share.

נַכָּשׁ m. (preced.) *he who lops trees*; v. נִיכּוּשׁ.

נְכַת (v. next w.) *to bite.* Cant. R. to III, 4; v. נְכִיתָה.

נְכַת, נְכֵית (cmp. כתת; v. נכש) *to wound, bite, injure.* Targ. Num. XXI, 9. Ib. 6 (ed. Berl. נַכִּיתוּ *Pa.*); a. fr.—Gen. R. s. 98 חיויא דבעי לְמִיכַּת וכ׳ the serpent that is to bite my son. Y. Peah I, 16[a] bot. [read:] ... אילולי דאתאמר נְכוֹת לא הוינא נָכֵית had I not been told from on high, 'bite', I should not bite. Koh. R. to VII, 1 מאן דנַכְתֵּיה דנכתיה חמרא וכ׳, v. הִיחִל. Gitt. 67[b] (expl. קורדייקוס) וכ׳ young wine from the press has bitten him (made him delirious). B. Mets. 60[b] נשך איכא דקא נכית ליה וכ׳ it is *neshekh* (usury, v. נֶשֶׁךְ), for he bites (injures) him, by taking from him something which he (the creditor) had not given him; a. fr.

Pa. נַכֵּית 1) same. Targ. O. Num. XXI, 6, v. supra.—Ab. Zar. 35[b] הוה מְנַכֵּית ואכיל וכ׳ took a bite and ate of the bread (of a non-Jew) &c.—2) *to cause to bite.* Yeb. 76[a] מייתינן .. ומְנַכְּתִינַן ליה וכ׳ we get a big ant and let it bite (insert its head into the opening) and cut its head off.

Ithpe. איתְּנְכֵית, אִיתְנְכֵית *to be bitten, stung.* Targ. O. Num. XXI, 8. Targ. Y. II ib. 9.

נְכִתָה, v. נְכִיתָה.

נַכְתָּמָא m. (כתם) (*wooden*) *lid* of a water pitcher. Bets. 30[a]. B. Bath. 26[a] top כדנייד נ׳ וכ׳ as much as a lid on a pitcher shakes. Sabb. 105[b]. Pes. 112[a].

נָם perf. of נום.

נָמָא, נְמָה, *Pi.* נִימָּה, נִימָּא, v. נום I.

נְמוֹרִיָה, v. נְמִירָה.

נָמוֹךְ m., **נְמוּכָה** f. *low, lowly*, v. מָךְ.—*Pl.* נְמוּכִים; נְמוּכוֹת. Num. R. s. 19 בגבוה שבגבוהים ובנמוך שבנ׳ with the highest of the high (the cedar) and the lowest of the low (the hyssop). Sot. 5ᵇ נְמוּכֵי הרוח the humble. Koh. R. to IX, 10 נ׳ פנירתם with downcast countenances, opp. זקופות; a. fr.

נְמוֹס *law*, v. נִימוֹס.

נְמוֹס, v. מְסַס.—[Tosef. Bekh. IV, 16, read: גָּמוּס, v. גְּמַס.]

נְמוֹק, v. מְקַק.

נְמוֹק, v. נִימוּק.

נְמוֹר m. (נְמַר) *speckled*. Targ. Gen. XXX, 32, sq.—*Pl.* נְמוֹרִין; f. נְמוֹרְתָא. Targ. O. ib. 39. Ib. 35 נְמוֹרְתָּא; Y. ib. נְמוֹרְתָא (corr. acc.).

נְמוֹרֵי pr. n. pl., v. נְמִירֵי.

נְמוֹרִין pr. n. pl., v. נִמְרִין.

נמורקין, v. במורקין.

נַמְטָא f. (מוּט or מְטֵי) *felt-mattress, felt-cloth*. Yoma 69ᵃ; Bets. 15ᵃ, v. נְמַד.—*Pl.* נַמְטֵי. B. Mets. 84ᵇ, v. מוּךְ ch. B. Kam. 119ᵇ מאי בגדים נ׳ what kind of garments is meant? Felt-spreadings; ib. 93ᵇ.

נְמִי, v. טוּמִי.

נַמִּי adv. (= נְהִי מִי; cmp. ויהי מה II Sam. XVIII, 23) *at all events, really, even, likewise*. Pes. 102ᵃ נימא נידחו (נימא מהא נ׳ תיובתיה תיובתא Ms. M. (ed. תיובתיה נ׳ מהא I mean to say, at all events (even if the previous objection could be met) he will stand refuted from this citation; Erub. 30ᵃ. Pes. 114ᵃ, a. fr. חכא נ׳ (abbrev. ח״נ), v. הָכָא. Yoma 64ᵃ נהר נ׳, v. נְהַר II.—הכי נ׳ (abbrev. ה״נ) *it is really so; is it really so?* Ḥag. 11ᵇ ה״נ will you say, it is really so (that this subject must be taught only in the presence of three students)? Ḥull. 11ᵇ sq. ה״נ דלא וכ׳ (will you say) it is really so that he ate no meat?; וכי תימא ה״נ וכ׳ and if you will say, 'yes, it is so', what about sacred meat? Ib. 12ᵃ אפי׳ תרומה נ׳ then you must say 'yes' even with regard to T'rumah; אפי׳ שחיטה נ׳ לא then you must say 'no' even with regard to slaughtering. Ib. אי נ׳ שמע אינש אחרינא Rashi (ed. incorr.) even if another person did overhear it. Ib. 51ᵃ והאי נ׳ וכ׳ and this animal has really measured its strength. B. Mets. 98ᵃ, a. fr. אי נ׳ or indeed (which would be better).—R. Hash. 22ᵇ, a. fr. הכי נ׳ מסתברא so, indeed, it stands to reason. Ib., a. fr. תניא נ׳ הכי so, indeed, it has been taught. Ber. 4ᵇ … מה קימה אף שכיבה נ׳ וכ׳ as on getting up you must recite …., so on lying down likewise &c.; a. v. fr.

נְמָיָא, v. נְמִיָּה.

נְמִיגָה f. (denom. of נָמוֹג, Nif. of מוּג) *melting, loss of courage*. Mekh. B'shall., Shir., s. 9 (ref. to נמוגו, Ex. XV, 15) אין נ׳ אלא נמיסה the root מוג is synonymous with מסס; Yalk. Ex. 251 אין נ׳ אלא מסייה.

נְמִיָּיה, נְמִיָּה f. (supposed to be) *marten*. Ḥull. 52ᵇ. B. Bath. II, 5. Y'lamd. to Gen. XVI, 5, v. חָמַס; a. fr.

נְמִיָּיה, נְמִיָּה f. (נמי, dialect. corresp. to נבי; cmp. Arab. *namay*) *sproutings*, v. נְבִיָּיה.

נמימרין, Yalk. Ps. 868, v. מִימְרִין.

נְמִיָּיה, v. נְמִיָּה.

נְמִיָּיה, v. נְמִיָּה.

נְמִיל, v. נְמַל.

נְמִיסָה f. (denom. of נָמַס, Nif. of מָסַס) *melting, loss of courage*. Mekh. B'shall., Shir., s. 9, v. נְמִיגָה.

נְמִירֵי pr. n. pl. *N'miré*, a twin-town of (Hash-)Shulami, separated from it by the Jordan. Tosef. Bekh. VII, 3 כגון חשולמי ונ׳ ed. Zuck. (Var. מנרי, corrupt.) like Hash-Sh. and N., being two autonomous places (v. אַבְטוֹנְיָיוֹת); Bekh. 55ᵃ של נמר ונמורי (corr. acc.); Y. B. Bath. III, 14ᵃ top שלומי ונבירו.

נְמַךְ (v. מוּךְ, a. נָמוֹךְ), *Hif.* הִנְמִיךְ *to lower*. Sifré Num. 83 הגבוה מַנְמִיכוֹ וכ׳ every hilly place he lowered, and every depression he raised; Yalk. Ex. 228.—Ber. 45ᵃ יַנְמִיךְ הקורא קולו Ms. F. (v. Rabb. D. S. a. l. note 6; ed. ימעך) the reader must temper his voice.

נְמֵל m. (a popular corrupt. of לְמֵין, q. v.) *haven, bay*. Erub. IV, 2, v. לְמֵין. Tosef. Yoma II, 4 נְמָלָהּ של יפו (Var. נְמֵי׳) the harbor of Japho; Yoma 38ᵃ נ׳ של עכו; a. e.

נְמָלָה f. (b. h.; perh. a contr. of נמלה, נכמלה, fr. עָמַל) *ant*. Hull. 63ᵃ (in Chald. dict.) כי הוה חזי נ׳ וכ׳ when he saw ants (at work), he used to say, 'thy righteousness &c. (Ps. XXXVI, 7). Deut. R. s. 5; Yalk. Prov. 938 חנ׳ שלשה וכ׳ in the house of the ant there are three stories. Ib. מעשה בנ׳ אחת וכ׳ once an ant dropped a grain of wheat &c.; a. e.—*Pl.* נְמָלִין, נְמָלִים. Peah IV, 11. Tosef. ib. I, 8; Men. 71ᵇ; a. fr.—Y. Yeb. VIII, 9ᵇ מביא נימולין, v. נָשַׁךְ.—[Chald. שׁוּמְשְׁמָנָא.]

נַמְנוּמָא m. (נַמְנֵם) *sleeping couch*. Y. Keth. II, 26ᵃ bot., v. חִינוּמָא.—[נַמְנוּמֵי, inf. of נַמְנֵם.]

נַמְנֵם, נִמְנֵם, v. נום II h. a. ch.

נָמֵס m. (b. h.; מָסַס) *decayed*. Ex. R. s. 15 מי שהיה של עץ היה נ׳ that (idol) of wood appeared rotten; a. e.—V. מָסַס.

נמסיאות, Tosef. Toh. VII, 11, read: דִּימוֹסְיָאוֹת or אִסְטְוָנִיוֹת (v. Toh. VI, 10).

נמסינן, v. נִימְסִיוֹן.

נְמָקִים m. pl. (מָקַק) *decaying sores*. Sabb. 62ᵇ.

נָמֵר m. (b. h.) *tiger* or *leopard*. Y. Yeb. VIII, 9ᶜ top, v. חוּש II. Snh. I, 4; B. Kam. I, 4, v. בַּרְדְּלִיס; a. e.—*Pl.* נְמֵרִים. Gen. R. s. 34. Midr. Till. to Ps. LXXVIII, 45; a. e.—[From Sabb. 107ᵇ, ref. to Jer. XIII, 23, it would appear that נמר, in Talmudic days, meant *leopard*.]

נָמַר, *Pi.* נִמֵּר (denom. of preced.) *to give a checkered* or *striped appearance*, esp. נ׳ שדה *to take out* or *cut the ripe plants* of a field, leaving the unripe stand for later crops. Peah III, 2. Men. 71ᵇ בִּמְנַמֵּר לקליות when he cuts portions of the grain field with the intention of using the ears for roasting; במנמר לאוצר when he cuts for storage.—*Part. pass.* מְנוּמָּר *striped, speckled*. B. Kam. 119ᵇ לוקחין מהן בגד מנ׳ you may buy from them (weavers) (even) a checkered web (for which they may have used remnants of other people's wool). Gitt. 54ᵇ משום דמיחזי כמנ׳ because (if he were to pass his pen over all the Divine Names in the scroll) the writing would look speckled; Men. 29ᵇ bot. משום דמיחזי כמ׳ it would look speckled (if he were to insert omitted vowel letters). Y. Succ. III, 53ᵈ bot.; Y. Maasr. I, 49ᵃ המ׳ a speckled Ethrog.

נְמַר, נִמְרָא, (נְמִרְתָּ) נִמ׳ ch.=h. נָמֵר. Targ. Jer. V, 6; a. e.—Y. Peah III, 17ᶜ top (expl. המנמר ib. III, 2) כהדין נימרה making the field look checkered like a tiger (or leopard), v. נְמֵרִידָה.—*Pl.* נִמְרַיָּא, נְמָרִין, נִי׳. Targ. Cant. IV, 8 (ed. Vien. נְמָרִין). Targ. Hab. I, 8.—[בית נמרי, בית נמרין, נמרא, v. next w.]

בֵּית נִ׳, נִמְרָה (b. h.) pr. n. pl. (*Beth*) *Nimrah*, modern *Nimrîn*, in Peraea. Tosef. Shebi. VII, 11; Y. ib. IX, 38ᵈ bot.; ib. (expl. בית נמרה, Josh. XIII, 27) בֵּית נִמְרִין.—Targ. O. Num. XXXII, 3 ed. Berl. (ed. Vien. מכוור דבית נִמְרִין, read with Y. מכוור ובית נ׳); Targ. O. ib. 36; Y. בית נִמְרִין, נִמְרִי.—Tosef. Shebi. IV, 11 נמרין מלי׳ (Var. נמרים); Yalk. Deut. 874 נימרין מיליה; Sifré ib. 51 נימרון עליה (corr. acc.); Y. Shebi VI, 36ᶜ only נמרין.—[Sifré l. c. טרכונא דנימרא; Yalk. l. c. טרכונ׳ דוימרה; Y. Shebi. l. c. טרכונא דמתחום לבוצרא; Tosef. l. c. טרכונא דבתחום בצרה.] V. Hildesh. Geogr. p. 60.

נמרידה, v. נְמֵרִידָה.

נִמְרִין, נִמ׳, נִמְרֵי pr. n. pl. *Nimrin*, 1)=בית נמרה, v. preced. art.—2) *Nimrin* in Syria, the last station of messengers proclaiming the new moon. Y. Keth. II, 26ᵈ top עד מקום ששלוחי .... עד נ׳ as far as the messengers to announce the new moon go, as far as N. Y. R. Hash. I, 57ᵇ bot. אילין דאזלין לְנִמְרִין those messengers who go to N.—Tosef. Yoma V (IV), 3 ככותבת הנימרין, v. נִמְרִית.

נְמֵרִידָה f. (sub. שדה; v. נָמַר) *a checkered field*. Y. Peah III, 17ᶜ top (in a corrupt and defective passage) מקום ... נ׳ קריי לה (not נמרידה) the manured spots mature their plants earlier (and such a field) is called *nimrirah*.

נִמְרִית f. *of Nimrah* or *Beth Nimrah*. Y. Yoma VIII, 44ᵈ bot כותבת הנ׳; Tosef. ib. V (IV), 3 הנימרין; v. כּוֹתֶבֶת.

נַן, *pl.* of נָא I.

נָנָאִי, v. נָאנָאִי.

נַנַּי, נַנַּאי pr. n. m. (prob. abbrev. of חנניה) *Nannai*, a name frequent in Maḥoza. Yeb. 115ᵇ bot., v. חָבֵר.

ננגרי, v. קַרְיְנָנַי.

ננהא, Sabb. 140ᵃ Ar. ed. pr., v. נִיוְנְיָא II.

נַנְחוּ, *pl.* of נִידוּ.

נַנּוּס, נַנּוּסָא, נַנָּס, v. נַנָּס, נַנָּסָא.

נַנַּי, v. נַנַּאי.

נָנְיָא, נַנְרִיא, v. נִירְנְיָא.

נַנְּיס, v. נַנָּסָא.

נַנָּס m. (νᾶνος, nanus, of Semitic origin, fr. נסס, cmp. טלל fr. טלל) *dwarf*; (adj.) *puny, stumped*. Nidd. 24ᵇ, opp. אָרוֹךְ; Num. R. s. 9. Ber. 58ᵇ נ׳ one whose limbs are too small for his body, opp. כִּיפֵּחַ; Tosef. ib. VII (VI), 3 ננוס ed. Zuck. (Var. ננס); Y. ib. IX, 13ᵇ bot.; Tanḥ. ed. Bub., Pinḥas 1. Sifra Emor, Par. 3, ch. III; Bekh. VII, 6 (45ᵇ, of animals and of men). Cant. R. to II, 15; Gen. R. s. 65 נ׳ שבננסים a puny dwarf. Midr. Till. to Ps. CXXXVII; Pesik. R. s. 31 הנ׳ הזה that dwarf (Nebuchadnezzar); a. fr.—Ḥull. 63ᵃ וסימנך ננס פסול and thy sign (to remember that the small species of שקיטנא is unclean) be, 'the dwarf is unfit' (for priesthood).—*Pl.* נַנָּסִין, נַנָּסִים. Cant. R. l. c.; Gen. R. l. c., v. supra. Ib. s. 37; Yalk. ib. 62 כפתורים נ׳ Caphtorites (Gen. X, 14) are dwarfs; a. fr.—Tam. III, 5; Midd. III, 5 עמודים נ׳ small columns. Ib. V, 2 הנ׳ (sub. עמודים).—*Fem.* נַנֶּסֶת. Bekh. 45ᵇ. Par. II, 2; a. e.

נַנְּיס, נַנָּסָא ch. same. Targ. Y. II Lev. XXI, 20 נניס (h. text דק).—Pesik. Dibré, p. 112ᵃ sq. נ׳ דבבל (Ms. Parma ננוסא) the Babylonian dwarf (Nebuchadnezzar); Yalk. Dan. 1062 (ref. to Dan. IV, 14 שפל אנשים) זה נבוכדנצר נ׳ וכ׳ that means N. the dwarf &c. (v. 'Rashi' to Gen. R. s. 16, end).

נַנְעָה, נַנְעָא m. ch.=h. נַעֲנָע, *mint*. Y. Maasr. V, end, 52ᵃ והא נ׳ וכ׳ (not והיא) but there is mint (which has a quadrangular stem, whereas you say, there is nothing quadrangular in nature)? (Answ.) It is full of knots; Y. Ned. III, 37ᵈ bot. והא כנעה (corr. acc.); Y. Shebu. III, 34ᵈ bot. והנעה (corr. acc.).

ננקפ״ך, a fictitious word made up of every second letter in מנא מנא תקל ופרסין, v. אאלר״ן.

נֵס I m. (b. h.; נסס *to lift up*, cmp. נָסַח) 1) *flag*. B. Bath. V, 1, v. אַדְרָא II. Gen. R. s. 55, beg. (ref. to Ps. LX, 6) כנס הזה וכ׳ like the flag of a ship; ib. (ref. to נסה, Gen. XXII, 1) גדלו כנס וכ׳ he lifted Abraham up like &c.; Yalk. Ps. 777 כנסו של וכ׳ (read: כנס זה); a. e.—2) (cmp. אוֹת, מוֹפֵת) *sign, wonder, providential event*. Nidd. 31ᵃ אפי׳ בעל הנס אינו מכיר בנסו even he to whom the providential sign happens, does not recognize it. Yoma 21ᵃ כרובים בנס וכ׳ the cherubs (above the ark in the Solomonic Temple) stood by a miracle. Ib., a. e. נס גדול היה וכ׳ a great miracle was connected with the show-bread which was as fresh at its removal &c. Sot. 47^a, a. fr. נס בתוך נס a double wonder. Ned. 41^a גדול נס שנעשה וכ׳ the wonder of recovery which the sick man experiences, is greater than that which happened to Hananiah, Mishael &c. Sabb. 23^a, a. e. אַף הן היו באותו הנס the women, too, were concerned in that wonderful delivery. Ib. תימטוט נס why not omit the benediction mentioning the wonder (שעשה נסים וכ׳)?; a. v. fr.—*Pl.* נִסִּים, נִסִּין, נִי׳. Ber. IX, 1 הרואה מקום שנעשו בו נ׳ .. ברוך שעשה נ׳ וכ׳ he who sees a place where miracles happened to Israel, must say, Blessed be he who performed wonders &c. Ib. 60^a, a. fr. מעשה נ׳ (abbrev. מ״נ) a miraculous event, v. זֵכֶר. Yoma 29^a אסתר סוף כל הנ׳ the Book of Esther is the last record of miracles. Taan. 25^a; Snh. 109^a top, v. לָמַד; a. v. fr.

***נֵס II** *island.* Deut. R. s. 2, v. נִיסָא.—*Pl.* נִיסִים, נִיסִין, נֵסִין, v. נִיסָא.

נֵס, נִסָּא, נִי׳ I m. ch.=h. נֵס I, 1) *flag, sign, miraculous event.* Targ. Y. Num. XXV, 8; a. fr.—Y. Pes. V, 32^c bot. נסא הוה רב a great event (delivery from danger) had occurred; Y. Taan. III, end, 67^a ניסא. Ber. 54^a נ׳ דרבים a providential event which concerns the community, opp. נ׳ דיחיד. Meg. 3^b משום פרסומי נ׳ because it is a duty to proclaim the wonderful event (in the Book of Esther); Sabb. 23^b פרסומי נ׳ to proclaim the wonderful events (of the Maccabean days, by lighting the candles); a. v. fr.—*Pl.* נִסִּין, נִסַּיָּא, נִסֵּי, נִי׳. Targ. O. Ex. XVII, 15. Targ. Y. II Num. XXI, 14; a. fr.—Y. Ter. VIII, end, 46^c. Yoma 21^a נ׳ דגואי wonders which happened within the Temple; נ׳ דבראי outside of the Temple. Ib.^{b} נ׳ דקביעי permanent, regularly recurring wonders; a. fr.—2) (=נִסָּיוֹן) *trial.*—*Pl.* as ab. Targ. Y. II Ex. XV, 25.—Y. Maas. Sh. V, end, 55^c (oneirocritical play on נִיסָן) וניסין לית את חמי and thou shalt experience no trials; (Lam. R. to I, 1 רבתי (ולא אחית לידי נסיון; Ber. 56^b נִסְיוֹנִין (חד מחלם׳)).

נִסָּא II, נִסָּה, נִי׳ pr. n. m. *Nissa*, an Amora. Y. Erub. II, 20^a bot. Y. B. Bath. II, beg. 13^b. Y. Ter. XI, end, 48^b; a. fr.

נְסָא, נְסָא, v. נסי.

נסאטאר, v. נְסִיוֹטָאֵר.

נְסִיב, נְסַב (corresp. to h. נָשָׂא a. נָטַל) *to lift up; to take; to carry.* Targ. Gen. II, 21; a. fr.—נ׳ ויהב (= h. נשא ונתן) *to deal.* Targ. Zech. V, 6, sq.—(איתתא) נ׳ *to take to wife, marry.* Targ. Gen. IV, 19; a. fr.—נ׳ אפין (= h. נשא פנים) *to be partial, favor.* Targ. O. Gen. XXXII, 21. Targ. Y. Ex. XXIII, 3.—Part. pass. נְסִיב; f. נְסִיבָא, נְסִיבְתָא; *pl.* נְסִיבִין; נְסִיבָן. Targ. O. Gen. II, 23. Targ. Y. Num. V, 22 נסיבתא wedded.—נ׳ אפין *respected.* Targ. Is. III, 3 (not נְסֵב); a. fr.—Y. B. Mets. II, 8^c bot. והוא נָסֵיב כולא וכ׳ and he takes everything (entrusted to him) and runs away. Gen. R. s. 84, beg. דיִסַּב מאה וכ׳ that he should receive one hundred lashes; Yalk. Job 904; Yalk. Gen. 140 דיהיב (corr. acc.). Lam. R. to I, 1 סַב מובלא וכ׳ take that load &c. Ib. סב לי טימיתהון וכ׳ take their price at my hands and carry them &c. Y. Kidd. IV, 66^a נהות דרג וסב איתתא; Yeb. 63^a נְסֵיב איתתא וכ׳, v. הֲרַג. Macc. 11^a; Gen. R. s. 80, v. גְּזַר; a. v. fr.—Zeb. 11^b הדיא אַגְּרָיָה נַסְבָה the redactor took this up (inserted it) by the way, v. גְּרָיָא II.—Cant. R. to II, 16 והוה נ׳ נפש and he took courage, felt better; ib. ואיתנסיב נפש read: והוית נסיב נפש and I felt better.—Y. Sabb. I, 3^a bot. נ׳ לידוי washed his hands (v. נָטַל). Y. Ber. VIII, 12^a bot. נַסְבוּן ידיכון (not נסבין) wash your hands; ib. סב בריך wash thy hands and say grace.—[Y. Maasr. IV, 51^b bot. והוון סבין מיניה, perh. to be read: והוון נסבין, they took from him.]

Af. אַסֵּיב, אַסִּיב, אַנְסֵיב *to cause to take,* esp. *to give in marriage to, to allow to marry.* Targ. Zech. III, 5. Targ. Y. Gen. XXXVI, 3 דְּאַסִּיבָהּ (not בא ...); a. e.—Yeb. 121^a לדביתהו .. ואַנְסְבָהּ רב (not ואנסבי) and R. D. allowed his wife to marry again; ib. ואנסבוה (corr. acc.). Ib. 120^a top לְאַנְסוּבֵי לצרה וכ׳ (Rashi: לְאִינְּסֹ׳, *Ithpe.*) to permit her rival to marry before her. Lev. R. s. 34 ואַסְבוּן יתיה איתתא וכ׳ and they made him marry another wife; Yalk. Is. 352 אסבייתיה, read: אַסַּב יתיה; a. fr.—[Sabb. 123^a אַסּוּבֵי ינוקא *to handle,* treat the infant; v., however, אָסַב.]

Pa. נַסֵּב same. B. Mets. 105^a קא מְנַסְּבַת וכ׳ thou causest my land to bear a bad reputation. Yeb. l. c. מְנַסְּבִינַן לה לצרה we allow the rival to marry; a. fr.

Ithpa. אִתְנַסַּב, *Ithpe.* אִתְנְסִיב, אִינְּסִיב *to be taken; to be taken away; to be married.* Targ. O. Num. XXXV, 17. Targ. Y. Gen. II, 23. Targ. Jud. XVII, 2; a. fr.—Snh. 51^a משום דאִינְּסִיבָא להו לחוי because she is married to one of those. Yeb. 120^a (repeatedly) אינסיב (read אינסיבא). Ib. 43^b אִינְּסוּבֵי הוא דלא וכ׳ to marry she is not allowed, but to be betrothed &c.; a. fr.—Cant. R. to II, 16 איתנסיב, v. supra.

נִסְבָא f. (preced.) *selection, choice.* Targ. Ez. XVII, 5 גפן נ׳ ed. Lag. a choice vine (ed. נִצְבָא; h. text צפצפה).

נִסְבָא or **נִסְבְּתָא** f. (preced.) *free-will offering.*—*Pl.* נִסְבָתָא, נִסְבָאתָא. Targ. Ps. CXIX, 108 (ed. Wil. נִכְסִ׳, corr. acc.). Targ. Y. Deut. XII, 17 (ed. Amst. a. oth. נסכ׳, corr. acc.); v. נְסִיבָא.

נַסּוֹחַ, נַסּוֹחָא m. (נְסַח) *one who removes, sweeper.* Y. Yoma III, 40^c top, v. מְגַלְּיָינָא.

נְסוֹרֶת f. (נְסַר) *chips, saw-dust.* Sabb. IV, 1 (49^a) נ׳ של חרשין וכ׳ (Talm. ed. נְסוֹרוֹת *pl.*) (fine) saw-dust of the carpenters; Y. ib. 6^d bot. אנן תנינן נ׳ .. נעורת וכ׳ we read *n'soreth,* the teachers of the house of Rabbi read *n'oreth,* which shows that both mean the same. B. Kam. X, 10 (119^a) אף הנ׳ של בעה״ב Y. ed. (Mish. ed. הַנְּסֹרוֹת, some Bab. ed. הַנְּסָרִים; v. Rabb. D. S. a. l. note 200; Ar. הנסורות) even the saw-dust belongs to the employer.

***נְסוֹרְתָּה** f. (preced.) *saw-dust,* name of a certain *aromatic plant.* Y. Shebi. VII, beg. 37^b.

נְסַח (נְשַׁח) (b. h.; cmp. נסע) *to remove.* Sot. 42^b; Yoma 75^a (ref. to יַשְׁחֶנָּה, Prov. XII, 25) יְסִחֶנָּה מדעתו (Ms. M. 2 יַשִּׂיחֶנָּה, v. Rabb. D. S. a. l. note 50) let him banish it from his mind; Yalk. Prov. 950; Snh. 100^b יַשִּׂיחֶנָּה; v. סוּחַ.

Hif. הִסִּיחַ (with דעת) *to divert the mind, to discard.*

Sabb. 82a יסיח דעתו מדברים אחרים, expl. יַסִּיחַ דעתו he must discard from his mind everything else. Y. Ber. VI, end, 10d ה' דעתו (ed. Krot. הִסִּיעַ) if he has abandoned the thought (of drinking more wine); a. e.—Snh. l. c.; Yoma l. c., v. supra.—V. הֶסֵּיחַ.

נְסַח ch. same, 1) *to remove, take out.* Targ. Jud. XIV, 9 (h. text וירדה).—Part. pass. נְסִיחַ. Ib.—Cant. R. to V, 14 אימיה נָסְחָא וכ' his mother took the bread out of the oven, and he ate; Pesik. B'shall., p. 90b, sq. נשא (corr. acc.).—[2) *to lift, weigh.*—Denom. מְסַחְתָּא, מַסְחָא.]

Pa. נַסַּח *to remove, sweep out; to exile.* Lam. R. to I, 13 (expl. וירדנה, ib., with ref. to Jud. l. c.) נַסְּחָהּ (not נסחא) he removed (exiled) her.—Part. pass. מְנַסַּח. Targ. Prov. XXIX, 21 (h. text מנון).

Ithpe. אִתְנְסַח *to be pulled out.* Targ. Esth. VII, 9 (fr. Ezra VI, 11).

Af. אַסַּח as preced. *Hif.* Zeb. 20b אַסּוּחֵי מַסַּח דעתיה he discards (the service) from his mind; לא מַסַּח he does not. Pes. 103b אַסַּחְתּוּ דעתייכו you have abandoned the thought (of drinking). Gitt. 53b א' דעתיה he ceased to have his mind on it (as sacred matter that must be guarded); a. fr.

נָסָא, נסי *to lift up, take, carry,* v. נְשָׂא.

נָסָה, נסי (cmp. preced.) *to lift up.*

Pi. נִסָּה 1) same; 2) (denom. of נֵס) *to put up a sign; to ask for a test* (cmp. Is. VII, 11, sq.); *to try, test.* Gen. R. s. 55, beg. (interpret. נִסָּה, Gen. XXII, 1) .. בשביל לְנַסּוֹתָן לגדלן וכ' in order to lift them up (as a standard) for the world, to raise them &c., v. נֵס. Ib. (ref. to Gen. l. c.) R. J. says נ' גדלו כנס וכ' he raised him &c.; R. A. says, נ' אותן בוודאי he really tried him, v. יָדַאי. Ib. אין הקב"ה מְנַסֶּה וכ' the Lord does not test the wicked, but only the righteous; ib. s. 32; s. 34. Mekh. B'shall., Vayassa, s. 1 (ref. to Ex. XV, 25) שם נשא לו (ל)גדולה there he raised him (Moses) to greatness; ... שם נסה המקום את ישראל there God tested Israel. Ib. Yithro, Baḥod., s. 9 לבעבור נַסּוֹת אתכם בשביל לגדל אתכם (Ex. XX, 28) 'to lift you up', to raise you. Arakh. 15a עשר נסיונות נִיסּוּ וכ' ten times did our ancestors try the Lord; Ab. V, 4; a. fr.

Hithpa. הִתְנַסָּה, *Nithpa.* נִתְנַסָּה *to be tried.* Ib. 3. Yalk. Ps. 777 הראשונים מִתְנַסִּים ביד הקב"ה ... אבל האחרונים נִתְנַסּוּ וכ' the ancients were tried by the Lord ..., but the latter generations were tried by the nations; a. fr.

(נְשָׂא) נְסָא, נְסֵי ch. same, 1) *to lift up.* Targ. O. Deut. XXVIII, 56 נְסִיאַת ed. Berl. (oth. ed. נַסִּי, Pa.); Y. נַסְיַית (h. text נִסְּתָה). Targ. Ps. IV, 7 נְשָׂא (h. text נְסָה).—[Pesik. B'shall., p. 91a, v. נְסַח.]—2) *to take, receive, carry* (v. נְסַב). Lam. R. to II, 2 לא נָסְיָין לחון they (the areas described) could not receive (would have no room for) them; Y. Taan. IV, 69b לא נָסְיָיה. Y. Maas. Sh. IV, 54d נַסְתֵּיהּ לקניא וכ' נְסָתוֹן בר קפר Bar K. took them. Lev. R. s. 6 he took the cane and knocked it down. Ib. s. 34, end נסאתיה וחמאי ליה וכ', read: נסא יתיה ואחמי וכ' he took him along and showed to him &c.; (Yalk. Is. 355 נסבוה ואחמתיה וכ').—Pesik. R. s. 22 נשא ואפקדיה וכ' he took (his money) and put it in trust with him. Ib. נַסְתֵּיהּ ויהבה ליה she took it (the deposited money) and gave it to him; a. fr.

Pa. נַסֵּי 1) *to find out by sign, to divine.* Targ. O. Gen. XXX, 27.—2) *to try, test; to attempt.* Targ. O. Deut. XXVIII, 56, v. supra.—Targ. Esth. V, 14 לְמְנַסְיָא צליבא to test the (strength of) the gallows. Targ. Ex. XVI, 4; a. fr.—Snh. 107a אמר מינסנא לך מְנַסֵּינָא לך I will try thee. Ib. (corr. acc.). Ab. Zar. 15a ניסייה נידולי, read: נִינַסְּיֵיהּ let us try the animal for me; a. e.

Af. אַנְסֵי, הַנְסֵי same. Targ. Ps. LXXVIII, 56 (Ms. *Pa.*). Targ. Y. II Gen. XXII, 1.

Ithpa. אִיתְנַסֵּי, אִינַּסֵּי 1) *to be lifted up.* Targ. Ps. LX, 6.—2) *to be tried.* Targ. II Esth. V, 14.—Snh. l. c. איתנהו מִינַּסּוּ לי .. מִינַּסֵּית לי they have been tried (proved true) to me, thou hast not.

נסיא, נסיא נ', אתא, v. אֲתָאנַסְיָא.—נ' חניס, v. חֲנִיסְנַסְיָא.

נְסִיב, v. נְסַב.

נְסִיבָא I m. (preced.) *that which is taken, assessment, tax.* Targ. O. Num. XXXI, 28 (h. text מכס); ib. 39; a. fr.—Targ. O. Lev. XXVII, 23 (h. text מכסת).

נְסִיבָא II, נְסִיבְתָּא f. 1) same. Targ. Y. Num. XXXI, 37; 39; a. fr.—2) *that which is lifted up* (תרומה), *free-will offering.* Targ. Y. Lev. XXII, 23; 21; a. e.—[נְסִיבְתָּא *married,* v. נְסַב.]—V. נִסְבָּא.

נְסִיוּבֵי m. pl. (=נסיבבי; preced. wds.; cmp. פָּרַשׁ a. פֶּרֶשׁ) [*that which is separated,*] נ' דחלבא, or נ' *whey.* Pes. 42a. B. Mets. 68b נ' ותותרי whey and refuse of wool. Ab. Zar. 35b איכא נ' דלא קיימי there is the whey which does not curdle (and which may contain unclean milk).

נְסִיוּמָאֵי, v. גְּסִיוֹמָאֵי.

נִיסּ', נִסָּיוֹן m. (נָסָה) 1) *lifting up.* Gen. R. s. 55, beg. נ' אחר נ' גידולין וכ' (ref. to Ps. LX, 6) a repeated elevation, dignity &c.—2) *trial, test; temptation.* Snh. 107a דוד ... הביא עצמו לידי נ' David ... placed himself in the power of trial (asked to be tried, Ps. XXVI, 2). Ber. 60b אל תביאני .. לידי נ' suffer me not to come within the power of sin, iniquity, or temptation. Sifré Deut. 21 נותן אתה לי לנ' wilt thou let me have (the animal) for a trial?; a. fr.—*Pl.* נִסְיוֹנוֹת, נִסְיוֹנִין. Ab. V, 3 עשרה נ' נתנסה וכ' Abraham underwent ten trials and stood all of them. Arakh. 15a עשר נ', v. נָסָה. Num. R. s. 17 נ' אחרים additional trials; a. fr.

נִסְיוֹן, נִסְיוֹנָא, נִסְ' ch. 1) same, *sign, test, trial.* Targ. Y. Num. XXVI, 10 (h. text נֵס). Targ. Y. II Gen. XXII, 1. Targ. Y. Ex. XV, 25; a. e.—Ib. XVII, 7, v. נִשְׂיוּתָא.—Ber. 56b, v. נְשָׂא I.—2) *wonder, providential escape, salvation.* Y. Ter. VIII, end, 46c לנ' הוא מיתחמי he appears as a messenger of salvation; (Gen. R. s. 63 על נסין).—*Pl.* נִסְיוֹנִין, נִסְיוֹנֵי. Targ. II Esth. V, 1; a. e.—Ab. Zar. 15a משום נ' on account of the trials (connected with the purchase of animals, and which the Jewish seller may be induced to attend on the Sabbath eve). Lam. R. to I, 1, v. נְשָׂא I; a. e.

נְסִיוּתָא, v. נְשִׂיאוּתָא.

נְסִייא, v. נסיא.

נְסִיךְ, v. נָסַךְ.

נָסִיךְ m. (b. h.; נָסַךְ) [*anointed,*] *viceroy, prince* (contradist. to מֶלֶךְ). Num. R. s. 20 (ref. to Num. XXII, 4) והלא מתחלה נ׳ היה וכ׳ but was he not originally a viceroy? ... But when Sihon was slain, they appointed him king in his place; Yalk. ib. 765.

נְסִיכָה f.=נִיסּוּךְ, q. v.

נָסִיס m. (נסס) *falling away, grief.* Tem. 16ᵃ (interpreting עצבי, I Chr. IV, 10) הרידי הולך בנסיסי לשאול (not לנסיסי) I shall go with my grief to the grave (cmp. Gen. XXXVII, 35; XLIV, 31; a. e.); Mekh. Yithro, Amal., s. 2 יורד כבן סיסי (corr. acc.); Yalk. Josh. 27 (a. Ar. s. v. בר) ברסיסי (corr. acc.).

נְסִיס ch. 1) same, *evil, trouble.* Targ. II Esth. I, 3 נ׳ לנונין a trouble to the fish. [Targ. Koh. V, 16 בִּנְסִיס, ב radical, v. בְּנַס; perh. to be read: בְּנִסָּא.]—*Pl.* נְסִיסִין. Koh. R. to II, 17 תלת נ׳ בישין three great evils.—2) adj. constr. *suffering, weak.* Targ. Y. Lev. XXII, 22 נ׳ עיני Ar. (ed. עירי לקיין).

נְסִיע, or **נְסִיעָה**, Koh. R. to I, 11 ענחה נ׳, read: אֲחָאנַסְיָא.

נְסִיעָה f. (נָסַע) *moving, marching.* Y. Erub. V, 22ᶜ bot.; Men. 95ᵃ בִּנְסִיעָתוֹ when marching, opp. חֲנָיָה. Mekh. Yithro, Bahod., s. 1; a. e.

נִסָּיְתָא, נִסְתָא, נ׳ f. (נְסִי) *trial;* pr. n. pl. *Nissetha, Nistha.* Targ. O. Ex. XVII, 7 (Y. נִסְיוֹנָא); Targ. O. Deut. XXXIII, 8 (h. text מסה); a. e.

נָסַךְ (b. h.) *to pour, cast.* Y. Ber. I, 2ᵈ top, v. מָסַךְ II.

Pi. נִסֵּךְ 1) *to offer a libation.* Succ. IV, 9 ולְמְנַסֵּךְ אומרים לו וכ׳ and they said to him who offered the libation (of water), raise thy hand. Ib. שפעם אחת נ׳ אחד וכ׳ for once it happened, that a priest poured the libation out at his feet. Snh. 62ᵇ זיבח ... ונ׳ וכ׳ if one sacrificed, burnt incense, and offered a libation (to an idol) &c.; a. fr.—Cant. R. to IV, 12 מַאן היו ישראל מנטרים כל וכ׳ (read: מְנַסְּכִים, v. Matt. K. a. l.) whence did the Israelites take wine for their festive gatherings during the forty years &c.?—2) *to make wine forbidden* (יֵין נֶסֶךְ) *by the manipulation of a gentile suspected of dedicating it to idolatrous purposes.* Keth. 27ᵃ; Sabb. 41ᵃ אין פנאי לְנַסֵּךְ they do not take the time to manipulate the wine. Ab. Zar. 56ᵇ (in Chald. dict.) והא קא מנסך בידיה but might he not dedicate it to idolatry by putting his hand into it?; והא קא מנסך ברגל might he not do it with his foot (while treading the wine)? Gitt. V, 4 המנסך he who does damage to his neighbor by touching his wine for idolatrous purposes (v. interpret. ib. 52ᵇ). Y. Ab. Zar. IV, 44ᵃ bot. מנסך כל הבור he causes all the wine in the pit to be forbidden; a. fr.

Nif. נִיסַּךְ *to be offered as libation, to be poured on the altar.* Pes. 22ᵃ כמים הנִיסָּכִין like the water which is poured on the altar, opp. הנשפכין which is poured out at the foot of the altar.

Hithpa. הִתְנַסֵּךְ, *Nithpa.* נִתְנַסֵּךְ; 1) same. Ib. המתנסכים; a. fr.—2) *to be made forbidden (as dedicated to idolatry).* Y. Ab. Zar. l. c. נתנ׳ הבור וכ׳ if the wine in the pit has been manipulated and become forbidden, the jet of wine poured into the pit becomes forbidden (affecting the wine in the vessel).

נְסַךְ, נְסִיךְ ch. same, esp. *to offer a libation.* Targ. Cant. IV, 15; a. e.

Pa. נַסֵּךְ, נַסִּיךְ as preced. *Pi.* Targ. Ex. XXX, 9; a. fr.—Sabb. 41ᵃ לא מְנַסְּכֵי they will not take the time to manipulate &c., v. preced.

Ithpa. אִתְנַסֵּךְ, *Ithpe.* אִינְּסִיךְ as preced. *Hithpa.* Targ. Num. XXVIII, 7; a. e.—Ab. Zar. 71ᵇ קמא קמא אינ׳ ליה every drop as it comes out becomes forbidden.

נֶסֶךְ m. (b. h.; preced.) 1) *libation.* Ex. R. s. 15 יין נ׳ wine from which a libation has been poured on the altar.—*Pl.* נְסָכִין, נְסָכִים; constr. נִסְכֵי, נ׳. Zeb. IX, 1 הנ׳ ירדו the libations brought on the altar illegally, may be taken down. Tosef. ib. V, 1; Men. 15ᵇ, a. e. נסכי בהמה the libations connected with an animal sacrifice. Ib. II, 4 ונְסָכָיו and the libations belonging thereto; a. v. fr.—2) יין נ׳; יין שנתנסך לע״ז; abbrev. (י״נ) *wine known* (or *suspected*) *to have been manipulated by an idolater, wine forbidden to Jews because of such (known or suspected) manipulation.* Ab. Zar. IV, 8 (55ᵃ) ואינו נעשה י״נ וכ׳ (Bab. ed. עושה) it does not become (the gentile does not make it) forbidden wine until &c. Ib. V, 1 לעשות עמו ביין נ׳ to work with him in wine dedicated to an idol. Ib. 2 יין נ׳ שנפל וכ׳ if forbidden wine was poured over grapes. Ib. 74ᵃ bot. יין נ׳ really idolatrous wine, opp. סתם יין suspected; a. fr.

נִסְכָּא, נ׳ I ch. same. Targ. O. Ex. XXIX, 40 (Y. נִיסּוּכָא); a. fr.—*Pl.* נִסְכִּין, נ׳. Targ. Jer. XIX, 13; a. fr.

נִסְכָּא, נ׳ II (preced. wds.) *cast metal.* Sabb. 59ᵇ, v. אַנְסְכָא.—Esp. *a piece of silver* or *gold, bar,* opp. to מטבע, coined metal. B. Kam. 96ᵇ תאר מאן דגזיל נ׳ וכ׳ if one steals a piece of metal and makes it into coins. Ib. 98ᵃ שבח לעניין נ׳ he profits by the increased value of the metal. Keth. 110ᵇ ואימא נ׳ but may not 'silver' in the agreement mean metal (not coins)?; Men. 107ᵃ; a. e.—B. Bath. 33ᵇ היינו נ׳ דר׳ אבא וכ׳ this is a case corresponding to that of a metal bar which R. Abba decided, the case being that one took by force a piece of metal &c.; Shebu. 32ᵇ; a. e.

נִסְכָּא*, נ׳ III m. (סכך) *weaving manipulation.* Sabb. 96ᵇ בנ׳ בתרא (Ms. M. מַסְכָּא) at the last manipulation (when the weaver throws the clue through the web for the last time).

נָסַל, v. נִיסֵל.

נָסַס (b. h. נָסַס) [*to pine away,*] *to be sick; trnsf. to be troubled.* Targ. Esth. IV, 17.

Pa. נַסֵּיס *to trouble.* Targ. II Kings IV, 28 (h. text תשלה).

Ithpa. אִתְנַסַּס, אִיתְנַסַּס, *Ithpe.* אִינְּסִיס, אִתְנְסִיס *to be troubled; to grieve; to be weak.* Targ. Gen. XLV, 5. Ib.

XXXIV, 7 (O. ed. Berl. אִיתְנְשִׁיאוּ; v. Berl. Mass., p. 77). Targ. II Chr. XVI, 10; a. e.—Sabb. 145b; Gitt. 56a; v. אִיתְּנִים. Gen. R. s. 50 (expl. וילאו, Gen. XIX, 11) אִינְּשׁוֹן or אִיתְנְשׁוֹן they became weak.

נָסַע (b. h.) *to move, march.* Tosef. Sot. VIII, 1 בכל יום נוֹסֵעַ אחר וכ׳ .. every day the ark moved behind two standards (divisions), ..., but on that day it moved in front; Sot. 33b. Num. R. s. 2 לאחר שהיו נוֹסְעִים .. נוסעים את המשכן after these two standards had moved, the Levites marched (carrying) the Tabernacle. Yalk. ib. 686 מתקרבים לִיסַּע came together to make ready for the march. Mekh. B'shall., Vayass'a, s. 1 ה׳ נסיעה לא נָסְעוּ וכ׳ this march they undertook by the order of Moses, but all other marches they made at the order of the Deity, a. fr.

Hif. הִסִּיעַ 1) *to remove, cause to depart, to separate, take apart.* Mekh. l. c. הִסִּיעָן בעל כרחן במקל he forced them to march, against their will, with the staff. Ib. ע״ז עברה ... וְהִסִּיעָהּ משה וכ׳ an idol went with the Israelites across the sea, and Moses removed it &c. Kel. V, 7 צריך לְהַסִּיעוֹ he must (not only divide, but) separate the parts of the stove entirely. Sot. 8a בית דין מַסִּיעִין את העדים וכ׳ the court orders the witnesses to change their places; Tosef. Snh. IX, 1 (ed. Zuck. מַשִּׂיאִין). Gen. R. s. 38 (ref. to Gen. XI, 2) הִסִּיעוּ עצמן מקדמונו וכ׳ they removed themselves from the Originator of the world; ib. s. 41 ה׳ עצמו וכ׳ he removed himself &c. Mekh. B'shall., Shir., s. 10 גפן שֶׁהִסַּעְתָּה ממצרים the vine (Israel) which thou didst transfer from Egypt (Ps. LXXX, 9); a. fr.—B. Bath. 8b לְהַסִּיעַ על קיצתן to remove (place outside of the protection of the law, Rashi) those who disregard the terms fixed by the authorities.—Erub. VIII, 5 (86a) הסיע מלבו (Ms. M. הסירה; ed. Sonc. הסירוה מדעתו, v. Rabb. D. S. a. l. note) he has removed from his mind (the thought of returning to his residence). Mekh. B'shall. s. 3 (ref. to ויסעו, Ex. XIV, 15) יַסִּיעוּ דברים (שהיו דוברים) מלבן let them remove from their hearts the (evil) words which &c.; Ex. R. s. 21.—הסיח דעת=ה׳ דעת, v. נָסַח. Y. Ber. V, 9c bot.; a. fr.—[Y. Taan. IV, beg. 67b מפני מסיע, read: הָשֵּׁיעַ.—Tosef. Shebi. II, 20 מסיעין, read מְסַיְּיעִין.]—2) *to signalize,* v. נָשָׂא.

Hof. הוּסַּע *to be removed.* Tosef. Yoma I, 4 ה׳ מן הכהונה was removed (deposed) from the high priesthood; Y. Hor. III, 47d top.

נְסַע ch. same. Gen. R. s. 38 (ref. to Gen. XI, 2) נְסָעוּ מן מדינחא וכ׳ they moved from the east to go further east.

Af. אַסַּע *to remove.* Y. Meg. IV, 75c top אנא מסתכל ולא מַסַּע דעתי I can look (at the priests) without diverting my attention (from my prayers); Y. Taan. IV, beg. 67b מַסְּעָה; v. הָסַע.

***נֶסַע** m. (preced.) *march.*—*Pl.* נְסָעִים. Num. R. s. 2 תחלה לנ׳ (Judah was) the first in marching in the desert, opp. חֲנִיּוֹת.

נָסַק (b. h. נשק) *to go up, ascend;* v. מָסַק.

Hif. הִסִּיק 1) *to impose a tax, to assess,* v. מַסִּיק II.—2) *to bring to a conclusion,* v. מַסִּיק I.—3) *to put on wood, to make the flame rise;* [cmp. עָלָה *Hif.*] *to start a fire, to heat.* Bets. 32a, a. e. מַסִּיקִין בכלים וכ׳ you may, on the Holy Day, use wooden vessels for heating &c. Pes. 27b המַסִּיק he who put the wood on. Ib. תנור שֶׁהִסִּיקוֹ וכ׳ if one heated an oven with wood belonging to the sanctuary &c. Sabb. III, 1 כירה שֶׁהִסִּיקוּהָ בקש וכ׳ a range which they heated with straw &c. Tosef. Yoma II, 5; Yoma 38a מַסִּיקִין מבפנים placed the fire deep into the stove. Sabb. 41a; a. fr.—[Midr. Till. to Ps. XXVIII, v. infra.]

Nif. נִיסַּק, נִיסּוֹק; *Hof.* הוּסַּק *to be heated.* Y. Ber. IV, 8b top נִסּוֹקֶת; ib. IX, 14b top נִיס׳, v. מֶרְחָץ.—Pes. 30b top הא ה׳ התנור but if the oven has been made glowing. Midr. Till. to Ps. XXVIII אם הוא נ׳ .. יהא נ׳ וכ׳ if it (the furnace) is usually heated with one bundle, let it now be heated with seven; ib. אם הוא מסיק בשבעה יהא מסיק וכ׳ (corr. acc.) if it is heated with seven bundles, let it be heated &c. Kel. V, 4. Tosef. Hull. I, 22 עד שלא הוּסְּקוּ before they are hardened by heating; a. fr.

נְסַק ch. same, *to go up.* Impf. יִסַּק, יִיסַק; inf. מִיסַּק, מִיסַק; imper. סַק, סַק. Targ. II Sam. V, 22, sq. Targ. O. Num. XX, 19 נִיסַּק ed. Berl. Targ. Gen. XLIV, 17; a. fr.—Kidd. 50a אדעתא לְמִיסַק וכ׳ with the idea of going up to Palestine. Bets. 27a אזכי ואסק; M. Kat. 22a ואיסק (not ואסיק), a. e., v. זְכִי; a. fr.

Af. אַסִּיק, אֲסֵיק 1) *to cause to rise, to bring up, offer.* Targ. Lev. II, 9, a. fr. (h. text הקטיר). Targ. II Sam. VI, 2 לְאַסָּקָא ed. Wil. Targ. Lev. XI, 3, sq.; a. fr.—Targ. Josh. XVII, 13 מַסְּקֵי מסין *tributaries.*—Y. Keth. XI, 34b bot. והוה מַסִּיק לון מזונין וכ׳ and he offered them support as long as they lived. Gitt. 56b, a. fr. אַסְּקִיה וכ׳, v. נְגִידָא III. Y. Peah I, 15c אַסְּקוּנֵיה למאתים וכ׳ they raised the offer to two hundred, to one thousand; Y. Kidd. I, 61b top אַסְּקוּנֵיה. Y. Maas. Sh. IV, end, 55c מַסִּיק חסין will produce lettuce; a. fr.—2) (sub. בישרא) *to produce new flesh, to heal.* Gitt. 69a לְאַסּוּקֵי וכ׳ for healing let him take &c.—3) *to heat.* Targ. Koh. II, 6.—4) *to finish.* Succ. 39a אַסּוּקֵי מילתא the winding up of a proceeding; Yeb. 106b Ar. (ed. אאסוקי).—5) (with בִּשְׁמָא) *to name after, to adopt a name.* Yoma 38b לא מַסְּקִינַן בשמייהו we do not name children after them. Gitt. 11b דלא שכיחי ישראל דמַסְּקֵי בשמהתייהו names which Israelites are not in the habit of adopting. Shebu. 29a ואסיק להו (שמא) זוזי and named them coins; a. e.—6) (with זוזי, a. ב of person) *to produce a claim against.* Shebu. 41b הב לי .. דמַסִּיקְנָא בך give me the one hundred Zuz which I claim against thee (which thou owest me). Keth. 85a הוה מַסְּקֵי בירח זוזי וכ׳, v. הוּוָאֵי. B. Kam. 97a אינשי דמסיק בהו זוזי persons against whom he had a claim; a. e.—7) (with אדעתא) *to have in mind.* Shebu. 29a דמסקי אדעתייהו וכ׳ they might have in mind an idol.

Ittaf. אִיתַּסַּק 1) *to be offered up.* Targ. O. Lev. II, 12 יִתַּסְּקוּן ed. Berl. (oth. ed. a. Y. יִתְּסְקוּן); a. e.—2) *to be kindled, burnt.* Targ. Ps. LXXVIII, 21; a. e.

נִסְקָא, v. נִקְצָא.

נָסַר (b. h. נשר, a. שׂוּר; cmp. סער a. שׂער) [*to produce a rough, grating sound*; cmp. גָּרַר I,] *to saw, plane.* Gen. R. s. 6 כמסר הזה שהוא נוסר בעץ (the light of the sun produces a sound) like (that of) the plane which planes wood, opp. שָׁף to glide; Midr. Sam. ch. IX. Y. Ber. I, 2ᶜ bot. עד שתחמה נוֹסֶרֶת ברקיע וכ׳ while the sun passes in the sky a journey of &c. Gen. R. s. 8, beg.; Lev. R. s. 14, beg. נְסָרוֹ וכ׳ he sawed him apart &c., v. גַּב.

Pi. נִסֵּר same. Yoma 20ᵇ גלגל חמה שמְנַסֵּר ברקיע וכ׳ the globe of the sun which saws in the sky like a carpenter sawing cedars, v. supra. Gen. R. s. 65, end … נתנו והיו מְנַסְּרִים בו they placed him on a sawing-jack (v. חֲמוֹר) and sawed his body; a. e.

Nif. נִנְסַר *to be sawed.* B. Kam. X, 10 נְסָרִים, נְסָרוֹת, v. נְסוֹרֶת.

נְסַר ch. same. Targ. Y. I Ex. XIV, 25 (h. text וַיָּסַר; cmp. I Chr. XX, 3).

Pa. נַסַּר same, *to split.* Targ. Ps. XXIX, 7.—Yeb. 49ᵇ אתיוה לארזא ונַסְּרוּהָ they brought the cedar and sawed it through; Yalk. Is. 274. B. Bath. 75ᵃ מְנַסְּרֵי אבנים וכ׳ Ms. M. (ed. מינסרי, corr. acc.) who were cutting precious stones.—V. נְסַר II.

נֶסֶר m. 1) (preced.) (*planed*) *board.* Cant. R. to I, 11 שחיפה בין נ׳ לנ׳ he put gold on between one board and the other; Y. Shek. VI, 49ᵈ bot. Y. Ḥag. II, 78ᵇ bot.—*Pl.* נְסָרִים, נְסָרִין. B. Bath. IV, 6 הנ׳ the boards in the bath house. Ib. 67ᵇ בית הנ׳ the room in which the boards are stored. Ib. מכר את נ׳ sold (with the press) the boards, v. יְצִירִין. Kel. XXII, 10, v. שֶׁנֶם. Y. Sabb. III, 6ᵃ top להיות מגלין את הנ׳ to remove the boards (which covered the bathing tank). Bab. ib. 40ᵃ; a. e.—[2) *wicker*, v. נֵצֶר III.]

נִיסְרָא, נִ׳ ch. 1) same, *board.*—*Pl.* נִסְרִין, נִסְ׳, נִיסְ׳. Targ. I Kings VI, 15; a. fr.—Ib. VII, 30 נ׳ דנחש bronze plates (to cover the laver (?); h. text סרני).—2) *veneer.* Sabb. 98ᵇ דני׳ veneered boards, opp. שלמין solid.—Pl. constr. נִסְרֵי. Targ. Hos. VIII, 6 נ׳ לווחין gold foils for boards (h. text שבבים; cmp. שִׁיבָא).

נֵסֶת, v. נְסִי.

נִסְתָּא, v. נְשִׁיתָא.

נְעָא, v. נְעֵי.

נָעָא, v. נְיָעָא.

נָעֶה m. = נָאֶה; pl. נָעִים, v. נָאֶה.

נַעֲוָא, נַעֲרָא m. (עור) [*hollowed out,*] *tank* of the press (h. יֶקֶב). Targ. Y. Ex. XXII, 28.—*Pl.* נַעֲוַיָּא, נַעֲוֵי. Targ. Joel II, 24. Targ. O. Gen. XLIX, 12.—[Sachs, Beitr. II, 27: adaptation of Lat. *navia.*]

נַעֲוָה f. h. same. Ab. Zar. 74ᵇ נ׳ אריתחו (Ms. M. אריתחוד) as to a tank (used by gentiles), cleanse it with hot water.

נְעוֹר, v. עור.

נְעוּרִים m. pl. (b. h.; נַעַר) *youth.* Ex. R. s. 1 חופת נ׳ canopy of youth (bridal canopy).

נעוריתא, v. נְשִׁירְתָּא.

נְעוֹרֶן, v. נַעֲרָן.

נְעוֹרֶת f. (b. h. נְעֹרֶת; נער) [*light matter,*] *scraps, chips.* Y. Sabb. IV, 6ᵈ bot., v. נְסוֹרֶת.—Esp. (של פשתן) נ׳ *hatcheled flax.* Sabb. IV, 1 (49ᵃ) נ׳ של פ׳ דקה thoroughly beaten flax (cmp. דִּקְתָּא). Ib. 11ᵃ, a. e., v. אֵשׁ. Snh. 37ᵃ, v. הַבְהֵב; a. fr.

נְעוֹרְתָּא ch. same; constr. נְעוֹרַת. Targ. Is. I, 31 (Regia נְעֹרֶת).

נְעוֹת, v. שוח.

נְעֵי, נְעָא, q. v. (cmp. נצץ).

נְעִילָה f. (נָעַל) 1) *closing, shutting.* Y. Erub. III, 21ᵃ היא קשירה היא נ׳ tying a door (the stem קשר) means the same as shutting (the stem נעל). Num. R. s. 14 (play on נעלי, Ps. LX, 10) בִּנְעִילַת גרונו by tying up his throat (strangulation).—נעילת שערים *the time of closing the Temple gates*; (sub. תְּפִלַּת) *the concluding prayer on the Day of Atonement, on public fasts and Maʿămadoth* (v. מַעֲמָד); *the prayer called Nᵉʿilah* (נְעִילָה). Taan. IV, 1 בשחרית … בנ׳ שׁ׳ during the morning prayer, the Musaf, the Minḥah and the Nᵉʿilah. Y. Ber. IV, 7ᶜ top אימתי הוא נ׳ when is the time for the N.? בנעילת שערי שמים when the gates of heaven are closed (sunset); בנ׳ שערי היכל when the Temple gates are closed. Ib. דנצלי נ׳ שערים that we may offer the N. prayer. Ib. נ׳ פוטרת וכ׳; Yoma 87ᵇ תפלת נ׳ וכ׳ the concluding prayer exempts from reading the evening prayer; a. fr.—Trnsf. *locking up, interruption of business.* Cant. R. to VII, 2 (play on בנעלים, ib.) שתי נעלים נ׳ בפסח ונ׳ בחג two cessations of business, one shutting up on Passover, and one &c.—2) נעילת הסנדל (or נעילה) *putting on sandals, wearing shoes.* Yoma VIII, 1. Ib. 74ᵃ. M. Kat. 15ᵇ; a. fr.—Gen. R. s. 100 נ׳ רשות wearing shoes (by the mourner on the Sabbath) is a matter of choice, v. נת״ר.

נָעִים I m., **נְעִימָה** f. (b. h.; נָעֵם) *pleasing, lovely.* Ruth R. to II, 5 כיון שראה אותה נ׳ ומעשיה נאים when he saw that she was lovely and her conduct becoming.—*Pl.* נְעִימוֹת; נְעִימִים. Ib. מעשיה נאים ונ׳ her conduct is becoming and lovely. Midr. Till. to Ps. V כל מה שנתתה לנו טובים ונ׳ הם all the things which thou hast given us are good and pleasing. Gen. R. s. 23, v. נַעֲמָה. Cant. R. to IV, 4 כולכם נ׳ וחסידים וכ׳ all of you are welcome, all of you are pious &c.; a. e.

נְעִים ch. same. Targ. Y. Ex. XIX, 19.

נְעִים II pr. n. pl. *Naʿim* (*Nain*), in Isachar. Gen. R. s. 98.

נְעִימָה f. (preced.) 1) fem. of נָעִים.—2) *taste, disposition.* Ab. d'R. N. ch. IV, end (Snh. 38ᵃ דעת).—*Pl.* נְעִימוֹת. Ib. שינה הקב״ה נ׳ בני אדם זה מזה the Lord made the dispositions of men different one from the other.—3) *tune, chant; trill.* Y. Shek. V, 48ᵈ bot. נ׳ יתירה היה יודע he knew an extraordinary way of singing; Yoma 38ᵇ כשהוא נותן קולו בנ׳ when he tuned his voice to a trill. Kidd. 71ᵃ הבליע שם בנְעִימַת וכ׳ he let the Divine Name (the Tetragrammaton which he pronounced) be drowned in the chant of his brother priests; Num. R. s. 11, end אמרו בתוך נעימת וכ׳ he pronounced it during the chant &c. Y. Shek. V, 55ᶜ bot. סורח את הנ׳, v. אַרְדִּבְלִים.

Meg. 32a חקורא בלא נ׳ he who recites Bible verses without chanting; Treat. Sof'rim III, 10. Cant. R. to VIII, 14 בנ׳ אחת in one accord; a. fr.

נְעִימְתָא, נְעִימָתָא ch. same, *sweetness, melody.* Targ. II Esth. I, 1 נְעִימַת constr. Targ. Y. Ex. XIX, 19 ונ׳ מַלְיָא and full melody.

נָעִיץ m. (נָעַץ) *a wedge-like ditch.—Pl.* נְעִיצִים, נְעִיצִין. B. Kam. V, 5 (50b). Mikv. V, 6; a. e.

נָעַל (b. h.) 1) *to tie* (the door), *to lock up, close.* B. Kam. VI, 1 נ׳ בפניה כראוי if he locked it in (secured the flock) properly. Tosef. B. Bath. II, 11, a. e. נ׳ וגדר וכ׳ if he fastened (something on the property), fenced in or tore down, it is possession (חֲזָקָה). Sabb. XIII, 6 ונ׳ אחד בפניו and one blocked it (by placing himself in the entrance). Ib. 7 לנוֹעֵל את ביתו וכ׳ it is like one locking up (sitting at the entrance of) his house to guard it. Mekh. Mishp. s. 18 שלא לִנְעוֹל בפני וכ׳ in order not to close the door to future proselytes (not to discourage them on account of advanced age). Snh. 32a, a. fr. כדי שלא תִנְעוֹל וכ׳, v. הֶלֶת.—Y. Naz. VIII, 57a bot., v. וָעַד. Tosef. Sot. V, 9 [read:] שנעל דלת וכ׳ who locked his wife up (to prevent her from going astray); Y. ib. I, 17a bot.; Gitt. 90a; Y. Kidd. IV, 66a; a. fr.—Cant. R. to VII, 2 (play on בנעלים, ib.) אתם נוֹעֲלִים לפני .. ואני נועל וכ׳ you lock up (interrupt business) for my sake on Passover ..., and I lock up (the rain) for your sake, v. נְעִילָה. Ib. מה היה ... שהיו נועלין בעד כל הצרות how great wa is the beauty of thy steps (pilgrimage to the Temple) which locked up (protected against) all troubles.—Part. pass. נָעוּל; f. נְעוּלָה; *pl.* נְעוּלִים, נְעוּלוֹת; נְעוּלִין. Midr. Till. to Ps. IV שערי תפלה ... נ׳ וכ׳ the gates of prayer are sometimes open, sometimes closed, but the gates of tears are never closed; a. e.—2) *to tie a sandal, to put shoes on.* Tosef. Sabb. IV (V), 8 לא יִנְעוֹל אדם וכ׳ one must not put on a nail-studded sandal &c. Y. M. Kat. III, 83c התירו .. לנעול בו ביום R. .. allowed (the people mourning for R. Yassa) to wear shoes on the same day. Tosef. Kidd. I, 5 נ׳ לו סנדלו וכ׳ if the slave tied his sandals for him (the new master) or untied them, it is possession (v. supra); B. Bath. 53b (Ms. M. הִנְעִיל); a. fr.—Part. pass. as ab., *shod.* Yalk. Josh. 7 וכי במנעלים אתה נ׳ וכ׳ dost thou wear shoes and observest not mourning?

Hif. הִנְעִיל *to put shoes on a person.* B. Bath. l. c.; Kidd. 22b הלבישו הִנְעִילוֹ וכ׳ if the slave helped him put on his clothes or his shoes or lifted him up (helped him into a conveyance), it is possession.

Nif. נִנְעַל *to be closed.* Ber. 32b מיום .. נִנְעֲלוּ שערי וכ׳ since the day the Temple was destroyed, the gates of prayer have been closed. Ib. שערי דמעה לא ננעלו; Midr. Till. to Ps. IV נִנְעָלִים, v. supra. B. Mets. 59a כל השערים נִנְעָלִים חוץ וכ׳ all gates (of prayer) are (at times) closed, except the gates for the cry of oppression. Ib. הפרגוד ננעל, v. פַּרְגּוֹד. Erub. 6b, a. e. אילמלא דלתותיה נִנְעָלוֹת if its gates were not shut by night; a. fr.—Sabb. 67a bot. (in an incantation for a swallowed fish-bone) נִנְעַלְתְּ כתריס (Ms. M. מנעלתה בתריס) thou art locked up as (within) a cuirass.

נְעַל ch. same, *to tie* a shoe. Part. pass. נְעִיל, נְעִיל. Targ. Y. Deut. XXV, 9 ויהא נ׳ וכ׳ and there shall be tied on the foot ... a sandal which &c.

Af. אַנְעֵיל *to provide with shoes.* Targ. II Chr. XXVIII, 15. [Dan. II, 25, a. e. הַנְעֵל *to bring up,* fr. עֲלַל.]

נַעַל m. (b. h.; preced.) 1) (cmp. Gr. ὑπόδημα) [*tied under the foot,*] *shoe.* Yeb. 102a התורה ... נַעֲלוֹ ולא מנעלו the Law (Deut. XXV, 9) says, what is tied to his foot, but not what covers his foot (a full shoe, v. מִנְעוֹל). Sifré Deut. 291 (ref. to Deut. l. c.) נעלו שלו his own shoe; a. e.—2) *lock, locking up.—Pl.* נְעָלִים. Cant. R. to VII, 2, v. נְעִילָה.

נעלא, Targ. Y. Lev. XI, 22, Ar., v. נִישּׁוּלָא.

נָעֵם (b. h.) *to be pleasing, lovely.*

Hif. הִנְעִים 1) same. Snh. 24a (ref. to נֹעַם Zech. XI, 7) אלו .. שמַנְעִימִים זה לזה וכ׳ this refers to the scholars in Palestine who are polite to one another in discussion, opp. מחבלים.—2) *to sweeten* the voice; *to sing, accompany.* Y. Shek. V, 48d bot. היה מַנְעִים את קולו וכ׳ he sweetened his voice when singing, v. נְעִימָה. Gen. R. s. 23 שהיתה מַנְעֶמֶת בתוף וכ׳ she sang to the timbrel in honor of idolatry, v. נַעֲמָה. Cant. R. to IV, 4 מי מנעים זמירותיהם וכ׳ who sweetens Israel's songs? David &c.; a. e.

נַעֲמָא, v. נַעֲמִיתָא.

נַעֲמָה (b. h.) pr. n. f. *Naamah,* 1) sister of Tubal-Cain. Gen. R. s. 23 (ref. to Gen. IV, 22) למה היו קורין אותה נ׳ וכ׳ why was she (the wife of Noah) called N.? Because her doings were pleasing; ib. נ׳ אחרת היתה וכ׳ Tubal-Cain's sister was a different Naamah, and she was so named &c., v. נָעֵם Hif.; Yalk. ib. 38.—2) N., the Ammonite, mother of King Rehoboam. Gen. R. s. 41; Yeb. 77a. Ib. 63a; a. e.

נָעֳמִי (b. h.) pr. n. f. *Naomi,* the mother-in-law of Ruth. B. Bath. 91a, v. חָוָה. Snh. 19b. Ruth R. to I, 2; a. e.

נָעֳמִית f. (נָעֵם; v. Fl. to Levy Targ. Dict. II, p. 569 sq.) *ostrich.* Kel. XVII, 14 ביצת נ׳ המצופה the glazed shell of an ostrich egg; Tosef. ib., B. Mets. VII, 6. Y. Sabb. I, 3d את בת היענה זו ביצת נ׳ 'the child of a *ya'ănah'* (Lev. XI, 16), this intimates that the egg of an ostrich (and of all other unclean birds) is forbidden; a. e.—*Pl.* נַעֲמִיּוֹת. Tosef. Sabb. XIV (XV), 8; Sabb. 128a מפני שהוא מאכל לנ׳ because glass pieces are given to ostriches to swallow. Y. Yoma IV, 41d top. Midr. Sam. ch. XVIII; a. e.

נַעֲמִיתָא, נַעֲ׳, נַעֲמָא ch. (בת נ׳, ברת נ׳) same. Targ. Lev. XI, 16 (ed. Berl. נְעָ׳). Targ. Is. XXXIV, 13 בת נַעֲמָא ed. Wil. (ed. Lag. נעמין; some ed. נעמנין, corr. acc.). Targ. Job XXX, 29.—Sabb. 110b ביעתא דנ׳ an ostrich egg. Y. M. Kat. III, 83b bot. נ׳; Bab. ib. 26a בת נ׳.

נַעֲמָן I (b. h.) *Naaman,* a Syrian general. Gitt. 57b נ׳ גר תושב היה N. was a convert &c., v. גֵּר. Ned. 40a שיזדמנו לו ריעים כנ׳ וכ׳ that he may meet with friends like those of N. who cured him of his leprosy. Deut. R. s. 2; a. fr.

נַעֲמָן II m. *Naaman,* name of a planet. Pirké d'R. El. ch. VI חלון נ׳ window of N. (a station of the sun).

נַעְנַע, נַעְנָא m. (cmp. נִינְיָא II) *mint.* Y. Sabb. VII, 10ª נענע ed. Krot. (oth. נענא).

נִע׳, נִעְנוּעַ m. (נִעְנַע) *shaking* (the Lulab). Succ. 37ᵇ.

נִעְנַע, נַעְנֵעַ, v. נוּעַ h. a. ch.

נַעְנַע, v. נַעְנָא.

נָעַץ (cmp. אוּץ, עוּץ) 1) *to prick, stick; to wedge in.* Men. 64ᵇ נ׳ צפרניו וכ׳ the swine pressed its nails against the wall; Sot. 49ᵇ; Y. Ber. IV, 7ᵇ, a. e.—Y. Shek. V, 48ᵈ bot. כשהיה נוֹעֵץ גודלו וכ׳ when he inserted his thumb into his mouth. Sabb. 17ª נָעֲצוּ חרב וכ׳ they stuck a sword into the floor of the college; a. fr.—Part. pass. נָעוּץ. Bets. 7ᵇ, v. דָּקַר. Erub. III, 3; a. e.—2) *to cut a wedge-like ditch* (נָעִיץ). Y. Sabb. V, 9ᵈ bot.; Y. Kil. VII, 31ᵇ bot., v. חָרִיץ; a. e.

Nif. נִנְעַץ *to be fixed, stuck in.* Sabb. 67ª bot. (in an incantation, v. נָעַל) נִנְעַצְתְּ כמחט (not תא...) thou art stuck in like a pin.

נְעַץ (transp. נְצַע) ch. same. Targ. Y. Gen. XXX, 38 (O. דעץ). Targ. Y. Deut. XV, 17; a. fr.—*Part. pass.* נְעִיץ; f. נְעִיצָא; *pl.* נְעִיצִין; נְעִיצָן *inserted; perforated.* Targ. O. Gen. XXVIII, 12. Targ. Cant. II, 2.—Y. Ter. VIII, 45ᵈ top; Y. Ab. Zar. II, 41ª bot. (ל)מִיעַץ סכינא וכ׳ (or לְמִיעַץ) to stick a knife into a radish.

Pa. נַעֵץ (transp. נַצַּע) same, *to plant.* Cant. R. to I, 16 וּכדון אפי׳ את מְנַעְצַת וכ׳ (not מצנעת) and now, even if you tried to stick into it sixty myriads of reeds &c., v. נְסֵי; Y. Taan. IV, 69ᵇ; Y. Meg. I, 70ª bot. מבצע (corr. acc.); Lam. R. to II, 2 כד את נַעֲצְתּוֹן (not נצעתון).

נַעֲצוּץ m. (b. h.; preced.) *thorn;* (homilet.) *a wicked person.* Meg. 10ᵇ (ref. to Is. LV, 13); Yalk. Is. 345.

נַעֲצוּצָא ch. same.—*Pl.* נַעֲצוּצַיָּא. Targ. Is. VII, 19.

נָעַר I (b. h.; cmp. next w.) [*to be excited, noisy,*] esp. (of the ass) *to bray.* Ber. 3ª. Ib. 56ª (in Chald. dict.) דקאי אאיסדן ונוֹעֵר standing at the head of the bed and braying. B. Kam. 18ᵇ; Kidd. 24ᵇ; a. e.—[Cant. R. to IV, 8 בתחלה הוא נוער, read: נֵעוֹר, v. עוּר.]

נָעַר II (b. h.; cmp. עור, ערר) *to shake, stir.* Makhsh. I, 4 הנוֹעֵר אגודה וכ׳ he who shakes (the rain off) a bundle of vegetables. Ib. V, 7. Pesik. R. s. 26 לאיוב נָעַרְתִּי מן האשפה וכ׳ I shook Job (making him rise) from the dunghill, and concerning thee (Israel) it is written (Is. LII, 2), shake thyself &c.; a. e.

Pi. נִיעֵר 1) *to shake.* Pesik. Shek., p. 17ª נַעֲרָהּ קפלה shake it (the garment), fold it; Lev. R. s. 2. B. Mets. II, 8 מצא כסות מְנַעֲרָהּ וכ׳ if one found a garment (and holds it in charge waiting for the owner to claim it), he must shake it once in thirty days. Sabb. 147ª top; a. fr.—2) *to stir.* Hull. VIII, 3 נ׳ את הקדרה if he stirred (the meat in) the pot. Y. Ab. Zar. I, 39ᵈ top שמא נ׳ הגוי בקדרה the gentile might have stirred the pot; a. fr.—3) *to empty; to cause evacuation.* Toh. II, 1 מְנַעֶרֶת את הקדרה she may empty (or *stir*) the dish. Kel. XXVIII, 2 לְנַעֵר בו וכ׳ used for (lifting and) emptying the pot. Tosef. ib. B. Mets. II, 10 שהחנוני מְנַעֵר בו׳ which the shop-keeper uses when pouring out &c. (or through which he pours for straining), v. נַתִּיךְ; a. e.—נ׳ את הצאן *to use means by which to expedite the discharge of excrements of the flock on the spot to be manured* (v. הדר I, *Pi.*). Tosef. Shebi. II, 20; M. Kat. 12ª; Y. Shebi. III, 34ᶜ bot. Ib. השוכר ... לְנַעֲרָהּ he who hires a flock (for manuring) is forbidden to use means &c.; expl. ib. מוליכה ממקום וכ׳ by driving it from place to place.—*Part. pass.* מְנוֹעָר; f. מְנוֹעֶרֶת; *pl.* מְנוֹעָרִין, מְנוֹעָרִים; מְנוֹעָרוֹת *empty, vacant.* Y. Ber. IV, 7ᵇ bot. (play on שִׁנְעָר) שהם מנ׳ מן המצות וכ׳ they (the Babylonians) are vacant of (cannot perform) certain religious observances &c.; Koh. R. to XII, 7; Gen. R. s. 37 שהיא מנ׳ וכ׳ she (Babylonia) is deprived &c. Hag. 14ª (play on נערים, Is. III, 4) אלו בני אדם שמנ׳ וכ׳ that means persons empty of good deeds, opp. ממולא; Yalk. Is. 261.—[B. Bath. 74ᵇ ור״א נוער some ed., v. עור I.—Hull. 51ᵇ ניערה, v. infra.]

Nif. נִנְעַר 1) *to be stirred up; to bestir one's self.* B. Bath. 74ᵇ ונ׳ ר״א and R. El. was stirred up (awoke). Sot. 5ª אין עפרו נ׳ his dust will not be stirred up (for resurrection). Ex. R. s. 1 (play on חלאה ונערה, I Chr. IV, 5) חלתה וְנִנְעֲרָה מחליה וכ׳ she (Miriam) was sick, but she bestirred herself (arose) from her sickness, and the Lord restored her to youth. Y. Ber. III, 6ᵈ top (play on מנעריו, Gen. VIII, 21) משעה שהוא נ׳ ויוצא וכ׳ from the moment the embryo bestirs itself to come out into the world; Gen. R. s. 34; Yalk. ib. 61. Hull. 51ᵇ ננערה לעמוד וכ׳ Rashi (ed. נִיעֲרָה) if the animal made an effort to get up, although it did not succeed; a. e.—2) (of flax) *to be hatcheled.* Y. Sabb. II, beg. 4ᶜ (expl. חוסן, ib. II, 1) פשתן שלא ננערה flax which has not yet been hatcheled.—3) *to be emptied, poured out.* Y. Ber. l. c. (play on שנער) ששם נִנְעֲרוּ וכ׳ for into that valley the dead of the generation of the flood were dumped; Gen. R. s. 37; Koh. R. l. c.—Snh. 92ª קשתו נִינְעֶרֶת his bow will be empty (his sexual vitality broken).

Hif. הִנְעִיר *to stir up, to keep awake.* Erub. 53ᵇ (play on נערה &c., v. אַחֲרוֹנִית) וְהִנְעִירַתְהוּ and she kept him awake.

Hithpa. הִתְנַעֵר *to be emptied*; trnsf. *to be displaced.* Zeb. 116ª (ref. to Cant. IV, 16) תִּתְנַעֵר אומה ... ותבא וכ׳ (v. Rabb. D. S. a. l. note) removed be the (Roman) nation whose sacrifices are slaughtered northward (Lev. I, 11, which is entitled only to burnt-offerings), and let the nation enter &c.

נְעַר ch. same, *to shake, stir.*—*Part. pass.* נְעִיר *waking.* Targ. Job XXI, 32 (Ms. נְעִיר; ed. Wil. יְעִיר, v. עור).

Pa. נַעֵר *to shake; to empty.* Yalk. Zech. 570; Cant. R. to IV, 8 (ref. to Zech. II, 17) (דמְנַעֲרָא) דמְנַעֲרָה וכ׳, v. גַּו ch.; Gen. R. s. 75. Sabb. 142ª וּלְינַעֲרִינְהוּ נִעוּרֵי let him shake the fruit out of the basket.

נַעַר m. (b. h.; preced., cmp. נְעוֹרֶת, a. meanings of דַּק, זְעֵר, דַּרְדְּקָא &c.) *tender, young; lad.* Tanh. Hayé 1 שיתכבד הזקן בְּנַ׳ that the old may be honored by the young. Ex. R. s. 1 ילד היה ומנהגו כנ׳ he was a child, but his behavior was like that of a lad; a. fr.—*Pl.* נְעָרִים. Yoma 75ᵇ לנ׳ לחם וכ׳ the manna was bread to the young, oil to the old &c. Tanh. Sh'mini 11 אם נ׳ הם וכ׳ if they (the elders) are young &c., v. קָפַץ. Ib. הבחורים והנ׳ the young men and the lads. Sot. 46ᵇ נ׳ היו וכזבח וכ׳ they were young men, but behaved contemptibly like children; a. fr.—*Fem.* נַעֲרָה *lass, maid*, esp. (law) *a girl between twelve and twelve and a half years of age*, v. בַּגְרוּת. Esth. R. to V, 1; a. fr.—Keth. III, 8, contrad. to בוגרת a. קטנה. Ib. IV, 1; a. fr.—*Pl.* נְעָרוֹת, constr. נַעֲרוֹת. Ib. III, 1 (29[a]). Esth. R. l. c. שתי נַעֲרוֹתֶיהָ her two maids; a. fr.

נַעֲרוּת f. (preced.) *youth; vitality; puerility*. Ex. R. s. 1, v. נָעַר II *Nif.*—Kidd. IV, 14 משמרתו … בנַעֲרוּתו the Law guards him from all evil while he is young. Deut. R. s. 8, end. Gen. R. s. 84 (ref. to Gen. XXXVII, 2) שהיה עושה מעשה נ׳ he acted puerilely (was vain); a. fr.—Esp. *maidenhood, the age* or *the legal status of a* נַעֲרָה. Y. Yeb. I, 3[a] top, v. בַּגְרוּת; Kidd. 4[a] bot. סימני נ׳ the symptoms of maidenhood (puberty); a. fr.

נַעֲרוּתָא f. (v. נָעַר I) *roaring, camel's cry*. Yeb. 120[b] ולא אפסקיה לנַעֲרוּתֵיה Rashi (ed. אפסיקתיה) and this did not make the camel cease from crying (until life was entirely extinct).

נַעֲרָן (b. h.) *Naaran*, near Jericho. Lev. R. s. 23 (ref. to Lam. I, 17) כגון … יריחו לנ׳ as hostile as Jericho to N.; Cant. R. to II, 2; Lam. R. to l. c. נועדן (corr. acc. or נוֹעֲרָן).—Hull. 5[a] (ref. to נערה קטנה, II Kings V, 2) קטנה דמן נ׳ (ed. נְעוֹרָן) a little girl from N.; Sot. 46[b] נעורן.

נְעֹרֶת, v. נְעוֹרֶת.

נַעֲרַת, v. נְעוֹרְתָא.

נַעֲתָא, v. נָאֲתָא.

נָפָא, v. נָפֵי.

נָפָא, *pl.* נָפָן, v. נַפְיָא.

נָפָה I, *Pi.* נִיפָּה, v. נפי.

נָפָה II (b. h.; נוף) *fan; winnow; sieve*. Men. VI, 7; X, 4, v. נפי. Y. Keth. VII, 31[b] bot., v. נָדַר. Hull. 45[a] ניקבה כנ׳ if the windpipe has perforations like a sieve. Sot. 48[b]; Y. ib. IX, 24[b] bot., v. נוֹפֶת. Tanh. Ekeb 1; Yalk. Ps. 676, v. נוֹפֶת; a. fr.—Ab. V, 15 נ׳ a scholar who retains the best teachings.—*Pl.* נָפוֹת. Men. 76[b].

נְפָוָתָא, v. נְפָפָא, a. נַפְיָא.

נְפוֹל, נִפּוֹל, v. sub נִיס׳.

נְפוּלָא, v. נְפִילָא II.

נִפּוֹלִין, v. נִיפּוֹלִין.

נָפוֹס, (נָפוֹץ) m. (נפץ, נפס) a kind of *radish*, resembling the carrot as to foliage, and the radish as to taste. Kil. I, 3; 5; Y. ed. a. Ms. M. ס … (Mish. a. Bab. ed. ץ …). Ukts. I, 2. [Lat. *napus* is a kind of *turnip*.]

נָפַח (b. h.; cmp. פּוּחַ) 1) *to blow, breathe*. Y. Sabb. VII, 10[d] הנוֹפֵחַ כלי זכוכית he who shapes glass vessels by blowing (on the Sabbath); Bab. ib. 75[b] הַמְנַפֵּחַ בכלי וכ׳. Makhsh. I, 6 הנופח בעדשים וכ׳ he who breathes at lentils to ascertain their quality. Tosef. Sabb. XV (XVI), 2 נופח בחוטמו וכ׳ you blow into its nostrils and put the teat into its mouth; Sabb. 128[b]; Y. ib. XVIII, end, 16[c] מביא יין ונופח וכ׳ you take wine and squirt it &c. B. Mets. 60[b] אין נוֹפְחִין בקרביים it is not permitted to blow up entrails (for sale, to give them a delusive appearance); a. fr.—2) *to be blown up, to swell*. Tanh. K'dosh. 8 נָפְחוּ פניו his face was swollen. Ib. עיניו נְפוּחוֹת his eyes swollen.

Nif. נִיפַּח same. Sabb. 75[b], v. supra. Maasr. IV, 5 מְנַפֵּיחַ .. ואם ני׳ וכ׳ Y. ed. (Bab. ed. מנפח .. נפח; Ms. M. מנפיח; Mish. ed. מנפח .. נפח, v. Rabb. D. S. a. l. note 7) he may blow out (the chaff of the wheat-ears) from hand to hand and eat, but if he blows and puts the grain in his lap, he is bound (to pay tithes); Bets. 13[b]. Ib. 14[a]. Ber. 19[b]; Nidd. 57[a], a. e., v. פְּרַס; a. fr.—[Y. Peah VIII, 21[b] top המנפח, read המכפח, v. קָפַח.]

Pu. נוּפַּח *to be blown, fanned*. Treat. S'maḥ. ch. VIII מוטב .. אש שנוּפְּחָה ולא אש שלא נופחה וכ׳ it is better that a fire consume me which has been blown (by man), than a fire that has not been fanned (Gehenna; Job XX, 26).

Nif. נִיפַּח *to be blown up, to swell*. Num. R. s. 7 תִּנָּפַח כרסי וכ׳ my belly may swell and burst.

נְפַח ch. same, 1) *to blow*. Targ. Gen. II, 7; a. fr.—Y. Bets. II, end, 62[b] (ל) מִנְפּוֹחַ וכ׳ to blow meat up. Gitt. 69[a] bot. לִינְפַּח ליה חבריה וכ׳ let his neighbor blow white cress-seeds (into his throat) through a straw. Hull. 46[b] ונַפְחִינָא לה and we blow the lungs up; a. fr.—*Part. pass.* נְפִיחַ; f. נְפִיחָא; *pl.* נְפִיחִין, נְפִיחָן *blown, ignited; blown up, swollen*. Targ. Job XX, 26. Targ. O. Num. V, 21; a. fr.—Hull. 47[b] א״ד דנפיחא (not דנפיחה) some explain דמיא לאופתא (v. אוּפְתָּא) as meaning lungs which look as if distended (white). Sabb. 33[a] נְפִיחַי כפן, v. כַּפְנָא; a. fr.—2) *to be blown up, to swell*. Targ. O. Num. V, 27, v. *Ithpa.* (Y. וְיִנְפַּח, prob. to be read: וְיִתְנְפַּח).—Lev. R. s. 33; Cant. R. to II, 14, v. קוּלְתָא.

Pa. נַפַּח same, *to blow, cause swelling*. Targ. Y. Num. V, 22 (O. לְאַפָּחָא, *Af.*; ed. Amst. לַאֲפָחָא); a. e.—Part. pass. מְנַפַּח; f. מְנַפְּחָא; *pl.* מְנַפְּחָן, מְנַפְּחִין. Targ. Y. ib. 21.—Lam. R. to I, 1 רבתי (1 חד כות׳) כל עמא מְנַפְּחִין לי וכ׳ (I dreamt) all the people were blowing at me with their full cheeks. Ib. דאינון מנפחין (it meant) that it (the wheat) was swollen (through rain drippings). Snh. 43[a]; B. Bath. 134[b] מְנַפַּח רב ששת וכ׳ R. Sh. blew into his hand (intimating that the question raised was scurrilous); a. e.

Af. אַפַּח, אַפֵּח 1) *to blow, swell*. Targ. O. Num. V, 22, v. supra. Targ. Ps. XI, 6 מַפְּחִין דאשתא (Ms. מפ׳ אש׳) blowers (winds) of fire (h. text פחים אש).—2) (with נפש) *to incite longing, to cause despair*. Targ. Job XXXI, 39. Targ. I Sam. II, 33 (h. text לאדיב).—V. נְפַח.

Ittaf. אִתַּפַּח, *Ithpa.* אִתְנַפַּח, אִינַּ׳; *Ithpe.* אִתְנְפַח, אִינְ׳ 1) *to be swollen*. Targ. Y. Num. V, 27 (v. supra; O. וְיִתְפְּחוּן, ed. Berl. וְיִתְפְּחוּן). Targ. Job XIX, 26 (ed. Wil. אִתְּפַח; h. text נקפו). Targ. Koh. XII, 5.—Y. Maas. Sh. IV, end, 55[c] אִינְּפְחָן the wheat shall swell (v. supra).—2) *to be blown, ignited*. Sabb. 26[a] אינפח בה נורא she caught fire.

נֶפֶח m. (preced.) *swelling; bulk, volume* (v. אַפּוּתָא). B. Mets. VI, 5 הנ׳ קשה למשאוי an increase of volume makes the load harder for the animal (Bab. ed. 80^a 'דנ' קשה כמשאוי an increase of size is as hard for the animal as an increase of weight), v. נִפְחָא. B. Kam. 47^a נִיפְחָה, v. נִפְחָא.

נַפָּח m. (preced. wds.) *smith.* Gen. R. s. 84, beg. [read:] נ׳ שהיה מפוחו פתוח באמצע פלטיא ופתח בנו זהבי מפוח כנגדו a smith whose open shop was in the middle of the road, and whose son, a jeweler, opened a smithy opposite him; Tanh. Vayesheb 1; a. fr.—Y. R. Hash. II, 58^b top, a. e. בן הנ׳ the smith's son, i. e. R. Johanan, v. next w.—*Pl.* נַפָּחִין. Y. B. Bath. II, beg. 13^b ולא של נ׳ nor dare an oven for smiths be put up (without the precautions mentioned in the Mishnah).

נַפָּחָא, נַפְּחָא ch. same. Targ. Is. XLIV, 12.—Gitt. 69^b בנורא דבי נ׳ Rashi (ed. only בי נ׳) by the fire of the smithy. Ib. מיא דבי נ׳ water used in the smithy. Sabb. 25^b, a. fr. ר׳ יצחק נ׳ R. Isaac, the smith. Hull. 77^a יצחק בר נ׳ (corr. acc.)—בר נ׳ a) the smith's son, v. יוֹחָנָן. Snh. 96^a טבא דנ׳ מדבר נ׳ better is what the smith (R. Isaac) said, than what the smith's son (R. Johanan) said. B. Mets. 85^b; a. e.—b) name of *a bird.* Hull. 62^b.—*Pl.* נַפָּחִין. Targ. Jer. VI, 29. Targ. Jud. V, 26 נַפָּחִין.

נִפְחָא, נִי׳ ch.=h. נֶפַח. B. Mets. 80^a (expl. קשה כמשאוי, v. נֶפַח) נ׳ כי תקלא וכ׳ the volume of the load is like the weight, i. e. loads of the same volume are considered of the same weight as regards the stress on the animal, and if he added three Kab to the volume bargained for, he is responsible for any injury to the ass; ib. (expl. קשה למשאוי) תקלא .. ונ׳ דוזי וכ׳ weight is weight, and the volume is an addition, i. e. if he changed the load for a more voluminous one although of the same weight, he is responsible for the additional volume. Tem. 30^b ניחא ליה בנִיפְחָהּ its fuller appearance is welcome to him; Ab. Zar. 34^b בנפחיה. B. Kam. 47^a נ׳ מאי (Ms. F. נִיפְחָהּ) how about the gain in value from its fuller appearance?

נִפְחַיָּא pr. n. pl. *N'fahaya.* Targ. Y. Num. XXI, 30 (h. text נֹפַח).

נָפַט, *Pi.* נִיפֵּט (cmp. נפץ) *to beat* (*cotton*). Sabb. 73^b הדש המנפץ והמְנַפֵּט וכ׳ threshing, beating flax and beating cotton are all one kind of labor (threshing). [Ar. s. v. פץ reads: והמנפס, v. נָפַס.]

נֵפְט m. (prob. a transpos. of נטף, a readaptation of νάφθα) *naphtha.* Sabb. II, 2. Ib. 26^a אין מדליקין בנ׳ לבן וכ׳ white naphtha must not be used for lighting ... because it is explosive. Ib. ומה יעשו ... אלא נ׳ and what shall the Cappadocians do who have .... only naphtha? Yoma 38^b, sq. Y. Snh. VII, 24^b bot. (v. שְׂרֵפָה) בפתילה של נ׳ the Mishnah, describing capital punishment by burning, means a wick saturated with naphtha. Y. Sot. VII, beg. 22^b אש כנגד נ׳ שלהן 'fire' (Ps. XVIII, 13) corresponds to the arrows of the human armies tipped in naphtha; Pesik. R. s. 17 רמה בהן נ׳ he (the besieger) throws naphtha &c. (βέλη πυροφόρα or πυροβόλα).

נִפְטָא ch. same. Targ. Y. II Ex. XIV, 24. Targ. II Esth. I, 2.—Sabb. 46^a.

נַפְטוֹרָיא m. (preced.) *dealer in naphtha.*—*Pl.* נַפְטוֹרֵי. Ned. 91^b.

נָפָה, נפי, *Pi.* נִיפָּה (denom. of נָפָה) *to fan, winnow, sift.* Maasr. IV, 5, v. נָפָה. B. Bath. 94^a אם בא לְנַפּוֹת מְנַפֶּה וכ׳ if the buyer winnows (a sample of the wheat, and it is found to contain more than the legally allowed refuse), he winnows the entire quantity, and the seller has to indemnify him for the entire quantity lost by winnowing. Y. Maasr. IV, 51^b bot. ובלבד שלא יְנַפֶּה וכ׳ (better יְנַפֵּחַ) but he must not blow the chaff out over a basket; a. e.—Part. pass. מְנוּפֶּה; f. מְנוּפָּה. Men. X, 4; VI, 7 מנ׳ בשלש עשרה נפה sifted thirteen times. Ib. סלת מנ׳ כל צרכה fine flour sufficiently sifted. Tanh. T'tsavveh 5, v. סֹלֶת; a. e.—Pesik. R. s. 3 (ref. to כברת, Gen. XLVIII, 7) בזמן שהארץ מנ׳ .. בכברה (not ככברה) at a season when the ground can be sifted and be shaken in the sieve.

נְפָא, נַפֵּי, *Pa.* נַפֵּי, same. Y. Sabb. VII, 10^a bot. כד מְנַפְיָא וכ׳ when she fans (blows the chaff out, on the Sabbath), she is guilty of an act coming under the category of winnowing. Ruth R. to III, 3 [read:] אזל נַפְיָיהּ והיא וכ׳ go and winnow it (again), and it will yield the remainder; Yalk. ib. 604 זיל נַפֵּי תיבנא וכ׳ (not כפי).

נַפְיָא f. (preced.)=h. נָפָה, *fan, winnow, sieve.* Pes. 111^b והדר ביה כנ׳ (Ms. M. כיתופא) and he moves to and fro like a fan. B. Kam. 97^b אפי׳ כי נ׳ (Ms. R. מנפיא, v. Rabb. D. S. a. l. note 80) even if the new coin be of the size of a sieve?; Hull. 124^a אפי׳ כנ׳ even if the flesh on the hide be of the size &c.?—Gitt. 69^a bot. פארי דדייש נ׳ the bran which comes up to the top of the sieve when shaken.—Hull. 45^a וסימניך נ׳ to remember the process required to ascertain the condition of the trachea perforated like a sieve, think of the construction of a sieve; a. e.—*Pl.* נַפְוָותָא, נְפָוָתָא. Sabb. 134^a, v. נִסְפָּא. B. Mets. 74^a איפשר בנ׳ the winnowing may be done with a fan (independently of the wind). Succ. 20^b חזו לפרסי וכ׳ can be used for covers and sieves, v. פַּרְסָא.—Y. Sabb. VII, 10^c top נָפָן (fr. נָפָא).—[Tosef. Hull. III (IV), 27 נפיא, v. אַפְיָין.]

נְפִיוֹרָא, v. נִיפְרָא.

נְפִיחָה f. (נָפַח) *blowing, breath.* Y. Sabb. II, 5^a bot. הבעיר וכיבה בנ׳ אחת if he ignited and extinguished in one continued act of blowing. Gen. R. s. 14, end בעולם הזה בנ׳ וכ׳ in this world the breath of life is put in by blowing (Gen. II, 7), ... but in the coming world by placing (Ez. XXXVII, 6). Ib. ומה אם זה שעשוי בִנְפִיחָתוֹ של בשר ודם וכ׳ if this (glass) which is produced by the blowing of a human being, can be restored (when broken) &c.; a. e.—Y. Meg. III, 74^b bot. בנ׳ אחת in one breath (v. נְשִׁימָה).—[Ruth R. to III, 3 אזל נפיחה, v. נְפִי.]

נָפִיל, נְפִ׳, נְפִילִים m., *pl.* (b. h.; cmp. פלא) *giants.* Gen. R. s. 26 נ׳ שהפילו וכ׳ they are called *n'filim*, because they caused the downfall of the world; a. e.—בֶּן נְפִ׳ a) name of *a demon.* Bekh. 44^b רוח בן נ׳ *nervous prostration*, v. נָאלָא II.—b) name of a *species of lizards*, living in the water. Sifra Sh'mini, ch. VI, Par. 5; Hull. 127^a (not כן). Ex. R. s. 15 בן הפילי׳ some ed. (corr. acc.).

נְפִיל m., **נְפִילָא** I f. ch. same, 1) *giant.* Ruth R. to II, 1 נפיל נ׳ לנ׳ when a giant marries a giantess.—2) *Orion.* —*Pl.* נְפִילִין, v. נִיפְלָא I.

נְפִיל, נְפִילָא II (**נִפְלָא**) m.=h. נֵפֶל, *untimely birth, not viable.* Targ. Y. I Lev. XXII, 27 דלא נְפִיל (ed. Vien. נְפִיל, ed. Amst. נֵפִיל) that it is not an untimely birth. Targ. Ps. LVIII, 9 Ms. (ed. נְפוּלָא). Targ. Job III, 16 נִפְלָא (Bxt. נֵפְלָא; Ms. נִפְלָא).—*Pl.* נְפִלֵי, נִי׳. B. Bath. 101^b בדנ׳ (v. Rabb. D. S. a. l. note 30, ed. בנ׳) it means a lot set aside for burying untimely births. Ib. 102^b תרתי בנ׳ וכ׳ we do not presume two lots to be set aside for &c.

נְפִילָה f. (נָפַל) 1) *falling.* Sot. VIII, 6, a. e. v. נִיסָה. B. Kam. V, 7 (54^b) לִנְפִילַת הבור as to the laws relating to an animal falling into a pit (Ex. XXI, 33 sq.). Y. Ber. I, 3^d top שתסמכנו מנְפִילָתֵנוּ that thou mayest support us in our downfall.—*Pl.* נְפִילוֹת. Yalk. Esth. 1058 (ref. to Esth. VI, 13) שתי נ׳ הללו למה why this double use of *nafal?*—2) (v. מַפּוֹלֶת) *quantity of seed required for a field.* Peah V, 1 נותן לעניים (ב)כדי נ׳ (Y. ed. לעניים נְפִלָּה) he must give to the poor as much as the field requires for seed (v. Maim. a. l.; oth. opin.: as much as is generally dropped at cutting); B. Mets. 105^b. Ib. IX, 5 אם יש בה כדי נ׳ (Y. ed. נִיפְלָה) if the field yields as much as is required for seed, expl. Y. ib. 12^a כדי הזרע הנופל בה; Y. Peah. V, 18^d כדי ניפלת (corr. acc.).—[Y. Orl. I, 60^d top כדי נפילתה R. S. to Orl. I, 2, v. טְפִילָה.]

נְפִיצָה f. (נָפַץ) *shattering.* Y. Orl. I, 60^d bot. [read:] היא עשייה היא הקמה היא שבירה היא נ׳ (some ed. נְתִיצָה) 'making' an idol is the same as putting up, 'breaking' the same as shattering (v. Y. Ab. Zar. IV, 44^a).

נְפִיק, v. נְפַק.

נָפִיק m. (preced.; cmp. Syr. נפסקא, P. Sm. 2424) *quick, alert.* Targ. I Sam. XXIII, 22 ערים ונ׳ (h. text ערם יערים).

נפיקא, Lev. R. s. 26 מאנין נ׳ (מאנויין) some ed., oth. פניקא, v. פַּנְנִיקָא.

נְפֵיש (interch. with פוש a. פְּשַׁר, q. v.) 1) [*to be blown up,*] *to be large; to increase.* Targ. Ex. I, 7; a. e. Imper. פוש. Targ. Gen. I, 28; a. e.—*2) [*to be blown away,*] *to be gone.* B. Bath. 121^a; Ned. 78^a אתא לנהרדעא .. נ׳ Ar. (ed. ולא אשכחיה) he came to N. to see R. S.; he was gone.

Af. אַפִּישׁ (interch. with אַפִּישׁ, a. אַפְשַׁר) *to extend, enlarge.* Targ. Gen. XLVIII, 4 (some ed. מַפְשַׁר׳). Targ. Y. Num. XIX, 6 אַפּוּשֵׁי; a. fr.—Men. 23^b דא׳ לה תבלין טפי וכ׳ when he made the quantity of spices larger than &c. Bets. 7^a לא מַפְשִׁירְנַן ... אַפּוּשֵׁי (or אַפּוּשֵׁי .. מַפְשַׁר׳) we must not extend the range of unclean things by rabbinical enactments. Sot. 26^a לא לִיפַּשׁ .. אפושי we ought not to increase the number of illegitimate births (by allowing intermarriage between bastards). B. Bath. 12^b בעינא דא׳ אריסי (Rashi ניחא לי לאפושי) I desire (it is an advantage to me) to have a large number of tenants around me (whom my neighbor must employ). Ib. אפושי לאו מילתא היא this plea about a large number &c., is no plea; a. e.—Y. Kil. IX, 32^c top; Y. Keth. XII, 35^b top נַפִּישׁ לר׳ וכ׳ let us make room for R. H.

נְפִישׁ m., **נְפִישָׁא** c. (preced.) [*blown up,*] *large, numerous* (cmp. אֲנַשׁ). Targ. Y. Deut. XXV, 9.—B. Bath. 73^b כמה נ׳ חיליה וכ׳ how great is the strength of the tree. Keth. 66^b דנ׳ זיונא the management of which is a large concern, v. זִיוּנָא III.; a. fr.—*Pl.* נְפִישִׁין, נְפִישֵׁי; נְפִישָׁן. Targ. II Esth. VI, 10; a. e.—Snh. 52^a, v. חוּגְנָא. Yeb. 74^b הנך נ׳ those (laws relating to dedicated objects) are extensive. B. Bath. l. c. משום דנ׳ מיא because the water is deep; a. fr.

נָפִישׁ, *pl.* נְפִישִׁים, v. נֶפֶשׁ.

נְפִיתָא, v. נְפִיתָא.

נֹפֶךְ, נו׳ m. (b. h.) name of *a jewel* in the high priest's breast plate, *emerald.* Ex. R. s. 38, end על נ׳ היה כתוב וכ׳ on the *nofekh* the name of Judah was engraven.

נָפַל (b. h.) *to fall, lie down; to be dropped; to occur.* Sabb. XVI, 2 נָפְלָה דליקה if a conflagration takes place. Pes. II, 3, v. מַפּוֹלֶת. Y. Sot. VII, 21^d top (ref. to יקים, Deut. XXVII, 26) וכי יש תורה נוֹפֶלֶת is there a falling law (to need erection)? Ned. 65^b כל הנוֹפֵל אינו נופל לידי וכ׳ he who falls (becomes poor) does not immediately fall into the hands of (become dependent on) the charities (but his friends support him for a time). B. Kam. IX, 11, a. fr. יִפְּלוּ דמיו לנדבה its equivalent must be surrendered as a donation to the Temple. B. Bath. IX, 4 האחין .. שנ׳ אחד מהן לאומנות נ׳ לאמצע if one of two partner brothers (heirs) has been summoned to public service, his salary goes into the common fund. Y. Shek. V, 49^b top בשביל ששמעתי שנפלה לך ירושה וכ׳ since I heard that an inheritance has fallen to thy share at a distant place, take (this as a loan) &c.; a. v. fr.—Imperat. פּוֹל. Tosef. Dem. VI, 4 ופול תחתיי וכ׳ (Var. טול, some ed. צול) and surrender thyself to public service in my place (v. supra).

Hif. הִפִּיל *to cause to fall; to throw down.* Gen. R. s. 26, v. נְפִיל. B. Kam. III, 10 ה׳ את שינו struck out his tooth; Tosef. ib. IX, 23; a. fr.—Esp. *to miscarry.* Nidd. III, 1 המַפֶּלֶת וכ׳ if a woman loses a lump-shaped embryo; a. fr.

Hithpa. הִתְנַפֵּל *to prostrate one's self.* Deut. R. s. 2, v. נִיפּוּל.

Nif. הִנָּפֵל (denom. of נִיפּוּל) *to fall apart, be spoiled.* Tosef. Sabb. VI (VII), 14 שלא תִינָּפֵל הפת, v. צָוַות.

נְפַל ch. same. Targ. II Sam. I, 4. Targ. Koh. XI, 3 לְמִנְפַּל; a. v. fr.—Imperat. פּוֹל. Targ. Is. L, 11.—Part. נָפֵיל, part. pass. נְפִיל. Targ. Prov. XI, 5 (ed. Wil. נְפַל). Targ. Ps. CXLV, 14; a. e.—Ḥull. 51^a אי נְפוּל לארעא if they were thrown down (violently). Ib.^{b}, v. נְגִירְתָּא. Ned. 65^b כל דמסכין לאו עלי נפיל not every one that becomes poor, falls on me (for support). B. Mets. 105^a בזרא דנ׳ נ׳ a seed (of weeds) once fallen, has fallen (cannot be destroyed by the plough). Meg. 15^b נְפַלָה ליה מילתא בדעתיה something (a suspicion) had entered his mind; a. fr.

Af. אַפֵּיל, as preced. *Hif.* Targ. Ps. LXXVIII, 28. Targ. Y. Ex. XXI, 22; a. fr.—Ḥull. 42^a top אַפּוּלֵי אפיל (read אַפְּלָא)

she may have miscarried. Snh. 109[b] וְהִפִּילָא ליה and she miscarried through his fault; a. fr.

Ithpe. אִיתְנְפִיל *to be upset, fall in.* M. Kat. 2[a] דאתי לְאִיתְנְפוּלֵי a caving in (of the ground through which the water makes a road) might occur; ib.[b]; a. e.

נְפַל, *pl.* **נְפָלִים**, v. נָפִיל.

נֵפֶל, בֶּר' נ' m. (preced. wds.) 1) *capacity for seed,* v. נְפִילָה.—2) (b. h.) *abortion; premature, not viable birth.* Tosef. Ohol. XVI, 13; Pes. 9[a], a. e.—Y. Yeb. XI, end, 12[b] אינו נ' is not considered a non-viable birth (for legal purposes); a. v. fr.—*Pl.* נְפָלִים. Gen. R. s. 26 (play on הַנְּפִלִים, Gen. VI, 4) שמלאו את העולם נ' וכ' they filled the world with abortions by their lascivious life. Tosef. l. c.; a. fr.

נִפְלָא I (נִפְלָא, נְפָלָא) ch. same, v. נְפִיל.

נִפְלָא II m. *giant,* v. נָפִיל ch., a. נִיפְלָא I.

נִפְלָא III m., **נִפְלָאָה** f., *pl.* **נִפְלָאוֹת** (פְּלָא) *miracles.* Midr. Till. to Ps. CVI; v. פֶּלֶא.

נְפַלֵי, בַּר נ', v. נָפִיל ch.

נְפַנֵּף, v. נוּף h.

נְפַס, נְפָסָא, נַפָּס, v. נפץ, נפצא.

נָפַע (cmp. פּוּעַ, פָּעָה) *to blow, squirt into the mouth.* Ex. R. s. 1 (play on פועה, Ex. I, 15) שהיתה נוֹפַעַת יין וכ' she squirted wine into the child's mouth after having given its mother to drink, v. נָפַח.

Hif. הִפִּיעַ *to blow air into the lungs, to revive.* Ib. שהיתה מַפִּיעָה (or מְפִיעָה, fr. פּוּעַ) את וכ' she revived the child when they said it was dead.

נְפַע (interch. with נְפַץ) *to shake.*

Pa. נַפַּע *to shatter.* Targ. Jer. XXIII, 29 ed. Lag. (ed. מפגע, מפגע, corr. acc.; Bxt. נפץ).

Ithpa. אִתְנַפַּע *to be shattered.* Targ. II Chr. XXXIII, 13 (ed. Wil. אתכ', corr. acc.).

נָפַף, *Pi.* נִפֵּף, v. נוּף h.

נְפַף, *Pa.* נַפֵּף (preced.) *to fan, inspire.* Sabb. 134[a], v. next w.

נַפְפָא f. (preced.) *fan.* Sabb. 134[a] לִינַפְּפֵיה בנ' Ms. M. (not לִיכ'; ed. בִּנְפָוָותָא *pl.*, Rashi בנפ', v. נַפְיָא) let one fan the child with a fan.

נְפָפִיתָא f. (preced. wds.) *remnant of flour in the sieve.* Yeb. 114[b] ס"ד בהאי פורתא דנ' וכ' (Ar. דנפיתא) can it be imagined that he could live on that little remnant of flour which thou hast left to him?

נָפַץ (b. h.; cmp. פּוּץ) *to scatter, shake out, empty.* Bicc. I, 8 נוֹפֵץ וכ' he scatters them on the ground, and does not read. Tosef. B. Bath. IV, 2 נוֹפְצוֹ he shakes the bag out. Keth. 72[a] (the Mishnah means) שתְּקַבֵּלָא ונוֹפֶצֶת that she should receive (the semen) and then discharge it (by violent movements); a. e.

Pi. נִפֵּץ 1) same. Kil. V, 7 יְנַפֵּץ he must shake the grain out of the ears; Y. ib. 30[a] bot. Deut. R. s. 3 וִינַפֵּץ אבני וכ' and scatter the stones prepared for rebuilding the Temple. Lev. R. s. 10; s. 19 בשעה שאתה מְנַפְּצוֹ אין וכ' as soon as you shake it out (of its marrow), it is good for nothing. Midr. Till. to Ps. XVII אני מְנַפֵּץ ... כשם שאתה נִפַּצְתָּ וכ' I will dash thy babes against the rock, as thou didst my babes; a. e.—2) (interch. with נפס) *to beat* flax, *to hatchel* wool. Sabb. XIII, 4 והמְנַפֵּץ (Y. ed. a. Ar. המְנַפֵּס). Ib. VII, 2. Ib. 73[b], v. נָפַס. Ber. 58[a] ונִפֵּץ; Tosef. ib. VII (VI), 2 וניפס, ed. Zuck. (Var. נפץ); Y. ib. IX, 13[c] top וניפס; a. fr.—3) *to spread.* Midr. Till. to Ps. XXII מְנַפֶּצֶת, v. נָצַץ.

נְפַץ ch. same, 1) *to scatter, shake out.* Targ. O. Gen. XXIV, 20 (ed. Berl. נְפַצַת). Targ. Jud. VI, 38 ed. Lag. (ed. נפק, incorr.).—Nidd. 31[a] (prov.) פוץ מלחא ושדי וכ' shake the salt off, and throw the meat to the dog (when life escapes, the body decays). Gen. R. s. 36 (ref. to נפצה, Gen. IX, 19) לדגה .. דנַפְצָה עוברה וכ' like a large fish that scatters its roe &c.; a. e.—Snh. 67[b] דנַפֵּיץ (Rashi מְנַפֵּץ) he scattered, i. e. *blew his nose.*—2) *to shatter, break.* Targ. Jud. VII, 19.—3) *to beat, hatchel.* Yoma 20[b], v. אֲגַר II.—Part. pass. נְפִיץ. Hull. 51[b], a. e. כיתנא דדייק ולא נ' flax which has been pounded, but not carded (freed of hard substances).—4) *to snap* a chalked cord for marking. Targ. Is. XLIV, 13.

Pa. נַפֵּיץ same. Targ. Jer. LI, 34.—Ib. XXIII, 29, v. נְפַע.—Targ. Esth. I, 11 וּמְנַפְּסָן.—Part. pass. מְנַפַּץ. Targ. Is. XXVII, 9.—B. Kam. 93[b] נַפְּצֵיה נַפּוּצֵי, v. פְּרַק II. Sabb. 147[a] מְנַפְּצֵי גלימייהו shaking their cloaks. Ib. נַפּוּצוּ וכ' shake them in his face. Hull. 113[a] וּמְנַפֵּיץ ליה and shakes the salt off. Ib. 76[b] נַפְּצֵיה וכ' he split it, and found two nerves; a. e.—[B. Bath. 45[a] מפצי; Keth. 91[b], sq. מפצינא, v. פְּצָא.]

נַפָּסָא, נַפָּצָא m. (preced.) *flax-beater, carder.* Yeb. 118[b]; Keth. 75[a] דנ' גברא תיקרייה וכ' though the husband be a carder, his wife will call him out to the threshold and sit down (proud of her husband); [Ar. נפסא: *a guardsman in the vegetable garden,* denom. of נָפוֹס.]

נַפְצָא f. (preced. wds.) *scattering.* Nidd. 30[b] סמא דנ' וכ' he made them drink a scattering drug (which destroys the semen in the womb).

***נָפַק** (cmp. פוק) *to go out.* Cant. R. to III, 4 (play on פלצות, Is. XXI, 4) על ידי שנפקו לדבר לֵצוּת because they went out for lascivious purposes.

נְפַק ch. (corresp. to h. יצא) same, 1) *to go out, come out; to result, end.* Targ. O. VIII, 7 מִיפַּק ed. Berl. (oth. ed. a. Y. מֵיפַק); a. v. fr.—Y. Ber. I, 2[c] top שרי מלכא נ' וכ' when the king begins to march out, even if he has not yet gone out, we say, he has gone out. Ib. 3[c] bot. הוינן נָפְקִין לתעניתא we went out for fast and prayer. Koh. R. to X, 8 מִינְפַּק ליה (=מן נ') after he came out. Y. Taan. IV, 69[a] מִנְפְּקִין when they came out; Lam. R. to II, 2 מן דנַפְקִין. Y. l. c. לא נפקין טבאות (Matt. K. to Lam. R. l. c. לא נַפְקַת לחוך) they did not end well. Pesik. B'shall., p. 94[a] וגוש חלבאי נפקין וכ' and the men of Giscala went out after them with sticks &c.; Koh. R. to XI, 2 וגוש חלב אנפקין (corr. acc.); a. v. fr.—Imperat. פּוּק. Targ. Gen. VIII, 16; a. fr.—Erub. 14[b], a. e. פ' חזי וכ', v. הְבַר. Sabb.

106ª, a. e. פ׳ תנר וכ׳, v. פַּר I ch.—Part. נָפִיק. Targ. I Kings XV, 17; v. next w.; a. fr.—כד נפיק בירח (נ׳) = h. כיוצא בו (v. יְצָא) *similar to, corresponding*. Targ. Y. II Gen. II, 18. Targ. Y. Deut. XIV, 8 (not פְּנַפֵּק, בִּנְפִיק).—Y. Ber. VI, 10ᵇ bot. נ׳ אנא ידי חובתי do I do my duty?, v. יְצָא. Succ. 36ᵇ ונ׳ בה and used it for doing his duty (for the ceremony of Ethrog).—Y. Sabb. VI, 8ª top, a. e. מה נ׳ מן בינייהון what is the outcome from between them?, i. e. what is the difference between them in practice?—נפקא מינה וכ׳ the practical difference is &c. Bets. 6ᵇ למאי נ׳ מינה in regard to what practice is there a difference (whether or not eggs found in a chicken can be hatched)? למקח וממכר it makes a difference in trade (if one bought eggs for breeding). Keth. 72ª מאי נ׳ לה מינה תיעביד what difference does it make to her? let her do it; a. v. fr.—Tem. 7ª נ׳ לירח וכ׳ it is derived from the Biblical word &c. Ib. תֵּיפּוּק לירח זריקה וכ׳ let 'sprinkling' be derived from &c.—Gen. R. s. 52 וניפוק ידוי and do justice to it (to the verse to be explained), v. supra.—2) *to take out, exclude*. Sabb. 74ª וליפוק חדא וכ׳ let him take out one (of the enumerated categories) and insert another one. Hull. 43ª לא תיפק, v. infra.—[Targ. Am. IX, 13, v. infra.]

Af. אַפִּיק, *Haf.* הַנְפֵּק 1) *to lead forth, carry forth; to bring forth, produce; to derive; to take out, exclude*. Targ. Ex. XVI, 3. Targ. Am. IX, 13 במפיק ed. Lag. (oth. ed. בְּמַפֵּק, corr. acc.). Targ. Job XV, 13; a. fr.—Ber. 38ª (ref. to המוציא in the benediction over bread) דא׳ משמע it means 'who has brought forth'; דמַפֵּיק משמע it means 'who brings forth'. Ib. אַפִּיקוּ ליה ריפתא they brought out bread (and placed it) before him. Ib. (ref. to המוציא, Ex. VI, 7) כד מַפֵּיקְנָא לכו ... דאַפֵּיקִית וכ׳ when I lead you forth, I shall do for you a thing that you may know that it is I who led you forth. Sot. 16ᵇ; R. Hash. 13ª לא תַפֵּיק נפשך וכ׳ do not let thyself go beyond the established rule. B. Bath. 60ª דהוה מַפֵּיק וכ׳ which led to (opened towards) etc. Tem. 3ᵇ מפיק שם וכ׳ utters the name of the Lord in vain. Ib. 7ª מַפְּקִינַן לבמת יחיד we derive from it a rule for individual high-places.—Hull. 42ᵇ אַפֵּיק חדא וכ׳ take out one category and insert another. Ib. 43ª top חנך דאַפֵּקְתְּ לא תַפֵּיק Tosaf. (ed. לא תיפק) the two which thou didst exclude, do not exclude; a. v. fr.—לְאַפּוּקֵי or לְאַפּוּקֵי *to the exclusion of*, v. אֲפַק.—2) *to take out by legal decision; to collect; to claim*. Keth. 76ᵇ מייתי אב ראיה ומפיק the father brings evidence and gets a verdict for collecting, opp. ומוקים for letting the money stand where it is. Y. Gitt. I, end, 43ᵈ ואַפְקוּן מיניה and collected from him. Ib. בעון מִיפְקָא (v. supra *Pe.* 2) they wanted to collect. Y. Shebu. VII, 38ª top אתון ואַפְקוּן דלא וכ׳ they came and claimed that he had not given them anything; a. fr.

Ittaf. אִיתְּפַק, *Ithaf.* אִתְהַנְפַּק *to be carried forth*. Targ. Gen. XXXVIII, 25; a. fr.—Y. Gitt. VI, 48ª bot. אתא׳ למקטלא was led out to be executed.

נֶפֶק m., constr. נְפַק (preced.) *going out*; נ׳ בַּר *a male prostitute; fem.* נִפְקָא, constr. נִפְקַת; נִפְקַת בָּרָא a) *a female prostitute*. Targ. Y. II Deut. XXIII, 18. Targ. Gen. XXIV, 35.—b) (sub ביה) *brothel, prostitution*. Targ. I Kings XIV, 24; a. fr.

נִ׳, נַפְקָא m. (preced. wds.) 1) = h. צֵאָה, *excrements*. Gitt. 69ᵇ top.—2) = h. מוֹצָא, *outlet, opening*; [Ar.: *projection*].—*Pl.* נִ׳, נַפְקֵי. Erub. 87ᵇ.

נַפְקוּתָא f. (preced. wds.) = h. הוֹצָאָה, *expense*. Ned. 7ª לנ׳ בעלמא for general expense (not charity). Tosef. B. Mets. IX, 13 (in a farming contract) ואנא בעמלי ובנַפְקָתִי ידיי וכ׳ and I shall get one half for my labor and my outlay; B. Mets. 105ª.—[In Talmud. comment. and casuists: נ׳ *outcome, difference*, v. נְפַק.]—*Pl.* (fr. נפקתא) נַפְקָתָא. Pesik. R. s. 31, v. מַעֲלָתָא.

נִפְקַת, constr. of נִפְקָא, v. נֶפֶק.

נַפְקָתָא, v. נַפְקוּתָא.

נַפְרְזָא m. (an adapt. of λεόπαρδος) *leopard*. B. Kam. 16ª (Ms. M. נפריא), v. אֲפָא.

נָפַשׁ m. (נָפַשׁ, b. h. *Nif.*) *breathing, resting*.—*Pl.* נְפָשִׁים, נִפְשֵׁי, נְפָשִׁין. Tanh. Vaëra 6 (expl. ישעו, Ex. V, 9) אל יהיו משתעשעין כלומר אל יהיו נ׳ (not ואל יהוו) let them not play, that is, let them not rest (on the Sabbath); Ex. R. s. 5.

נְפַשׁ, v. נְפִישׁ.

נֶפֶשׁ f. (b. h.; preced. wds.) 1) *resting place*, esp. *a structure next to* or *over a tomb*. Ohol. VII, 1 נ׳ אטומה a solid tomb-structure (to which there is no access). Shek. II, 5 מותר המת בונין לו נ׳ וכ׳ from what is left over of the appropriation for funeral expenses, we build a monument &c.; (Gen. R. s. 82 בִּירָה). Tosef. Erub. VI (V), 4, sq.; Erub. 55ᵇ (contrad. to קבר).—*Pl.* נְפָשׁוֹת. Ib. V, 1 נ׳ sepulchres (containing a place of shelter). Y. Shek. II, 47ª top; Gen. R. l. c. אין עושין נ׳ וכ׳ no monuments need be put up for the righteous, v. זִכָּרוֹן. Tosef. Ohol. XVII, 4 חזקת נ׳ שבא״י וכ׳ the presumption in the case of sepulchres in Palestine is that they are levitically clean, except those marked.—2) *soul, life; person; will, desire, disposition*. B. Mets. IV, 6 שאינו אלא נ׳ רעה for it (the refusal of a coin on the ground of a slight abrasion) proves merely a malevolent soul (illiberality in dealing); ib. 52ᵇ, v. קְפִיד. Gen. R. s. 14 (names of the soul) נ׳ רוח וכ׳. Ib. נ׳ זו הדם *nefesh* means blood (life). Ib. (ref. to Gen. II, 7, a. VII, 22) כאן הוא עושה נשמה נ׳ וכ׳ here the text calls the soul (נשמה) *nefesh*, and there, *ruaḥ* (spirit); ib. s. 32.—Snh. IV, 5 נ׳ אחת one (person's) life. Y. Taan. III, beg. 66ᵇ טכיון שנתנו ב״ד נַפְשָׁן וכ׳ as soon as the court has declared its will to do a thing. Nidd. 65ᵇ, a. fr. בעל נ׳ one who is master over his desire, *a conscientious man*.—Ber. 44ᵇ כל נ׳ משיב את הנ׳ all life (animal food) restores life; וכל קרוב לנ׳ וכ׳ and what is nearest life (the neck which contains the jugular vein) &c.—Y. Keth. V, 30ᵇ top דברים שהן קיום נ׳ things required for sustaining life. Yoma 74ᵇ אבידת נ׳, v. אֲבֵידָה; a. v. fr.—נחת נ׳, v. הֲנָחָה.—Sifra M'tsor'a, Zab., Par. 3, ch. VI ואם נַפְשְׁךָ לומר וכ׳ (= ואיבעית אימא, v. בְּעֵי) or if you prefer (another argument); Hull. 78ᵇ bot. Ib. מה ואם נפשך לומר why should you prefer another argument?, i. e. what objection can there be to the argument offered before?—(מ׳בח נמשך), v. מַח.—Hull. IV, 7 (77ª) נ׳ הדשה *one not fastidious.*— B. Bath. 89ª נ׳ מאזנים *the opening in which the tongue of scales rests* (agina).—*Pl.* as ab. דיני נ׳, v. דִּין II. Snh. l. c. עדי נ׳ witnesses in capital cases.—Yoma VIII, 6 ספק נ׳ the possibility of danger to human life; Sabb. 129ª; a. fr.

נַפְשָׁה, נַפְשָׁא, נְפַשׁ ch. same, 1) *monument.* Pesik. B'shall., p. 79ᵇ ועבדון ליה נ׳ וכ׳ and they erected a monument to him (the dog that saved their lives), and to this day they call it נ׳ דכלבא the dog's monument. Y. Erub. V, 22ᵇ bot. נ׳ דסירייקין, v. סְרִיקִין; a. e.—2) *soul, will* &c. (v. preced.). Targ. Gen. I, 20. Ib. XXIII, 8; a. fr.—Cant. R. to II, 16, v. נְכַב. Sabb. 129ª בשר נ׳ חלף נ׳ meat (is a necessary of life), life for life, v. preced.—נח נַפְשֵׁיה, v. נְחַת ch. Pes. 68ᵇ נַפְשָׁאִי, v. חַדֵּי. Ib. אדעתא דנפשיה with the intention of benefiting himself. Sot. 16ᵇ, a. e. לא תפיק נַפְשָׁךְ, v. נְפַק; a. v. fr.—*Pl.* נַפְשָׁתָא, נַפְשָׁן. Targ. Jud. XVIII, 25 (ed. Lag. sing.). Targ. Gen. XIV, 21; a. fr.—[Targ. Y. Lev. XXVI, 15 נַפְשָׁתְהוֹן (sing.).]—Y. Ab. Zar. III, 42ᶜ, v. סְכַן II.

נֶפֶת, v. נוֹפֶת.

נַפְתַּאי, v. נִפְתִּי.

נַפְתּוֹחָא, נַפְתּוֹחָאָה, נַפְתָּח׳, v. נַבְטְיָיא.

נִפְתִּי, נִפְתַּיָּיא, נַ׳...יָּיה, נַ׳ m. (preced.) *Nabataean.* Y. Sabb. XIV, beg. 14ᵇ, v. נִיוְיתֵי. Ib. XVI, end, 15ᵈ; Y. Yoma VIII, 45ᵇ.—*Pl.* נִפְתָּאֵי. Y. B. Bath. VIII, 16ᵇ bot. Y. Snh. IX, end, 27ᵇ.

נֵץ I m. (b. h.; נָצַץ) 1) *sprouting, flower, blossom.* Ukts. II, 1 והנץ שלה and the flower-like substance on cucumbers. Ib. 3 הנץ שלו the sproutings on the pomegranate; (Tosef. ib. I, 8 שיער, סיאר). Y. Shebi. IV, end, 35ᶜ (ref. to משיתצו, ib. IV, 10) לאי דו נץ שורא וכ׳ what blossoming is meant? Such as promises one Rob'a of olives. Cant. R. to II, 3 נִיצוֹ קודם לעליו its blossoms come out before its leaves. Tosef. Par. XII (XI), 1 משישיר את ניצו when it has shed its blossoms; a. fr.—Gen. R. s. 28 נץ השדרה Ar. (ed. לוז q. v.).—חַלְב, v. נץ החלב.—2) נֵץ, חֲנִץ name of *a coin* (Blossom)=7/8 of an As (v. הֶדְוֹסְת). Kidd. 12ª; Tosef. B. Bath. V, 12 ed. Zuck. (Var. חונץ, some ed. חוצץ, corr. acc.).—*Pl.* נִיצִים, חֲנִיצִין. Y. Kidd. I, 58ᵈ; Bab. ib. l. c.; Tosef. l. c.; v. חֲנִץ.

נֵץ, נֵיץ, נִיצָא ch. same, *blossom.* Targ. O. Gen. XL, 10. Targ. O. Num. XVII, 23 (ed. Berl. נֵץ). Targ. Job XIV, 2 (ed. Lag. ציצא). Targ. Y. II Deut. XXVIII, 40 נַצְיָה; a. e.—*Pl.* נִיצִין, נִצִּין. Targ. Y. Num. l. c. Targ. Job XXXI, 8 נִצַּיי (not נצרי); a. e.—נִצְּיָא *the blooming stage.* Y. Maasr Sh. IV, 55ᵇ bot., v. חֲבָבָא; Lam. R. to I, 1 (זהר כיה׳) רבתי נצבא (corr. acc.).

נֵץ II m. (b. h.; prob. fr. its far-sightedness, cmp. צִיץ, *Hif.*) *hawk.* Hull. III, 1; Tosef. ib. III, 3; a. e.

נָצָא, נִצָּא I ch. (mostly בר נ׳) same. Targ. O. Lev. XI, 16; Deut. XIV, 15. Targ. Job XXXIX, 26 (Ms. נִיצָא).—*Pl.* נִצִּין. Targ. II Esth. I, 2.

נַצָּא II c. (נְצַר) 1) (adj.) *shrunk, withered.*—*Pl.* f. נַצָּן. Targ. Gen. XLI, 23 (h. text צנמות).—2) *lean (low) ground.* M. Kat. 10ᵇ נצא (Ms. M. צנא, v. Rabb. D. S. a. l. note); B. Bath. 54ª, v. מַלְיָא.

נְצָא *to quarrel,* v. נְצֵי.

נַצָּא III (or נְצָא) m. (preced.) *strife;* pr. n. m. *Natsa.* Sabb. 56ᵇ (transl. מריב, I Chr. VIII, 34, a. ref. to וירב, I Sam. XV, 5) נ׳ בר נ׳ Strife (Mephibosheth), son of Strife (Saul), v. נְחַל.

נָצַב *to put up, place,* v. יָצַב.

Nif. נִצַּב *to stand (defiantly).* Num. R. s. 18, v. חֲצָבָה.

נְצַב, נְצִיב ch. same, *to put up, plant.* Targ. Gen. IX, 20 (h. text נטע). Targ. Y. Deut. XXXII, 50 (cmp. נְטַע); a. fr.—Lev. R. s. 25 לְמִנְצַב נציבין to plant (trees); Koh. R. to II, 20 לְמִנְצַב. Y. Orl. I, 61ª top ונ׳ לון בארץ and planted them in the land (Palestine); a. fr.—Part. pass. נְצִיב, נְצִיבָא. Lam. R. to I, 1 חד גופנא .. והות נ׳ (רבתי) וכ׳ we had a vine which was planted on our father's grave.

Af. אַנְצֵב *to point, sharpen* (cmp. נצבתא, Dan. II, 41). Targ. I Sam. XIII, 21 לְאַנְצָבָא, (Ar. לאנצא, v. אֲנַץ; h. text להציב).

נִצְבָא, נִצְבְּתָא, נִ׳ c., נִ׳ f. (preced.) *plant, shoots.* Targ. Job XIV, 8, sq. (Ms. נְצִיב). Targ. Is. LVII, 3. Targ. Mic. I, 6 ed. Lag. (ed. מַצְבַת). [Targ. Ez. XVII, 5, v. נִסְבָּא.]—*Pl.* נִצְבִין, v. נִצְבָא.

נָצָה, v. נצי.

נָצוֹחַ, v. ניצוח.

נָצוֹחָא m. (נְצַח) *victor.* Lev. R. s. 30 ולית .. מאן הוא נ׳ (some ed. נצח) and we do not know which is the victor; Yalk. Lev. 651 הוי ניצוחיה הוי דין (corr. acc.); (Pesik. Ul'kaḥ., p. 180ª הדידין נצח). Lev. R. l. c. דהוא נצוחייא (corr. acc.)—*Pl.* נְצוֹחַיָּא. Ib. דישראל אינון נ׳ that the Israelites are the victors; Pesik. l. c., p. 180ᵇ. Ib. ניצוחייא (corr. acc.); Yalk. l. c. נוצח׳ (corr. acc.).

נְצוּחוֹת m. pl. (preced.) *illustrious men.* Cant. R. to II, 13 (play on הנצנים, ib. 11) הנ׳ נראו וכ׳ the illustrious appear in the land.

נְצוֹלֶת f. (נָצַל; v. ניצולת) *place for refuse, dumping ground, mire.* Ber. 9ᵇ כנ׳ שאין בה דגה Ar. (ed. כִּמְצוּלָה).

נִצּוֹק, נִיצ׳ m. (יָצַק) *uninterrupted flow* of a liquid poured from vessel to vessel. Toh. VIII, 9 הנ׳ ... אינו חבור וכ׳ an uninterrupted flow, a current on slanting ground and ..., are not considered a connection (of the two liquids) either for communicating uncleanness or for producing cleanness. Ab. Zar. 56ᵇ, a. fr. נ׳ חיבור, v. חִיבּוּר. Yad. IV, 7. Naz. 50ᵇ יש נ׳ לאוכלין וכ׳ does, or does not, the law regarding a connected flow apply to eatable things (e. g. melted fat)? a. fr.

נָצוֹר, v. נְצַר IV.

***נְצוֹרָא** m. (יצר) *joiner's frame, clasps* to keep glued objects in shape. Targ. Is. XLIV, 13 ed. Lag. (oth. ed. נְצוֹרִין *pl.*; Var. ed. Lag. נצוריין; ed. Ven. I a. Levita Var. נִצְמִין; h. text מחוגה).

נָצַח (b. h.; cmp. צח) [*to be bright, pure,*] (cmp. זָכָה)

to be victorious, win, prevail. Y. Sabb. VII, 5[b] top אם לִנְצוֹחַ אם לְהִינָּצֵחַ whether to conquer or to be conquered. Pes. 119[a] (play on לַמְנַצֵּחַ) זמרו למי שנוֹצְחִין אותו ושמח sing to him who rejoices when they conquer him (prevail over him to change his evil decrees); Midr. Till. to Ps. IV. Pesik. R. s. 40 נָצַחְתִּי לדור וכ׳ I conquered the generation of the flood and was the loser by it, because I destroyed &c. Ib. נְצָחַנִי משה וכ׳ Moses conquered me…, and I gained all those masses; a. fr.—Part. pass. נָצוּחַ. Ib. בשעה שאני נוצח…ובשעה שאני נ׳ וכ׳ when I prevail, I lose, but when I am prevailed over, I gain; a. e.

Pi. נִצַּח 1) *to make illustrious, to glorify.* Midr. Till. l. c. (expl. למנצח) למי שהוא נאה לְנַצֵּחַ to him whom it is befitting to glorify.—2) *to conquer, prevail over.* Ib. מלך ב״ור מְנַצְּחִים אותו וכ׳ a human king is angry when people defeat him (in argument; cmp. זָכֵי *Pa.*); Pes. l. c.—B. Mets. 59[b] נִצְּחוּנִי בני (or נְצָחוּנִי) my children have won over me. Ib. תלמידי חכמים שמנצחים וכ׳ scholars who defeat one another in discussion. Snh. 91[a] אם יְנַצְּחוּנִי..נִצַּחְתֶּם if they defeat me, say to them, you have defeated an ignoramus among us; ואם אני אֲנַצֵּחַ … תורת משה נִצַּחְתְּכֶם and if I defeat them, say to them, the law of Moses has defeated you; a. fr.—Part. pass. מְנוּצָּח. Midr. Till. l. c. למי שמנ׳ וכ׳ to him who allows himself to be won over by his creatures (v. supra); a. e.

Nif. נִיצַּח *to be defeated.* Y. Sabb. II, 5[b] top v. supra.

נְצַח ch. same, 1) *to be glad, to sing.* Targ. II Esth. I, 2 והוה נָצַח וכ׳ it flew singing among &c.—2) *to succeed, thrive.* Targ. Koh. XI, 2.—3) *to be victorious.* Targ. O Ex. XXXII, 18, v. נִצְחָא; a. e.—Y. Sot. IX, 24[b] נִצְחוּ טליא the boys (John Hyrcan's sons) have won the battle; Bab. ib. 33[a]; Tosef. ib. XIII, 5. Tam. 32[a], v. סִטְנָא; a. e.

Pa. נַצַּח *to conquer, overpower.* Targ. Y. Num. XVI, 14; a. e.—Lam. R. to I, 13 (expl. וירדנה ib.) נַצְּחָהּ (not נצחא) he conquered her.

Af. אַנְצַח *to cheer up, play.* Y. Ter. VIII, end, 46[c] ואי׳ קדמיהון and played before them; (Gen. R. s. 63 מוזגה, v. מְזַג).

Ithpe. אִתְנְצַח 1) *to be bright, shine, excel.* Targ. Ez. XIX, 11. Ib. XXXI, 8; a. e.—2) *to be defeated.* Targ. Y. Ex. XXXII, 18.

נַצֵּחַ m., **נַצַּחַת** f. (b. h.; preced.) *successful, convincing, irrefutable.* Snh. 105[a] (ref. to Jer. VIII, 5) תשובה נ׳ השיבה וכ׳ the congregation of Israel defeated the prophets with an irrefutable argument.

נֵצַח m. (b. h.; preced.) *success, endurance*; (adv.) *forever.* Erub. 54[a] כל מקום שנאמר נ׳ וכ׳ wherever the Biblical text has the words *netsaḥ*, *selah*, or *va'ed*, it means &c., v. הֶפְסֵק.—*Pl.* נְצָחִים. Midr. Till. to Ps. IV, v. נִיצּוּחַ.

נַצְחָא m. (preced. wds.) *victor.*—*Pl.* נַצְּחִין. Targ. II Esth. I, 2 כליל רייש נ׳ the crown of the chief of victors. Targ. Ex. XXXII, 18 (O. ed. Berl. דְנַצְּחִין, v. נְצַח).

נִצְּחוֹן, נִי׳ m. (preced. wds.) 1) *victory, strength.* Sot. VIII, 1 בְנִיצְחוֹנוֹ של וכ׳ (Y. ed. בנצחת ב״ור, corr. acc.) relying on the strength of &c.; a. e.—2) *praise, song.* Midr. Till. to Ps. LXXXIV; Yalk. Ps. 833 כל מי שרואה … נותן עליה נ׳ whoever sees that wine press (Is. LXIII, 1 sq.), gives forth songs over it.

נַצְחָן m. (preced. wds.) *victorious, strong.* Targ. Job XXII, 8 Ms. (ed. v. next w.).

נִצְחָן, נִצְחָנָא, נִי׳ m. ch. = h. נִצָּחוֹן, *strength, victory.* Targ. Job XXII, 8 (h. text זְרוֹעַ; Ms., v. preced.). Targ. Jud. VII, 18. Targ. Ps. XXXV, 23; a. fr.—*Pl.* נִצְחָנִין, נִי׳; constr. נִצְחָנֵי, נִי׳. Targ. Jud. V, 28. Targ. Y. II Ex. XIV, 14; a. e.

נִצְחָנָה pr. n. pl. *Nitsḥana.* Koh. R. to II, 8.

נִצְחָנוּתָא f., constr. נִצְחָנוּת = נִצְחָנָא. Targ. Y. I Ex. XIV, 14; a. e.

נִצַּחַת, v. נִצֵּחַ.—[Sot. VIII, 1 (3), Y. ed. נצחת ב״ור, v. נִצָּחוֹן.]

נָצָה, נצי *to press; Nif.* נִצָּה (b. h.; cmp. חָבַל) *to wrangle, fight.*

Hithpa. הִתְנַצֵּה same. Tanh. Huck. ed. Bub. 1; Num. R. s. 18, end ראה שני צפרים מִתְנַצִּין וכ׳ saw two birds fight &c.

נְצָא, נְצֵי ch. same, 1) *to be pressed; to shrink, be lean,* v. נְצָא II.—2) *to wrangle.* Targ. Gen. XXVI, 20, sq.; a. fr.—Part. נָאצֵי, נָצֵי; f. נַצְיָא; *pl.* נָצָן. Targ. Prov. XXVI, 17 נא׳ ed. Lag. (ed. Wil. נְצֵי, corr. acc.). Ib. XXVII, 15. Targ. Ex. II, 13; a. e.—M. Kat. 16[a] דִּנְצֵינָן וכ׳ that we (the court) must contend (with persons disregarding legal summonses) and curse &c.

Ithpa. אִתְנַצֵּי, *Ithpe.* אִתְנְצֵי, אִינְ׳ same. Targ. O. Lev. XXIV, 10. Targ. Gen. XLV, 24; a. fr.—B. Mets. 84[b] הוה קא מִינַּצְיָא וכ׳ his wife was quarrelling with &c. Kidd. 76[a] נשי דכי מִינְּצוּ בהדי הדדי בעריות הוא דמִינְּצוּ when women quarrel with one another, they will eventually reproach one another with unchaste conduct; גברי . . ביוחסין הוא דמינצו when men quarrel, they will reproach each other with spurious descent (if there is any rumor about it). Ib[b]. כיון דמִינְּצוּ בהדי אינשי (or דמְנַצּוּ *Pa.*) because they (charity collectors) expose themselves to reproaches. Ib. והוה קא מִינְּצֵי איהו וכ׳ (or מְנַצֵּי) he and Rab Bibi strove with each other, one saying, I want the town office &c. Meg. 24[a] משום דאתי לְאִינְּצוּיֵי because it may come to quarrels between them. Ib.[b] אינצי אביו ומינצי רבו Ms. M. (ed. נִיצּוּיֵי) his father may take up the quarrel for him, or his teacher. B. Kam. 117[a] מנצו, v. שׁוּתָא III; a. e.

Pa. נַצֵּי same. Targ. Koh. III, 7; a. e.—Meg. 24[a] קטן בר נַצּוּיֵי הוא will a minor quarrel (about precedence)? Ber. 56[a] מְנַצּוּ (Beth N. מִינְּצֵי); a. e. (v. supra).

נַצְיָא, v. נַץ ch.

נְצִיב, v. נְצַב.

נָצִיב m. (נָצַב; cmp. יַצִּיבָא) *permanent resident*, opp. גֵּר. Gen. R. s. 64 (ref. to שְׁכֹן, Gen. XXVI, 2) עשה שכונה בא״י. . הוי נוטע הוי זורע הוי נ׳ make a settlement in the land of Israel, be a planter, be a sower, be a citizen.

נְצִיב m. (b. h.; נָצַב) *officer, post*; (in a secret letter) *month.* Snh. 12[a] לקבוע נ׳ אחד to establish one post (to intercalate one month).

נְצִיבָא, נְצִיב m. ch. = נְצָבָא, q. v. Targ. Job XIV, 8, sq. Ms.—*Pl.* נְצִיבִין. Targ. Ps. CXLIV, 12.—Lev. R. s. 25, v. נְצַב; a. e.—Targ. Y. Ex. XXVI, 15 כאורח נְצִיבֵיהוֹן the way they grow, v. גְּדִילָה I.

נְצִירָא* m. (v. נְצָא II) *lean land.* Targ. Ps. LXV, 11 נְצִירָתָא תבריך ed. Lag. (ed. Wil. צְמַחְתָּא; h.text צְמַחְהּ). Ib. נְצִירָנָא רוי Ms. (ed. מרביעי צמחתא; h. text תלמיה).

נְצִירְנָא, v. preced.

נְצִיף, v. נְצַף.

נָצִיר m. (b. h. Kethib; נצר) *guarded;* (homiletically interpreted = יצר) *that which is being formed, embryo, premature birth.*—*Pl.* נְצִירִים, constr. נְצִירֵי. Y. Shebi. IV, end, 35[c] אפילו נפלים וכ׳ even premature births will have a share in the resurrection, as we read (Is. XLIX, 6) &c.

נְצִית, v. צות.

נָצַל (b. h.; cmp. אצל) *to remove, set aside.*

Pi. נִצֵּל *to empty, ransack.* Esth. R. to III, 9 עד שנִצְּלוּ את מצרים so that they ransacked Egypt.

Nif. נִצַּל, נִיצּוֹל, נִיצַּל *1) *to be fit for throwing away* (as נֶצֶל), *to be decayed.* Y. Naz. VII, 56[b] bot. בשר המת שנִצַּל Ar. (Ar. ed. Rome שנצול; ed. שנתוק), v. נֶצֶל.—2) (b. h.) *to be rescued, saved.* Midr. Till. to Ps. I לא נִצַּלְתִּי מידו I did not escape his power; Yalk. Num. 750 ניצלתי (read: נִיצַּ׳; ed. Liv. נִצּוֹלְתִּי). Yoma 86[b] כגון שבאת ..... וכ׳ חורמנה when an opportunity to sin offered itself to him once and again, and he escaped it; Kidd. 39[b]. Esth. R. to II, 7 עתידין לִינָּצֵל וכ׳ עתידין להִנָּצֵל are destined to be saved through me; על ידיה be saved through her. B. Bath. 164[b] שלש .. אין אדם ניצול מהן וכ׳ there are three sins which man cannot escape &c.; a. fr.

Hif. הִצִּיל *to save, rescue.* Num. R. s. 18 אשתו הִצִּילַתּוּ his wife saved him. Ib. משה .. הַצִּילֵנוּ O Moses . . ., save us! Sabb. XVI, 1 מַצִּילִין אותן וכ׳ we must save them from fire (on the Sabbath). Snh. VIII, 7 שמצילין אותן בנפשן whom we must save (prevent from committing a crime) even at the risk of their lives. Ib. 73[a] ניתן לְהַצִּילָהּ בנפשו it is a duty to save her (from rape) at the expense of the assailant's life; a. fr.—Trnsf. (in ritual and levitical law) *to protect.* Hull. 55[b] כל ... מַצִּיל בגלודה every part of the skin (which has remained unaffected) protects a flayed animal from being declared *t'refah.* Ib. מהו שיַצִּיל וכ׳ does it form a protection from &c.? Ohol. V, 3 מַצֶּלֶת על הכל protects everything in it from uncleanness; a. v. fr.

Hof. הוּצַּל *to be saved.* Esth. R. to V, 3 כבר הוּצְּלוּ חנניה וכ׳ Hananiah and his colleagues have long ere this been delivered from the furnace; a. e.

נְצַל ch. same, *to save.* Taan. 9[b] פִּרְשׁוּפָא, v. רחמנא לִיצְּלַן; a. e.

Af. אַצֵּיל same. Snh. 72[b] דלא מצי אַצּוֹלֵיהּ when he cannot save him. Sabb. 115[a] השתא אַצּוֹלֵי מַצְּלִינַן וכ׳ since we are bound to save them (on the Sabbath), is it necessary to say that they require burying (when defective)?; a. fr.

Ittaf. אִתַּצַּל *to be saved.* Ab. Zar. 18[a] bot. וּמִתַּצְּלַת and thou shalt be saved.

נֶצֶל, נֵי׳ m. (preced. wds.) [*that which is thrown away,*] *decayed matter,* esp. (in levitical law) *liquid and coagulated portions of a corpse.* Ohol. II, 1; Naz. VII, 2. Y. ib. VII, 56[b] bot. איזהו נ׳ בשר המת שנתוק ומוהל וכ׳ (Ar. שנצל) what is *netsel* (in levitical law)? A corpse which is dissolving &c., v. מוֹהַל; Bab. ib. 50[a] איזהו נ׳ בשר המת שקרש ומוהל שהורתיח a secretion from a corpse which became coagulated, and a liquid secretion exposed to heat. Tosef. Ohol. III, 6; a. e.

נִצְמִין m. pl. (צמם) *clasps,* v. נְצוֹרָא.

נִצְנֵץ, נַצְנֵץ, v. נצץ.

נֶצַע transpos. of נֶעֶץ q. v.

נְצִיף, נְצַף (cmp. צפצף) *to chirp, squeal.* Targ. Is. XXIX, 4; a. e.

Pa. נַצֵּיף same. Ib. XXXVIII, 14 (some ed. מְנַצֵּיף *Af.*). Ib. XIII, 22; a. fr.

נִצְפָּה f. *caper-bush.* Dem. I, 1 וה׳; expl. Ber. 40[b] פִּרְחָה the flower of the caper-bush. Ib. 36[a] מיני נ׳ (identical with צָלָף) the various products of the caper-bush which are eatable; the leaves &c.—Y. Sabb. XV, end, 15[b] סיכה אחת של נ׳ one bush of &c.; Lev. R. s. 34, end אילן של נ׳; (Sabb. 150[b] צלף).

נָצַץ (נוּץ) (b. h.; cmp. צוץ) *to sparkle, blossom.* Erub. 54[a] חֶלְוַת, v. נוֹצְצִין.

Hif. הֵנֵץ 1) *to sparkle.* Y. Ber. I, 2[c] עד שֶׁתָּנֵץ החמה; Gen. R. s. 50, a. e. (Pes. 93[b] עד הנץ), v. הָנֵץ.—2) *to blossom, sprout.* Shebi. IV, 10 משיָנֵצוּ; Pes. 53[a] משיְנֵיצוּ (or משינֵיצוּ) as soon as they blossom (expl. Y. Shebi. IV, end, 35[c] משתכנימו רובע, v. נֵץ). B. Bath. 147[a] בשעה שיונצו (Ms. M. שהֵנֵיצוּ) when they are in blossom. Koh. R. to XII, 5, v. צוץ; a. fr.—2) *to cause to sprout.* Gen. R. s. 28 מֵנֵיץ Ar. (ed. מציץ), v. צוץ.

Pilp. נִצְנֵץ 1) *to sparkle, be enkindled.* Gen. R. s. 84 נִיצְנְצָה בו רוח״ק the spirit of prophecy was enkindled within him; Cant. R. to I, 12. Midr. Till. to Ps. XC, end, נ׳ עליו מזיו וכ׳ a ray of the Divine Glory shone upon him, v. זָהַר.—2) *to sprout, grow.* Cant. R. to VI, 10 מִתְנַצְנֶצֶת ובאה spreads wider and wider; (Midr. Till. to Ps. XXII מנצצת).

נְצַץ ch. same, *to sprout, grow forth, bloom.* Targ. Ps. XCII, 8. Ib. LXXII, 16 יְנַצֵּץ Ms. (ed. *Pa.*).

Pa. נַצֵּץ 1) same, v. supra.—2) *to sparkle.* Targ. Ez. I, 7 Levita (ed. מְנַצְנְצִין *Palpel*).

נִצְצָא, נִיצְצָא m. = נָצָא, בַּר נ׳ *hawk.* Targ. Y. Lev. XI, 16; Targ. Y. Deut. XIV, 15 (נִצְצָא). Targ. Y. Lev. XX, 25 ני׳.

נָצַר (b. h.; cmp. אצר, צרר) *to preserve, guard.* B. Bath. 91[b] (play on והוצרים, I Chr. IV, 23) שנָצְרוּ שבועות וכ׳ who guarded their father's oath (of abstinence). Ber. 17[a] נְצוֹר לשוני מרע, תורתי וכ׳ keep my law in thy heart. Ib. guard my tongue from evil. Tanh. B'midbar 13 עד היכן נְצָרָן up to what degree did He guard them?; Num. R. s. 2. Midr. Till. to Ps. CXL רצונך שאֶצָּרְךָ נצור וכ׳ if it is thy desire that I guard thee, guard thou my law; a. fr.

נְצַר (cmp. Arab. ṣarṣara, a. צַרְצוּר) *to chirp*. Lev. R. s. 33 end (play on נבוכד נצר) נבח .. נ׳ כצרצרא bark like a dog ..., chirp like a cricket; מיד ... נ׳ וכ׳ presently he ... chirped &c.; Cant. R. to II, 14.

נֵצֶר I m. (preced.) *cricket*.—*Pl.* נְצָרִין. Tosef. Ḥull. III, 25 (Ḥull. 65^b צרצור).

נֵצֶר II m. (b. h.; cmp. Arab. naḍara, a. נצץ) *sprout, offshoot*. Tanḥ. Lekh, ed. Bub. 9 אם נוטלין נ׳ מהם וכ׳ if you take a shoot of them (the felled trees) and plant it &c.; Tanḥ. ib. 5 ונוטעין מִנִּצְרָה שלהן.

נֵצֶר III m. (cmp. מֵצַר II) [*twist*,] *willow, wicker*. Erub. 58^a (חבל) של נ׳ a wicker rope.—*Pl.* נְצָרִים. Ib. Kel. XX, 2 כלי נ׳ (ed. Dehr. נְסָרִים) vessels of wickerwork. Bicc. III, 8 סלי נ׳ (Ms. M. נס׳) wicker baskets; a. fr.—Tosef. Toh. XI, 16 נוֹצְרִין.

נֵצֶר IV pr. n. m. 1) *Netsar*, one of the alleged disciples of Jesus of Nazareth. Snh. 43^a Ms. M. a. ed. Ven. (omitted in later edit., v. תַּלְמִי).—2) בֶּן נ׳ *Ben-Netsar* (*son of Nassor*) name of a chief of robbers who became founder of a dynasty, i. e. *Odenathus* of Palmyra (v. Cyclop. Brit. s. v. Palmyra, Ersch u. Gruber II, Vol. 27, p. 185, Fürst Gloss., p. 145). Keth. 51^b (opp. to מלכות אחשורוש the legitimate Persian dynasty). Gen. R. s. 76; Yalk. Dan. 1064 בן נָצוֹר. Y. Ter. VIII, 46^b bot. בר ניצור.

נִצְרָא, נִצְרָה, נ׳ I, m. ch.=h. נֵצֶר III, *wicker-basket*. Y. Maasr. IV, 51^b אפי׳ נ׳ even an ordinary basket of figs, opp. to כַּלְכָּלָה.—*Pl.* נִצְרִין, נִ׳. Y. Ab. Zar. IV, 44^a bot.—[Targ. Job XXXI, 8 נצרי, read with ed. Lag. a. oth. נִצַּי, v. נֵץ ch.]

נִצְרָה II f. *shoot*, v. נֵצֶר II.

נִצְרְפֵי m. pl. (fr. צרף, a cacophemistic disguise of נוֹצְרִי, v. נוֹצְרָאֵי); בי נ׳ *a Christian place of worship*, contrad. to בֵּי אֲבִידָן. Sabb. 116^a (Ms. O. נצרפו, v. Rabb. D. S. a. l. note 30).

נָקָא, v. נָקֵי.

נָקָא, v. נָאקְתָא.—[Y. Shek. VII, 50^c bot. נ׳ בר קא, v. נוּקְנִיקָה.]

נַקַּאי, נַקַּי pr. n. m. *Nacai* (*Lucas*, v. Neub. Stud. Bibl. I, p. 61); 1) נ׳ ספרא N. the scribe (or teacher). Gen. R. s. 79 שמע קליה דנ׳ ס׳ he heard N. say; Koh. R. to X, 8 קליה דנ״ ס׳; Yalk. Gen. 133 דנקא׳; Pesik. B'shall., p. 90^a דמינקי (corr. acc.).—2) N., one of the disciples of Jesus of Nazareth. Snh. 43^a Ms. M. a. early eds. (v. נֵצֶר IV).

נקאני, נ׳ קא, v. נוּקְנִיקָה.

נָקַב (b. h.; cmp. קבב s. v. קַב) 1) *to bore, perforate*. Snh. 97^b מקרא זה נוֹקֵב וכ׳ this verse bores and penetrates to the depth. Ib. 6^b, a. e. יִקּוֹב הדין וכ׳, v. דִּין II; a. e.—Part. pass. נָקוּב; *f.* נְקוּבָה; *pl.* נְקוּבִים, נְקוּבִין; נְקוּבוֹת. Y. Keth. XII, 35^a top; Y. Kil. IX, 32^b top; (Gen. R. s. 100 נקופה), v. אָרוֹן. Cant. R. to VIII, 5 מצאתי חככם נ׳ וכ׳ I found your palate perforated, unable to receive blessings.—Esp. נקובה *the case of an animal found to have a vital organ perforated*. Ḥull. III, 1 נְקוּבַת הושט, v. וֶשֶׁט. Ib. 43^a; a. fr.—Esp. נְקוּבִים (נְקָבִים) *female parts*. Y. Meg. I, 71^d bot. (reported as one of the changes adopted in the Greek translation of the Pentateuch, ref. to Gen. I, 27, a. V, 2) זכר ונְקוּבָיו בראם a male with corresponding female parts created he them; Gen. R. s. 8; Mekh. Bo, s. 14 (v. Gen. R. l. c., beg.).—[Y. Meg. I, 71^c לנקוביו, v. נֶקֶב.]—2) (cmp. אָרַר) *to curse, blaspheme*. Snh. 56^a (ref. to Lev. XXIV, 16) ממאי דהאי נוֹקֵב וכ׳ whence do you prove that this *nokeb* is used in the sense of blasphemy? .... perhaps it means *to perforate*? Ib. למימרא דנוקב וכ׳ to indicate that *nokeb* means curse.—3) *to point out, to pronounce*. Ib. אימא פרושי שמיה הוא I might say, *nokeb* means uttering His name (the Tetragrammaton)? Tanḥ. Emor 24 התחיל לִנְקוֹב וכ׳ he began to pronounce the Name and curse Him.—[Midr. Till. to Ps. I ונקובות ירדים; ed. Bub. נקיבת ירק, read: קְנִיבַת ירק, v. קְנִיבָה.]

Nif. נִקַּב, נִיקַּב *to be perforated, punctured*. Ḥull. III, 1 הריאה שנִיקְּבָה if a lung is found to be perforated. Ib. עד שתִּינָּקֵב וכ׳ until the puncture reaches &c. Ib. 43^a בלא נ׳ זה אם זה if only one of the two is perforated. Bekh. 44^b אם נִקְּבוּ זה וכ׳ if there is a perforation going from one channel to the other; a. fr.

נְקַב ch. same, *to perforate*. Targ. II Kings XII, 10; a. fr.—Ḥull. 48^a אי האי נְקִיב וכ׳ whether this lobe is perforated or the other; a. e.

Pa. נַקֵּיב same. Ib.^{b} נַקּוּבֵי נקיב ואתאי the needle perforated (the entrails) and came into the lungs.

Ithpe. אִתְנְקֵב, אִיתְּקִיב *to be perforated* Ib. Ib. 45^a; a. e.

נֶקֶב m. (b. h.; preced.) *hole, perforation, incision*. Ḥull. 45^a נ׳ אחד ארוך one lengthy incision; a. fr.—*Pl.* נְקָבִים, נְקָבִין. Ib. נ׳ שיש בהן חסרון perforations connected with loss of substance (holes); נ׳ שאין בהן חסרון mere punctures. Bekh. 44^b שני נ׳ יש בו וכ׳ two channels are in the membrum. Gen. R. s. 1, beg.; a. fr.—Esp. *the organs of the extremities, urinary organ* &c. Tosef. Ber. II, 18 ויהא צריך לִנְקָבָיו when needing to ease himself; Ber. 23^a; Y. Meg. I, 71^c לִנְקוּבָיו. Sabb. 152^a; a. fr.

נִקְבָא, נִ׳, נו׳ ch. same. Lev. R. s. 12 חזא נ׳ בתרעא saw a hole in the door. Sabb. 90^a בנ׳ דמרגניתא in the cavity wherein the pearl is seated; a. e.—*Pl.* נִקְבִין, נִיקְבִין, constr. נִקְבֵי, נִ׳. Targ. Ez. XXVIII, 13 נִקְ׳ (ed. Lag. נִיקְ׳). Targ. II Chr. XXXIII, 11; a. e.—Nidd. 62^a נ׳ מרגניתא, v. supra; a. e.

נְקֵבָה, נְקֵי׳ f. (b. h.; preced. wds.) *female sex, female; female gender*. Nidd. III, 2, a. fr. תשב לנ׳ she must observe the laws of cleanness for the birth of a female child (Lev. XII, 5). Ib. 31^b, v. נָקִי I; a. v. fr.—לשון נ׳ feminine gender. Kidd. 2^b, v. זָכָר; a. fr.—Y. Yeb. VIII, end, 9^d ממקום נ׳, v. next w.—*Pl.* נְקֵבוֹת, נְקֵי׳. Kidd. 82^b; a. v. fr.—Succ. 12^b חציך נ׳, v. חֵץ.

נְקֵבוּת, נְקֵי׳ f. (preced.) 1) *female genitals, female sex*. Snh. 82^b; (Y. ib. X, 28^d bot., a. e. קיבה). Yeb. 83^b בנ׳ שלו

at his (the hermaphrodite's) female organ; (Y. ib. VIII, end, 9[d] מקום נְקֵיבָה). Ib. צד נְקֵיבוּתוֹ (ed. Krot. נְקֵיבָתוֹ) inasmuch as he is a female, v. זַכְרוּת.—2) *the broadside of a double tool.* Bets. 31[b], v. זַכְרוּת.

נְקַבְתָּה, נִקְבְּתָא, v. נְקֵיפְתָּא.

נָקַד I (cmp. קָדַר) *to sting, point, puncture, break through.* Y. Keth. II, 26[b] bot. לבי נוֹקְדֵינִי my conscience stings me (I am afraid that I may have sinned); Y. Yeb. X, 11[a] top נוקדיני (corr. acc.). Gitt. 56[a] (play on נַקְדִּימוֹן) שנָּקְדָה לו חמה בעבורו for his sake did the sun break through again (after being obscured); Yalk. Deut. 809; Taan. 20[a] Ms. M. (ed. שנקדרה). Ib. אילו לא נ׳ החמה Ms. M. (ed. נקדרה). [Ib. שלשה נקדה Ms. M. (ed. נקדמה, read, as Ab. Zar. 25[a]: עמדה.]—2) (Massorah) *to dot, mark with diacritical points.* Ab. d'R. N. ch. XXXIV, כבר נָקַדְתִּי עליהן I (Ezra) have marked these words with dots.—Part. pass. נָקוּד. Ib. נ׳ על י׳ שבינֵיך there is a dot over the Yod of *benekhah* (Gen. XVI, 6). Snh. 43[b] למה נ׳ על לנו וכ׳ why are there dots over *lanu* &c. (Deut. XXIX, 28)? Pes. IX, 2 לפיכך נ׳ על וכ׳ therefore the Hé (of רחקה, Num. IX, 10) is marked &c.; a. fr.

Nif. נִיקַּד *to be spotted.* Maasr. I, 3 החרובים משיִּנָּקְדוּ carobs are subject to tithes as soon as they get dark spots; Y. ib. 48[d] bot. משיִּנָּקְדוּ.

נָקַד II (dialect. interch. with נָקַר) *to be clean,* v. נָקַר II.

נְקַד ch. same, v. נְקַר.

נַקְדּוֹד m. (v. נוֹקֵד) *herder.* Lev. R. s. 1 אין גנאי.. נַקְדּוֹדוֹ it is not beneath a king's dignity to speak with his herder (the Lord spoke to Noah).—Y. Ber. I, 3[c] bot. (ref. to 1 Kings VIII, 54) כגון הדין נקדים הוה עימד (Var. נקרים; corr. acc.) Solomon stood before the Lord like a herder (giving an account of the Temple expenses), expl. by R. El. bar A. ככסים הללו וכ׳.

נקדים, v. preced.

נַקְדִּימוֹן pr. n. m. *Nakdimon* (Nicodemus) ben Gorion, a wealthy citizen of Jerusalem during the siege by Vespasian and Titus. Gitt. 56[a]. Taan. 20[a] (ed. Pes. נִיקוֹדֵימוֹן); Ab. Zar. 25[a]; Yalk. Deut. 809; Yalk. Josh. 21. Gen. R. s. 42. Lam. R. to I, 16; Pesik. R. s. 29—30—30.

נוֹקְדָן, נַקְדָּן m. (נָקַר I) *a punctilious person, caviller.* Der. Er. Zuta ch. VI (נקד׳).—*Pl.* נוֹקְדָ׳, נַקְדָּנִין. Tosef. Ber. V, 18 והנו׳ חופשין וכ׳ ed. Zuck. (Var. והנקד׳) the cavillers (overscrupulous) take him to task for it; Y. ib. VII, 11[c] top הנו׳ (ed. Lehm. הנוקדנין); Bab. ib. 50[a] נקד׳ (Ar. נקר׳), v. נַקְרָן.

נוֹקְדָ׳, נַקְדָּנָא ch. same. Y. Ber. VII, 11[c] top בגין דצוות... נו׳ (ed. Lehm. נוקר׳) because R... called R.... a caviller.—*Pl.* נַקְדָּנֵי. Ned. 49[b] הלין נ׳ דהוצל those fastidious persons of Hutzal.

נָקָה I f., v. נְאָקָה II.

נָקָה II *to be clean,* v. נקי.

נָקוּב m., pl. נְקוּבִים, v. נָקַב a. נֶקֶב.

נְקוּבָא m. ch. = h. נְקוּבָה, v. נֶקֶב.—*Pl.* נְקוּבֵי. Hull. 42[b] תמניא הוו נ׳ there are eight cases of perforations (which cause the animal so afflicted to be declared *t'refah*). Ib. 54[b].

נְקוּבָה f., 1) v. נֶקֶב.—2) בֵּית נ׳ *anus, buttock.* Pes. VII, 1 בית נְקוּבָתוֹ; a. e.

נְקוּבְתָּא, v. נְקֵיפְתָּא.

נְקוּד, v. נִיקּוּד.

נָקוֹד m. (b. h. נָקֹד; נָקַר I) *speckled.*—*Pl.* נְקוּדִים. Tanh. Vayetsé 11 היה מתהפך עליו מן העקודים לנ׳ ומן הנ׳ וכ׳ he turned around (changing his wages) from the ring-streaked to the speckled and from the speckled to the ring-streaked; a. e.

נְקוּדָה f. (b. h. נְקֻדָּה; preced.) *point, dot, drop.* Y. Sabb. VII, 10[d] top יש שהוא כותב נ׳ אחת וכ׳ sometimes a man writes one dot (a touch of the pen by which a Daleth is changed into a Resh &c.). Y. Hag. II, 77[c] והוא מראה להן בנ׳ (של מעלן) וכ׳ and it (the letter Beth) points with its upper stroke (saying), He above (has created me); ib. נ׳ לאחריו the projecting point (of the Beth) beneath to the right side; Pesik. R. s. 21; (Gen. R. s. 1 (עוקץ); a. fr.—*Pl.* נְקוּדוֹת. Y. Gitt. II, 44[b] top אפי׳ עירב נ׳ even if he connected the dots (which he had dropped to form letters, v. נָטַף); a. fr.—Esp. (Massorah) *mark by diacritical dots above letters.* Ab. d'R. N. ch. XXXIV אעביר נ׳ (מעליהן (not אעבור) I will remove the dots from above them. Gen. R. s. 48, v. כָּתַב; a. fr.—*Pl.* as ab. Ab. d'R. N. l. c.; Treat. Sof'rim VI, 3 עשר נ׳ בתורה there are ten passages in the Torah marked with dots; a. fr.

נְקוּטָאֵי m. pl. (נְקַט) *(laborers) gathered from different places.* B. Mets. 83[b] (Ms. H. לְקוּטָאֵי).

נְקוּר, v. נִיקּוּר.

נְקוּנִיקָא, נְקוּנִיא, v. מַקְנִיקָה.

נַקּוֹסָה, נַקּוֹסָא pr. n. m. *Nakosa.* B. Kam. 81[b] יהודה בן נ׳ Ms. M. (ed. קַטּוֹסָא); Y. Ber. II, end, 5[d] ed. Lehm. (ed. פסוס). Koh. R. to I, 8; VII, 26 (some ed. נקיסא).

נְקוּף, v. נִיקּוּף.

נְקוֹפָא m. (נְקַף I) *striking against, bruise.* Targ. Ps. LVI, 14 (ed. Wil. נְקִיפָא).

נְקוֹרָא, נְקוֹר, v. sub נִיק׳.

נַקּוֹרוֹת m. pl. (נָקַר I) *those sharpening the millstones, chisellers.* Tosef. Kidd. V, 14; Kidd. 82[a].

נְקוּשָׁא, v. נִיקּוּשָׁא.

נָקַז (cmp. קָזַז a. נָקַר I) *to puncture.*
Hif. הִקִּיז (mostly with דָּם) *to let blood; to be bled.*

Bekh. V, 2 אין מַקִּיזִין לו דם you must not bleed it; יַקִּיז one may &c. Sabb. 129ª הִ' דם ונצטנן if one feels chilly after having been bled. Ib.ᵇ הִ' דם ועמד if one stands up after &c. Ab. Zar. 29ª. Ned. 54ᵇ אין מקיזין על וכ' you must not be bled after having eaten &c. Sot. 22ᵇ (expl. פרוש קיזאי) הַמַּקִּיז דם לכתלים who bleeds himself by striking against the walls (walking with closed eyes from sanctimoniousness). Ber. 60ª הנכנס לְהַקִּיז דם he who enters (the surgeon's office) to be bled; a. fr.

נְקֵז ch., *Af.* אַקִּיז same. Y. Ber. III, 5ᶜ bot. [V. קְזַז.]

נָקַט (cmp. לָקַט) *to hold in hand, take, seize.* [נקטה Pesik. B'shall., p. 81ᵇ; Yalk. Ex. 225, v. קוּט.]

Pi. נִיקֵּט *to cause to hold, to procure.* Ex. R. s. 1 וּמְנַקֶּטֶת לחם שני וכ' (some ed. ומלקט) and provided for them two balls (breast-shaped stones); (Sot. 11ᵇ ומלקט; Yalk. Ex. 164 ומלקט; Yalk. Ez. 354 ומוחן).

נְקַט ch. same (corresp. to h. אָחַז). Targ. Esth. VI, 1; a. fr.—Part. act. נָקֵיט, pass. נְקִיט *holding.* Ib. VIII, 15; a. fr.—Shebu. 38ᵇ נ' חפצא וכ' he held an object in his hand (on being sworn). Ab. Zar. 30ª הוה נקיט חמרא בהדיה was carrying wine with him. Ib. סירכא דגברא נְקִיטָה she holds fast (clings to) the habit of her (deceased) husband. Sanh. 5ª נְקִיטְנָא רשותא I hold a license (to teach). M. Kat. 28ª, a. e. נְקוֹט לך מידיא וכ' hold at least half of it in thy hand, i. e. admit as certain &c.; Snh. 90ᵇ נְקוֹטוּ (not נקוטי); a. v. fr.—Hull. 53ª, a. fr. נְקִיטִינָן, נְקִטִינַן we hold a tradition.—Sabb. 116ᵇ top נקיט שמא וכ' quoted in Levy Talm. Dict. (ed. שקיל) had the reputation that &c. Gitt. 56ª נְקוֹט נפשך בקצירי have thyself counted among the sick, i. e. have the report spread that thou art sick. Hull. 87ª נקוט לי זימנא וכ' keep time for me &c., i. e. allow me three days' time.—Trnsf. *to contract a habit.* B. Kam. 57ª, v. נִירְגָּא.

Af. אַקֵּיט, אַנְקֵיט, *Pa.* נַקֵּיט 1) *to cause to hold, to give, hand.* Targ. II Esth. IV, 16.—Pes. 110ª מְנַקְּטָא ליה אימיה וכ' (not מנקיט, v. Rabb. D. S. a. l. note) his mother was ready to hand him two cups. Ib. מְנַקֵּיט ליה וכ' (or מְנַקְּטָא) his servant was ready to hand him &c. B. Kam. 85ᵇ לְאַנְקוּטֵיה גוונא דבישריה to make him regain the natural color of flesh; a. e.—B. Bath. 22ª נַקֵּיט ליה שוקא make him take the market, i. e. give him the monopoly of sale.—2) *to pick up, gather.* Ned. 50ª (read מְנַקְּטָא .. חוות) הוה קא מנקיט וכ' she picked the straw out of his hair.—3) *to cause to contract a habit, train.* B. Kam. 118ᵇ; B. Bath. 88ª אַנְקְטִינְהוּ וכ', v. נִירְגָּא.—4) **to carry.* Targ. Y. Ex. XXI, 37 אַקְטֵיה בגנבותיה he carried it (on his shoulder) when he stole it.

Ithpe. אִתְנְקֵיט *to receive.* Yeb. 42ᵇ מִתְנְקֵיט ואזיל הלכתא וכ' received instruction from him while walking.

נַקְטְמוֹן, v. נִיקְטֵ'.

נָקָה, נקי (b. h.) [*to be rubbed off, be white,*] *to be clean, clear* (cmp. זָכָה).

Pi. נִיקָּה 1) *to cleanse.* Ex. R. s. 1 וּמְנַקָּה אותם and cleansed them (the new-born); Yalk. ib. 164; Yalk. Ez. 354; (Sot. 11ᵇ מנקיד). B. Kam. 93ᵇ פשתן וְנִיקָּהוּ if he stole flax and cleansed (bleached) it; Tosef. ib. X, 2; a. e.—2) *to clear, let go unpunished.* Yoma 86ª (ref. to Ex. XXXIV, 7) מנקה הוא וכ' he clears the repentant sinners &c. Tem. 3ᵇ. Pesik. R. s. 42 כדי לְנַקּוֹת את שרה in order to clear Sarah (from suspicion); a. fr.—Part. pass. מְנוּקָּה, *pl.* מְנוּקִּין *clear, clean, bare.* Snh. 49ª מנ' מגזל innocent of robbery. Sot. 28ª. Snh. 36ᵇ, a. e. מנ' .. כשם שב"ד מנ' בצדק as the judges must be clear (from suspicion) as to righteousness, so must they be clear of every blemish (of descent). Gitt. 86ª מ' מכל מום free from all objectionable qualities; a. e.

Nif. נִיקָּה, נִקָּה, *Hithpa.* הִתְנַקָּה *to be cleared, vindicated.* Tosef. Sot. II, 3 שנ' ונקתה נִקְּתָה מכל פורענויות וכ' (v. ed. Zuck. note) the text says (Num. V, 28) 'and she shall be cleared', she shall be cleared (released) from all the evils which might come upon her deservedly (because she gave rise to suspicion through her conduct). Ib. שניקללה גדולה (Var. שנקל) read: שניקתה בניוולה she is released from further visitation (being sufficiently punished) by her exposure to disgrace. Pesik. R. l. c. מִתְנַקָּה ... והיאך by what severe means has Sarah been vindicated!

**Hif.* הִנְקָה *to clear, remove.* Kidd. 62ª (ref. to הִנָּקִי, Num. V, 19) הַנְקִי כתיב it may be read *hanki*, clear thy life out of thy body (die, if thou art guilty); v. חָנַק.

נְקָא, נְקֵי ch. same. [Targ. Prov. XVII, 3, v. בְּקָא.]

Pa. נַקִּי *to cleanse, clear.* Targ. Is. I, 25.—Keth. 87ª נַקּוֹ נפשך בשבועתא clear thyself by means of an oath. Part. pass. מְנַקַּי. Ib. מְנַקֵּית משבועתא thou art free from the obligation of an oath.

Ithpa. אִתְנַקִּי, אִתְנַקָּא *to be cleansed.* Targ. Ez. XVI, 4; v. נְקַר II.

נָקִי I m. (b. h.; preced.) *clean, clear; bare.* Tosef. Toh. III, 8, opp. מלוכלך. Pes. 22ᵇ (ref. to Ex. XXI, 28) as one says to his neighbor יצא פלוני נ' מנכסיו that man went out of his possessions empty-handed; B. Kam. 41ª. Ib.ᵇ נ' מתשלומי כופר free from paying the half-fine. Taan. 23ª (ref. to Job XXII, 30) דור שלא היה נ' וכ' thou hast saved with thy prayer a generation which was not clear from sin. Y. Meg. I, 71ᶜ; Y. Ber. II, 4ᵈ top (ref. to Koh. V, 17) שמור ... שתהא טהור ונ' guard thy foot, that thou be pure and guiltless when thou art called to the house of God; a. fr.—Erub. 62ᵇ, a. fr. קב ונ' only a Kab (little in quantity), but well-sifted (v. infra).—(Adv.) נ' שבועה, נְקִי נדר without vow (as an oath), without oath; or: cleared by means of a vow &c. Keth. 87ª.—*Pl.* נְקִיִּין, נְקִיִּים. Gen. R. s. 98, v. נִקָּיוֹן. Gitt. IX, 10 נְקִיֵּי הדעת the pure-minded; a. e.—*Fem.* נְקִיָּה, נְקִיָּיה. Nidd. 31ᵇ נְקֵבָה נְקִייה באה a female comes into the world poor (without the means of making a livelihood). Y. Maasr. II, 49ᵈ דעתו נ' his mind is clear (he is wise). Y. Hag. II, 77ᵇ top אין דעתן נ' their minds are not clear enough (for esoteric wisdom). Num. R. s. 9 כדי שתהיי נ' לבעליך וכ' in order that thou be clean for thy husband through these waters. Y. Shek. V, 48ᵈ bot. פת נ' bread of fine (sifted) flour; Pes. 37ª, v. הַדְרָאָה. Kidd. 82ᵇ אומנות נ' וקלה a cleanly and easy trade; Tosef. ib. V, 15; a. fr.

נָקִי II m. (preced.) *a young lamb* (v. Syr. נקיא, P. Sm. 2446). Sabb. 54ª; Shebu. 6ᵇ, v. פְּבֵן.

נָקִי, v. נְקַאי.

נְקִיבָה, נְקִיבוֹת, v. sub נְקֵב׳.—[נקיבת ירק, Midr. Till. to Ps. I ed. Bub., v. קְנִיבָה.]

נָקִיד pr. n. (נָקַד II) *Naḳid* (*Cleanliness*). Pes. 111ª, v. אִיסְרָא.

נְקִידָא c. (preced.) *pure, clear.* Gitt. 69ª bot. חמרא נ׳ clear (not dark) wine.—*Pl.* נְקִידֵי. Sabb. 110ᵇ מוניני נ׳ Ms. O. (Ar. דנקידי; ed. דנקירי) clear fish-brine, v. נְקִירָא.

נְקִיָּה, v. נָקִי I.

נִקָּיוֹן, נִק׳ m. (b. h.; נָקָה) *purity, innocence; clearness.* Ruth R. to I, 1 (play on ולבן שנים וכ׳, Gen. XLIX, 12) שהיו סודרין ... בִּשְׁנַיִם עד שהיו מוציאין אותה בנ׳ כחלב (the Sanhedrin) that used to discuss the points of law in couples (v. Snh. V, 5), until they brought them out with a clearness like that of milk; Gen. R. s. 98 שוהו .. בשינים עד שהן מוציאין אותן נְקִיִּים כחלב (read בִּשְׁנַיִם).

נְקִיּוּת f. (preced.) 1) *cleanliness.* Yeb. 46ᵇ ודילמא נ׳ בעלמא perhaps mere cleanliness of appearance is intended? (not levitical purification). Sot. IX, 15; Y. Shek. III, end, 47ᶜ; Ab. Zar. 20ᵇ זריזות מביאה לידי נ׳ zeal leads to cleanliness, נ׳ מביאה וכ׳ cleanliness leads to levitical purity. Y. Pes. VII, 35ᵇ bot. אינה אלא נ׳ it is a mere matter of cleanliness.—2) *innocence, expiation.* Tem. 3ᵇ ואימא .. נ׳ כלל may I not say, it means that there is no expiation for him?; a. e.—3) *respectability, dignity.* Sifra K'dosh., Par. 2, ch. IV מתפרנס בנ׳ he will make a decent living (not be dependent on charity). Gen. R. s. 99; a. e.

נְקִיוּתָא or **נְקִיוּתָא** ch. same, *cleanliness*; v. מְנַקְּיוּתָא.

נָקִיט m., **נְקִיטָה** f. (קוט) [*shrinking,*] *feeling aversion, disgusted.* Pesik. Dibré, p. 111ª ונפשו נ׳ עליו ממנה and he has a disgust for it; Yalk. Lam. 998; Yalk. Prov. 932 קניטה (corr. acc.); v. קָנִיט.

נְקִיט, נְקִיט, נְקִיטָא, v. נְקַט.

נִקִּיטָא, נִיקִיטָה m. (read: נִיקֵיט׳, νικῆτα, Vocat. of νικήτης) *O, conqueror!* Lam. R. introd. (R. Josh. 2), v. בַּרְבַּרוֹן; Lev. R. s. 22 נ׳ ברבריא.

נְקִיָּיה, v. נָקִי I.

נְקִימָה f. (נָקַם) *revenge, retaliation; use of the root* נקם. Sifra K'dosh., Par. 2, ch. IV; Yoma 23ª (defining the difference between נ׳ and נְטִירָה). Snh. 52ᵇ נ׳ זו סייף *n'ḳimah* (Ex. XXI, 20) means putting to death by the sword; Y. ib. VI, 24ʰ bot.

נְקִיפָא, v. נְקוּפָא.

נְקִיפֵי, בֵּית נ׳ pr. n. gent. *Beth N'ḳifê.* Y. Yeb. I, 3ª bot. כשפחת בית נ׳; v. קוּפָאֵר.

נְקִיפְתָּא, נ׳ דְעִיּוֹן pr. n. pl. *N'ḳifta* (*Hollow*) *of Iyon* (Merg ʿAyun), in the north of Palestine (v. Hildesh. Beitr., p. 37, sq.). Tosef. Shebi. IV, 11 (Var. נְקַבְתָּא, נְקִיב׳, נְקוּב׳); Sifré Deut. 51 נקבתה רעיון; Y. Shebi. VI, 36ᶜ מקב׳ רעיון; Yalk. Deut. 874 נקיב׳ רעיון (corr. acc.).

נָקִיק m. (b. h.; cmp. נקע) *cleft.* Yalk. Cant. 986 ... ליונה ונכנסה לנ׳ הסלע like a dove that, fleeing before a hawk, entered the cleft of a rock.—*Pl.* נְקִיקִים, constr. נְקִיקֵי. Tosef. Zab. II, 9; Pes. 81ᵇ; a. e.

נְקִירָא m., pl. נְקִירֵי (נָקַר I) 1) name of *small birds* (*pickers*). Sabb. 110ᵇ מוניני דנ׳ brine of small birds; v. נְקִידָא.—2) *bite*, v. יְקוּרָא.

נְקִירָה f. (preced.) *picking, bite.* Toh. III, 8 נְקִירַת תרנגולים (Ar. נְקָרַת) traces of hens' pickings.

נְקִירְתָּא f. (preced. wds.; cmp. b. h. נִקְרָה) *cave, underground passage.* Ab. Zar. 10ᵇ נְקַרְתָּא.—*Pl.* נְקִירָתָא. Targ. Job XXX, 6 (h. text חֹרֵי).—Ber. 54ᵇ top (Ms. M. מחילתא); Yalk. Num. 764.

נְקִישׁ, v. נְקַשׁ.

נְקִישָׁא, v. נְקָשָׁא.

נִקְלְבָּס, v. sub נִיק׳.

נַקְלָה, v. אוּנְקְלִי II.

נקלוגוס, v. נִיקוֹלוֹגוֹס.

נִקְלְוָּס, v. sub נִיק׳.

נַקְלְמִין m. pl. ch. = next w. Targ. Esth. I, 6.

נַקְלִיטִין m. pl. (קָלַט, cmp. נָדִיר fr. נדר) [*retirement*] *the poles of the bedstead, connected by a cross-pole* over which a net is spread so as to form a slanting cover, *curtain-frame.* Kel. XII, 2. Ib. XVIII, 3 נַקְלִיטֵי המטה; Succ. I, 3; Y. ib. 52ᵇ bot. נִיקְלִיטֵי. Bab. ib. 10ᵇ נ׳ שנים וכ׳ *naḳliṭin* means a frame with two poles (one on each side), *ḳinofoth*, one with four poles; a. fr.

נָקַם (b. h.; cmp. קום) 1) *to take revenge.* Sabb. 63ª נוֹקֵם ונוטר כנחש revengeful and grudge-bearing like a serpent. Yoma 23ª; a. fr.—2) *to be hostile, do evil.* Midr. Till. to Ps. CXLIX, 7 מה שנָּקְמוּ, v. נְקָמָה.

נְקַם ch. same. Targ. Lev. XIX, 18.

Ithpa. אִתְנַקַּם *to be punished.* Targ. Y. II Ex. XXI, 20.

נִקְמָא, נִקְמְתָא f. (preced.) *revenge; judgment.* Targ. Y. I Deut. XXXII, 43 (ed. Amst. נִקְמָא); Y. II (ed. Amst. נִקְמְתָא). Targ. Y. II ib. 35.

נְקָמָה f. h. (b. h.) same. Ber. 33ª (ref. to Ps. XCIV, 1) גדולה נ׳ וכ׳ divine judgment is something great, for it is placed between two divine names. Ex. R. s. 20 עד שאנקום נִקְמָתָן וכ׳ until I execute judgment for the slaughter of the Ephraimites. Midr. Till. to Ps. CXLIX, 7 איזו היא נ׳ ... מה שנקמו לישראל what revenge is meant here? ... the revenge for the evil they did to Israel. Ib. ולא נִקְמַת אדם nor will it be a revenge executed by man; a. fr.—*Pl.* נְקָמוֹת. Ib. כל הנ׳ האילו יש וכ׳ all these retaliations are reserved with the Lord for the wicked; a. e.—[Ber. l. c. שתי נ׳

הללו וכ׳ why these two judgments (*n'kamah* in the plural)? v., however, הוֹפָעָה.]

נַקְמָן m. (preced.) *revengeful.* Gen. R. s. 99, end כשם שנחש נ׳ וכ׳ as the serpent is revengeful, so was Samson.

נִקְמְתָא, v. נִקְמָא.

נקסטן, v. פִּיקְסִינוֹן.

נֶקַע m. (cmp. נָקִיק) *cleft, cavity, ravine.* Kil. V, 4. Tosef. Erub. III (II), 3; a. e.—*Pl.* נְקָעִים. B. Bath. VII, 1. Ib. 103ᵃ; Kidd. 61ᵃ נ׳ מלאים מים ravines filled with water; v. נְאַגְנָא.—Y. Sabb. VII, 10ᵃ top נ׳ שתחת הזיתים cavities under olive trees; cmp. אוּגְיָא.

נָקַף I (b. h.; cmp. נגף) *to bring in close contact; to knock, strike against, wound.* Hull. 7ᵇ אין אדם נוֹקֵף וכ׳ no one on earth bruises his finger, unless it is decreed &c. Ber. 7ᵇ; Meg. 6ᵇ מי שלבו נוֹקְפוֹ he whom his heart smites (who has no clear conscience). Nidd. 3ᵇ, a. e. לבו נוקפו ופורש he may have scruples and separate himself entirely from his wife. Midr. Till. to Ps. IX, v. נְקַף.—Maas. Sh. V, 15; Sot. IX, 10 הנוֹקְפִים those who knocked the sacrifices on their heads; expl. ib. 48ᵃ; Y. ib. IX, 24ᵃ bot.—Part. pass. נָקוּף; f. נְקוּפָה; *pl.* נְקוּפִים, נְקוּפִין; נְקוּפוֹת. Tosef. Hull. III, 24 ביצים נ׳ לקערה eggs cracked open into a dish (Hull. 64ᵃ טרופות).

Hif. הִקִּיף, הִנְקִיף 1) *to cause a knocking together.* Sot. 22ᵇ (expl. נקפי) המַנְקִיף את רגליו he who knocks his feet against each other (by his mincing walk; Rashi: who causes his feet to strike against objects on the road); cmp. נָקַשׁ.—2) *to bring closely together.* Bekh. VII, 6 שמַקִּיף, v. נָקַשׁ. Nidd. X, 7 ומַקֶּפֶת and brings the vessel which contains the Hallah near the dough; T'bul Yom IV, 3, sq. Bets. IV, 5 ואין מַקִּיפִין שתי וכ׳ and you must not move two wine vessels together to put upon them &c.—Esp. (ritual law, in examining an organic defect found in a slaughtered animal) *to create a defect similar and near to the one found,* in order to ascertain whether the latter was not the result of an accident after slaughtering; in gen. *to compare.* Hull. 50ᵃ מַקִּיפִים בבני מעים we may compare defects in entrails in which was found a perforation the origin of which is doubtful by making a hole next to it. Ib. מקיפין בקנה we may compare defects in windpipes; a. fr.—Kidd. 40ᵃ אין מקיפין בחילול השם no comparing (balancing of sins against good deeds) is granted when the Name of God is profaned; (oth. interpret., v. נָקַף II).—*Part. pass.* מוּקָּף *brought near.* Erub. 30ᵇ; Hull. 7ᵃ; a. fr. לתרום שלא מן המ׳ to take T'rumah out of a mass which is not in close neighborhood of those products which are to be redeemed; Bicc. II, 5; Ter. IV, 3; a. e.

נְקַף ch. same, *to strike, knock, push down.* Targ. Ps. CXL, 5. Targ. O. Ex. XXXIV, 20 ותִיקְפֵיה ed. Berl. (oth. ed., a. Y. ותְנַקֵּף; ed. Vien. ותַנְקֵף *Af.*; h. text וערפתו). Targ. Deut. XXI, 4 (O. ed. Berl. ויַקְ׳, *Af.*); a. e.—Part. pass. נְקִיף; f. נְקִיפָא. Ib. 6 (O. ed. Vien. נְקַפְתָּא).—Erub. 53ᵇ (enigmatic speech) עלת נקפת בכד ידאון וכ׳ the ladle strikes against the jug, shall the eagles fly to their nests (the wine is gone, shall the students go home)?

Pa. נַקֵּף same. Targ. Ps. CXL, 12 (Ms. *Pe.*).—Part. pass. מְנַקַּף. Ber. 6ᵃ כרעי דמְנַקְּפֵי bruised feet; Yoma 53ᵃ, v. נְגַף.

Af. אַקֵּף, אַנְקֵף 1) same; v. supra.—2) *to knock the feet against each other, to mince* (v. preced. *Hif.*). Targ. Is. III, 16 (h. text טפף).—2) *to compare defects* (v. preced. *Hif.*). Hull. 50ᵃ אַקְפִינְהוּ ולא וכ׳ they compared them, and they did not look alike.

Ithpa. אִתְנַקַּף *to knock against, to stumble.* Targ. II Esth. IV, 13.—Yoma l. c. מִיתְנַקְּפִין Ar. ed. Koh., v. נְגַף.

נָקַף II (b. h.; cmp. קוּף a. נָקַב) *to circle; to bore.*—Part. pass. נָקוּף; f. נְקוּפָה. Gen. R. s. 100, v. נָקַב.

Hif. הִקִּיף 1) *to surround.* Erub. I, 8 (15ᵇ) והִקִּיפוּהָ (ב)כלי בהמה and they surrounded it (the camp) with utensils of travel (wagons, saddles &c.). Ib. 9 מַקִּיפִין שלשה וכ׳ you may surround the camp with three ropes &c. (for Sabbath purposes). Ib. 53ᵇ מצאתי שמקיפין אותה גנות וכ׳ I found that gardens and orchards surrounded the town (making it inaccessible); a. fr.—2) *to cause to go around.* Mekh. B'shall. s. 1 אַקִּיפֵם במדבר וכ׳ I shall make them go around in the desert forty years; ib. הריני מַקִּיפָן וכ׳. Snh. VIII, 1 עד שיַקִּיף וכ׳ until he has grown hair around &c., v. זָקָן.—3) *to cut all around,* esp. (with ref. to Lev. XIX, 27) *to cut around the corners of the hair of the head.* Naz. 57ᵇ אחד המַקִּיף ואחד הנִיקָּף he who cuts and he whose hair is cut are alike guilty; a. fr.—4) *to sell on terms* (v. הַקָּפָה), *to lend.* Ab. III, 16 החנוני מַקִּיף the shopkeeper allows credit (the Lord is long-suffering). B. Kam. 79ᵃ top גנב והק׳ if he stole an animal and sold it on credit (and has received no pay); a. fr.—Kidd. 40ᵃ אין מַקִּיפִין וכ׳ no loan on time is granted (no chance for repentance is allowed), when the Name of the Lord is profaned; (oth. interpret., v. נָקַף I).

Hof. הוּקַּף *to be surrounded.* Arakh. 33ᵇ; Meg. 3ᵇ שהו׳ ולבסוף וכ׳ it was surrounded (a fort was built) and then settled; a. fr.—Part. מוּקָּף; f. מוּקֶּפֶת; *pl.* מוּקָּפִין; מוּקָּפוֹת. Ib. I, 1 מו׳ חומה וכ׳ fortified since the days of Joshua. Ib. 2ᵇ. Ib. 4ᵇ. Gen. R. s. 39, v. פְּרִיל; a. fr.—Mekh. B'shall., s. 1 מוקפות *semicircular.*

Nif. נִיקַּף *to have one's hair cut all around.* Naz. l. c., v. supra. Ib. כל היכא דנ׳ מיחייב וכ׳ whenever he who has his hair cut &c. is punishable (is not a minor or a woman), the cutter is punishable; a. e.

Pi. נִיקֵּף 1) *to collect fruit which remained in the crown of the tree* (v. נִיקּוּף II), *to glean olives* (corresp. to פֵּאֵר, Deut. XXIV, 20). Gitt. V, 8 עני המְנַקֵּף ... מה שתחתיו גזל when the poor man does the gleaning on the top of the olive tree, what falls down under him is forbidden to any other person; Y. ed. המנ׳ בראש הזית גזל (corr. acc.; v. ib. 47ᶜ top).—2) *to cut all around, trim.* B. Kam. 119ᵇ; Tosef. ib. XI, 18 מְנַקְּפֵי הורגין those who trim shrubs. Ib. השוכר ... לנַקֵּף עמו וכ׳ if one hires a laborer to help him trim &c.

נְקַף ch. same.—*Af.* אַקֵּף as preced. *Hif.* Targ. Jud. XI, 18.—Targ. Lev. XIX, 27; a. fr. Part. pass. מְקַּף (= h. מוּקָּף, v. preced. *Hof.*). Ib. XXV, 31. Targ. Is. XXIX, 2; a. fr.—Snh. 69ᵃ מקמיה דלַקִּיף זקן before his hair around the genitals is grown.—Y. Ber. IX, 14ᵇ bot., a. e. (expl. נקפי) אַקִּיף לי וכ׳ (the Pharisee that says,) Lend me that I may do a certain pious work; a. fr.

נֶקֶף m. (נָקַף I) 1) *bruise.—Pl.* נְקָפִים. Sabb. 62^b (expl. נִקְפָּה, Is. III, 24); Yalk. Is. 264.—2) *beating* (of the heart), *scruples, doubt.* Midr. Till. to Ps. IX, 2 שלא יהא בלבי נ׳ that there be no struggle in my heart (ed. Bub., a. Yalk. ib. 642: שלא יהא לבי טוֹקֵף, v. נָקַף I).

נִקְפְּתָא, v. נָקַף I.

נַקְפִּי, נַק׳ m. (נקף) *knocker,* or *borrower,* an opprobrious epithet for a sort of sanctimonious Pharisees. Sot. 22^b, v. נָקַף I; Y. ib. V, 20^c bot.; Y. Ber. IX, 14^b bot., v. נָקַף II.

נִקְצָא, נִק׳ m. (קצץ) *piece, splinter.* Targ. Prov. XXVI, 8 נ׳ דטסא ed. (ed. Lag. a. oth. נִיסקא, transp. of נִיקסא, cmp. קִיסָא) a splinter of foil (*mica*; h. text צרור אבן).

נָקַר I (b. h.; cmp. קָרַר I) 1) *to dig, chisel,* esp. *to whet a millstone.* M. Kat. 10^a נוֹקְרִין ריחים וכ׳ you may roughen a millstone during the festive week. Sot. 46^b וְלִנְקוֹר, v. infra.—2) *to bore, perforate; to put out.* Sabb. 130^a יִקְּרוּ את מוחו they shall perforate (or put out) his brain. Sot. I, 8 נָקְרוּ פלשתים וכ׳ (or נִקְּרוּ) the Philistines put out his eyes; a. e.—3) (of birds, mice, serpents &c.) *to pick, gnaw at.* Tosef. Ter. VII, 17. Y. ib. III, beg. 42^a בשראו אותו נוֹקֵר when they saw the bird pick; a. fr.—[Y. Yeb. X, 11^a top לבי נוקריני, v. נָקַד I.]—Part. pass. נָקוּר; *pl.* נְקוּרִים, נְקוּרִין. Y. Ter. l. c. Tosef. l. c. שמא נ׳ היו may be they were already picked at (by birds); a. e.

Pi. נִיקֵּר same. M. Kat. l. c. מְנַקֵּר ריחים, v. supra. Sot. IX, 5 ולְנַקֵּר שם וכ׳ (ib. 46^b ולנקור) and to chisel stones there.—Pes. 8^b תרנגולתך מְנַקֶּרֶת וכ׳ (not מלקר) thy hen shall be picking in the dunghill &c. Toh. IV, 3 היו מְנַקְּרִין בהן וכ׳ if they have been picking them (the pieces of carrion) on the ground; a. e.

Nif. נִיקַּר *to be picked at.* Y. Ter. VIII, 45^c top תאנים ... שֶׁנִּיקְּרוּ figs or grapes which have been picked at.

נְקַר ch. same. Targ. Y. Num. XXI, 35. Targ. I Sam. XI, 2 מִיקַּר (ed. Wil. מִיקַּר); a. e.—Yalk. Prov. 963 דין נָקֵיר וכ׳ the one (the raven) picks the eye out, and the other (the eagle) eats it; Midr. Sam. ch. VII נָאקַר.—Pesik. B'shall., p. 93^b one worm דעתידא דִּנְקְרָא וכ׳ which shall bite me behind the ear.—Y. Sabb. XII, beg. 13^c הרין דנ׳ כיפין וכ׳ he who chisels stones, columns, millstones &c.; a. e.—Part. pass. נְקִיר. Kidd. 80^b אם איתא דנ׳ וכ׳ if it had been picked at (by the hens after drinking of a red liquid), it would have been noticeable.

Pa. נַקַּר same. Y. Ter. VIII, 45^c top חוה מְנַקְּרָא בתאיניא a serpent had been biting at figs.—M. Kat. 10^a דקא מְנַקַּר ריחיא (Ms. M. נְקַר) whetted millstones &c.

נָקַר II (interch. with נָקַד; cmp. נָקָה) *to be clean.* [Sifra Aḥăré, Par. 9, ch. XIII שלא תִנְקוֹר 'Rabad', be not *foppish* in dress in order to attract the admiration of women; v., however, נָחַשׁ.]

Pi. נִקֵּר *to keep clean.* Ḥull. 41^b הרוצה לְנַקֵּר וכ׳ (Ar. לְנַקֵּד) he who wishes to keep his court clean.

Hif. הִנְקִיר *to cleanse.* Sot. 11^b מַנְקִיר, v. נָקָה.

נְקַר ch. same; *Ithpa.* אִתְנַקַּר, *Ithpe.* אִתְנְקִיר, אִת׳ *to be cleansed.* Targ. Ez. XVI, 4 ed. Lag. לְאִתְנַקָּרָא (Var. לְאִתְנְקָרָא; ed. Wil. לאתנקאה; h. text למשעי).—B. Mets. 108^b בעינא דתִּתְנְקַר ארעאי (Ar. דתִתְנְקִיר) I desire that my field be clear (of stubble).

נֶקֶר m. (נָקַר I) *bite, trace of a bite.* Tosef. Ter. VII, 16 נ׳ בתאינה וכ׳ if there was a bite to be seen in a fig, and it shrivelled (v. גְּרוֹגֶרֶת,—which is an indication that it was not a serpent's bite). Y. ib. VIII, 46^a top מקום הנ׳ אכלו they (the birds) ate from a spot which had been bitten at (by a serpent); a. e.—V. נִיקּוּר.

נִקְרָא, נִק׳ m. (נְקַר I) 1) *cleft.—Pl.* נִקְרַיָּא. Targ. Y. I Num. XXIV, 21 (Y. II כבקרית, read: בִּנְקְרָתָא, v. נְקִירְתָּא).—2) *rag, lint.* Sabb. 134^b יהאי נ׳ מסי Ms. O. a. Ar. (ed. הני כתיתין מסו) a compress of lint has a healing effect (and is not merely a protection).—3) *pickings, worms which hens pick.* Ab. Zar. 28^a נ׳ מקילקלתא (Ms. M. נִיקְרֵי *pl.*) worms from a dunghill.

נְקָרָה f. (נָקַר I) 1) *offal at chiselling, stone-dust.* Ḥull. 88^b נְקָרַת פסולין dust of chiselled millstones.—2) *bite.* Toh. III, 8 Ar., v. נְקִירָה.

נקריס, v. נָקוּהּ.

נַקְרָן, נוֹקְרָן m. (נָקַר I) [*picker,*] *carper, fault-finder.—Pl.* נַקְרָנִים, נַקְרָנִין, נו׳. Y. Snh. X, 28^d bot.; Num. R. s. 20, end; Sifré Num. 131 והוקרנים (some ed. התיקר׳; corr. acc.); Yalk. ib. 771 נקדנין (some ed. נקרבין; corr. acc.).—V. נַקְדָּן.

נַקְרְתָּא, v. נְקִירְתָּא.

נָקַשׁ (v. קִשְׁקֵשׁ I) *to strike against; to touch closely.* Bekh. VII, 6 (45^a) (expl. עיקל וכ׳) כל שמקיף ... נוֹקְשׁוֹת (Mish. ed. נשקות) he whose legs do not touch each other when he puts his feet together. Meg. 12^b, v. infra.

Hif. הִקִּישׁ 1) *to cause striking against; to knock.* Bekh. l. c. (44^b) המַקִּישׁ בקרסוליו וכ׳ he who knocks his ankle-bones against each other (in walking, because his legs are bent outward), or rubs his legs against each other (his feet being bent outward). Midr. Sam. ch. IX מַקֶּשֶׁת ברגליה ומקשת בקרניה she knocks (creates a loud sound) with her feet and with her horns. Zab. IV, 1, sq. הי׳ על וכ׳ if he knocked against &c. Meg. 12^b (play on בן קיש, Esth. II, 5) שהי׳ על וכ׳ (Ms. M. שֶׁנָּקַשׁ) he (Mordecai) knocked at the gates of mercy &c.; a. fr.—Esp. (cmp. נָבָה, נָגַן) *to strike an instrument, play.* Tam. VII, 3. Gen. R. s. 18 (play on הפעם, Gen. II, 23) עתידה לְהַקִּישׁ עלי כזוג ('Rashi': לקשקש) she is destined to be loud against me like a bell. Pesik. R. s. 31; Midr. Till. to Ps. CXXXVII אני מבקש שתעמדו ותַקִּישׁוּ ... כדרך שהייתם מַקִּישִׁין וכ׳ I desire that you play on the cithern before me and the idol, as you played before your God. Ib. אנו עומדים לְהַקִּישׁ וכ׳ shall we stand playing before this dwarf (Nebuchadnezzar) and this idol? Ib. to Ps. XCII, end (play on יקשן, Gen. XXV, 2) שהיו מקישין בתוף לעכו״ם they struck the timbrel before idols; Yalk. Chr. 1073; Gen. R. s. 61 מקשין בית׳ (corr. acc.).—2) (cmp. נָקַף) *to bring under the same category by juxtaposition, to compare.* Kidd. 5^a, a. fr. (ref. to ויצאה a. והיתה in the same verse, Deut. XXIV, 2) מקיש הויה ליציאה, v. הֲוָיָה. Snh. 60^b (ref. to Ex. XXII, 19 a. XXXIV, 14) זביחה בכלל ... לְהַקִּישׁ אליה slaughtering for the idol would have been included in worshipping, and why is it singled out? To compare all other idolatrous functions with it: as slaughtering is a function performed inside &c. Zeb. 5b הִקִּישׁוֹ הכתוב וכ׳ the text (Lev. VII, 37) places it side by side with peace offerings; a. fr.

Hof. הוּקַשׁ *to be placed side by side, to be compared.* Ker. 3a (ref. to Num. XV, 29, sq.) הוּקְשָׁה כל התורה וכ׳ all the laws of the Torah are here placed on an equality with idolatry (as regards conditions of punishment). Ib. 2b הוּקְשׁוּ כל העריות כולן וכ׳ all laws concerning incest are put on an equality with &c. (Lev. XVIII, 29); a. fr.— Part. מוּקָשׁ. Gen. R. s. 35 (play on קשתי, Gen. IX, 13) דבר שהוא מ׳ לי something comparable with me (with the Divine Glory); Yalk. ib. 61; v. קִישּׁוּת II.

נְקַשׁ ch. same, *to strike against; to knock, drive in.* Targ. II Esth. VI, 10, sq. Targ. Jud. IV, 21 (ed. Wil. נקיש׳); a. e.—Snh. 25b אנא ידענא למִנְקַשׁ וכ׳ Ar. (ed. לְנַקּוּשֵׁי, *Pa.*; Rashi בְּנִקְשָׁא) I know better how to clap (at the pigeon-race). B. Kam. 52b איבעי ליה למיזל ומִינְקַשׁ עליה it was his duty to go and knock upon it (to try the soundness of the board). B. Mets. 59a (prov.) כִּמְשָׁלַם ... נָקֵישׁ ואזיל תיגרא when the barley is gone out of the pitcher, quarrel knocks and comes in; a. e.

Pa. נַקֵּשׁ same, v. supra.

Af. אַקֵּישׁ 1) same. Y. B. Bath. IV, end, 15c; Y. Gitt. III, end, 45b מַקְשִׁין על גרבא וכ׳ they knock at the vessel outside and know what is in it. Lev. R. s. 6 נסתיה .. ואַקְשֵׁיה לארעא he took the cane and knocked it against the floor; a. e.— 2) *to compare.* Targ. Job XXX, 19 (sec. Vers.).—Zeb. 5b מאי חזית דאַקְשַׁתְּ ... אַקְשָׁהּ לחטאת (ed. אַקֵּישׁ) why do you compare it with peace offerings? Compare it with sin offerings; Yalk. Lev. 470. Snh. 15a לְאַקּוּשֵׁי וכ׳ to place on an equal footing &c.; a. e.

Ithpe. אִתְנְקַשׁ *to be knocked together.* Targ. Koh. XII, 3 (of the trembling hands of the age-stricken; h. text ויזעו).

Ittaf. אִיתַּקַּשׁ *to be set side by side, be compared.* Pes. 61a (ref. to Ex. XII, 4) א׳ אוכלין למנויין those who partake of the Passover lamb are placed on an equal footing with those who are entered as shareholders, i. e. it must be slaughtered in behalf only of those entered and of such among them as are able to partake. Snh. 15a עבד א׳ לקרקעות a slave is classed with landed estate. Ib. 63a אִיתַּקּוּשֵׁי אִיתַּקּוּשׁ they (the bowing and the sacrificing to the idol) are legally alike; a. fr.

נִקְשָׁא m. (preced.) *knocking, rattling.* Snh. 25b בנ׳ תליא מילתא (Ar. בִּנְקִישָׁא) the winning of the race depends on the clapping, v. preced.—V. נִיקוּשָׁא.

נקשנון, נקשונין, v. פִּיקְסִינוֹן.

נֵר c. (b. h.; v. נור) *light.* Sabb. 22b; Men. 86b נר מערבי שנותנין וכ׳ the westernmost light (on the candle-stick in the Temple) into which as much oil was put as all the others together contained. Sabb. 22a מדליקין מנר לנר you may light one Ḥanuckah light on the other; a. v. fr.—Ber. 28b, a. e. נר ישראל light of Israel (great scholar).—Ex. R. s. 36 נֵרִי my (the Lord's) light (the Law), נֵרְךָ thy (man's) light (the soul); Lev. R. s. 31 נֵרִי (the Lord's light in the Temple).—*Pl.* נֵרוֹת. Tam. VI, 1 שני נ׳ מזרחיים (Talm. ed. שתי נ׳ מערביים, corr. acc.) the two easternmost lights. Ib. III, 9 (30b) שתי נ׳ מזרחיות (Talm ed. ב׳ נ׳ מערבית, read מערביות or מערביים); a. fr.

נָרָא m. (v. preced.) *violet* (color), *violet* (flower). Gitt. 19b בדקינן ליה במיא דנ׳ we examine the sheet with a violet-colored liquid (to bring out any faded writing). Ab. Zar. 28b אודרא דנ׳ Ar. (ed. אודרא דנדא; Ms. M. דטרא) violet-dyed wool. [R. Ḥan.: מיא דנ׳ decoction of the bark of the *pomegranate-tree*, Pers. nâr, Perl. Et. St., p. 37, sq.]

נַרְגָּא c. (transpos. of נַגְרָא, v. נַגָּרָא) *axe.* Targ. Y. Num. XXI, 35.—Ber. 54b שקל נ׳ בר וכ׳ Moses took an axe measuring ten cubits. Keth. 10b, v. דִּקְלָא. R. Hash. 13a שדא ביה נ׳ he swung an axe at it, i. e. disproved the opinion; Succ. 12a; Snh. 30b; Pes. 32b; a. e.—*Pl.* נַרְגִּין, נַרְגֵּי, נַרְגַּיָּא. Targ. II Esth. I, 2 (3). Targ. Job XLI, 21 (ed. Wil. נַרְ׳).—Yoma 37b; Bets. 33b קתתא דנ׳ וחציני (Ms. M. a. Ar. נגרי, v. Rabb. D. S. a. l. note) the helves of axes and adzes. Snh. 96b תלת .. נ׳ וכ׳ (not נרגא) three hundred mule loads of axes of iron that has power over iron (steel).

נֵרְגוֹל, v. נַרְגַּל.

נַרְגָּז, v. רְגַז.

נרגזא, Midr. Till. to Ps. LXXVIII, 45 ed. Bub. (oth. ed. נרגזין), read: בַּר גַּזָּא or בַּר גַּזִּין, v. גַּזָּא.

נַרְגִּילָא m. (Pers. nârgil, Perl. Et. St. p. 38) *cocoanut, cocoanut-palm* the bast of which is used for making ropes. Erub. 58a, v. נְבָרָא.

נֵרְגַל (b. h.) pr. n. *Nergal,* 1) a deity of the Cutheans (v. Schr. KAT², p. 282, sq.). Snh. 63b (quoting II Kings XVII, 30 נרגול), expl. תרנגול a cock; Y. Ab. Zar. III, 42d top ריגליה דיעקב וריגליה דיוסף וכ׳ Nergal has the meaning of *luck* in the sense in which the Scripture speaks of the luck of Jacob (Gen. XXX, 27 בגללך, for which לרגלי in verse 30) and the luck of Joseph (ib. XXXIX, 5 בגלל), v. רִגְלָא.—2) *N. Sarezzar,* one of the princes of Nebuchadnezzar. Targ. II Esth I, 2 (3).

נִרְגָּל, v. רְגַל.

נִרְגָּן, v. רְגַן.

נֵרְדְּ m. (b. h.) *Nard,* an aromatic herb, *Valerian.* Ker. 6a; Y. Yoma IV, 41d, v. שִׁיבּוֹלֶת.—B. Mets. 86a bot. ככריין דנ׳ וכ׳ talents' worth of N. [Cant. R. to I, 12 נרדי, expl. by R. M. סירחי my ill odor, v. next w.]

נִרְדָּא, נִר׳ ch. same, believed to smell badly. Targ. Cant. I, 12 (ed. Lag. a. oth. נירדא, corr. acc.).

נַרְדִּינוֹן m. (νάρδινον, sub. μῦρον) *nard-oil.* Cant. R. to IV, 14 (expl. נֵרְדְּ ib.).

נַרְדְּשִׁיר m. (Pers. a. Arab. *nard,* also *nardshir*) *Nardshir,* name of a game, *checkers.* Keth. 61b Ar. (ed. מרד׳).

נרווד, Neg. VII, 4 Ar. (ed. גרווד, ed. Dehr. נדויד) pr. n. pl., prob. a corrupt fragment of בְּרוּנְדִּיסִין *Brundisium*, v. בלדרסין.—[Ohol. VI, 1 Ar., v. נִדְבָּךְ.]

נָרוּס m. (naurûz, Koh. Ar. Compl. s. v.) *narus*, the Persian and Median *New-Year's Festival*, at the vernal equinox. Y. Ab. Zar. I, 39[c].

נָרוֹק, v. רָקַק.

נרמקי, Yeb. 102[b] top זוגי נ׳ Ar., misreading of רמוקי (ed. זוזי מוקי).

נרקום, נרקוס, v. next w.

נַרְקִיס, נַרְקָס m. (νάρκισσος) *narcissus*, prob. *White Daffodil*. Targ. Cant. II, 1 (some ed. ברקום, corr. acc.).—Ber. 43[b] נרקס דגנוניתא Ar. (ed. נרקום; Ms. M. נרכום) garden narcissus, דדברא wild n.

נָרָשׁ pr. n. pl. *Narash* (*Ners*), *Narse* in Babylonia. B. Mets. 93[b] גמלא דנ׳ the crossing of N. (v. גַּמְלָא). Nidd. 67[b]. Erub. 56[a]; Hull. 127[a], v. בִּירַאי. Yoma 81[b] בירי דנ׳ Beray near N.; a. e. (v. Berl. Beitr. z. Geogr., p. 54).—B. Kam. 115[a] bot. נַרְשָׁא.

נַרְשָׁאָה m. (preced.) *of Narash*. Hull. 127[a] נ׳ נשקיך וכ׳ if a Narashean kissed thee, count thy teeth. B. Kam. 115[a] נ׳ גנב וכ׳ a Narashean stole &c. Sabb. 60[a]; 140[a] אדא נ׳ Ada of N.; a. e.—*Pl.* נַרְשָׁאֵי. B. Mets. 68[a] חכירי נ׳ Narashean tenancies, i. e. the owner gives a field in pledge for a debt and takes it back in tenancy, v. מַשְׁכַּן.

נַרְתֵּק, נַרְתֵּיק m. (νάρθηξ) [*narthex*, a small umbelliferous plant with a hollow pithy stalk, which may be used as a receptacle; in gen.] *case*, *casket*. Y. Ber. V, 9[b] top נַרְתֵּיקוֹ של רופא a physician's medicine chest. Y. R. Hash. I, 57[b]. [Lam. R. to I, 9 נוורתוק Vers. in Ar. (corr. acc.), v. לַבְרָטוֹן.]—Y. Erub. I, 19[b] bot. (של קרן) נרתיקו the pithy hollow part of the horn, opp. זַכְרוּת. Gen. R. s. 6 גלגל חמה יש לו נ׳ the globe of the sun has a sheath; ib. הקב״ה מערטלו מנרתיקו (Ar. מנושתקו) the Lord will denude it of its sheath; Koh. R. to I, 5 (v. נַשְׁתֵּק); Ab. Zar. 3[b] bot., a. e.—[Y. Yoma IV, 41[d] top, v. נַשְׁתֵּק.]

נַרְתֵּקָא, נַרְתֵּיקָא ch. same. Targ. Ruth IV, 7 sq. נרתק יד *sleeve* (h. text נעל).—*Pl.* נַרְתֵּיקִין. Targ. Y. I Deut. XXV, 13 (weight-chests).

נרתיקות, Cant. R. to IV, 4 נ׳, read: נַרְתְּקוֹת, v. רָתַק.

נַרְתֵּק, נַרְתֵּקָא, v. נַרְתֵּיק, נַרְתֵּיקָא.

נָשָׁא, נָשׁ I m.=אֱנָשׁ, only in בַּר נ׳ *son of man, human being*. Targ. Job VII, 1; 20; a. fr.—Y. Dem. I, 22[a] top; a. v. fr.—*Pl.* בְּנֵי נָשׁ, נָשָׁא, also בְּנֵי נָשֵׁי. Targ. Ps. LXII, 10; a. fr.—Gen. R. s. 60. Y. Shek. V, end, 49[b]; a. fr.

נְשָׁא I f. (preced.) *woman*. Targ. Y. Deut. XXII, 5.—*Pl.* נְשִׁין, נְשַׁיָּא, נְשֵׁי. Targ. Ruth I, 4. Targ. Gen. VI, 2; a. fr.—Tam. 32[a] מחוזא דכוליה נ׳ a place inhabited by women only. Ber. 17[a] הני נשי מאי זכיין Ms. M. (ed. נשים) whereby can women acquire merits? M. Kat. 28[b] נ׳ דשכנציב the lamenting women of &c.; a. v. fr.—בֵּי נ׳ a) *the wife's family, father-in-law* &c.—b) *the paternal house after the father's death*. B. Bath. 12[b] אמצרא דבי נְשֵׁיה contiguous to the estate of his father-in-law (Rashi: of his deceased father). Sabb. 23[b]. Ib. 156[a] בי נשיה in the house of his deceased father (Ms. M. נשיאה, v. נַפְלָא). Yeb. 35[a] בי נְשֵׁיהוּ their (the women's) paternal home; a. e.

נָשָׁא II, נְשָׁא II *to forget*, v. נשי.

נָשָׁא III m. name of a *plant* the sap of which is used as a depilatory. B. Kam. 86[a] סָכוֹ נ׳ וכ׳ he smeared *nasha* over it so that the hair will not grow again. Macc. 20[b]. Naz. 40[a].—V. נֶשֶׁם.

נָשָׂא (b. h.; cmp. נָסָה) 1) *to lift up, carry*. Sot. 35[a] נ׳ ארון את נוֹשְׂאָיו the Ark carried its carriers. Ab. ch. VI נוֹשֵׂא בעול וכ׳ helps his brother to bear his yoke. Ber. III, 1 נוֹשְׂאֵי המטה, v. מִטָּה. Meg. 9[a] (one of the changes in translating the Bible into Greek) נוֹשֵׂא בני אדם a carrier of men (for חֲמֹר, Ex. IV, 20); a. v. fr.—Pesik. R. s. 6 אני מרומם ונושא את ראשם I will raise and elevate their head; v. infra.—נ׳ כפים, v. כַּף.—נ׳ פנים *to lift up the face, to respect, favor, spare, be partial*. Hag. 14[a] (expl. נשוא פנים, Is. III, 3) זה שנוֹשְׂאִין פ׳ לדורו בעבורו he for whose sake his generation is favored in heaven. Sabb. 13[b] שלא נ׳ פ׳ לתורה who spared him not for the sake of his scholarship. Yoma 87[a] שנָּשְׂאוּ לו פ׳ בעה״ז that indulgence was shown him (by the Lord) in this world. Num. R. s. 11 לא אֶשָּׂא פ׳ מפניך shall I not favor thee for thy own sake? Ib. כשם שהם נוֹשְׂאִין לי וכ׳ as they (the Israelites) honor me (by saying grace even after a scanty meal), so do I favor them; a. fr.—נ׳ נפש אל *to lift up the soul to, to long for*. Midr. Till. to Ps. XXV, 1 למה אתה נושא נפשך אלי why dost thou lift up thy soul to me (why dost thou depend on me)?; Yalk. ib. 701.—נ׳ קרבן *to offer up a sacrifice*. Ib. 702 אדם חוטא ונושא ק׳ if a man sinned, he offered &c.; Midr. Till. l. c. נושא ומביא ק׳ (corr. acc.)—Part. pass. נָשׂוּא, f. נְשׂוּאָה &c. Ib. עכשו ... הרי נפשנו נ׳ לךָ now that we have no sacrifices, our soul is lifted up to thee.—2) *to lift, remove*. Pesik. R. l. c. (ref. to the double meaning of נ׳, *to raise* a. *to remove*) לכו שְׂאוּ את ראשו go and remove (or lift up) his head; a. fr.—נ׳ עון *to forgive*. Y. Snh. X, beg., 27[c] (ref. to Ex. XXXIV, 7) נושא עונות אין וכ׳ the text does not say, 'removing iniquities', but 'removing iniquity', the Lord takes away (from the scales) one bond of man's sins, and the merits prevail &c.; Y. Peah I, 16[b] bot. (corr. acc.); Yalk. Ex. 400; v. שְׁטַר. Pesik. R. s. 45; a. e.—3) *to take*, esp. נ׳ ונתן *to take and give, to deal; to transact, argue*. Sabb. 31[a] נָשָׂאתָ ונתת באמונה hast thou (while on earth) been dealing honestly? B. Mets. 48[a] הנושא ונותן בדברים he who concludes a bargain verbally. Tanh. Sh'moth 18 כשם שנושאין ונותנין בהלכה וכ׳ as well as they debate on the law below, so do they above. Ib. שנושאין ונותנין בדין וכ׳ they argue in court, and the Lord argues with them; a. fr.—4) נ׳ אשה, or נ׳ *to take a wife into one's house, to marry*. Keth. II, 1 בתולה נְשָׂאתַנִי thou hast married me as a virgin; אלמנה נְשָׂאתִיךָ I married thee as a widow. Yeb. 37[b] לא יִשָּׂא אדם וכ׳ one may not marry in one country and go away &c. M. Kat. I, 7 אין נושאין נשים וכ׳ no marriages may take place during the festive week; a. v. fr.—*Part. pass.* נָשׂוּי (followed by accus.) *having married*; f. נְשׂוּאָה (followed by לְ) *being married to*; *pl.* נְשׂוּאִים, אֵין...;

נְשׂוּאוֹת. Yeb. III, 6 ואחד מ׳ נכריות one of them has married a stranger. Ib. ומתו הנ׳ את האחיות and those brothers who had married two sisters died. Ib. I, 2 (2^b) ... היתה נשואה לאחיו Y. ed. (Mish. ed. נשואת, corr. acc.; Bab. ed. נשואות) if his daughter or ... was married to &c.; a. fr.—Tosef. ib. VI, 5 נְשׂוּאֵי.

Nif. נִישָּׂא 1) *to be lifted up, removed* &c. Pesik. R. l. c. כבר .. שיִנָּשְׂאוּ את ראשם וכ׳ it had been decreed that their head should be lifted (v. supra): turn its meaning and elevate their head.—2) f. נִישֵּׂאת, נִישֵּׂית, נִשֵּׂ׳, נִישֵּׂאת *to be married.* Keth. I, 1 בתולה נ׳ וכ׳ a virgin's marriage takes place on the fourth day of the week. Ib. V, 2 הגיע .. ולא נִשְּׂאוּ if the time set for marriage expired and they were not taken in marriage. Yeb. II, 10 מותרות לִינָּשֵׂא להם they may marry them. Ib. 88^b הרי זו לא תִנָּשֵׂא ואם ניסת וכ׳ she must not marry again, and if she does &c.; Keth. 22^b; a. v. fr.

Hif. הִשִּׂיא 1) *to lift up, to announce by signals* (the New Moon). R. Hash. II, 2, a. e. מַשִּׂיאִין, v. מַשּׂוּאָה. Y. ib. II, 58^a top אין משיאין לילי זמנו we do not raise signals in the night of the regular New Moon (from the 29th to the 30th) &c.; a. fr.—Tosef. ib. II (I), 2 מַשִּׂיאִין את החודש ed. Zuck. (מסיא׳, משיא׳ על) we signalize the New Moon.—2) *to transfer.* Deut. R. s. 11 (ref. to ישא, Ps. LXXV, 5) יַשִּׂיא ברכה לאחרים he will bring blessing upon others.—3) *to move, remove, pass.* Bets. III, 7 מַשִּׂיאָהּ על גבי חברתה he may pass one knife over the other (to whet it). Tosef. Par. X (IX), 3 הִשִּׂיאוֹ לדבר אחר he diverted his mind towards another subject; Ab. Zar. II, 5. Y. ib. II, 41^c bot. היה לו לְהַשִּׂיאוֹ וכ׳, v. הַשִּׂיאָה.—4) *to transfer, transcribe, translate.* Tosef. Sot. VIII, 6 הִשִּׂיאוּ את הכתב וכ׳ they transcribed the inscription on the stones in seventy languages; Sot. 35^b; Y. ib. VII, 21^d bot.—5) *to give away in marriage; to cause to marry.* Keth. 111^b כל המַשִּׂיא בתו וכ׳ he who marries his daughter to a scholar. Ib. 67^b top מַשִּׂיאִין את היתומה וכ׳ we must first help the fatherless maiden to marry, and then the fatherless lad. Kidd. 29^a האב חייב .. ולְהַשִּׂיאוֹ אשה a father is bound to ..., and to provide a wife for him; a. fr.

Hithpa. הִתְנַשֵּׂא *to be raised; to exalt one's self, to boast.* Ab. Zar. 44^a, v. הֲלָם. Ber. 63^b לְהִתְנַשֵּׂא, v. נָבַל; a. e.

נְשָׂא ch. same, 1) *to lift up,* v. מְסֵי.—2) *to bring, offer.* Pesik. B'shall., p. 90^b, sq. אימיה נשא (Ms. O. נָסְבָה) his mother was bringing (the bread); v., however, נְסַח.—3) (neut. verb) *to move, stir.* Taan. 24^a; B. Mets. 85^b, v. נְשַׁב.

נָשַׁב (b. h.) *to blow.* Ber. 3^b בא .. ונוֹשֶׁבֶת בו (Ms. M. ומְנַשֶּׁבֶת *Pi.*) the north wind came and blew at him. Ab. III, 17 אפילו .. ונוֹשְׁבוֹת בו even if all the winds of the world came and blew at it (to uproot it) &c.; Taan. 20^a; a. fr.

Pi. נִשֵּׁב 1) same. Cant. R. to IV, 16. Yoma 21^b; a. fr.—2) *to cause to blow.* Keth. 111^b הקב״ה .. ומְנַשְּׁבָהּ עליה the Lord brings a wind ... and lets it pass over it (the wheat).

Hif. הִשִּׁיב same. מַשִּׁיב הרוח ומוריד הגשם 'who causes the wind to blow and the rain to descend', a clause inserted in *G'buroth* (v. גְּבוּרוֹת) during the winter season. Taan. 3^b אמר משיב הרוח אין וכ׳ if he said in his prayers, 'Who causes the wind to blow' only. Ib. 24^a אמר מ׳ הרוח וכ׳ as soon as he said, 'Who causes &c.', a wind arose; a. e.

נְשַׁב ch. same. Targ. Is. XL, 7; a. e.—Taan. 24^a, sq. וכ׳ זיקא (ed. once ונשא, v. נְשָׂא), v. preced.; B. Mets. 85^b ונַשְׁבָה זיקא (Ms. M. נשא; Ms. R. נַשְׁרָא; v. Rabb. D. S. a. l. note).

נִשְׁבָּא, נִשְׁ׳ m. ch. = next w. Targ. Prov. VI, 5 (some ed. נשבא, corr. acc.). Ib. XXII, 5 (some ed. *pl.*).—*Pl.* נִשְׁבֵּי, נִשְׁ׳. B. Mets. 85^b גדילנא נש׳ וכ׳ I plaited nets and caught deer; Keth. 103^b.

נִשְׁבִּים, נִשְׁבִּין, נִשְׁ׳ m. pl. (נשב; cmp. פַּח) *trap, snare, net.* Y. Sabb. XIII, 14^a bot.; Y. Bets. III, 62^a top מחוסר נ׳ that which must be caught by snares to be available. Sabb. 90^b מצניעין אותן לנ׳ they (the horse's hairs) are laid aside to be used for bird snares. B. Kam. VII, 7 (79^b) אין פורסין נשבים וכ׳ (Talm. ed. נישובים; Ms. M. נשבין; Rashi to Hull. 116^a quotes ניישבין) you must not spread gins for doves, unless &c.

נִשְׁדּוֹר, v. נִישְׁהוּר.

נָשָׁה, v. נשי.

נָשֶׁה m. (b. h.; preced.) *movable*; גִּיד הַנָּ׳, v. גִּיד.

נָשׁוּא* m. (נָשָׂא) *burden, affairs* (v. מַשּׂוּא). Num. R. s. 3 נשא נְשׂוּאָן של וכ׳ (some ed. נְשׂוּאִין, *pl.*) he administered the affairs of Israel.—V. נָשָׂא.

נִשּׂוּאִין, v. נִישּׂוּאִין.

נִשְׁוָאר, v. ניזוואר.

נִשְׁוָורָא m. (collect. noun; שאר, *Pa.* שַׁיֵּיר) *crumbs, leavings.* Pes. 111^b נ׳ בביתא וכ׳ to leave crumbs lie around in the house, is bad for poverty. Hull. 105^b (not ראה ...).

נשוותא, v. נְשִׁיאוּתָא.

נִשּׁוּפוֹת, v. נִישּׁוּבָה.

נְשַׁט (v. P. Sm. 2475) *to flay*, v. נְטַשׁ.

נָשָׁא, נָשָׁה, נשי (b. h.; cmp. נָשָׂא) 1) *to move, slip.* Hull. 91^a it is called *gid hannasheh* (v. גִּיד), שנ׳ ממקומו וכ׳ because it slipped from its place and went up; Yalk. Gen. 133. Ib. א״ר חנינא .. שנשא את מקומו R. H. said, ... because it left its place; Gen. R. s. 78 שנשה ממקומו; a. e.—2) *to discard, forget.* Ned. 50^b אבותינו אמרו נָשִׁינוּ טובה וכ׳ our fathers said (Lam. III, 17), we have forgotten the good times: we have not even seen them &c. Snh. 102^b (play on מנשה) שנשה יה he forgot Yah. Pesik. R. s. 45 (ref. to נְשׂוּי, Ps. XXXII, 1) אל תהי .. ש״ן נְשׁוּי read it not with Samekh (*n'suy*), but with Shin, *n'shuy*, whose sin is forgotten; a. e.—3) (with ב, cmp. נְסַק *Af.*) [*to raise, collect,*] *to have a claim against; to be a creditor of.* B. Mets. 75^b נוֹשֶׁה בחבירו מנה he who has a claim &c., to whom his neighbor owes money. Men. 85^b נושה בי וכ׳ I owe him &c.; a. e.

Hif. הִשִּׁיא 1) *to carry away; to incite, allure.* Gen. R. s. 19 (expl. השיאני, Gen. III, 13) הטעני he led me astray; v. גָּרָה.—2) *to make a loan to; to collect, distrain; to pledge.* Ib. (expl. השיאני) חייבני he made me a debtor (guilty, v. חוב). Cant. R. to II, 7 (ref. to אֶשָּׂא, Ps. XXV, 1) אַשִּׁיא כתיב it may be read *ashshi*, I pledge (my soul); שהיו מַשִּׁיאִין נפשם על וכ׳ they (the martyrs) pledged their lives for the sanctification &c. (v. Midr. Till. to Ps. XXV שנתמשכנו

וכ׳); ib. מדום ... משיאין they (the torturers) take their lives as pledges; Midr. Till. to Ps. XVI; Yalk. Ps. 667 משירוך (corr. acc.).—3) הִנְשִׁי to cause to forget. Snh. l. c. (play on מְנַשֶּׁה) שהנשי את ישראל לאביהם וכ׳ he made Israel forget their Father in heaven; Yalk. Kings 245 שהִנְשִׁיא.

נְשָׁא, נְשֵׁי ch. same, *to forget*. Targ. Deut. VIII, 19 (O. ed. Berl. *Ithpe.*).

Af. אַנְשִׁי 1) same. Targ. Ps. CXXXVII, 5; a. e.—Y. Dem. IV, 24ᵃ [read:] דילמא אַנְשִׁיתָה מתקנה perhaps thou didst forget to prepare it (by giving tithes)? Keth. 20ᵃ ואַנְשֵׁי חד וכ׳ and one of the witnesses has forgotten (that he knows of the case). Ḥull. 93ᵇ אַנְשְׁיוּהָ לדר׳ וכ׳ they have forgotten R. Judah's opinion. Gen. R. s. 77 דילמא אַנְשִׁינָן כלום perhaps we forgot something (left behind). Ib s. 78 אַנְשִׁית מאה I forgot one hundred (of the fables); a. fr.—2) *to cause to forget*. Targ. Lam. II, 6 (ed. Vien. ארנשי, corr. acc.); a. e.

Ithpe. אִתְנְשִׁי, אִינְּשֵׁי *to forget*. Targ. O. Deut. VIII, 19 (v. supra); a. e.—Y. Shek. VII, 50ᶜ bot. ואִינְשִׁיתָה and forgot to take it out; a. e.

נְשַׁח, v. נְסַח.

נִשְׁיָא m. ch.=h. נָשֶׁה. Targ. Gen. XXXII, 33 גידא דנ׳.—Ḥull. 97ᵇ גידא נ׳, v. גִּידָא.

נָשִׂיא m. (b. h.; נָשָׂא) 1) *prince, chief, ruler, officer*. Num. R. s. 1 לנ׳ שנכנס וכ׳ like unto a chief that entered a country. Ib. שלא מנה נ׳ לשבט וכ׳ he appointed no prince for the tribe of Levi. [Ib. נשיא שבטים, read נְשִׂיאֵי]. Hor. II, 6; a. v. fr.—*Pl.* נְשִׂיאִים. Num. R. s. 12 למה נזדרזו הנ׳ וכ׳ why were the princes so anxious to be the first &c.? Ib. s. 3; a. v. fr.—Esp. *Nasi*, the chief of the Great Sanhedrin in Jerusalem and of its successor in Palestinian places (v. אָב). Taan. II, 1. Pes. 66ᵃ מינוהו נ׳ עליהם they elected him as their Nasi; a. fr.—R. Judah the Nasi, v. רַבִּי.—*Pl.* as ab. Ḥag. II, 2; a. e.—2) *pl.* as ab. *clouds*. Kidd. 32ᵇ .. הק״בה מעלה נ׳ וכ׳ the Lord causes the wind to blow and brings up clouds and lets rain come down &c.

נְשִׂיאָה I נְשִׂיָּא, נְשִׂיָּה, נְסִ׳ ch. same, *prince, Nasi*. Ḥull. 98ᵃ a. fr. דבי נ׳ those of the Nasi's (R. Judah's) house. Ib. 124ᵃ חתניה דבי נ׳ the son-in-law of the Nasi's (the Resh Galutha's) house. Y. Ḥag. II, 77ᵈ bot. אין אנא מתעביד נ׳ if I am made Nasi; a. fr.—Y. Erub. VII, end, 24ᵈ ר׳ יודן נסייא.

נְשִׂיאָה II f. (נָשָׂא) 1) *lifting up*; נְשִׂיאַת כפים *pronouncing the priestly benediction*, v. נָשָׂא, a. פֶּה. Taan. 26ᵇ; a. fr.—2) *carrying, loading*. Ex. R. s. 4, v. עֲמִיסָה. Gen. R. s. 89 (ref. to Ps. LXXII, 3) נשאו הרים נְשִׂיאָתָן וכ׳ when the mountains bear their load (of fruits), there is peace for the people.—3) נְשִׂיאַת ראש *taking the sum, census*. Num. R. s. 6 (ref. to Num. IV, 2, sq.) למה הקדים ... לנ׳ ר׳ why does the Biblical text give Kehath the first place in taking the census?; v. next w.

נְשִׂיאוּת f. (נָשָׂא, v. preced.) 1) *lifting, carrying*. Num. R. s. 6 נאמר בהן נ׳ ראש the expression 'lifting up the head' (Num. IV, 1; 21; v. preced.) is used in connection with them. Ib. נ׳ ראש של בני קהת .. בנ׳ הארון the taking the census of the sons of Kehath (v. preced.) is not made dependent on their genealogical descent but on their office of carrying the Ark. Ib. s. 16 (ref. to Ps. CVI, 26, a. Num. XIV, 1) נ׳ יד כנגד נ׳ קול lifting up the hand (for oath) against lifting up the voice (for murmuring).—נ׳ עון *carrying sin, responsibility*. Tosef. Shebu. III, 4 (ref. to Lev. V, 1) תלה הכתוב נ׳ ע׳ וכ׳ the text makes the responsibility dependent on the telling. Y. Ter. I, 40ᶜ bot. (ref. to Num. XVIII, 32) את שהוא בנ׳ ע׳ וכ׳ only he who is responsible can separate T'rumah; ib. II, end, 41ᵈ ממה שהוא בנ׳ ע׳ וכ׳ from the fact that he is made responsible, you learn that his act is valid. Y. Shebu. I, 33ᵃ bot.; a. e.—2) (denom. of נָשִׂיא) *elevation to office, dignity*. Num. R. s. 4 (ref. to Num. IV, 2) אינו אומר פקוד ... לשון נ׳ the text does not read *p'ḳod*, but *naso* .., which expresses elevation; קבלו נ׳ מתוך וכ׳ they were given a superiority over the other sons of Levi.—Esp. *the office of the Nasi*. Keth. 103ᵇ נהוג נְשִׂיאוּתְךָ וכ׳, v. הָמִים. Sabb. 15ᵃ נהגו נְשִׂיאוּתָן וכ׳ occupied their office &c.; a. e.

נְשִׂיאוּתָא, נְשִׂיּוּתָא, נְסִ׳ ch. same, *the office of the Nasi, the house of the Nasi*. Y. Pes. VI, 33ᵃ bot. דשרון גרמון מן נ׳ וכ׳ who resigned from the Nasiate and appointed him (Hillel) &c.; Y. Kil. IX, 32ᵇ מנשיאותיה (corr. acc.) Y. Sabb. XII, 93ᶜ bot. אתחתנון בנ׳ they married into the Nasi family. Y. Peah III, 21ᵃ bot. Y. Kil. IX, 32ᵃ bot. ביתא דנְשִׂיּוּתָה הוא משועבד הוא לנשיותה it is the Nasi's official residence, and is pledged to those who occupy the office (and the widow must leave); Y. Keth. XII, 35ᵃ top נשוותא (corr. acc.); Gen. R. s. 100. Y. Ab. Zar. III, 42ᶜ אילין דנְשִׂיּוּתָא those of the family of the Nasi. Y. Sot. IX, end, 24ᶜ ניסיותיה (corr. acc.), v. הָתַן.

נְשִׂיָּא, v. נְשִׂיאָה.

נְשַׁיָּא, pl. of נְשָׁא I.

נְשִׂיּוּתָא, v. נְשִׂיאוּתָא.

נְשִׁיכָה f. (נָשַׁךְ) *biting, bite*. Mekh. Mishp., N'zikin, s. 12; Y. B. Kam. I, beg. 2ᵃ. Bab. ib. 2ᵇ נ׳ תולדה דשן היא is not biting a species of damage by the tooth? Ab. II, 10 נְשִׁיכָתָן נְשִׁיכַת וכ׳ their (the scholars') bite is the bite of a fox; a. e.—[Y. Ter. VI, end, 44ᵇ נשיכת פיאה, read נשירת, v. נְשִׁירָה.]

נְשִׁילָה f. (נָשַׁל) *falling off, chopping off; dropping*. Y. Macc. II, beg. 31ᶜ מה נ׳ שנ׳ להלן נשירה וכ׳ as the verb *nashal* there (Deut. XXVIII, 40) means dropping, so here it means (ib. XIX, 5) the slipping (of the iron from the helve). Ib. מה נ׳ שנ׳ להלן מכה וכ׳ as well as *nashal* there (Deut. VII, 1) means striking (diminishing), so here it means (Deut. XIX, 5) striking (the iron will cause a chip to fly off the wood). Koh. R. to IX, 12 בנְשִׁילַת אברים they died from decaying limbs; a. e.

נְשִׁימָה f. (נָשַׁם) *breath*. Meg. 16ᵇ צריך למימרינהו בנ׳ אחת you must recite them (the names of the sons of

Haman) in one breath; (Y. ib. III, 74^b bot. בנפיחה). Gen. R. s. 14, end (ref. to כל הנשמה, Ps. CL, 6) על כל נ׳ וכ׳ שאדם נושם וכ׳ for every breath that one takes one must praise &c.; Deut. R. s. 2, end.—[Tanh. R'eh 9, v. next w.]

נְשִׁיפָה f. (נָשַׁף) *blowing.* Tanh., ed. Bub., R'eh 3 מתו בנ׳ אחת they died from one current of wind; Tanh. ib. 9 בנשימה (corr. acc.).

נְשִׁיק, v. נָשַׁק.

נְשִׁיקָה, v. נָשַׁק.

נְשִׁיקָה f. (b. h.; נָשַׁק) 1) *kissing, kiss.* Gen. R. s. 70; Ex. R. s. 5, a. e. נ׳ של גדולה the kiss of homage; נ׳ של פרקים the kiss of meeting again; נ׳ של פרישות the kiss of parting; נ׳ של קריבות the kissing of relations. Deut. R. s. 11, end ונטל .. בִּנְשִׁיקַת פה and took his (Moses') soul with a kiss of the mouth. B. Bath. 17^a מרים נמי בנ׳ מתה Miriam, likewise, died with a (divine) kiss (without agony); M. Kat. 28^a. Ber. 8^a נ׳ דמיא וכ׳ death without agony is like taking &c., v. פִּירְנָא II; a. fr.—*Pl.* נְשִׁיקוֹת. Ex. R. l. c. Cant. R. to I, 2 מה״ש אמרוהו יתן לנו מנ׳ וכ׳ the ministering angels said the verse, 'May he give us of those kisses which he gave to his sons' (at Mount Sinai). Ib. בסיני נאמרה יוציא לנו נ׳ מתוך פיהו at Mount Sinai the verse was said (by the Israelites), 'May he let kisses go forth to us out of his mouth'; a. e.—2) *contact of sexual membra.* Yeb. 55^b.

נְשִׁיקוּת f. (preced.) *attachment, love.* Cant. R. to I, 2 יוציא לי קול נ׳ וכ׳ may He issue forth unto me the voice of attachment.

נְשִׁיקְיָא pr. n. pl. (or district) *N'shikya* in Babylonia. Sabb. 121^a Abin נ׳ דמן (Ms. M. מִנְּשִׁיקְאָה?) of N.

נְשִׁיקְתָא, constr. נְשִׁיקַת ch.=h. נְשִׁיקָה. Targ. Y. I Deut. XXXIV, 5.

נְשִׁירָה f. (נָשַׁר) *falling off, dropping* (of fruits). Y. Macc. II, beg. 31^c, v. נְשִׁילָה. Y. Peah II, 20^a bot. פרט בִּנְשִׁירָתוֹ קדש the dropping grapes are dedicated (to charity, cease to be private property) at the moment of dropping (before they reach the ground). Ib. לקט בנשירתו וכ׳ if one intercepts the grapes in falling &c.; Y. Ter. VI, end, 44^b. Ib. במשיכת פיאה וכ׳, read: בִּנְשִׁירַת פרט it refers to grapes intercepted in falling. Tem. 25^a אמר על הלקט עם נשירת רובו וכ׳ if he said concerning gleanings, As soon as the larger portion of them drops (before they reach the ground) they shall be free to all (הֶפְקֵר); a. e.

נְשִׁירְתָא f. (v. נְשַׁר II) *birds of prey.* Midr. Till. to Ps. LXXVIII, 45 (expl. ערוב ib.) נ׳ (some ed. נַשְׁרִיתָא; ed. Bub. נעוריתא, corr. acc.; Yalk. Ps. 820 פוריתה).

נְשִׁיתָא, v. נְשִׁיאוּתָא.

נָשַׁךְ (b. h.; cmp. נשק) 1) *to bite.* Gen. R. s. 74, beg. שארץ נוֹשְׁכִין ואוכלין וכ׳ they do not bite off and eat, but out &c.; Pesik. Par., p. 34^a; Koh. R. to VII, 23. Pirké d'R. El. ch. XXXVII אל תהי קורא וישקהו אלא וַיִּשָּׁכֵהוּ read not, 'and he kissed him' (Gen. XXXIII, 4) but, 'and he bit him.' Tosef. B. Kam. I, 5 אינה מועדת ... לִישּׁוֹךְ is not considered as forewarned (v. מוּעָד) as regards.... biting; a. fr.—Part. pass. נָשׁוּךְ, f. נְשׁוּכָה &c. Num. R. s. 20 רופא ... בלשונו נָשׁוּךְ נחש a physician that comes to heal with his tongue (charm) one bitten by a serpent. Ter. VIII, 6 נְשׁוּכַת הנחש וכ׳ any food showing traces of being bitten at by a serpent is forbidden &c.; a. fr.—Trnsf. *to adhere to, be affixed.* Pes. 48^b ככרות .. שֶׁנְּשׁוּכוֹת זו מזו Babylonian loaves which stick to one another; T'bul Yom I, 1 נשוכות זו בזו; Hall. II, 4 עד שישׁוכו (*Nif.*) until the pieces of dough have grown together in rising, contrad. to נגע. Sabb. 17^a הנשוכות clusters of grapes which stick together (and cannot be separated without squeezing some grapes open); a. fr.—Part. pass. as ab. Y. Hall. I, 57^b בנ׳ if refers to pieces of dough sticking together, contrad. to בלול kneaded. Ib. III, 59^c top עיסה הנ׳ dough made one lump by sticking; נ׳ מאליו sticking together of itself (by rising), opp. הִשִּׁיכוֹ בידיו he pasted it together with his hand. Ib. 58^b bot., sq. חנ׳ תורה the liability to T'rumah, Hallah &c. of joined lumps of dough is Biblical law. Y. Kil. IX, end, 32^d אין אסור אלא נ׳ בלבד the combination of heterogeneous materials (כִּלְאַיִם) is forbidden only when they are interlaced. Ib. והוהן נו נ׳, v. נוּ.—2) (denom. of נֶשֶׁךְ) *to take interest.* B. Mets. V, 1; a. e.

Nif. נִישַּׁךְ same, *to bite.* Gen. R. s. 78 לִנָּשְׁכוֹ to bite him. Tanh. Vayishl. 4 וִינַּשְּׁכֶנּוּ and may bite him; a. e.—Part. pass. מְנוּשָּׁךְ. Tosef. B. Kam. III, 6 או מ׳ or he is found to have been bitten.

Hif. הִשִּׁיךְ 1) *to cause to bite.* Snh. IX, 1 ה׳ בו וכ׳ he brought the serpent near him to bite him, contrad. to שיסה to set on. Ib. 78^a; B. Kam. 23^b, v. נָכַשׁ. Y. Yeb. VIII, 9^b top [read:] מביא נמלין ומַשִּׁיכָן וקוצץ he gets ants and makes them bite (the open wound) and cuts their bodies off (and so the gap is filled), v. Bab. ib. 76^a.—Trnsf. *to paste or press together.* Y. Hall. III, 59^c top, v. supra. Ib. מביא ארבע רובעין ומַשִּׁיךְ he takes four lumps of dough which joined contain four fourths of a Kab and presses them together into one lump; a. e.—2) *to pay interest.* B. Mets. 70^b (ref. to Deut. XXIII, 21) מאי תשיך לאו תַשּׁוֹךְ לא תַשִּׁיךְ what is meant by *tashshikh?* Does it not mean thou mayest (or must) take interest? No, it means, thou mayest (or must) pay him interest.

נֶשֶׁךְ m. (b. h.; preced.) [*bite,* trnsf., cmp. חֲבוּלְיָא] *usury, interest.* B. Mets. V, 1 איזהו נ׳ המלוה וכ׳ what is *neshekh?* If one loans a Sela stipulating the debt at five Denars, contrad. to תַּרְבִּית. Ib. 60^b נ׳ איכא דקא נכיה וכ׳ in this case it is *neshekh*, for he bites (injures the debtor) by receiving what he had not given him; a. fr.

נַשְׁכָנִית f. (preced.) *an animal wont to bite, biter.* Tosef. B. Bath. IV, 6; B. Mets. 80^a.

נָשַׁל (b. h.; cmp. שָׁלָה) 1) *to strike off, chip.* Tosef. Macc. II, 6 נ׳ הברזל מן העץ המתבקע if the iron (axe) chipped a piece off the wood which was to be split (and the chip struck a person dead); v. נְשִׁילָה.—2) *to slip off, fall off.* Lev. R. s. 22 נָשְׁלוּ איבריו his limbs fell off (by decay; Gen.

R. s. 10 נָשְׁרוּ; Koh. R. to V, 8 (נשרין, נשרין, ch.). Macc. 7[b] וְנָשַׁל קריתן, v. infra.

Pi. נִישֵּׁל to strike off, to cause chips to fly off. Ib. וְנִישֵּׁל כתיב *v'nashal* (Deut. XIX, 5) may be read *v'nishshel* (*Pi.*) and the iron chips off a part of the wood &c., v. supra; וְנָשַׁל קריתן the traditional reading is *v'nashal*, and the iron slips out of the helve (v. אֵם).

Nif. נִישּׁוֹל, נִישַּׁל to fall off, decay. Lev. R. s. 37, end שהיה נ׳ ממנו אבר אבר וכ׳ limb after limb fell off his body and was buried each in a different place; ib. נ׳ אבר אבר; Koh. R. to X, 15; Gen. R. s. 60. Num. R. s. 9 ידוא בשרה נ׳ her flesh (limbs) shall fall off; a. e.

Hif. הִשִּׁיל to let fall, drop. Bets. V, 1 מַשִּׁילִין פירות וכ׳ you may let down fruit (that was spread on the roof) through the aperture &c.; (versions ib. 35[b]: משחילין, משחירין, מנשירין, משירין).

נְשַׁל* ch., *Af.* אֲשֵׁיל to send off. Targ. Y. Deut. XXIV, 1 ed. pr. (oth. ed. וְיִתְשֵׁיל; h. text ושלחה).

נָשַׁם (b. h.; cmp. נשב) to breathe. Gen. R. s. 14 end, v. נְשִׁימָה.

נְשַׁם ch. same.

Ithpe. אִיתְנְשֵׁם, אִתְנְשֵׁים, *Ithpa.* אִיתְנַשַּׁם 1) to take breath, to rest. Pesik. B'shall., p. 93[a] בעי את לְמִתְנַשְּׁמָא וכ׳ wouldst thou rest a while?—2) to recover, get well. Y. Sabb. XIV, 14[d] bot.; Y. Ab. Zar. II, 40[d] לחש ... ואי׳ he whispered ...., and the person recovered, v. רָשַׁשׁ. Lam. R. to II, 11 כחול .. ואת מִתְנַשְּׁמָה use my eye-paint, and thou shalt get well. Y. Kil. IX, 32[b] bot. אִיתְנַשְּׁמַת it (the tooth) was cured; Y. Keth. XII, 35[a] bot.; Gen. R. s. 33 אִתְנַשְּׁמִית (some ed. אִתְחַשְּׁמִית I feel better). Lev. R. s. 9 רוקי .. ואנא מִיתְנַשֵּׁים spit in my face seven times, and I shall be cured.

Ittafel אִיתַּנְשְׁתַּם to breathe, to give signs of life. Sabb. 134[a] דלא מִיתַּנְשְׁתַּם ... דאי Rashi a. Ms. O. (ed. מנשתיה, מנשתי; Rashi Ms. בִּנְשִׁים, v. Rabb. D. S. a. l. note 40; Ms. M. מנשותין) an infant which gives no signs of life.

נֶשֶׁם m. (cmp. נָשָׁא III) *neshem*, a medicine which produces depilation. Neg. X, 10 אכל נ׳ סך נ׳ if one ate *n.* or smeared *n.*; Sifra Thazr., Neg., Par. 5, ch. X.

נִשְׁמָא m. (נשם) breath, respiration.—*Pl.* נִשְׁמֵי. Succ. 26[b]; Yalk. Prov. 938 שתין נ׳ sixty respirations.—נִשְׁמָא f., v. נִשְׁמְתָא.

נְשָׁמָה f. (b. h.; preced.) breath, spirit, soul. Gen. R. s. 14, end, v. נֶפֶשׁ. Snh. 52[a], a. e. שריפת נ׳ וגוף וכ׳ burning of the breath of life while the body remains intact. Y. Gitt. VII, beg. 48[c] בחזקת שהנ׳ תלויה בו under the presumption that he is still alive. Y. B. Kam. VII, end, 6[a] דבר שהנ׳ תלויה בו a part of an animal's body the removal of which results in death; a. fr.—*Pl.* נְשָׁמוֹת. Yeb. 62[a], a. e., v. גּוּף II. Sabb. 152[b] נִשְׁמוֹתָן של צדיקים (not נשמתן) the souls of the righteous; a. fr.

נִשְׁמָא, נִשְׁמְתָא ch. same. Targ. Deut. XX, 16; a. fr.—*Pl.* נִשְׁמָתָא. Targ. Is. LVII, 16; a. e.

נָשַׁף (b. h.; cmp. נָשַׁב) to blow, breathe. Num. R. s. 20 וכי לא .. לִנְשׁוֹף וכ׳ could not the angel have blown at him, and he (Balaam) would have given up his spirit?; Tanh. Bal. 8. Yalk. Cant. 986 והיה ... נוֹשֵׁף בה and a serpent blew (hissed) at it (the dove); a. e.—נ׳ עִסָּה (or עִיסָה) to make the leaven swell, to stir up passion, hatred. Esth. R. introd. (ref. to Am. V, 19) the serpent, that is Haman שהיה נוֹשֵׁף עִסָּא כנחש who stirred up passion like the serpent (Gen. III, 13); Lev. R. s. 13 שנשף עיסה כנחש (not שמשך); ib. s. 15 end שנשף כנחש (insert עסה); Gen. R. s. 16 שהיה המן שף עסה וכ׳ (fr. שוּף); Yalk. ib. 22 שף כנחש (corr. acc.).—[*Nif.* נִישּׁוֹף, נְשׁוֹף, v. שוּף II.]

נְשַׁף I ch. same. Ber. 3[b] (expl. נֶשֶׁף) נ׳ ליליא וכ׳ the night blows (expires), and the day comes in; the day blows, and night sets in (Rashi: *retires*), v. נֶשֶׁף, נִשְׁפָּא.

Ithpe. אִיתְנְשֵׁף to be covered with breath, to become dim. Men. 50[b] אִיתְנַשְׁפָּא לה (Ar. 'אית, Var. 'איג; some ed. Ar. אינשבא) the bread loses its glistening surface (when it gets stale).

נְשַׁף II (cmp. שוּף I ch.) to slip, glide, move. Meg. 3[a] לִינְשׁוֹף מדוכתיה וכ׳ let him move (Rashi: *skip*) from his place four cubits.

Ittaf. אִיתַּנְשְׁפָא to be made to slip. B. Mets. 23[a] מִיתַּנְשְׁפָא it slips from its place (by people's stepping against it).

נֶשֶׁף m. (b. h.; נָשַׁף) [*zephyr*,] early morning; sunset. Keth. 111[b] קדמית בנ׳ (fr. Ps. CXIX, 147) I got up early in the morning. Ber. 3[b] (ref. to Ps. l. c.) ממאי דהאי נ׳ אורתא וכ׳ how do we know that *neshef* means evening? (Answ. ref. to Prov. VII, 9). Ib. וכ׳ אורתא הוא הא נ׳ וכ׳ does *neshef* mean evening? does it not mean morning?—Lam. R. introd. (R. Joh. 2) הרי נ׳ the mountains of darkness. Lev. R. s. 23 אימתי נ׳ בא וכ׳ when will the dusk come, when the evening?; a. e.

נִשְׁפָּא, constr. נְשַׁף, נֶשֶׁף ch. same. Targ. Job III, 8. Ib. XXIV, 15 (ed. Wil. נֶשֶׁף).—*Pl.* נִשְׁפֵּי. Ber. 3[b] תרי נ׳ הוו וכ׳ there are two *neshef*, the night expires &c., v. נְשַׁף.

נָשַׁק (b. h.; cmp. נָשַׁךְ) 1) to touch closely; to kiss. Y. Yeb. XV, 14[d] (ref. to נשק, Ps. CXL, 8) ביום שתקיץ נוֹשֵׁק וכ׳ when the summer kisses the autumn (at the change of seasons, when disease is rife). Ib. ששני עולמות נוֹשְׁקִין וכ׳ when the two worlds touch eath other (the moment of death). Gen. R. s. 90, beg. (ref. to Gen. XLI, 40) שלא יהא אדם נוֹשְׁקֵנִי וכ׳ none shall kiss me (the kiss of homage) but thou. Ber. 8[b], a. e. כשנוֹשְׁקִין אין נושקין אלא וכ׳ when they (the Medians) kiss, they do so only on the hand. Yalk. Gen. 159 בדבר שהוא נוֹשְׁקוֹ על ערפו וכ׳ with a thing which one puts close to one's neck, that is the bow; a. fr.—*Part. pass.* נָשׁוּק (cmp. אָחוּז fr. אָחַז) kissing. Sot. 42[b] (ref. to Ruth I, 14) יבאו בני הנְּשׁוּקָה ... הדבוקה let the children of her that kissed (and parted) come and fall into the hands of the children of her who clung (to Naomi); Yalk. Sam. 156 הַנְּשִׁיקָה .. הַדְּבֵקָה.—2) (denom. of נֶשֶׁק) to arm, equip. Cant. R. to I, 2 (expl. ישקני, ib.) ידיינני ישחרני ידביקני may he arm me (ref. to I Chr. XII, 2), may he purify me (v. infra), may he attach me (ref. to Ezek. III, 13).

Pi. נִשֵּׁק 1) to kiss. Snh. VII, 6 הַמְנַשֵּׁק he who kisses (an idol); a. fr.—2) to arm, equip. Part. pass. מְנוּשָּׁק; f.

אם עסקת.. ששפתיך מְנוּשָׁקוֹת, *pl.* מְנוּשֶּׁקֶת Cant. R. l. c. כל וכ׳ if thou studiest the words of the Law so that thy lips be equipped (ready for contest), all shall kiss thee &c.

Hif. הִשִּׁיק 1) *to bring in close contact, to close* (lips). Y. Ab. Zar. II, 41[d] top יש דברים שמַשִּׁיקִין וכ׳ there are things on which you must seal your mouth (v. חָשַׁק).— 2) (Levitical law) *to restore a liquid to cleanness by contact or levelling with a clean well.* Mikv. VI, 8 מביא ... ומושכו ומַשִּׁיקוֹ he takes a pipe ... and draws (the water from the clean pond) and makes it touch the surface of the unclean pond; Tosef. ib. V, 5. Cant. R. l. c. (expl. ישקני, may He cleanse me, v. supra) כאדם שהוא מַשִּׁיק וכ׳ as one brings in contact or levels &c., v. גָּבָא. Bets. II, 3 ושוין שמַשִּׁיקִין וכ׳ and they agree that you may (on the Holy Day) dip a vessel with an unclean liquid into a well so that the two surfaces are on a level, v. הַשָּׁקָה. Hull. 26[a] sq. עד שלא החמיץ מַשִּׁיקוֹ וכ׳ before it is sour, you may cleanse it by levelling &c.; a. e.

נְשֵׁיק, נְשַׁק ch. same. Targ. Gen. XXIX, 11; 13 (O. ed. Vien. נַשֵּׁיק *Pa.*). Targ. Prov. XXIV, 26 נִנְשְׁקוּ וכ׳ let them *close* the lips of &c. Targ. Job XXXI, 27; a. fr.—M. Kat. 25[b] נָשׁוּק, v. פְּרִיסָא I. B. Bath. 74[a] הדכא דנָשְׁקָא ארעא וכ׳ where earth and heaven meet. Y. Maas. Sh. IV, 55[b] bot. חמית .. נשקה וכ׳ I saw in my dream one of my eyes touch the other. Gitt. 57[b] bot. ואֶינַשְׁקֵיה פורתא that I may kiss him a little (before he is put to death); a. fr.

Pa. נַשֵּׁק, נַשֵּׁיק same. Targ. O. Gen. XXXI, 28; a. e.

נֶשֶׁק m. (b. h.; preced.) [*hostile meeting*, cmp. זָוַג, מִלְחָמָה &c.,] *going to war*; כלי נ׳ (or sub. כלי) *weapon, armor.* Y. Yeb. XV, 14[d] (ref. to Ps. CXL, 8) נִשְׁקוֹ של גוג the day of war against Gog (v. זְיוּן); Yalk. Ps. 888.

***נַשְׁקִי** f. (preced. wds.) *kiss* (of the foot), a form of *taking possession of a slave.* Gitt. 43[b] מאי נמוסו ... נ׳ what is meant by the gentile's doing to the slave his *nomos* (v. נִימוֹס)? (Answer.) נ׳. Ib. שדה בת נ׳ היא can a field be taken possession of by *nashki?*—[Ar. *armor*, Rashi *seal*, suspended from the slave's neck].

נָשַׁר (cmp. נָשַׁל) *to drop, fall off.* Peah VII, 3 איזהו פרט הנּוֹשֵׁר וכ׳ by *peret* (Lev. XIX, 10) is understood that which drops on cutting grapes. Bets. 2[b] פירות הנּוֹשְׁרִין fruit which drops from the tree (on the Holy Day). Y. ib. I, beg. 60[a] ספק מהיום נָשְׁרוּ וכ׳ where it is doubtful whether they fell off to-day (on the Holy-Day) &c. Gen. R. s. 10, v. נָשַׁל; a. fr.—Sabb. XXII, 4 (146[b]) מי שנשרו כליו בדרך (במים) if one's garments (cloak) fell into a puddle on the road.

Hif. הִשִּׁיר (הִנְשִׁיר) 1) *to let fall, drop.* Ib. 67[a] אילן שמַשִּׁיר פירותיו a tree that drops its fruit prematurely. Naz. VI, 3 מפני שמַשֶּׁרֶת וכ׳ because it causes falling out of the hair. Y. Peah VIII, 20[a] bot. מַשִּׁיר (not משייר), v. מַחְבּוֹא. Midr. Till. to Ps. XIV עתיד .. לְהַשִּׁירוֹ the Lord will cause him to drop, v. נוֹבֶלֶת. Keth. 6[b] אע״פ שמַשִּׁיר צרורות although (by walking through the breach) he causes pebbles to break loose; Y. Ber. II, 5[b] top אפי׳ מַשֶּׁרֶת צרורות even if the wall is so brittle as to drop &c.; a. fr.—Bets. 35[b] מַנְשִׁירִין, מַשִּׁירִין (prob. to be read: מְנַשְּׁרִין as versions of מַשִּׁילִין, v. נָשַׁל).—Esth. R. to I, 14 ומַשִּׁירָן, v. פַּרְשְׁדָנָה II.

Pi. נִשֵּׁר 1) *to drop, let drop*, v. supra.—2) (cmp. Assyr. našâru, Del. Assyr. Handw., p. 487) *to tear, lacerate.* Ab. Zar. 11[a] sq. איזהו עיקור ... המְנַשֵּׁר פרסותיה וכ׳ what mutilation of an animal's feet does not affect its vitality (v. טְרֵפָה)? Cutting the tendons of its hoofs beneath the ankle; ib. 13[a]. Pesik. R. s. 31 מְנַשְּׁרִים בשערו they pluck his hair.

נְשַׁר I ch. same, 1) *to fall off.* Koh. R. to V, 8 נָשְׁרִין, נָשְׁרָן, v. נָשַׁל.—2) *to lacerate.* Ber. 8[a] [a gloss, v. Ar. ed. Koh. s. v. נשר 4] דלאחורי נָשְׁרָא (Ar. נָשְׁרֵי) which tears backwards (when you attempt to pull it out), v. חֵיזְרָא I.

Af. אַשִּׁיר *to cause to fall off, drop.* Targ. I Chr. V, 23, v. סְרִי II.

נֶשֶׁר I or **נֶשֶׁר** m. (preced.) *dropping, dropped fruit.* Succ. I, 3 מפני הנ׳ to intercept the droppings (from the branches covering the Succah). Pes. 56[a] להאכיל נ׳ לעניים וכ׳ to give the poor an opportunity to eat of the fallen fruit (on Sabbaths &c.) in years of famine; Men. 71[a]; a. fr.—*Pl.* נְשָׁרִין, נְשָׁרִים. Tosef. Pes. II (III), 19. Y. Bets. I, bg. 60[a]; a. e.

נֶשֶׁר II m. (v. נִשֵּׁר *Pi.*) *eagle.* Hag. 13[b] מלך שבעופות נ׳ the king of birds is the eagle. Hull. 60[b] sq. (ref. to Lev. XI, 13) נ׳ מה נ׳ וכ׳ the text specifies the eagle to intimate, as the eagle has no additional toe ...., so all birds like him are unclean. Y. Peah I, 15[d] top נ׳ שהוא רחמן the eagle who is kind (to his young ones); Yalk. Prov. 963. Mekh. Yithro, Bahod., s. 2; a. fr.—Snh. 12[a] (in a secret letter) ותפשו נ׳ and the eagle (Roman) caught them (the messengers, v. נְצִיב).—*Pl.* נְשָׁרִים. Ib. 92[b] עושה להם כנפים כנ׳ וכ׳ he shall give them (the righteous) wings like those of the eagles, and they shall soar &c.; a. e.

נְשַׁר II, נִשְׁרָא, נִ׳ 1) same. Targ. Lev. XI, 13; a. fr.—*Pl.* נִשְׁרִין, נִשְׁרַיָּא, נִ׳. Targ. Ex. XIX, 4. Targ. II Sam. I, 23.—Erub. 53[b], v. נְקַף I.—2) *Nishra*, name of an Arabian deity (Sabaean: *Nasr*). Ab. Zar. 11[b].—[נשרא, Ber. 8[a], v. נְשַׁר I.]—קַן נִשְׁרַיָּיא pr. n. pl., v. קַן ch.

נַשְׁרִיתָא, v. נִשְׁרִיתָא.

נִשְׁתּ׳, Sabb. 134[a], מנשתיר, מנשתירה, v. נָשַׁם.

נִשְׁתִּיק, v. נִשְׁתַּק.

נִשְׁתַּם, v. נָשַׁם.

נִשְׁתַּן (v. שָׁתַן) *to urinate.* Sabb. 134[a] מְנַשְׁתֵּן Ms. M., v. נָשַׁם.

נִשְׁתֵּיק, נִשְׁתַּק m. (נָשַׁק, cmp. אינשתם, fr. נָשַׁם) *attachment*, a contrivance to prevent the handle of a coal-pan from getting too hot. Tosef. Yoma III (II), 3 בכל יום לא היה לה נ׳ on any other day the priest's coal-pan had no damper &c.; Yoma 44[b] נִיאַשְׁתֵּיק (Ms. M. נִיאוּשׁ׳; Rashi: 'a rattling ring'); Y. ib. IV, 41[d] top נרתיק. Koh. R. to I, 5 [read:] מערטלו מִנַּשְׁתְּקוֹ or כְּנַרְתְּקוֹ (v. חשתק).

נְתַב, נְתִיב=נְשַׁב, *to blow.* Targ. Ps. CXXIX, 6 (ed. Wil. נְתַק). Ib. CIII, 16 (ed. Wil. נתכת, some ed. חבת, corr. acc.).

Pa. נַתֵּב same. Targ. Y. I Deut. XXXII, 2 (ed. Vien. דמיתנתבין *Ithpe.*). Targ. Y. Gen. I, 2 (ed. Vien. מְנַתְּבָא).

Af. אַנְתִּיב *to cause to blow.* Targ. Ps. CXLVII, 18 (Ms. *Pa.*).

Ithpe. אִיתְנְתַב, אִיתְנְתִיב *to be blown,* v. supra.—[Targ. Y. Gen. XII, 10 לאיתנתבא, read: לְאִיתּוֹתָבָא, v. יְתַב.]

נִתְבְּרָא, v. נִדְבְּכָה.

נְתוּחַ, v. נִיתּוּחַ.

נְתוֹפְתִי, נְתוֹצָתִי, (נְתִיצָתִי), v. נְטוֹפָתִי.

נָתַז, *Pi.* נִתֵּז (sec. verb of נָזָה, v. Kidd. 25^a) 1) (neut. verb) *to squirt, fly off.* Kidd. 25^a הזה... מַזָּה וְנִתְּזָה הזאה וכ׳ (perh. *Nif.*) if a person (priest) was sprinkling for purification, and the sprinkling flew upon his (the unclean person's) mouth. Y. Yoma III, 41^a top, a. e. מְנַתְּזִין, v. נִיצוֹץ. B. Kam. II, 1 היו ... מנ׳ וכ׳ if stones flew off from under the animal's feet; a. e.—2) (act. verb) *to cause to fly off.* Ib. 19^a במקום .. אלא אם כן מְנַתֶּזֶת where the animal cannot help making stones fly off. Nidd. 61^a וְנִתְּזוּ בקרדומותיהן they chopped with their axes.

Hif. הִתִּיז (b. h. הַתֵּז) *to cause to fly off, to chop off; to squirt.* B. Kam. l. c. בעטה וְהִתִּיזָה וכ׳ she kicked and made stones fly off and thus did damage. Ib. 17^b. Snh. 102^a כשתי מקלות שמַתִּיזוֹת זו את זו like two sticks which splinter one another. Sabb. 62^b ומַתִּיזוֹת עליהם and caused the balsam to squirt at them; a. fr.—Esp. (with ראש) *to decapitate.* Snh. VII, 3 היו מַתִּיזִין את וכ׳ they decapitated him with a sword. Y. Ber. IX, 13^a חייבו לְהַתִּיז וכ׳ he sentenced him to decapitation; Cant. R. to VII, 5; a. fr.—Trnsf. *to separate syllables* or *words distinctly, to articulate (sybillants).* Y. Ber. II, 4^d צריך להתיז למען תזכרו (ed. Lehm. צריך לה׳ זי״ן וכ׳) you must articulate *tiz-k'ru* (emphasizing the *zayin,* Num. XV, 40). Ib. צריך לה׳ כי לעולם חסדו you must articulate *ḥas-do* (so as not to make it sound *ḥasto* or *ḥazdo.*—[Gitt. 70^a מַתִּיזִין גופו וכ׳ *scatter* the strength &c.; En Yaăk. מתישין.]

Hof. הוּתַּז *to be made to fly off, be cut off.* Ḥull. 27^a. Gen. R. s. 9, end יוּתַּז ראשו בסייף his head shall be cut off with a sword.

Nif. נִיתַּז *to fly off; to splash.* Cant. R. l. c. ... נִתְּזָה החרב והתיזה the sword flew off the neck of Moses and struck &c. Nidd. 13^a נִתְּזִין, v. נִיצוֹץ. Tosef. Macc. II, 1 נִיתְּזָה בקעת וכ׳ if a chip flew off &c., v. נָשַׁל.—Ḥull. VI, 6 דם הנִתָּז the blood which splashes forth at slaughtering; ib. 88^a הני׳. Zeb. XI, 3; a. fr.

נְתַז ch. same, *to gush forth, splash.* Targ. O. Deut. I, 44 יָתְזָן (ed. Vien. נַתְּזָן, of bees). Targ. Job III, 23 (h. text נתך).—Sot. 48^b (quot. fr. Targ. O. Deut. l. c.).

Af. אַתִּיז (with רישא) *to decapitate.* Targ. I Chr. X, 9 (h. text נשא).

Pa. נַתֵּיז *to cause to fly off.* B. Kam. 19^a קא מְנַתְּזָא צרורות, v. preced.

נִתְזָה pr. n. m. *Nithza.* Snh. 74^a נמנו וגמרו בעליית בית נ׳ they voted and passed a law in the upper chamber of the house of N.; Y. ib. III, 21^b top; Yalk. Deut. 838; Y. Shebi. IV, 35^a bot. לבוח. Kidd. 40^b; (Sifré Deut. 41 ערוד).

נִתְזוֹאִי* (prob. to be read נִתְזְוָאֵר) pr. n. m. Erub. 59^a (Ms. M. נִשְׁוָאֵר; v. Rabb. D. S. a. l. note; Ar. נתזור, prob. for נִתְזוֹר).

נָתַח (b. h.), *Pi.* נִתַּח 1) *to sever, dissect.* Zeb. 85^a יפשיט וִינַתַּח וכ׳ he must flay and dissect it in its place (where he slaughtered it). Ḥull. 28^b כיון שמְנַתְּחָהּ אבר אבר (not דמנ׳) since he cuts it into parts; a. fr.—2) *to distrain, take by force,* esp. *to seize* by waiting for the debtor to come out of the house with an object, opp. to מַשְׁכֵּן, to enter and seize. B. Mets. 113^a אימא לא יְנַתְּחֶנּוּ וכ׳ read in the Mishnah (IX, 13), he must not seize his goods outside of his house except through the court messenger.

נְתַח ch., *Pa.* נַתַּח same, 1) as preced. 2. B. Mets. 113^a נַתּוּחֵי אין וכ׳ the court messenger may distrain out side of the house, but enter and seize he dare not?—2) *to tear, pull.* Bets. 10^b גוזלות מְנַתְּחֵי מהדדי (not אהדדי; Ms. M. מנתקי) pigeons might pull against each other (and tear the bands); Gitt. 51^a.

נֵתַח m. (b. h.; preced.) *piece.*—*Pl.* נְתָחִים. Sifra Vayikra, N'dab., Par. 4, ch. V (ref. to Lev. I, 6) יכול ינתח נְתָחֶיהָ לִנְתָחֵיהֶם you might think, he may cut its parts into their parts again; Ḥull. 11^a ולא נתחיה לנ׳ but he must not cut &c.; a. e.

נְתִיב m. (b. h.) *highway, road.* Keth. 8^b נ׳ הוא משׁשת וכ׳ such is the road (the course of events) from the days of creation. Ex. R. s. 30 התורה אומרת באי זה נ׳ אני מהלכת the Torah says, what road do I follow?; a. e.—*Pl.* נְתִיבוֹת. Ib.

נְתִיבְתָּא f. ch. same. Targ. Prov. I, 15 Ms. (ed. שְׁבִיל׳).

נַתִּיךְ m. (נְתַךְ I; cmp. יָצוּק) *cast, firm.* Targ. Job XLI, 16 Ms. (ed. אַתִּיךְ).

נָתִין m. (b. h.; נָתַן) [*donated, dedicated to the Temple service,*] *Nathin,* a descendant of the Gibeonites (Josh. IX, 27). Macc. III, 1; a. fr.—*Pl.* נְתִינִים, נְתִינִין. Yeb. 78^b נ׳ דוד גזר עליהן as to N'thinim, David decreed concerning them (their exclusion from the Israelitish community with regard to intermarriages). Ib. VIII, 3 ממזרין ונ׳ אסורין bastards and N'thinim are forbidden (for intermarriage). Tosef. Kidd. V, 4; a. fr.—*Fem.* נְתִינָה. Macc. l. c.; a. e.

נְתִינָאָה ch. same.—*Pl.* נְתִינָאֵי. Targ. I Chr. IX, 2.—Kidd. 70^b (play on דורנוניתא) דרא דנ׳ Rashi (ed. דראי נ׳) village of N'thinim.

נְתִינָה I, v. נָתִין.

נְתִינָה II pr. n. m. *N'thinah,* father of Dama, (v. דָּמָא). Kidd. 31^a; Y. ib. I, 61^b top; a. e.

נְתִינָה III f. (נָתַן) 1) *donation.* Pes. 21^b, a. e. (ref. to Deut. XIV, 21) אין לי אלא לגר בנ׳ וכ׳ from this I would conclude that it is permitted to give it to the sojourner as a gift &c., contrad. to מכירה; a. fr.—2) *delivery.* B. Mets. 19ª עד שעת נ׳ up to the time of the delivery (of the letter of divorce). Y. Ḥag. II, 77ᵇ bot.; Cant. R. to I, 10 כנתינתן מסיני, v. שָׁמַח; a. fr.—3) *putting on,* opp. חליצה taking off. Y. Ber. III, beg. 5ᵈ הלכה .. בנ׳ the practice is in accordance with ... as regards putting on (the shoes by mourners); Y. M. Kat. III, 82ᵇ; Gen. R. s. 100.

נְתִינוּת f. (נָתִין) *the legal status of the Nathin; the class of N'thinim.* Tosef. Kidd. V, 4 'I shall cleanse you' (Ez. XXXVI, 25) אפי׳ מן הנ׳ even from the class of *n'thinim* (i. e. they shall be restored to full Jewish citizenship). Ib. 2 כל שאין בה לא משום נ׳ וכ׳ a family which is not suspected of intermarriage with N'thinim; Keth. 14ª. Ibᵇ; a. e.

נְתִינִי m. (preced.) *one belonging to the class of N'thinim.* Kidd. IV, 1; Tosef. ib. V, 1; v. מַמְזֵרִי.

נְתִיצָה f. (נָתַץ) *cutting out, breaking up.* Sifra Sh'mini, Par. 8, ch. X את שיש לו נ׳ that which can be broken up (brick-work &c.). Y. Sabb. IX, 11ᵈ top נ׳ נ׳ מבית המנוגע the breaking up of idolatrous structures (Deut. XII, 3) is analogous to the breaking up of leprous buildings (Lev. XIV, 45). Y. Orl. III, 63ª bot. דכתיב נ׳ נ׳ for the term נתץ is used for idolatry and for levitical purity (Lev. XI, 35). Tosef. Neg. VI, 10, contrad. to חליצה the removal of one affected stone. Mekh. B'shall., Shir., s. 10 נטיעה שאין בה נ׳ a putting up not to be followed by a tearing down. Y. Orl. I, 60ᵈ bot., v. נְפִיצָה. Y. Ab. Zar. IV, 44ª; a. fr.

נְתִיקָה f. (נָתַק) 1) *breaking loose.* Pesik. Shub., p. 163ª (ref. to אתקנך, Jer. XXII, 24) ממקום נְתִיקָתוֹ תהא תקנתו from where he will be torn away will arise his regeneration (through repentance); Cant. R. to VIII, 6 ממקום שנְתִיקָתָהּ שם וכ׳; Yalk. Jer. 303.—2) *forcing a door open.* Y. Snh. VII, 25ᵈ (in Chald. dict.) יהיב ליה (חד) בנ׳ struck him by opening the door forcibly; v. מְרִתּוֹקָא.

נָתַךְ (b. h.; cmp. נתק, נתח) *to cut, reduce, smelt.* [Tosef. Shebi. III, 19 לתוך, יתוך Var. ed. Zuck., v. נָתַק.]

Nif. נִיתַּךְ *to be smelted, reduced to slags.* Zeb. XII, 6 נ׳ הבשר if the flesh in the fire is burned to hard lumps; ib. 106ª, contrad. to נעשין אפר; v. חֲרוּכָא.

Hif. הִתִּיךְ *to smelt, cast, pour.* Ex. R. s. 15 ... של כסף הִתִּיכָן וכ׳ the idols of silver ..., he caused to melt and be shapeless as before they were cast. Y. Sabb. X, 10ᵇ bot. המַתִּיךְ אבר he who casts lead (on the Sabbath). Naz. 50ᵇ והִתִּיכוֹ and he melted it (the fat); Tosef. Ohol. IV, 3 והיתכו, והתכו (corr. acc.); Y. Naz. VII, 56ᵇ bot. Y. Ab. Zar. III, 43ᵇ; ib. IV, 44ᵇ top המתיך כוס לע״ז he who casts a cup for an idol.—[Pesik. R. s. 31 מנתכי׳ אחוריה, read: מכופתים לאחורייהם; v. ed. Fr. note 49.]

Hof. הוּתַּךְ *to be molten; to be reduced to slags.* Meïl. II, 3 (9ª) עד שיוּתַּךְ הבשר (Talm. ed. שיתיך, corr. acc.) until the flesh is charred in small lumps; Zeb. 85ᵇ; 104ᵇ.—Part. מוּתָּךְ. Sabb. 21ª, a. fr. חלב מ׳ Ar. (ed. מְהוּתָּךְ, v. התך) molten fat.

נְתַךְ I ch. same; *Af.* אַתֵּיךְ *to melt, cast, pour.* Targ. Job X, 10 Ms. (ed. סנן). Targ. Ex. XXV, 12; a. fr.—Part. pass. מַתַּךְ. Targ. II Chr. IV, 2, sq.—Midr. Till. to Ps. II, 6 (expl. נסכתי ib.) אַתִּיכְתֵּיה I cast him (made him strong, cmp. יָצַק *Hof.*); Yalk. ib. 620.

Pa. נַתֵּךְ same. Targ. II Chr. XXXII, 21.

***נְתַךְ** II (v. P. Sm. 2480; cmp. נָתַח *Pi.* 2) *to distrain, fine.* Targ. Prov. XVII, 26 (h. text ענש).

***נְתַל** (v. P. Sm. 2480) = נְתַן *to give answer, teach.* Targ. Prov. XXVI, 4; 7.

נָתָן (b. h.) pr. n. m. *Nathan,* 1) the prophet. Koh. R. to IV, 12. Midr. Till. to Ps. LI; a. fr.—2) N. the Babylonian, a Tannai. Ber. IX, 5. Tosef. Yeb. VIII, 4. B. Bath. 73ª; a. fr.—3) name of several Amoraim. Y. Erub. VI, 23ᶜ bot., v. הְרוּמָאָה; a. e.—Y. M. Kat. III, 82ª נ׳ בר אבא.—Y. Ter. VII, 44ᶜ נ׳ בר הושעיה.—Y. Ber. IV, 7ᵇ נ׳ בר טובי; a. fr.—4) N. d'Tsutsitha, a penitent. Sabb. 56ᵇ.—אבות דר׳ נ׳, v. אָב II.

נָתַן (b. h.) *to give; to place, put.* Gitt. I, 6 תֵּן גט וכ׳ give this letter of divorce to my wife. Ib. תְּנוּ גט וכ׳ give ye &c. Ib. לא יִתְּנוּ לאחר מיתה they must not deliver it after the man's death; a. v. fr.—נ׳ עיניו ל— (to put an eye upon) *to intend.* B. Mets. 19ª, a. e. כיון שנ׳ ע׳ לגרשה as soon as he has resolved to divorce her; a. fr.—נ׳ עיניו ב— (to have an eye on) *to desire, think of.* Ned. XI, 12 שלא תהא אשה נוֹתֶנֶת עיניה באחר lest the woman have a liking for another man. Ib. 20ᵇ שלא אֶתֵּן עיני וכ׳ lest I think of another woman. Ib. אל ישתה .. ויִתֵּן וכ׳ one must not drink of one cup (have connection with one woman) and think of another; a. fr.—Esp. נ׳ עיניו בו *to cast an angry eye at, to hurt by an angry look.* Ber. 58ª נ׳ ע׳ בו ונעשה וכ׳ he cast an eye at him and he was changed into &c., v. גַּל; Sabb. 34ª; a. e.—Y. Ber. III, beg. 5ᵈ, a. fr. נותן תפלין puts on T'fillin.—נ׳ טעם, v. טַעַם.—הדין נותן the conclusion *ad majus* gives it, it is a legitimate conclusion. Bekh. 59ᵇ, a. fr. Ib. היא הנוֹתֶנֶת (on the contrary,) it is thus we should argue.—Gen. R. s. 33 והדין נותן and it stands to reason.—Esp. נ׳ (sub. דם) *to put blood on the altar, sprinkle, smear.* Zeb. VIII, 4; a. fr.—[Tosef. Neg. VI, 10 נותן, v. נָתַץ.]

Nif. נִיתַּן *to be given, put* &c.; *to be intended.* Ned. 38ª לא נִיתְּנָה תורה אלא וכ׳ the Law was given only to Moses and his descendants. Ib. וכולן נִתְּנוּ וכ׳ and all those (gates of understanding) were granted to Moses; a. fr.—Keth. 81ª לא ניתנה כתובה וכ׳ the K'thubah is not intended to be collected during life-time. R. Hash. 28ª מצות .. נִיתְּנוּ, v. הֲנָאָה; a. fr.—[Tosef. Ab. Zar. V (VI), 8 עד שינתץ, v. נָתַץ.]—Esp. *to be put on the altar, sprinkled, smeared.* Zeb. VIII, 9 הנִתָּנִין למטה .... בנתנין למעלה blood which must be put below (the red line) which has been mixed with blood that must be put above. Ib. 10 יִנָּתְנוּ במתן וכ׳ shall be applied four times, v. מַתָּן a. מַתָּנָה; a. fr.

Hof. הוּתַּן *to be put.* Makhsh. I, 1 (הרי זה) בכי יוּתַּן it comes under the law (Lev. XI, 38), i. e. it is a liquid which, if put on eatables, makes them susceptible of uncleanness. Ib. 2 אינן בכי יותן do not qualify for uncleanness; a. fr.

נְתַן ch. same. Targ. Deut. XV, 10; a. fr.—[Targ. Is. LIII, 5 ובדנתתינה some ed., read: ובדניתנהי, v. נְהַי I.]

נָתַץ (b. h.) *to chip off; to tear down.* Neg. XIII, 2 בזמן שהוא נוֹתֵץ נותץ את שלו when he has to tear down (Lev. XIV, 45), he must chip off his part of the house, contrad. to חָלַץ; Tosef. ib. VI, 10. Ib. בנתיצה נותץ את וכ׳ (not נותן) when he has to tear down, he must chop those stones which are affected as well as those which are not; a. fr.

Nif. נִיתַּץ *to be torn down.* Ab. Zar. 53^b עד שיִּתָּתֵץ רובו until the largest part of it is torn down; Tosef. ib. V (VI), 8 שינתן (corr. acc.). Neg. XIII, 1; a. fr.

Hof. הוּתַּץ same. Ab. Zar. III, 9 אם חדש יוּתַּץ if the oven was new, it must be taken apart; Pes. 26^b; a. fr.

נָתַק (b. h.; cmp. preced. a. נתך) 1) *to break loose; tear out.* Y. Shebi. IV, 35^b bot. מקום שנהגו לקוץ יִתּוֹק לִתּוֹק וכ׳ where it is customary to cut the reeds, let him pluck them; where it is customary to pluck them &c.; Tosef. ib. III, 19 Var. יִתּוֹק לִתּוֹק. Cant. R. to VIII, 6 (ref. to Jer. XXII, 24) שהוא נוֹתֵק מלכות וכ׳ that he will tear the Davidic kingdom out of his hand; ib. משם אני נותק וכ׳ from there I shall tear loose the kingdom &c.; Pesik. Shub., p. 163^a. Bekh. 33^b נותק he who tears loose (testicles and throws them away); נותק אחר כורת who removes them after one has cut them (tearing off the roots). Sifra Thazr., Neg., ch. VII, Par. 5 אם נְתָקוֹ אדם if a man made it bald (נֶתֶק); (R. S. to Neg. III, 5 אם נִיתְּקוּ בידי אדם, Nif.); a. e.—*Part. pass.* נָתוּק (b. h.) *an animal whose testicles have been forcibly removed*; [oth. opin.: *whose membrum has been mutilated by a violent severance*]. Sifra Emor, Par. 7, ch. VII; Tosef. Yeb. X, 5.—2) *to cause oozing, to secrete.* Tosef. Ter. III, 13 ענבים רכות ונוֹתְקוֹת .. ואינן נוֹתְקִין וכ׳ grapes are soft and let their juice ooze out (when packed), but olives are hard and do not let their oil ooze out.; Y. ib. III, 42^b top, v. הִידָא.

Pi. נִיתֵּק 1) *to tear loose.* Cant. R. l. c. (ref. to Jer. l. c.) אֲנַתֶּקְךָ אין .. אֲתַקֶּנְךָ it does not say *ănattekkha* (I shall tear thee loose), but (it may be read) *athakkenkha* (I shall restore thee, v. תָּקַן); Yalk. Jer. 303 אֲתַקֶּנְךָ (*Hif.*); Pesik. l. c.—2) [*to tear, pull*] *to remonstrate, protest.* Sifré Num. 115; Yalk. Num. 750 התחיל הבן ההוא מְנַתֵּק that son began to protest (against doing slave's work); התחילו ישראל מְנַתְּקִים the Israelites remonstrated (against the laws imposed upon them); v. infra.

Nif. נִתּוֹק, נִיתַּק 1) *to be torn loose; to fall out.* Ḥull. 123^b שומר העשוי לִנָּתֵק מאליו a protection (cover) which is likely to come off of itself. Nidd. 65^a כיון שנִּתְּקוּ שניו וכ׳ when a man's teeth are gone; a. e.—2) [*to tear one's self loose,*] *to remonstrate, be discontented.* Sifra Aḥăré, Par. 9, ch. XIII גלוי .. לִינָּתֵק בעריות it was known before the Lord that they would bear unwillingly the restrictive laws concerning sexual relations; נִיתְּקוּ בעריות they did remonstrate &c. (ref. to Num. XI, 10; v. Sabb. 130^a; Yoma 75^a); Yalk. Lev. 590.—3) *to be shifted, transformed, modified.* Zeb. 5^b, a. fr. אשם שנ׳ לרעיה an animal dedicated as a guilt-offering which (on account of its owner's death &c.) has been condemned to pasture until natural death (v. סָאַב).—Y. Naz. IV, end, 53^c משנ׳ מלא תעשה לעשה since it (the cutting of the hair which is forbidden to the Nazarite) has gone over from a prohibition to a positive duty (Num. VI, 18).—לאו שנ׳ לעשה a prohibition transformed into a command, i. e. a prohibitive law the transgression of which must be repaired by a succeeding act, e. g. (Lev. XIX, 13) 'thou shalt not rob', and (ib. V, 23) 'he shall make restitution.' Ḥull. 141^a (for which ib. XII, 4 מצות לא תעשה שיש בה קום עשה). Yoma 85^b לא תעשה שנ׳ לעשה; a. fr.—4) (v. Kal 2) *to enter a stage of moist decomposition.* Y. Naz. VII, 56^b, v. בָּצַל.—5) (denom. of נֶתֶק) *to become hairless and blanched, to be afflicted with* נֶתֶק. Neg. X, 9 וכ׳ כל ראשו and his entire head became bald (v. קָרַחַת). Sifra Thazr. l. c. את שני׳ נתק בתוך נתק a person that became afflicted with a bald spot within a patch of hair surrounded by baldness (Neg. X, 7 שני נְתָקִין זה לפנים מזה; a. fr.).

נְתַק ch. same; *Af.* אַתִּיק *to pull, drag.* Targ. Jer. XII, 3 אַתִּיקִינוּן or אַתְקִינוּן (ed. אַתְקְנ׳, ed. Lag. אַתְקִינִי׳, v. תְּקַן; h. text התיקם).

Pa. נַתִּיק 1) *to tear, sever.* B. Kam. 9^b שור דרכיה לְנַתּוּקֵי an ox may be expected to tear (the rope). Beta. 10^b מְנַתְּקֵי Ms. M., v. נְתַח.—2) *to snatch, take away.* Yoma 46^b כיון דנַתְּקָהּ נתקה having snatched it (the coal from the altar), he has snatched it (and it has its sacred character no longer).—3) *to shift, transform.* Macc. 15^a ההוא לְנַתּוּקֵי לאוי וכ׳ Ms. M. (Rashi לאויה, ed. לאו) this (positive command) has the function of modifying the prohibitory law (intimating the reparation in the event of its transgression); v. preced. *Nif.*

Ithpe. אִיתְּתִיק, אִתְנְתַק 1) *to be severed, snatched.* Targ. Koh. IV, 12.—Yoma l. c. איתְּתִיקָה למצותה the taking it from the altar was done for an ordained use of it; a. e.—2) *to be set aside, be designated.* Erub. 13^a כיון דא׳ לשום רחל תו לא הדרא מִיתַּתְקָא וכ׳ having been originally designated (copied) for Rachel, it cannot again be converted and used for Leah; Sot. 20^b. Zeb. 3^a; a. e.

נֶתֶק m. (b. h.; preced.) [*torn out,*] *bald (blanched) spot* on the head or in the beard. Neg. X, 2; a. fr. *Pl.* נְתָקִים, נְתָקִין. Ib. 1; 7; a. fr.

נִתְקָא, נִ׳ ch. same. Targ. Lev. XIII, 30; a. fr.

נת"ר, a mnemotechnical abbreviation for נטילת הסנדל, תשמיש המטה, a. רחיצת ידים. M. Kat. 24^a.

נָתַר I (b. h.; cmp. נתק) *to sever, loosen.*

Nif. נִיתַּר, נִיתּוֹר 1) *to be torn loose, be released.* Y. Taan. II, 65^d top, v. נָטַשׁ II a. נָתוּשׁ.—Trnsf. *to be untied, released from an obligation; to become permitted.* Y. Yeb. IV, 6^b bot. (ref. to Deut. XXV, 10) בית שהוא נִיתָּר וכ׳ a house (of several wives) which is released (from the leviratical marriage) by means of one *ḥălitsah* (performed on one of the wives). Y. Bicc. I, 64^b top כל הביכורים שראו לִיתּוֹר .. אינן נִיתּוֹרִין וכ׳ .. all the first fruits which are to be released (become permitted by being brought to the Temple) in the land (of Palestine), can become so only by reciting the confession (Deut. XXVI, 5—10). Erub. 10^a; 12^a חצר נִיתֶּרֶת וכ׳ a court becomes permitted (for Sabbath purposes) by &c., v. פַּס. Ib. שהוא נִיתָּר וכ׳ that it is made available &c.; a. e.

Hif. הִתִּיר 1) *to loosen, untie, unscrew.* Tosef. Sabb. XVI (XVII), 5 שהִתִּירוֹ which one unscrewed; Sabb. XX, 5 מַתִּירִין, v. מַכְבֵּשׁ. Ib. 22^{a} מתירין (ציצית) מבגד לבגד you may untie show-fringes from one garment (and put them) on another garment. Gen. R. s. 5 מַתִּירָן ומוציא וכ׳ he unties them (opens the bags) and lets the air in them escape; a. fr.—[Tosef. Shebi. I, 7, v. וָתַר.]—2) *to permit, declare permitted*, opp. אָסַר. Sabb. 4^{a} הִתִּירוּ לו וכ׳ would they (the scholars) permit him to take it out &c.? Ib. II, 4 ור׳ יהודה מַתִּיר but R. Judah declares it permitted. Ib. 2 וחכמים מַתִּירִין; a. v. fr.—V. מַתִּיר.—3) *to free, surrender; to outlaw, proscribe.* Snh. 40^{b} ה׳ עצמו למיתה did he surrender himself to death?, i. e. did he declare that he would commit the act in spite of the warning which defined it to be a deadly crime? Ib. 41^{a} (ref. to Deut. XVII, 6) עד שיַּתִּיר וכ׳ until he declares himself ready to undergo capital punishment for his act. Ḥull. 41^{a}. Y. Peah I, 16^{a} עִילָא .. לְהַתִּיר דמן וכ׳ they wanted a pretext to outlaw the rebels; a. fr.

Hof. הוּתַּר 1) *to be loosened, untied.* Lev. R. s. 28, beg., a. fr. הוּתְּרָה הרצועה, v. רְצוּעָה. Sabb. XX, 5 אם היה מוּתָּר וכ׳ if it (the clothes press) was (partly) unscrewed on the eve of the Sabbath, he may unscrew it entirely. B. Kam. 9^{b} שור מותר an ox that is not tied, opp. קָשוּר. Erub. II, 1 קשורות אבל לא מוּתָּרוֹת closely tied together, but not tied in a loose way; a. e.—2) *to be permitted.* Y. Sabb. II, 5^{b} bot. ה׳ הנדר, v. נֶדֶר; Snh. 68^{a}. Ḥull. 17^{a} בתחילה ה׳ להן וכ׳ originally they were permitted to eat the flesh of an animal killed by stabbing (v. נְחִירָה). Ib. 9^{a} נשחטה הותרה when the animal has been slaughtered according to the ritual, it is (absolutely) permitted. Erub. 93^{b} שבת כיון שהותרה הותרה as regards Sabbath laws what has been permitted at the entrance of the Sabbath remains permitted the entire day; ib. 70^{b} כל שה׳ למקצת וכ׳ whatever is permitted for one part of the Sabbath &c.; a. v. fr.—Part. מוּתָּר; f. מוּתֶּרֶת; *pl.* מוּתָּרִים, מוּתָּרִין; מוּתָּרוֹת (*it is, they are*) *permitted* (of things and persons). Ter. X, 7. Yeb. I, 2 צרתה מ׳ her rival is permitted (to him as wife). Ib. III, 2 ומ׳ באחותה and he is permitted to marry her sister. Ib. II, 10 מותרות לינשא להן may be married to them; a. v. fr.—Pes. 48^{a}, a. e. (ref. to ממשקה ישראל, Ez. XLV, 15) מן המותר לישראל of what an Israelite is permitted to drink. Sabb. 108^{a} (ref. to בפיך, Ex. XIII, 9) מדבר המותר בפיך the Torah must be written on the skin of an animal which is permitted in thy mouth (a clean animal).

נָתַר II, *Pi.* נִתֵּר (b. h.; cmp. נתק) [*to move.*] *to leap.* B. Kam. 38^{a} (ref. to Hab. III, 6) מאי משמע דהאי ויתר לישנא דאגלויי הוא what evidence is there that this *vayyatter* has the meaning of sending into exile (causing to emigrate)? Answ. ref. to לְנַתֵּר (Lev. XI, 21). Lev. R. s. 20 (ref. to Job XXXVII, 1) מהו וְיִתַּר יקפץ וכ׳ what does *v'yittar* mean? It will leap, as we read (Lev. l. c.) &c.

Hif. הִתִּיר *to exile.* B. Kam. l. c., v. supra. Lev. R. s. 6, beg. ומַתִּיר את הגנבים and condemned the thieves to exportation (v., however, פְּיֵיד).

נְתַר ch. = h. נָשַׁר, *to fall off, drop; to fall apart, decay; to become wearied, faint.* Targ. Is. XL, 7. Ib. LXIV, 5; a. fr.—B. Mets. 21^{b} דנַתְרָא that it (the fig) dropped (and was not taken off the tree). Ib. אע״ג דנָתְרִין ויתי וכ׳ even when the olives have dropped &c. Sabb. 33^{b} וקא נָתְרָן דמעת עיניה and the tears fell from his eyes; a. fr.

Af. אַתִּיר *to drop, shed, let fall.* Targ. Ruth II, 16. Targ. Y. II Ex. IX, 32 ואַתְּרַת (not ואַתְּ׳).—Y. Kil. VII, beg. 30^{d} דמַתְּרָן טרפיהון וכ׳ where trees shed their leaves even in midsummer. Naz. 42^{a} ארעה דלא מַתְּרָא an earth which does not cause falling out of the hair; a. e.—Y. Yeb. XVI, 15^{d} אתרין, v. infra.

Pa. נַתֵּר 1) (neut. verb) *to crumble, fall in.* B. Kam. 9^{b} בור דרכה לנַתּוּרֵי a pit is liable to fall in (and mere covering it up is not a sufficient precaution).—2) *to drop, shed.* Targ. Is. I, 30; a. e.—Y. Yeb. XVI, 15^{d} (if one says of a person) נַתְּרֵי פלוני, 'I have dropped that man', you must not allow his wife to marry again (it does not necessarily mean that he saw him dead), for I may say, he means [read:] אַתְּרֵי לפלוני מאכל I dropped that man something to eat.

נֶתֶר f. (b. h.; preced.; v. esp. Naz. 42^{a} quot. in preced.) 1) (*nitron*,) *natron, native carbonate of soda* (v. Sm. Bibl. Dict. s. v. Nitre, a. Sm. Ant. s. v. Nitron). Sabb. IX, 5; Nidd. IX, 6. Ib. 62^{a}; Sabb. 90^{a}, v. אֲלֶכְסַנְדְּרִי a. אַנְטִיפַּטְרִית; a. e.—2) כלי נ׳ *a vessel made of alum crystals.* Kel. II, 1. Ab. Zar. 33^{b} (expl. כלי מחפורת וכ׳, v. מַחְפּוֹרֶת); a. fr. [v., however, Maim. to Kel. l. c.]

נִתְרָא, נִי׳ I ch. same. Targ. Jer. II, 22. Targ. Prov. XXV, 20 (Ms. יתרא as in Pesh.).

נִתְרָא, נִי׳ II ch. = h. נֶשֶׁר I, *dropping.* Targ. O. a. Y. I Lev. XIX, 10 (h. text פרט).

נָתַשׁ (b. h.; cmp. נתץ) *to break loose, tear off.*

Nif. נִיתּוֹשׁ, נִתַּשׁ, *to be torn loose, be released.* Lev. R. s. 29; Gen. R. s. 56, v. נָתַשׁ II a. נָתַר I.

Hif. הִתִּישׁ *to uproot.* Gen. R. s. 23, beg. (play on מתושאל, Gen. IV, 18) מַתִּישָׁן אני וכ׳ I shall tear them out of this world.—[הַתִּישׁ or הִתִּישׁ *to weaken*, v. תָּשַׁשׁ.]

***נְתַשׁ** h. same. Targ. Ps. CXVIII, 10, sq. אֶתְּשִׁינּוּן (ed. Lag. אֶתּוֹשְׁשִׁינּוּן; Regia a. Levita אֶתּוֹשְׁשִׁי׳), v. תְּשַׁשׁ.

ס

ס *Samekh*, the fifteenth letter of the Alphabet. It interchanges with שׂ, e.g. פָּרַס a. פָּרַשׂ, נָסָא a. נָשָׂא; a. fr.; with ז, q. v.; with צ, as סַוָּאר a. צַוָּאר.—ס preformative for Safel forms, as in סִרְהֵב, סקבל &c.

ס׳ as numeral, *sixty*, v. א׳.

סְאָא, v. סְאָה ch.

סָאַב [*to be rough, ugly,*] *to be filthy, unclean, repulsive.*

Pi. סִיאֵב *to soil, make unclean; to unfit for sacrifice* on account of repulsive appearance. Part. pass. מְסוֹאָב, f. מְסוֹאֶבֶת; *pl.* מְסוֹאָבִים, מְסוֹאָבִין; מְסוֹאָבוֹת.—ידים מס׳ *unwashed hands.* Hall. II, 2. Hull. II, 5; a. fr.—Tem. 8[a] ירעו ... הא מס׳ וקיימין (you say) 'let them go to pasture until they become unfit for sacrifice', but are they not already unfit (being blemished)?

Hithpa. הִסְתָּאֵב *to become filthy, repulsive, unfit for sacrifice.* Yeb. XI, 5 יהא רועה עד שיִסְתָּאֵב let it go to pasture, until it becomes unfit for sacrifice. Tem. l. c. עד שיִסְתָּאֲבוּ, v. supra. Ib. IV, 1 עד שתִּסְתָּאֵב; a. fr.

סְאֵב I ch. same.

Pa. סָאֵב, סָאֵיב 1) *to soil, defile, make unclean, unfit for sacrifice.* Targ. Lev. XV, 31. Targ. Gen. XXXIV, 5; a. fr.—Taan. 11[a] bot. ההוא דסָאֵיב נפשיה that is because he defiled himself (by touching a corpse &c.). Y. Maas. Sh. III, 54[b] top סָאֵב לה ופדי לה made the fruit unclean and also redeemed it. Y. Snh. I, 18[b] top חד בר נש ס׳ וכ׳ a man caused a priest to become unclean; a. e.—*Part. pass.* מְסָאַב, f. מְסָאֲבָא; *pl.* מְסָאֲבִין &c. Targ. Lev. XIV, 40. Ib. O. XII, 2. Ib. XI, 8; a. fr.—Tem. 22[a] הא מְסָאֲבָה וקיימא is it not already unfit for sacrifice?, v. preced. Ab. Zar. 37[a]; Eduy. VIII, 4 Ms. M., v. infra.—2) *to declare unclean.* Targ. Lev. XIII, 44; a. fr.

Ithpa. אִסְתָּאַב *to be made unclean, be unclean.* Targ. Num. VI, 12 (Regia מסאב). Targ. Y. ib. 11. Targ. O. Lev. XIII, 45. Targ. O. Deut. XXII, 9 (h. text תקדש); a. fr.—Eduy. VIII, 4 ודיקרב במיתא מִתְסָאֵב (Ms. M. מְסָאַב) only what is sure to have touched a corpse is unclean (v. Ab. Zar. 37[b]).

סְאֵב II or **סָאַב** (cmp. preced.; v. סִיב I) [*to be hairy,*] *to be old.* Targ. Prov. XXII, 6 נסאב ed. Lag. (oth. ed. נְסוּב, יְסוּב, נסאובא; Ms. נסאבא).—Y. Dem. III, 23[c] bot. כד תִּסְאֲבוּן וכ׳ when you are old (appointed elders, v. זָקֵן), I shall tell you.

סָאבָא m. (preced.) *old man*, v. סָב.

סְאָה f. (b. h.) *S'ah*, a measure of volume for dry objects and for liquids; in gen. *measure.* Men. XII, 4 בארבעים ס׳ וכ׳ in a reservoir containing forty S. he can bathe for purification, in forty less one drop &c. Mikv. I, 7; a. fr.—Sot. 9[a] אין ... עד שתתמלא סְאָתוֹ the Lord does not exact payment (punishment) of a man until his measure is full. Ib. 8[b]; Tosef. ib. III, 1 (ref. to בסאסאה, Is. XXVII, 8) אין לי אלא שמודד בס׳ וכ׳ this would prove only that the Lord measures by the S'ah (repays only great sins, overlooking the small ones) &c.; Y. ib. I, 17[a].—בֵּית ס׳ (or sub. בית) *a field requiring one S'ah of seed,* (a square measure) *Beth S'ah.* Shebi. III, 2. B. Bath. VII, 2 רובע לס׳ one fourth of a Kab for each (Beth) S'ah; a. fr.—Tanh. Ki Thissa 26 משקל ארבעים ס׳ forty S'ah in weight (weight of forty S'ah of wheat).—*Pl.* סְאִין, סְאִים, סָאוֹת. Y. l. c. (ref. to סאון, Is. IX, 4) ריבה כאן ס׳ הרבה the text intimates here a variety of measures (recompenses). Men. VII, 1 חמש ס׳ וכ׳ five Jerusalem S'ah which are equal to six Desert S'ah. Ib. 77[a]; a. fr.—*Du.* סָאתַיִם. Ter. X, 8. Shebi. III, 4; a. fr.

סְאָא, סְאָה ch. same. Targ. II Kings VII, 1; 16; a. e.—*Pl.* סְאִין, סָאוִוין, סָאוִין, סָאוֵי, סָאוָון, סְיָון, סָוָן. Targ. Gen. XVIII, 6. Targ. Y. Ex. XXIX, 4; a. fr.—Targ. Y. Deut. XXXIV, 12 (*a weight*, v. preced.).—Pes. 113[a] סָאוֵי Ms. M. (ed. סְאָה). M. Kat. 12[a] בר שית ס׳ וכ׳ a vessel containing six S'ah (of beer) but well closed, is better &c.; a. e.—*Du.* סָאתָן. Targ. II Kings l. c.—V. סָאתָא.

סְאוֹב m. (סְאֵב I) *unclean object; uncleanness.* Targ. Y. Lev. XXI, 1. Targ. Y. Deut. VII, 26 ס׳ שקצא (ed. Amst. סְאֵיב, not סָ׳) what has become unclean through an abomination.

סוֹבְתָא, סוֹאַבְתָא, סְאוֹבְתָא f. (preced.) 1) *uncleanness*, esp. *menstruation.* Targ. Ez. XXIV, 11. Targ. Y. Gen. XVIII, 11 (ed. Vien. סיבְתָא). Targ. Lev. XV, 25; 31 (some ed. סְאֵיב׳); a. fr.—2) cmp. (נִדָּה) *menstruant.* Targ. O. ib. 33 (Y. סיאובְתָא; some ed. סֵיאֵיב׳); a. e.—*Pl.* סוֹאֲבָתָא. Targ. II Chr. XXIX, 16. Targ. O. Lev. XVI, 16; 19 סוֹאֲבַת constr. (Y. סוֹאֲבוֹת Hebraism); a. e.

סְאוֹר, v. שְׂאוֹר.

סְאוּרָא, סְאוּר, v. סִיאוּר, סִיאוּרָא.

סָאט, v. סוּט.

סְאֵיב, סָאֵיב, v. סְאֵב I a. סְאוֹב.

סָאֵים, v. סוּם I ch.

סָאִין, v. סִין. [סְאִין *pl.* of סְאָה.]

סָאמָא *silver*, v. סִימָא I.

סָאן, v. סִין.

סָאנֵי, v. סְנֵי.

סאסא, סאניא Targ. Prov. XVI, 16; XVII, 3 some ed., v. סִימָא I.

סָאסָא, סָאסְאָה m. h. a. ch. (=סעסע, cmp. סער, שׂער; cmp. זְאזָא) *bristle, awn* or *beard of grain.* Sot. 5[a] (Ar. סָסָא). Ḥull. 17[b] דמיא לס׳ (Ar. לססא) if the slaughtering knife is rough like a bristle of &c.—*Pl.* סָאסִין, constr. סָאסֵי. Koh. R. to IX, 11 שהיה רץ על ס׳ שיבולין וכ׳ (not שיבולי׳א; some ed. שָׂאסֵי) he ran over the ears of standing grain, and they were not broken.

סָאפוֹן m. *soap, detergent,* v. צָפוֹן I.

סָאתָא I, סָאתָה f. ch.=h. סְאָה, *S'ah; measure.* Targ. Is. XXVII, 8. Targ. Job XX, 22; a. e.—Y. Ter. X, 47[b] top כמה ס׳ עבדא וכ׳ how much does a S'ah contain? Twenty four Log. Lev. R. s. 36; Y. Snh. X, 27[d] כארנש... והא ס׳ וכ׳ as if one says, here is the bag, here is the Sela, and here is the measure, rise and measure (said of one who asks immediate reward for a good deed); Ruth R. introd. (some ed. סאה); a. e.—*Pl.*, v. סְאָה ch.

סָאתָא II f.=סְחוּתָא, *sweepings, refuse.* Lam. R. to I, 15 (expl. סלה, ib.) עבדי ס׳ וכ׳ (some ed. סָאתֵי *pl.*) he made me like refuse before them. Ib. בבר גמזא צווחין לס׳ סריקי (read סלותא; Ar. לסחותא סולתא.. בבריגיא) in Bar Gamza they call sweepings *sallutha* (that which is thrown away); v. סְחוּיָתָא.

סַב, v. נְסַב.

סָאבָא I, סָבָא, סָב m. ch. (v. סְאַב II, סִיב)=h. שָׂב, *grey, old; elder; ancestor; scholar* (=h. זָקֵן). Targ. Is. III, 2. Targ. Gen. XXIV, 2; a. fr.—Targ. Y. II Lev. XXII, 27 סַבְיָא.—Targ. II Esth. VII, 9 כאגג אבא סב (ed. Lag. אבא. טב, corr. acc.) like Agag my *grandfather.*—Y. Yeb. XII, 12[d] bot., opp. טַלְיָתָא. Ḥull. 6[a] אשכחיה ההוא ס׳ an old man (or scholar) met him; Sabb. 34[a]. Gen. R. s. 74 (ref. to Ps. CXXIV, 1) ישראל ס׳ it means Israel the patriarch (not Israel the people); Midr. Till. to Ps. l. c. Y. Ned. X, end, 42[b] לְסָבִי to my ancestor. Ib. ר׳ דוסתי ס׳ R. Dostay senior; a. fr.—[Y. Maas. Sh. V, 56[c] top, v. כָּפָא I.]—*Pl.* סָבִין, סָבֵי, סָבַיָּא. Targ. Zech. VIII, 4. Targ. Joel I, 14. Targ. Prov. XX, 29 (Ms. סֵיבֵי); a. fr.—Y. Peah VII, end, 21[b] אית חוו ס׳ וכ׳ there were (poor) old men in our days &c. Kidd. 33[a] ר׳... ס׳ דארמאי R. J. used to rise before gentile old men. Snh. 17[b] ס׳ דסורא the scholars of Sura. B. Bath. 58[b] סאבי דיהודאי the Jewish scholars. Bekh. 8[b], v. אַתּוּנָס; a. fr.—*Fem.* (סָבָא), סַבְתָא. Y. Maas. Sh. III, 54[b] top אמר לון חד סבא (read: אמרה לון חדא ס׳) said to them a certain matron (prob. wife of a scholar). Ib. הדא סבתא.. מימר that matron was of the opinion. B. Bath. 125[b] נכסי לס׳ I bequeathe my property to my grandmother. Ib. אי קדים ס׳ וכ׳ if that grandmother had sold the property bequeathed to her before the claim could be preferred, the sale would have been valid; a. fr.—*Pl.* סָבָן. Targ. Zech. l. c.; a. e.—[סָב *to be old,* v. סִיב.]

סָבָא II 1) pr. n. m. *Saba.* Y. Yeb. IX, beg. 10[a] נירוא בר ס׳; Y. Kil. IX, beg. 31[d] סָבָה.—2) כְּפַר ס׳ pr. n. pl. *K'far Saba,* in Samaria. Y. Dem. II, 22[c] bot. (ed. Krot. כפרסבא, one word). Nidd. 61[a]; Tosef. ib. VIII, 5 (v. Hildesh. Beitr., p. 10).

סָבָא III (b. h.; cmp. שָׂבַע) *to drink freely.*—Part. pass. סָבוּא, *pl.* סְבוּאִים, סְבוּאִין *soaked, satiated.* Nidd. 24[b] עצמותיו ס׳ Ar. (ed. סכויין) his bones are found satiated with moisture, i. e. *porous,* contrad. to משוחין oily, smooth.

סְבָא ch. same. Part. סָבֵי. Targ. O. Deut. XXI, 20.—[Targ. I Sam. XXX, 20 וסבא some ed., read וּשְׁבָא.].

Pa. סַבֵּי *to retail wine* in the shop or tavern. B. Bath. 98[a] אדעתא לְסַבּוּיֵיה with the intention to retail it.

Af. אַסְבָּא *to satiate, soak;* trnsf. (cmp. סָפַג) *to lash.* Keth. 10[a] אַסְבוּהּ כופרי make him absorb (strike him with) palm switches. Ib. וּמַסְבְּרִנַן ליה וכ׳ and we lash him nevertheless.

סָבַב (b. h.) *to go around, turn.* Num. R. s. 18 כשהייתי... והולך וסוֹבֵב כל וכ׳ when I travelled ... and went around all the towns; הייתי סובב והולך מעיר וכ׳ I went around from town to town. Erub. 56[a] וסובב אל צפון בלילה 'and turns northward' (Koh. I, 6) by night; a. e.

Nif. נָסַב *to take a turn.* Num. R. s. 4 ונָסַבָּה ורחבה למעלה it turned upward and became wider.

Pi. סִיבֵּב 1) *to surround.* Erub. l. c.; B. Bath. 25[b] (ref. to Koh. l. c.) פעמים מְסַבַּבְתָּן ופעמים מהלכתן (Rashi סוֹבַבְתָּן, v. Rabb. D. S. a. l. note 4) at seasons the sun goes around them (making a circuitous route), and at seasons it passes straight through (from north-east to south-west). Erub. 23[b]; Num. R. s. 13 סַבֵּב tie around; a. e.—Trnsf. *to be around a person, to wait upon.* Deut. R. s. 1 (play on סב את ההר, Deut. II, 3) הרבה סי׳ עשו את הורו וכ׳ a long while has Esau been around his parent &c.—סי׳ על הפתחים *to go around from door to door, to beg.* Tosef. Peah IV, 8 המְסַבֵּב על... אין וכ׳ for the poor man that goes begging, the public charities are not bound to do anything. Y. ib. I, 15[d] top כבד.. אפי׳ את מסבב וכ׳ 'honor thy father and thy mother', even if thou have to go begging (thou must support them); Pesik. R. s. 23—24; a. e.—Ruth R. to I, 1 עכשיו.. מְסַבְּבִין פתחי וכ׳ now all Israel will surround my gate ..., waiting for distribution of food; Yalk. ib. 598 יהיו.. מסובבין.—2) *to carry around from place to place.* Kel. I, 7 וּמְסַבְּבִין לתוכן וכ׳ and you may carry a corpse from one (of the fortified places) to another; Tosef. ib. B. Kam. I, 14 ומס׳ בתוכן.—3) *to place around.* Num. R. s. 2 סי׳ לכסאו וכ׳ he placed four angels around his throne.—Part. pass. מְסוּבָּב, f. מְסוּבֶּבֶת *surrounded, closed.* B. Bath. 25[b], v. אַכְסַדְרָא.—*Pl.* מְסוּבִּים, מְסוּבִּין *assembled, arranged around.* Ab. Zar. 18[a] מס׳ לו וכ׳ (Ms. M. מְסוֹבְבִין אותו) (his sins) are arranged around him on the day of judgment (as witnesses). Yalk. Ruth l. c., v. supra.—Esp. *reclining on the dining couch around the tables* (v. מְסוּבָּה). Ex. R. s. 25 מס׳ ואוכלין וכ׳ lying on couches and eating and praising &c. Pes. 101[b] בני... מס׳ לשתות the members of a party that were assembled for a feast; ib. 102[a]. Tosef. ib. X, 12; a. fr.—[Tanḥ. Ḥayé 3 מסביב, read: מכתיב, v. כָּתַב.]

Hif. הֵסֵב, הֵסִיב, הֵיסִי׳ 1) [*to surround the table,*] *to recline for dining in company.* Ber. VI, 6 (42[a]) הֵסֵיבּוּ אחד וכ׳ (Bab. ed. הֵסֵבּוּ; Y. ed. הֵיסֵבּוּ) if they lie down for a meal, one says grace in behalf of all, opp. היו יושבין. Tosef. ib. IV, 20 בעל הבית שהיה מֵיסֵב ואוכל וכ׳ if a host has been reclining in company and eating, and a neighbor called him away to speak to him. Ib. V, 5; Y. Taan. IV, 68^a bot. בזמן שהן שתי ... ומיסב וכ׳ when there are two couches, the highest in rank goes up and reclines at the head of the uppermost couch &c., v. הֵסֵב. Pes. X, 1 אפי׳ עני ... עד שיָּסֵב even the poorest man in Israel must not eat (on the Passover night) without reclining (to indicate that he is a free man); a. fr.—2) *to cause to recline, to invite.* Ex. R. s. 25 (ref. to ויסב, Ex. XIII, 18, a. שלחן, Ps. LXXVIII, 19) הֵסִיבָן תחת ענני וכ׳ he invited them to recline under the clouds of glory (v. סִיגְמָטִין); a. e.—3) *to turn around.* Pesik. R. s. 14 עתיד אני לְהָסֵיב על עולמי וכ׳ I shall turn again to my world in mercy.

Hof. הוּסַב *to be transferred* from tribe to tribe (Num. XXXVI, 7). B. Bath. 112^a כבר הוּסַבָּה the field had been transferred (before the division of the land); שכבר הוסבה לא אמרינן we do not adopt the argument that a transfer before the division made any difference (v. comment., a. Rabb. D. S. a. l. notes 4 a. 5 for Var. Lect.).

Polel סוֹבֵב *to surround.* Ab. Zar. 18^a, v. supra.

סְבַב ch. same; *Af.* אַסְּב *to go around* (announcing). Y. R. Hash. II, 58^a top דהוון אילין מַסְּבִין יומא דין וכ׳ these went around (as messengers to announce the New-Moon) to-day, and others the day after. Ib. למה מתו דיַסְּבוּן; מַסְּבָה, v. צְפַת.

סִבְבָא m. (preced.; cmp. שִׁיבְבָא) *neighbor, borderer.*—*Pl.* סִבְבַיָּא. Targ. Is. VII, 20 בס׳ ובמגריא בעברי וכ׳ (ed. Lag. בסיבביא במגריא) read: בס׳ בעברי וכ׳ (במגריא being a gloss to our w.) among the borderers on the sides of &c.

סִבָּה, v. סִיבָּה.

סבהור, Targ. Prov. II, 7 ed. Lag., read שִׁבְחוֹר=סִבְחוֹר.

סַבְהֲלוֹם m.=h. יַהֲלֹם, name of *a jewel* in the high priest's breast-plate, *diamond.* Targ. O. Ex. XXVIII, 18 (some ed. סִ׳); XXXIX, 11. Targ. Y. Num. II, 10.

סֵבוֹ, v. v. סֵיבוֹ.

סַבּוֹאָתָא, v. סַבּוֹיָתָא.

סבוי, Yalk. Num. 773, סברוני ס׳, v. סִיפּוּיָא.

סַבּוֹיָתָא c. pl. (סְבָא) *wine-retailers.* Ab. Zar. 71^a (Ar. סַבּוֹאָתָא); ib. 72^b סַבְיָתָא.

סִבּוּךְ, v. סִיפּוּךְ.

סִבּוּל, v. סִיבּוּלָת.

סַבּוּלָאָה* m. (סְבַל) *load-carrier.* B. Mets. 93^b בר ס׳ ארא (Ms. R. סַבּוּלָא; Ms. H. סַבּוּלָאָה, Ms. F. סַקּוּלָא *of Saccola=Sacala* in Gedrosia?).

סִבּוּלֶת, סִבּוּלִית, v. סִיבּוּלֶת.

סִבּוּנָה, Y. Sabb. VI, 8^a bot. ed. Zyt., v. סִבְנִי.

סִבּוּר, סִבּוּרָא, v. sub. סִיבּ׳.

סָבוֹרָא m. (סְבַר I) 1) *a reasoner* (opp. to learned, v. גְּמַר II). Y. Sabb. III, 6^a ההדין ס׳ דלא ילִיף וכ׳ that reasoner who has neither studied nor attended scholars.—2) (adj.) *imaginative, fanciful.* Y. Kidd. III, 63^d bot. דחגיי אינשא ס׳ הוא (not אינשי) for Ḥ. is a fanciful man (whose traditions cannot be relied upon).

סְבוֹרָא m. *hope,* v. סִבְרָא.

סָבוּתָא, v. סֵיבוּתָא.

סַבְטָא pr. n. m. *Sabṭa.* Snh. 64^a ס׳ בן אלס (v. אָלָס, a. אַבְלַס); Y. ib. X, 28^d סובתה; Sifré Num. 131, a. Yalk. ib. 771 סבטיא.

סַבַּטְיָא, v. preced.

סַבַּטְיוֹן, סַמְבַּ׳, סַנְבַּ׳ pr. n., נְהַר ס׳ (Σαββατεῖον, Σαββατικός) *the river Sabbation,* said to rest on the seventh day (v. Plin. Hist. Nat. XXXI, 2; Jos. Bell. Jud. V, 5, 1; Neub. Géogr. p. 33). Snh. 65^b נהר ס׳ יוכיח let the river S. prove (that the seventh day is the Sabbath); Yalk. Lev. 617 סנ׳; Gen. R. s. 11 סמ׳; Tanḥ. Ki Thissa 33 סמ׳; Pesik. R. s. 23 סמ׳. Gen. R. s. 73 עשרת .. לפנים מנהר סמ׳ וכ׳ the ten tribes were exiled to within the confines of the river S., whereas Judah and Benjamin were scattered over all lands; Y. Snh. X, 29^c bot. סנ׳; Targ. Y. Ex. XXXIV, 10 מן לגיו לנהר סמ׳.

סַבְיָא m. 1) *old,* v. סָב.—2) *officer of the royal household.* Koh. R. to IX, 18 (expl. המזכיר, II Kings XVIII, 18) ס׳ (some ed. סָכְיָא).

סָבִיב (b. h.; סָבַב) *around.* Tanḥ. B'midb. 12 ס׳ למשכן around the Tabernacle; a. e.

סְבִיבָה f. (preced.) *neighborhood.*—*Pl.* סְבִיבוֹת. Num. R. s. 18 כיון שראו שנסתלקו ישראל מסְּבִיבוֹתֵיהֶם when they saw that the Israelites had removed themselves from their neighborhood; a. e.

סְבִיכָא m. (סְבַךְ)=b. h. סְבָךְ, *thicket.* Targ. Ps. LXXIV, 5. Targ. II Chr. XX, 2 סְבִיךְ דיקליא (h. text חצצון תמר).

סְבִילָה f. (סָבַל) *carrying a burden, use of the stem* סָבַל. R. Hash. 11^b אתיא ס׳ ס׳ Ms. M. (omitted in ed., v. Rabb. D. S. a. l. note) there is an analogy between סבל (Ex. VI, 6) and סבל (Ps. LXXXI, 7); Yalk. Ex. 177; Yalk. Ps. 831.

סבין, Y. R. Hash. II, 59^c top, v. סְבַי.

סְבִינְתָא, v. סַבְנִיתָא.

סְבִיסְקֵי m. pl. (v. Löw Pfl., p. 188 sq.) *mandrake flowers.* Snh. 99^b (expl. דודאים, Gen. XXX, 14) ס׳ (Var. סיבסוך, Ms. M. סכסוך; v. Rabb. D. S. a. l. note).

סְבִיעַ, v. שְׂבַע.

סבירניות, Y. Keth. I, 25^b top, v. טַבְרְיָא.

סַבְּיְיתָא, v. סַפְוֹיְיתָא.

סָבַךְ (b. h.) *to interweave, interlace*, esp. *to make a hedge* or *dam* with twigs, stones &c. Shebi. III, 8 לא יְסַבּוֹךְ בעפר Ms. M. a. R. S. a. l. (ed. יסמוך) he must not cover the dam with earth, opp. עושה חייץ, v. חַיִיץ.

Nif. נִסְבַּךְ *to be caught, entangled.* Lev. R. s. 29, a. e., v. נָטַשׁ II. Yalk. Num. 782, v. infra; a. e.

Hithpa. הִסְתַּבֵּךְ, *Nithpa.* נִסְתַּבֵּךְ same. Gen. R. s. 56 מִסְתַּבְּכִין בצרות entangled in troubles. Ib. [read:] עתידין בניך לְהִסְתַּבֵּךְ במלכיות ונמשכין ממלכות למלכות thy children will be entangled (come in conflict) with successive empires, and be drawn from empire to empire; Yalk. Num. 782 נִסְבָּכִין. Gen. R. s. 65 וכ׳ בשערו and the chaff stuck in his hair. Y. Sabb. VII, 10ª bot. נִסְתַּבְּכוּ בגדיו וכ׳ if his garments were caught in thorns; a. e.

Hof. הוּסְבָּךְ same. Peah VII, 3 [read:] עקץ .. הו׳ בעלים ונפל לארץ וכ׳ if he cut a cluster off by its stalk, and it was intercepted by the foliage, and in falling to the ground single berries fell off.

Pi. סִבֵּךְ *to entangle.* [Y. Kil. II, end, 28ᵇ מסבכין, some ed., v. סָכַךְ.]—Part. pass. מְסוּבָּךְ. Ḥull. 30ᵇ תחת צמר מס׳ if he put the slaughtering knife under the entangled wool (on the animal's neck). M. Kat. 6ª top בִּמְסוּבָּכִין when the trees in the field are irregularly scattered (not planted in rows). Sot. 48ª; Yalk. Is 292 (ref. to ארזה, Zeph. II, 14) בית המסובך בארזים a house which lies in a thicket of cedars.

סְבַךְ ch. same. Part. pass. סְבִיךְ. Ḥull. 48ª והוא דס׳ בבסרא provided the perforated lung is intergrown with the fleshy part of the ribs.

Pa. סַבֵּךְ *to weave a net.* Targ. Prov. XXX, 28 דִּמְסַבְּכָא ed. Lag. (Var. דִּמְסַבְּכָה).

סֶבֶךְ m. (preced.) *net-work, web.* Tosef. Kel. B. Bath. VII, 1 אם יש לחן ס׳ (ed. Zuck. a. oth. סכך) if the fringes form a web. Ib. ס׳ עולה וכ׳ a web of fringes is partly subject and partly not subject to the standard measure of &c.

***סַבָּךְ** m. (preced.) *net-weaver.* Erub. 72ᵇ top ר׳ יהודה הס׳ R. Ḥan. a. Alfasi (ed. הסבר, v. Rabb. D. S. a. l. note 20).

סִבְּכָא, ס׳ m. (preced. wds.) *net, head-dress.*—*Pl.* סִבְּכַיָא, סִיבְ׳. Targ. Is. III, 18 (h. text שהרנים); v. next w.—[Ib. VII, 20 סיבכיא, ed. Lag., v. סִבְּכָא.]

סְבָכָה, שְׂ׳ f. (b. h. שְׂ׳) 1) same. Tosef. Sabb. IV (V), 11 ס׳ המוזהבת (ed. Lag. סבכא, Var. סבכא, corr. acc.) a gold-embroidered hair net; Sabb. 57ᵇ. Y. ib. VI, 8ᵇ bot.; Neg. XI, 11, a. fr. שביס של ס׳, v. שָׁבִיס; Tosef. Kel. B. Bath. V, 15 שביס של ש׳. Sabb. l. c. כל שהוא למטה מן הש׳ whatever ornament is worn beneath the net; ib. 65ª הס׳; (Tosef. ib. IV (V), 7 חיפוי שלמטה משערה); a. fr.—2) *any net-work, mat* &c. Kel. XXVIII, 9 ס׳ של זקנה the old woman's net-work (mat to sit upon, v. Maim. a. l.). Ib. חלוק .. העשוי כס׳ the public woman's shirt which is like net-work (gauze, v. הוּץ II). Y. Ter. VIII, 45ᵈ אירס .. עומד כס׳ the venom of the serpent remains on top (of liquids) as a net-like film; Y. Ab. Zar. II, 41ᵈ top דומה לש׳; Y. Sabb. I, 3ᵈ top עשוי כש׳; a. fr.—Ib. VI, 7ᵈ סביסה, read שבכה, v. סְבִיסָל II.—*Pl.* סְבָכוֹת, שְׂ׳. Kel. XXIV, 16; Tosef. ib. B. Bath. II, 10 שלש ס׳ הן וכ׳ there are three categories of nets with regard to levitical cleanness; a. e.

סִבְּכַיִיר, v. סִיבְכַי.

סְבַכְתָּא f. ch.=h. סְבָכָה. B. Bath. 146ª (Ms. M. ספכ׳, oth. Mss. סבתכא, ספתכא, סככתא, v. Rabb. D. S. a. l. note), v. בַּיְיכָא.

סָבַל (b. h.) *to carry* a load; *to sustain; to endure.* Lev. R. s. 4, end הנפש הזו סוֹבֶלֶת... והקב״ה סובל את עולמו the soul supports the body, and the Lord sustains his world; (Tanḥ. Ḥayé 3 משמרת ... משמר). Pes. 113ᵇ ארבעה ... אין סוֹבְלָתָן there are four things which the mind (of man) cannot endure. Gen. R. s. 22 (ref. to Gen. IV, 13) לעליונים .. אתה סובל ולפשעי אין אתה סובל thou bearest those on high and those below, and my trespass thou wilt not bear? Y. R. Hash. II, end, 58ᵇ (ref. to Ps. CXLIV, 14 אלופינו מסבלים) בשעה שהגדולים סוֹבְלִין את וכ׳ when the great bear the small (take care of them), there is no breach &c.; ib. בשעה שהקטנים סובלין וכ׳ when the small bear the great (respect their superiority), there is &c.; Yalk. Ps. 888; Ruth R. introd (ושם). Ex. R. s. 5 סָבְלוּ מכות they endured maltreatment; a. fr.—Y. Peah I, 16ᵇ הפורק .. ואיני סוֹבְלָהּ he who throws off the yoke, that is, he who says, there is a law, but I will not bear it.

Pi. סִיבֵּל *to load.* Part. pass. מְסוּבָּל. Ber. 17ª (ref. to Ps. l. c.) מְסוּבָּלִים במצות laden with good deeds; מס׳ ביסורים laden with pains. Yalk. Deut. 963 מסובלים בכספם וכ׳ (Deut. R. s. 11 היו סובלים) carrying their silver and their gold; a. e.

סְבַל ch. same. Targ. Y. Deut. XXXII, 11. Targ. Job XXI, 3. Targ. Y. II Deut. XXIV, 15; a. fr.—Cant. R. to V, 14 לְמִיסְבַּל, v. סְבַנִי. Gen. R. s. 38 דְּסָבֵיל רוחא, v. רוּחָא; a. e.

Pa. סַבֵּל (v. סִבְלוֹן) *to send presents of betrothal.* Kidd. 50ᵇ מְסַבְּלֵי והדר מקדשי where it is customary to send the presents before betrothal; a. e.

סַבָּל m. (b. h.; preced.) *load-carrier.* Y. B. Mets. X, end, 12ᶜ; (Bab. ib. 118ᵇ כַּתָּף). Kidd. 82ᵇ; Y. ib. IV, end, 66ᵈ; Tosef. ib. V, 15 (ed. Zuck. note). Tanḥ., ed. Bub., M'tsora 11 בריאים כסבלו של עולם as strong as he who carries the world; Yalk. Ps. 808.—*Pl.* סַבָּלִין. Kel. XXVIII, 9 כסת הס׳ the cushion which load-carriers wear on their heads.

סְבָלָה f. (b. h.; preced.) *load, burden.*—*Pl.* סְבָלוֹת. Lev. R. s. 37 סִבְלוֹתָם, v. יָשַׁב. Ex. R. s. 1 שהיה רואה בסבלותם וכ׳ he saw their burdens and wept. Ib. היה הולך ומישב להן סִבְלוֹתֵיהֶן he went and helped them to arrange their burdens; a. e.

סִבְלוֹן, סִי׳ m. (preced. wds.) 1) *load.* Sifra introd. עשוי לסיבלון אחר made for the carrying of something else (than only persons).—2) *pl.* סִבְלוֹנוֹת, סִיבְ׳ (cmp. b. h. מַשָּׂא, מַשְׂאֵת) *presents*, esp. *presents of betrothal* (donatio propter nuptias). Kidd. II, 6 אע״פ ששלח ס׳ וכ׳ although he sent presents after that (after an invalid betrothal). Ib. 50[b] חוששין לס׳ we have an apprehension concerning nuptial presents, i. e. the fact of a man's having sent presents to a woman gives rise to the apprehension that a betrothal may have taken place (Tosaf.), or that the presents may have been meant as a means of betrothal (Rashi). Ib. אימא ... כי קא משדר ס׳ אדעתא וכ׳ I might think ... when he sent the presents he did so with the intention of making them the means of betrothal. B. Bath. IX, 5 השולח ס׳ ... ארץ נגבין if one sends presents ..., they cannot be reclaimed (in case of death or divorce before marriage). Ib. 146[a] ס׳ העשויין ליבלות presents intended for immediate consumption or wear; a. fr.

סבנה, v. next w.

סִיבְ׳, סוּבְ׳, סְבָנִי m. (cmp. Arab. *sabanu*, nomen oppidi ... a quo panni nomen acceperunt (Freytag); cmp. σάβανον, sabanum) *a cloth*, esp. *a head-cover which fell down over the shoulders, sibni*. Y. Sabb. VI, 8[a] bot. כריך סְבָנֵיה עליהון (ed. Zyt. סבונה, corr. acc.) he tied his *sibni* around them; Y. Yeb. XII, 12[d] top סְבָנָה. Gitt. 59[a] ס׳ (Ar. סוּ׳), v. חוֹמֵס. Cant. R. to V, 14 אפי׳ סבניה לא הוה יכיל למיסבל וכ׳ (he became so weak from studying that) he could not even carry his sibni (in his hand), but others had to take it off for him; v. next w.—*Pl.* סְבָנִין. Gen. R. s. 19 סכנין (corr. acc.) *a female head-cover*, corresp. to סודרין for males.

סְבִינְתָא, סְבָנִיתָא f. same. Sabb. 147[b] סבנ׳ צריך וכ׳ Ar. (ed. סב׳; Ms. O. סִיבְנִיְיתָא; Rashi Ms. סִיבְנָיָיתָא, *pl.*) if one carries a *sabnitha* (to be used at bathing, on the Sabbath), he must tie its two ends (around his neck, so that it be a part of his wearing apparel). Pesik. B'shall., p. 93[b] סְבָנִיתֵיה וכ׳ Ms. O. (ed. סבינתיה, v. Bub. notes a. l.) even his *s.*, if another person did not take it off for him, he could not &c. (Ar. אפי׳ ס׳ לא יכיל טעין, v. preced.). Y. Shebu. VI, end, 37[b] ארים סביניתיה וכ׳ tore his *s.* off his head and said, this sheet (סדינא) shall not go out of my hands &c.—*Pl.* סִיבְ׳, סְבָנָיִין, סְבִינָיָיתָא, סִיבְנָ׳, סַבְנָיָיתָא. Sabb. l. c., v. supra.—Y. ib. VI, 8[b] bot. (expl. מטפחות, Is. III, 22) ס׳ רברבן large head-covers.

סְבַסְטִי pr. n. pl. (Σεβαστή) *Sebaste*, built by Herod on the site of the old Samaria (Shomron). Num. R. s. 10 (ref. to Am. VI, 1) that means the ten tribes שהיו יושבים לבטח בס׳ (not שיושבים) who dwelt safely in S.; Tanh. Sh'mini 5 בסבַסְטְיָא. Arakh. III, 2 (14[a]), v. חוֹלֶת; Sifra B'hucḳ. Par. 4, ch. X סְוַוסְטִי; Tosef. Arakh. II, 8 ספוסטא (Var. ספיסטא, corr. acc.).

***סְבַסְטִין** m. pl. (σεβαστοί) *members of the imperial family, princes*. Tanh. B'midb. 2 [read:] הרבצתי אתכם כס׳ וכ׳ I caused you to recline on couches like princes; (ref. to ויסב, Ex. XIII, 8) כדרך שהמלכים מסובין וכ׳ just as kings recline; [Var. בסיגמטין, בסוג׳, taken fr. Num. R. s. 1, beg., v. סִיגְמָטִין].

סְבַע *to be satisfied*, v. שְׂבַע.

סִיבְ׳, סַבְעָא m. (preced.) *plenty*. Targ. O. Gen. XLI, 29; 30; 31 ed. Berl. (oth. ed. שׂוֹבְעָא, שֻׂבְעָא). Targ. O. Deut. XXIII, 25 ed. Berl. (oth. ed. שׂוֹב׳, שְׂבַ׳). Targ. Prov. III, 10 סובעא Ms. (ed. שׂוֹבְעָנָא, שׂוּבְעָא).

סבקין, v. סִיבַּק.

סָבַר (b. h. שָׂבַר *Pi.*; Saf. of ברר) [*to be bright,*] *to look for, be hopeful; to think, imagine. Part. pass.* סָבוּר; f. סְבוּרָה; *pl.* סְבוּרִים, סְבוּרִין; סְבוּרוֹת *hoping; thinking*. Ruth R. to I, 1 היו ... ס׳ עליו the citizens were relying on him; (Yalk. ib. 598 בטוחין).—Keth. VII, 10 ס׳ הייתי וכ׳ I was in hopes that I might be able to bear it. Gitt. 56[b] וכס׳ הרג וכ׳ and he was like thinking (he imagined) that &c., v. הָרַג; a. fr.—Tanh. P'kudé 3 היו סוֹבְרִים וכ׳ (perh. to be read: סבורים) they thought that he (Adam) was their creator; Pirké d'R. El. ch. XI כסבורין.

Hif. הִסְבִּיר *to brighten, illustrate, make clear*. Koh. R. to X, 10 (ref. to Koh. l. c.) אם נקהה ... והוא אינו בא לידך לְהַסְבִּירוֹ בפניך וכ׳ if thy study has been dull to thee like iron (difficult), and he ... does not come to thy side to make it clear before thee, denounce him with all thy might.—Esp. הס׳ פנים *to show a bright face; to be friendly; to encourage*. Ib. ואין הרב מַסְבִּיר פ׳ לתלמיד and the teacher does not show the pupil a kind face (will not relent); ib. ואין הרב מסביר לתלמיד (sub. פנים). Ib. ואין הקב״ה מסביר פ׳ לדור and the Lord does not look favorably at the generation. Y. Yoma VI, beg. 43[b] שלא יהא הדיין מסביר פ׳ ... ומעיז וכ׳ that the judge must not be friendly towards the one and severe towards the other (of the litigants). Midr. Till. to Ps. CXXXVII אלהיהן ... וכיון שמַסְבִּירִין לו פ׳ וכ׳ their God is merciful, and as soon as they show him a kind face, he takes pity &c.; Pesik. R. s. 28. Ber. 63[b] אני ואתה נַסְבִּיר פ׳ בהלכה let us cheer each other up in the *halakhah* (by discussion). Ib. כשם שאני הִסְבַּרְתִּי ... הַסְבֵּר פ׳ וכ׳ as I have been kind to thee, so be thou kind (forgiving) to &c.; a. fr.

סְבַר, סְבִיר I ch. same, 1) (with אַפִּין) *to show a bright face, be pleasant; to favor* (with ב or ל). Targ. Y. Gen. IV, 4, sq. Targ. Job XXXII, 22 יִסְבַּר Ms. (ed. יְסוֹבַר *Poël*; some ed. יְסַבַּר *Pa.*).—*Part. pass.* סְבִיר; סְבִיר אפין *looked up to with favor, honored, popular*. Ib. XXII, 8.—2) *to be bright, intelligent*. Targ. O. Lev. XIX, 32 סָבַר (Y. ib. סָבִירִין).—3) *to look out for, hope; to speculate, plan; to imagine, believe*. Targ. Hos. XII, 7. Targ. Ps. XXVII, 14. Targ. Y. Ex. X, 11 סַבְרִין. Targ. Prov. XIV, 12; a. fr.—*Part. pass.* סְבִיר, סָבִיר *looking for, planning, thinking, believing*. Targ. O. Ex. X, 10. Targ. O. Gen. XXXVII, 8; a. fr.—Y. Ber. III, 6[c] top תמן סָבְרִית הֲוֵית there I thought about it, v. סְבַר.—4) *to conclude, argue, understand; to have an idea*. Targ. II Sam. XII, 19; a. e.—B. Bath. 65[a], a. fr. סבור מינה וכ׳ they concluded from this that ..., but it is not so. Gitt. 56[a] סבור רבנן לקרוביה the scholars proposed to offer it up on the altar. Keth. 87[b], a. fr. ס׳ ... למימר וכ׳ R. ... had an idea to say &c. (but was refuted). Ber. 3[a], a. fr. מאי קס׳ what is R. E.'s opinion? אי קס׳ שלש וכ׳ if he holds that the night contains three watches &c. Ib. 4[b] ר׳ יוחנן ס׳ וכ׳ R. J. argues (thus) &c. Ib. 27[a] מי סָבְרַת דהאי וכ׳ do you think that &c.?—Yeb. 72b חזריה.. וסַבְרָהּ וכ׳ he learned it by heart in three days, and reasoned it out (drew the logical conclusions from it) in three months. Sabb. 63a לִיסְבַּר, v. גְּמַר II. Keth. 77a דקסַבְרָא וקבילא for she understood well (her husband's physical condition) and accepted it; ib. דא סַבְרָא וקבילא did she not understand and accept? B. Mets. 65a סַבְרַת וקבילת thou didst understand and accept; a. fr.—ס׳ כ־ to think like, *to agree with, adopt the opinion of.* Succ. 33b ס׳ לה כותיה בחדא ופליג וכ׳ he agrees with him in one point, and differs in another point; a. fr.—ל־ סַבְרָא *is of the opinion, shares the opinion.* Ib.a אי ס׳ לן וכ׳ if we accept the opinion that &c. Hull. 48a ולית לא ס׳ ליה (abbr. ל״ס) but he himself does not entertain that opinion; a. fr.—Tanh. P'kudé 2 סַבְרֵי מרנן have the gentlemen formed an opinion?, i. e. how do you vote?—Ib. (introducing the benediction over wine) סברי מרנן have you agreed (to allow me to say the prayer)?, i. e. with your permission!—B. Kam. 32a ותִסְבְּרָא how can you understand that?, i.e. is this not a contradiction?—Gen. R. s. 34; s. 38 הוה מַסְבַּר ליה ולא ס׳ he explained to him, but he could not comprehend; מאי טעמא לית את סבר why is it that you do not comprehend?

Pa. סַבַּר 1) *to look for, hope, trust.* Targ. O. Gen. XLIX, 18 סַבָּרִית (ed. Berl. סַבְרִית).—2) with אַפִּין *to favor.* Targ. Job XXXII, 22, v. supra.

Af. אַסְבַּר 1) *to trust.* Targ. Prov. XI, 28 מַסְבִּיר Ed. Lag. (oth. ed. מְסַבַּר *Pa.*); a. e.—2) *to make confident.* Targ. Ps. XXII, 10.—3) (with אַפִּין) *to be kind to, cheer up.* Targ. Y. Num. VI, 26 יַסְבַּר סְבַר אפוי. Targ. I Chr. II, 55.—4) *to illustrate, explain.* Hull. 48a אַסְבְּרָהּ לי.. רבין Rabin.. made it clear to me. B. Mets. 33a דאַסְבְּרָן זומא וכ׳ who explained to us what *zomalistron* meant. Erub. 21b ואַסְבְּרָהּ במאי דדמי ליה and illustrated it by a simile. Y. ib. X, beg. 26a אַסְבְּרֵי רב וכ׳ R. H. enlightened me (saying) &c. Gen. R. l. c., v. supra; a. fr.

Ithpa. אִסְתַּבַּר 1) *to look for, hope; to plan, intend.* Targ. Ps. CVI, 13.—Targ. Y. II Gen. XLIX, 17.—2) *to be understood, be intelligible, evident*; to be *rational, logical.* R. Hash. 31b sq. אמר מלתא וא׳ טעמיה וכ׳ he said something, and his argument appeared reasonable, and his teacher instituted the usage in his (R. Johanan's) name. Y. Ab. Zar. I, 40a לא מִסְתַּבְּרָא כאוִין סוברה וכ׳ it is not reasonable to follow this opinion that it is not forbidden. Ber. 36a מסתברא כוותך it is reasonable to follow thy opinion, i. e. thou art obviously right. Sabb. 76a אדרבא כדמעיקרא מס׳ on the contrary, that which he first said stands to reason; a. fr.

Poël סוֹבַר, v. supra.

Ithpoël אִסְתּוֹבַר (cmp. צָפַן) *provide one's self; to store up for one's self.* Targ. Ez. XXXIX, 9. V. תִּסְבְּרָא, טִסְבְּרָא.

סְבַר II, *Poël* סוֹבַר (cmp. סבל) [*to encompass,*] *to carry; to bear, endure; to sustain.* Targ. Y. Gen. XXI, 15. Targ. Deut. I, 31.—Targ. Prov. XXX, 21 לסוֹבָרָא Ms. (ed. לְמִסְבְּרָא, לְמַסְבְּרָא). Targ. Ps. XCVI, 8 אובילו וסוֹבַרוּ ed. Wil. (ed. Lag. תוברו ושׁוֹבְרוּ, corr. acc.). Targ. I Kings IV, 7 (h. text כלכל); a. fr.—Y. B. Bath. II, beg. 13b ולא הוות יכיל מְסוֹבַר and could not carry it (and dropped it).

סְבַר III, *Poël* סוֹבַר (*Saf.* of ברי; cmp. Arab. *sabar* exploravit vulnus &c., *misbâr* specillum vulnerarium) *to perforate, cut,* (only used in the sense of) *to let blood.* Part. pass. מְסוֹבַר. Pes. 112a top דמס׳ ולא משי וכ׳ Ms. M. (ed. מְסוֹבַר, v. סְבַר II) he who has been bled and has not washed his hands. Yeb. 72a לא מְסוֹבְרִינַן ביה Ar. (ed. מסוכ׳) and on it (that day) we must not be bled. Meïl. 20b דמס׳ ואכל וכ׳ (ed. דמסוכ׳; Ar. דסַפַּר, prob. clerical error, v. Koh. Ar. Compl. s. v.) he who eats fowl after blood-letting. Ab. Zar. 28b דכאיב ליה עינא ודמ׳ Ag. Hatt. (v. Rabb. D. S. a. l. note 7) one having pain of the eye and one who has been bled.—V. סִיבּוּרָא II.

סַבָּר m. (סְבַר I) *reasoner, fine scholar.* Targ. O. Lev. XIX, 32 Ms. a. some ed., (ed. Berl. סָבָר, v. סְבַר I).—*Pl.* סַבָּרִין. Targ. Y. II Gen. XLIX, 10 (ed. Vien. סב׳, corr. acc.; Y. I ספרין).

סֶבֶר m. (b. h. שֶׂבֶר; סְבַר I) 1) *hope.* Gen. R. s. 91 (ref. to Gen. XLII, 1) אל תהי קורא יש שבר אלא יש ס׳ ... שִׁסְבְּרוֹ וכ׳ read not *yesh sheber* (there is corn) but *yesh seber* (there is hope) &c., v. אִסְפַּקְלַרְיָא. Sifra Ahărê, Par. 9, ch. XIII ושמא תאמר אבד סִבְרִי ואבד סכויי ... אני סִבְרָךְ וכ׳ lest thou say, my hope is gone, my outlook is frustrated, therefore it reads, 'I am the Lord', I am thy hope &c. Yoma 72a אבד סִבְרָן ובטל סכויין their prospect of restoration is gone &c. Erub. 21b אבד סִבְרָם וכ׳ they are beyond hope (of return to God) &c. B. Mets. 33b פסק סברם ובטל סכוים there is no hope for them &c.; Yalk. Is. 371 .. שכרן .. שיכויין .. (read שִׁבְרָן).—2) with פָּנִים, *brightness, friendly expression;* in gen. *countenance.* Ab. I, 15 הוי מקבל.. בס׳ פ׳ יפות receive every man with a countenance of friendliness. Cant. R. to II, 5; a. fr.—3) *understanding, plain sense.* Yalk. Sam. 158 כך הוא סִבְרוֹ של דבר this is the plain sense of the thing (the common opinion), opp. to עיקרו של דבר the root, the deeper cause; v. סְבָרָא.

סוֹבְרָא, ס׳, סִבְרָא, סְבַר IV ch. same, 1) *hope.* Targ. Prov. XI, 7. Targ. Job V, 16. Targ. Prov. XIII, 12 סַבְרָא ed. Wil.—Targ. Ps. IX, 19 סוֹבָ׳ (Bxt. סבו׳); a. fr.—Gen. R. s. 68 סִבְרִי, v. בַּרְיָיא. Ib. s. 53 את לא אובדית סִיבְרָךְ וכ׳ (some ed. סוֹבְרָךְ) as thou didst not give up thy hope, so will I not suffer thy hope to be frustrated. Midr. Sam. ch. V; Yalk. ib. 86 (ref. to אפסי, I Sam. II, 10) ... אילין דסוֹבְרֵיהוֹן פסיק מן ברייהון that means the nations whose hope is cut off from their Creator (who have no faith); a. e.—2) with אַפִּין, *countenance.* Targ. Gen. XXXI, 2; a. fr.—Gen. R. s. 35, v. אַפָּא. Lev. R. s. 5 מאן יכיל למיחמי ס׳ אפוי וכ׳ who can ever see the face of Abba Judan?; a. fr.—3) *opinion.* Y. Ab. Zar. I, 40a סִיבְרָהּ (ed. Krot. סו׳), v. סְבַר I, *Ithpa.*

סְבַר, סְבָרָא m. (preced.) 1) *brightness of mind, ingenuity.* Targ. Cant. V, 10.—2) *speculation, logical argument.* Meg. 18b, a. e. (expl. מתנמנם, v. נָיִם) דקרו.. ולא ידע לאהדורי ס׳ you call him, and he answers but cannot recall an argument. Y. Ber. III, 6c top כל סבר קשי דהוה לי תמן סברתיה any hard thinking I had to do, there I did it. Ib. כל ההוא סברא קשיא וכ׳ all that difficult subject of T'bul Yom I studied there.—Esp. *logical deduction, conclusion by reasoning,* opp. to גמרא verbal tradition. Yoma

38ᵃ bot. גמרא גמירנא ס׳ לא ידענא I know the final decision as a tradition, the argument I do not know. Gitt. 6ᵇ בשלמא מילתא דתליא בס׳ לודיי וכ׳ if it were a thing which depends on reason, you might be right, but this is a tradition. B. Bath. 77ᵃ גמרא או ס׳ is this a tradition or a logical inference? Ab. Zar. 34ᵇ איבעית אימא ס׳ ואב״א קרא I may say, it is founded on reason, or I may say, it is intimated in the Scriptures; a. v. fr.—3) *common sense, ordinary conception*, opp. עיקר. Y. Ber. IX, 13ᶜ bot.; Midr. Till. to Ps. XVIII, 8 כך הוא ס׳ דמילתא, v. סְבַר 3.

סְבְרוֹנָא m. (dimin. of סִבְרָא) *dear hope*, or *dear little face*. Pesik. B'shall., p. 83ᵃ סְבְרוֹנִי, v. בְּרוֹנָא I; Yalk. Num. 773; Cant. R. to IV, 12.

סְבְרוֹסִי m. (prob. a. geogr. term; cmp. סְמַרְאֵי) *sibrosi*, name of a species of olive. Ber. 39ᵃ Ms. M. (ed. סמרוסי), v. אַבְרוֹסִי.

סִיבַר, סַבְרָתָא, סַבְרוּתָא f.=סִבְרָא, *hope*. Targ. Ps. IX, 11 סַבְרוּתָךְ (Ms. סִיבְ׳) the hope placed in thee. Targ. Job XI, 20 סַבְרְתְהוֹן ed. Wil. (ed. Lag. סיבר׳); a. e.

סַבְרִיקִין, סַבְרִיקִים, v. סְפַרְקִין.

סַבְרָתָא, v. סַבְרוּתָא.

סֵבְתָא, v. סִיבְתָא.—[Ab. Zar. 58ᵇ סבתא, v. סְמִיתָא II.]

סַג, v. סִיג.

סְגָא, v. סְגִי.

סְגַד, סְגֵד, סְגִיד (b. h. סָגַד) *to bend, bow; to worship*. Targ. Gen. XXIV, 26. Targ. O. ib. XXVII, 7; a. fr.—Part. סָגִיד, *pl.* סָגְדִין. Targ. II Esth. III, 2; a. e.—Gen. R. s. 38, end ווי ליה ... ובעי למסגד לבר יומיה woe to that man who is sixty years old and wants to bow to an idol made to-day!; Yalk. ib. 62 למסגוד לחדין דעביד יומא דין. Ib. נסגוד לנורא .. נסגוד וכ׳ let us worship the fire; said he to him, let us worship the water which extinguishes the fire. Cant. R. to II, 5 סְסַגִּיד, v. פְּדִיתָא; a. fr.—Hull. 62ᵇ סָגִיד, v. זָגִיד.

סְגִדָא, סִי׳ c. (preced.) *kneeling, worship*. Targ. O. Lev. XXVI, 1 סיגדא ed. Berl. (oth. ed. סְגִידָא; h. text משכית).—*Pl.* m. סְגִדִין, סִי׳; f. סְגִדָתָא, סִי׳. Targ. O. Num. XXXI, 10 בית סְגִדַתְהוֹן; Y. בית סְגִדֵיהוֹן (ed. Vien. סַגְ׳; h. text טירתם).

סְגִידוּ, סְגִדוּ f. (preced.) *idol-worship; trnsf.* m. *idol*. Targ. Y. I Gen. XI, 4; Y. II בית סגידו (strike out בית).

סַגְדּוּם, v. זַגְדּוּם.

סגדיות, read: סַגְרִיּוֹת; v. אַכְסִינָרוֹן.

סגדיס, v. זַגְדִּיס.

סֶגוּ, v. סִיגּוּ.

סָגוֹד, v. סְגַד.

סְגוֹדָא, סְגוֹד m.=סְגִדָא, *idol-worship*. Targ. Y. Ex. XXIII, 24.

סְגוֹיִינָא, v. סְגִינְיָנָא.

סְגוֹל, סְגוֹלָא, סְגוֹלָה m. (סְגַל)=h. אֶשְׁכּוֹל, *cluster* of grapes. Targ. Y. II Num. XIII, 23. Ib., sq. נחל סגולא Ar. (ed. לה ...). Targ. Y. II Deut. I, 24 נחלי סגולה.—Y. Peah VII, 20ᵇ top הוא ס׳ וכ׳ that (much spoken of) cluster in the vineyard. Ib. הדין תורא דאת סבר הוא ס׳ that ox which you think you see (at a distance), is a cluster.—*Pl.* סְגוֹלַיָּא. Targ. Y. I Gen. XL, 12. Targ. Y. ib. 10.

סְגוּלָא m. (v. next w.) *acquisition, property*. Targ. Y. II Gen. XIV, 21 (not סגי לא; h. text רכוש). Ib. XXXI, 18.—Hebr. form סְגוּלָּה (v. next art.). Targ. Y. II Deut. XXVI, 18.

סְגוֹלָה, v. סְגוֹל.

סְגוּלָּה f. (b. h.; סְגֻלָּה; סָגַל) *safe investment, heirloom, family relic, treasure*. Mekh. Yithro, Bahod., s. 2 (ref. to סגלה, Ex. XIX, 5) מה סְגוּלָּתוֹ של אדם וכ׳ as the heirloom a man possesses is dear to him, so &c.; Pesik. R. s. 11, end. B. Bath. 52ᵃ קבל מן הקטן יעשה לו ס׳ if one receives a trust from a minor, he must invest it safely (since he cannot return it to him until he is of age). Ib. מאי ס׳ וכ׳ what is a *s'gullah?* ... A scroll of the Law; ... a date-tree. B. Kam. 87ᵇ; Tosef. ib. IX, 8, sq.; a. e.

סגולה, Deut. R. s. 11 מגעת בו ס׳, read with Yalk. ib. 963: סריח בת אשר.

סְגוּלָרִין m. pl. (saeculares, sub. ludi) *the secular games of the Romans*. Y. Ab. Zar. I, 40ᵃ סגיל׳ (corr. acc.); Tosef. ib. II, 6 סגלריון (Var. סגרלאדין, corr. acc.); Bab. ib. 18ᵇ סלגורין (corr. acc.; v. Var. Lect. in Rabb. D. S. a. l. note); Yalk. Ps. 613 סגלרין.

סָגוֹס, סָגוּם m. (σάγος, sagus, sagum) *a coarse woolen blanket*, mostly mentioned as *a mattress* to sleep on. Sifré Deut. 277 ס׳ בלילה וכ׳ he must give him back the sagum for the night (B. Mets. IX, 13 את חבר). Sifré ib. 234 (ref. to Deut. XXII, 12, 'wherewith thou clothest thyself') פרט לס׳ this excludes the sagum. Kel. XXIX, 1. Ohol. XI, 3; a. fr.—*Pl.* סְגוֹסִין. Tosef. Kel. B. Bath. VII, 1 (ed. Zuck. סגסגין, oth. ed. סגסין, corr. acc.; v. R. S. to Kel. XXIX, 1). Ib. V, 11 חסגסין (corr. acc.; v. R. S. to Kel. XXVIII, 8); ib. Neg. V, 14 סגסין (corr. acc.).—[Tanh. ed. Bub., Vayera 21 הוא מהלך בסגן Ms. R. (Ms. Parma בסגו, printed text סגן; Gen. R. s. 50, a. e. כסגן) read: מהלך בסגום כסגן he travelled in a sagum like a commoner; (v. Sm. Ant. s. v. Sagum.]

סְגוֹף, v. סְגַף.

סְגוֹף, סְגוּפָא, v. sub סִיגּ.

סְגוֹרָא, m., constr. סְגוֹר (סגר) *lock, secret*. Targ. Job XXXVIII, 16.

סְגָא, סְגִי I (b. h. שָׂגָא, שָׂגָה; Saf. of גאי; cmp. Job VIII, 11) 1) *to swell, rise, grow, spread, increase, thrive*.

Targ. Lev. XIII, 12. Targ. Ex. I, 20. Targ. Ps. XCII, 13; a. fr.—Part. סָגֵי; f. סַגְיָא. Targ. O. Ex. IX, 9, sq. ed. Berl. (ed. Vienna, a. Y. סַגִּי). Targ. Lev. XIII, 42; a. fr.—Esth. R. introd. מן דסְגוֹ דייני שיקרא סְגוּן וכ׳ when faithless judges are numerous, false witnesses are frequent; מן דסגון ... סָגְיָן ממונהון וכ׳ when informers are numerous, the cases of people's properties being despoiled increase; Yalk. Esth. 1044 מדסְגָן ... סְגִיאוּ; Yalk. Job 920 מדסגן .. סְגִיאוּ. Sot. IX, 15 (49[b]) יִסְגֵּא, v. חוּצְפָּא; a. fr.—2) (=h. רַב) *to be sufficient.* Snh. 6[a] יִסְגֵּי בתרי let it be enough with two judges.—[Targ. II Esth. III, 8 סגיותיה, read סַג יָתֵיה, v. סוג ch.]

Af. אַסְגֵּי *to enlarge, increase, make great; to have much, do much.* Targ. Gen. III, 16. Targ. Ps. XLIV, 13. Targ. Ex. XVI, 17. Targ. II Sam. XXII, 36; a. fr.—Yoma 88[a] סָגֵי ומַסְגֵּי he will grow and multiply (his descendants will be numerous).

Pa. סַגֵּי same. Targ. O. Num. XIV, 17 סַגִּי (imperative).

Ithpe. אִסְתְּגֵי *to be multiplied; to increase.* Targ. Y. Gen. XLVIII, 16.

סְגֵי, סְגָא II, *Pa.* סַגֵּי (preced.; cmp. meanings of עֲבַר) *to progress, pass, walk.* Snh. 95[a] אורחא דבעא לְסַגּוּיֵי ... סְגָא וכ׳ a distance which one would have required ten days to make, he made in one day. Taan. 24[a] ועד השתא הוא דסַגָּאִי and I have been running until now. Sabb. 118[b] דלא סָגֵינָא וכ׳ that I never walk a distance of four cubits with my head uncovered. Keth. 62[a] לְסַגּוּיֵי בהדיה, v. מְצֵי I. B. Bath. 123[a] ומי שרי ... לסגויי ברמאותא are righteous men permitted to walk in the way of fraud (to deal fraudulently with a deceiver)? Erub. 18[b] הי מינייהו סַגֵּי ברישא which of them went ahead?; זכר ס׳ וכ׳ the male (part of the double body) went ahead; Yalk. Ps. 887 מְסַתְּגְיָא .. סַגְיָא.

Af. אַסְגֵּי same. Targ. Jer. VIII, 6; XXIII, 10.—Sabb. 77[b] עיזי מַסְגָן ברישא goats take the lead. B. Kam. 60[b] מַסְגֵּי להדיא passes openly, מחבי חבויי ומסגי passes secretly; a. fr.

Ithpe. אִסְתְּגֵי *to be marched, be set in motion,* v. supra.—Esp. א׳ ליה *he moved on.* B. Bath. 74[a] ולא הוה מִסְתְּגֵי לן and we did not start; לא מ׳ ליה he (the camel) will not start. B. Mets. 107[b], sq. מ׳ להו they will march along the river. Sabb. 7[a] לא מ׳ להו בהדיא they do not pass there openly (with ease); a. e.

סְגֵי III, סַגְיָא I m. (סְגֵי I) *multitude, greatness.* Targ. Gen. XXXII, 13 (12) מִסְּגֵי (O. ed. Vien. מִשְּׂגֵי; some ed. מלמִסְגֵּי from being too numerous). Ib. XXX, 30 (O. ed. Vien. לְמסגי, v. מִסְגֵּי). Targ. Y. II Ex. XXIII, 2 סִגְיָא *majority*; a. e.—V. next w.

סַגִּי, סַגִּיא m., **סַגִּיאָה** f. (preced.) 1) *spreading,* v. סְגֵי I.—2) *numerous, large, great.* Targ. Gen. XXVI, 14 (O. ed. Vien. סַגְיָא). Targ. Is. LXIII, 7; a. fr.—Lam. R. to I, 1 רבתי (חד כות׳ 1) נהור בנהור ס׳ light within a great light (many joys).—נְהוֹר, v. ס׳ נהור.—*Pl.* סַגִּיאִין, סַגִּיאֵי, סַגְיֵי; f. סַגִּיאָן, סַגִּיָּין, סַגְיָין. Targ. Ps. III, 2, sq. Targ. Jud. VIII, 30 סגיאן (not איך ...); a. fr.—B. Bath. 65[a], a. fr. וזמנין ס׳, v. זְמַן ch. B. Mets. 44[b] באתרא דס׳ where money is plentiful, opp. דס׳ פירא where goods are plentiful; a. fr.—3) סַגִּי, סַגִּיא, also סַגִּין *much, enough; greatly.* Targ. Num. XVI, 3. Targ. II Esth. VI, 10 סַגִּיא באיש (not סַגְיָא); a. fr.—Y. Ber. V, 9[a] bot., v. חֲגָא. Y. Shebu. VII, end, 38[a] אנן עבדין טבות ס׳ מינכון we will do much better than you did. Y. B. Mets. II, 8[c] bot. דהב ס׳ much gold. Y. Yoma IV, 41[d] top חסר ס׳ it loses much (v. בְּרָרָא); Num. R. s. 12 a. fr.—Y. B. Mets. l. c. אתון רחמין .. סגוּי you love gold very much; ib. סגגין.—[Yalk. Prov. 935 סגיי סוגייא, read: סייגין סייגא, v. סוג I ch.]

סַגִּי, סַגִּיא II m. (סְגֵי II, v. סוּגְיָא) *way;* לא ס׳ there is no way, *it is impossible.* Keth. 95[b] לא ס׳ דלא יהבו לה there is no way of not giving her, i. e. they *must* grant her alimentation. Tam. 32[a] לא ס׳ דלא אזלינא I must go; a. e.

סַגְיָא I, v. סְגֵי II, III.

סַגְיָא II m.=סִיגָא, *fence.* Targ. Y. II Num. XXII, 24.

סַגְיָא III pr. n. *Sagia,* name of a canal in Babylonia. Kidd. 33[a] נהר ס׳ (Mss. M. a. R. סגא).

סַגְיוּ׳, סְגִיוּתָא, סְגִיאוּתָא f. (סְגֵי 1) *multitude, greatness.* Targ. O. Gen. XXVII, 28. Targ. O. Lev. XI, 42. Ib. XXV, 16; a. fr.

סְגִיד, סָגֵיד, סְגִידָא, v. סְגֵד, a. סִגְדָא.

סְגִידוּ, v. סִגְדוּ.

סַגְיוּ׳, סְגִיוּתָא, v. סְגִיאוּתָא.

סגיין, Tanḥ. Ki Thissa 2 בשיחין ובס׳, read ובסְנָיִין, v. סְנָה (Pesik. R. s. 10 בסירים ובחוחים).

סְגִיינָא, v. סוּגְיָינָא.

סְגִילָא, v. סִיגְלָא.

סגילאדין, v. סְטִלָּרִין.

סְגִילַרְיָה, סְגִילַרְיָא m. pl. (sigillaria) *Sigillaria, the Image Feast,* the last days of the Roman Saturnalia, on which little images were given and received as presents. Y. Ab. Zar. I, 40[a] סגילרייה (missing or corrupted in Bab. ib. 18[b]; Ms. M. סגלורין; v. Rabb. D. S. a. l. note 5); Tosef. ib. II, 6 סגלרייא; Yalk. Ps. 613 סגלרין (corr. acc.).

סגינים, Gen. R. s. 52 some ed., v. סִינִים.

סְגִיעַ, v. סְגַע.

סַגִּיעָא c. (preced.)=סַגִּיא, *large, great, numerous.* Targ. Prov. XXII, 1.—*Pl.* סַגִּיעִין, סַגִּיעֵי; f. סַגִּיעָן. Targ. Ps. IV, 7 ed. Lag. Targ. Prov. XIX, 4. Ib. 21; a. e.

סְגִיעָתָא, סְגִיעוּתָא f. (preced.) *greatness, multitude.* Targ. Ps. LI, 3. Ib. V, 11 סְגִיעַת Ms. (ed. סגעא, סיגעא, read: סִגְעַת).

סְגִיעֵי m. pl., v. סוּגֵי a. סוּגְעָא.

סְגִיף, סַגִּיף, v. סְגַף.

סְגִיר, סְגִירָא m., **סְגִירְתָּא, סְגִירַת, סְגִירְתָּא** f. (סְגַר) [*locked up,*] *declared leprous after being locked up;* in gen. *leprous.* Targ. Lev. XIII, 44. Targ. O. ib. 45.— Targ. O. Num. XII, 10 סגירא ed. Berl. (ed. Vien. סְגִירַת). Targ. Y. Ex. IV, 6; a. fr.—*Pl.* סְגִירִין; f. סְגִירָן, סְגִירָתָא. Targ. II Kings VII, 3.—Tosef. Neg. VI, 1 סְגִירָתָה; Snh. 71^a ...תָא, v. תּוּרְתָּא II.

סְגִירָה f. (סְגַר) 1) *closing in, use of the root* סגר. Mekh. B'shall. s. 1.—2) *enclosure.* Num. R. s. 13 משלימים לסְגִירַת האהל וכ׳ completing the enclosure of the Tabernacle on its sides and that of the court from all sides.

סְגִירוּ, סְגִירוּת, סְגִירוּתָא f. (סְגִיר) *leprosy.* Targ. Lev. XIII, 2, sq. Ib. 42; a. fr.

סְגִירַת, סְגִירְתָּא, v. סְגִיר.

סָגַל, *Pi.* סִיגֵּל (*Safel* of גלל) [*to heap up,*] *to lay by, save; to treasure* as a relic. Y. B. Bath. IX, 17^a top בן שנראה חלוק ... מה שס׳ ס׳ לעצמו if a son appears to have kept a separate household during his father's life-time: what he has saved (of what he took out for his private expenses), he has saved for himself (does not belong to the estate). Lam. R. to I, 17 עמד וס׳ וקנה וכ׳ he made an effort and economized and bought himself sheep. Tanh. Emor, ed. Bub., 30 מְסַגְּלִין עונות וכ׳ they accumulate sins during the whole year. Gen. R. s. 9 .. כלום מסגלין ... אנו נְסַגֵּל מצות וכ׳ the righteous live because they lay by good deeds, we shall likewise lay by good deeds (in order to live). Koh. R. to I, 3 מְסַגְּלוֹת במצות וכ׳ provide for the future world by means of good deeds; (Lev. R. s. 28, beg. מגדלין במצות *heap up*; Yalk. Koh. 966 מגדלים מצות; Pesik. Ha'om., p. 69^a מתגדלין, corr. acc.); a. fr.— Pesik. R. s. 11 (ref. to סגלה, Ex. XIX, 5) יכול כמו שהעבד מְסַגֵּל מאחר רבו והבן ... והאשה .. כך אתם מְסוּגָּלִים לי וכ׳ you might think, as a slave lays by something from what his master gives him, or a son from what his father gives him, or a wife from what her husband gives her, so have you been given me as a keepsake: therefore it is written, For mine is the whole earth; Yalk. Ex. 276 כשם שהאשה מְסַגֶּלֶת ... כן אתם מסגלין לי מאחורי as a wife ..., so could you lay by something for my benefit from what I give you; Mekh. Yithro, Bahod., s. 2 אף אתם מסוגלין לי מאחורי (corr. acc.). Sifré Deut. 48 two brothers שהיו מסגלים ממון אחר אביהם that saved what money their father gave them; Yalk. ib. 873.—*Part. pass.* מְסוּגָּל *given as a keepsake,* v. supra.

סְגַל ch. *to be round,* v. next wds.—[Targ. Ps. XLI, 4 יסגל Ms., read as in ed. יתגלי, v. Ned. 40^a.]

Pa. סַגֵּל *to lay by, save.* Midr. Till. to Ps. VII כל מה דאנא מְסַגֵּל את נסבא whatever I may save, thou shalt have; [read:] הן אינון כל מה דסַגְּלִית where is all that I have saved?; Yalk. Gen. 56 (not דסגילות).

סגלגל, Targ. Y. Ex. XXVI, 28 מסגלגל some ed., read: מתגלגל.

סְגַלְגַּל m., **סְגַלְגֶּלֶת** f. (preced. art.) *round.* Ned. 66^b אמרו לו ס׳ they said to him, (her head is) round.—*Pl.* סְגַלְגַּלִּין, סְגַלְגַּלִּים; סְגַלְגַּלּוֹת. Sabb. 81^a מפני מה ראשיהן ... ס׳ (Ms. M. ראשם ... סגלגל, v. Rabb. D. S. a. l. note) why are the heads of the Babylonians round?

סְגַלְגַּל, סְגַלְגְּלָא ch. 1) (adj.) same. Targ. I Kings VII, 23; a. fr.—*Pl.* סְגַלְגְּלִין; סְגַלְגְּלָן. Ib. 31. Targ. Ez. I, 7; a. e.—2) (noun) *door turning on pivots, folding door* (v. גְּלָה).—*Pl.* סְגַלְגְּלִין. Targ. I Kings VI, 34 (h. text גלילים). Targ. Esth. I, 6, v. תַּשְׁא.

סְגֻלָּה, s. סְגוּלָּה.

סגמוס, Y'lamd. to Num. I, quot. in Ar., read: סִיגְמָא; v. סִיגְמָטִין.

סָגָן m. (b. h. *pl.* סְגָנִים; v. סְגַר I; cmp. רַב) *grandee, chief, viceroy.* Midr. Till. to Ps. CXIX, 134 כלי ... אין לס׳ רשות וכ׳ the viceroy is not permitted to use a vessel which the king has used.—[Num. R. s. 15; Tanh. Bhaăl. 11 למחר ס׳, v. פָּגָן.]—Esp. סְגַן הכהנים or הש׳ *the chief of the priests, adjutant high priest.* Ab. III, 2. Yoma III, 9. Y. ib. III, 41^a top לא היה ... עד שנעשה ס׳ none could be appointed high priest, unless he was made a Sagan first. Sifra Tsav, Milluim, Par. 1 נעשה משה ס׳ הכ׳ לאהרן Moses was Aaron's aid; וכשם שנעשה לו ס׳ בחייו וכ׳ and as he was his aid in his life-time, so was he his aid in his dying hour; a. fr.—*Pl.* סְגָנִים, סְגָנִין, constr. סְגְנֵי, סִי׳. Ex. R. s. 1 מי שם הס׳ אלמים וכ׳ who made the chiefs (Pharaoh's counsellors) mute &c.?; Tanh. Sh'moth 10. Cant. R. to VI, 12 כשנעשו ... ונעשו ס׳ על וכ׳ when they were made free men and were redeemed and made the primates of all entering this world; Yalk. ib. 992 נעשו חורין וס׳ וכ׳ they were made nobles and primates &c. Num. R. s. 18 אחיו כ״ג ובניו סגני כהונה his brother is high priest and his sons the high priest's aids; a. fr.—[סגנין, Midr. Till. to Ps. XX, end, v. סִיגְנוֹן.—סְגָנִים, Y'lamd. to Num. X, 2, quot. in Ar., v. סִיגְנוֹן.]

סְגַן, סִגְנָא, סִי׳ I ch. same. Targ. Jer. LII, 24 ס׳ כהניא (h. text כהן המשנה), v. preced.—Targ. II Kings XXIII, 4 (h. text *pl.*); a. fr.—*Pl.* סִגְנִין, סִגְנַיָּא, סִגְנַיָּה, סִגְנֵי, סִי׳. Targ. I Chr. XVIII, 16.—Snh. 110^a ס׳ דכהנא (Ms. M. סגני כהנים, v. Rabb. D. S. a. l. note). Ib. 106^a, v. זְנֵי. Esth. R. to I, 3, v. טַעְמָא.

סִגְנָא II, v. סוּגְרִינָא.

סִגְנָא III, **סִגְנַאי,** v. סִיגְנָא II.

סִגְנוּם, סִגְנוֹן (סגנוס), v. סִיגְנוֹן.

סִגְנִיּוֹת f. pl. (v. סְגַר I, cmp. מוּרְבִּית) [*made of twigs, leaves,*] *loosely woven mats* used for covering up fruit. Kel. XVI, 5 ס׳ של עלין (R. S. 'סוּג) mats made of leaves; ס׳ של נצר of wicker.—[סיגניות, Yalk. Ex. 232, v. סִיגְנוֹן.]

סִגְנַיי, v. סִיגְנָא II.

סְגַע, סְגִיעַ=סְגַר I (with which our w. interchanges in mss. a. eds.). Targ. Ps. CXXXIX, 18. Targ. I Chr. XXIII, 17; a. fr.

סִגְעָא, סִיג׳ f. (preced.) *greatness, multitude.* Targ. Ps. V, 11, v. סְגִיעוּתָא.—*Pl.* m. סִגְעֵי, v. סוּגְעָא.

סַגֵּף (*Saf.* of נגף) *to plague, afflict* (corresp. to b. h. עִנָּה). B. Mets. VII, 10 (93^b) סִגְּפָהּ if he maltreated (starved) her (v. סָכַם).—Part. pass. סְגוּף; f. סְגוּפָה; pl. סְגוּפִים, סְגוּפִין, סְגוּפוֹת (usu. combined with הַוּי, v. דַּוֶה). Sifré Deut. 24; Yalk. ib. 805. Gen. R. s. 74; (ib. s. 60 שְׁפוּפִין); a. e.; v. סְחַם a. סָכַם.

Pi. סִיגֵּף *to afflict.* Taan. 22ᵇ לסגף את עצמו בתעניות to afflict himself by fasting. Y. Dem. VII, 26ᵇ top .. לא ירעיב ולא יְסַגֵּף the hired laborer must not starve himself or undergo privations, because he lessens his employer's work; a. e.—[Yalk. Josh. 27 יסמגני שלא, v. סָגַב.]

Hithpa. וְסְגַּף *to feel privation; to suffer.* Gen. R. s.60 (וּרא) מסְתַּגֵּף he suffers; Ex. R. s. 26; Mekh. B'shall., Vayassa, s. 6; a. e.

סְגַף **ch.** same. Part. pass. סְגִיף. Targ. Y. Deut. I, 27 (ed. Vien. סְגִירִין).

Pa. סַגֵּף *to afflict.* Targ. Y. Gen. XV, 13. Targ. Ps. XC, 15 תְּסַגְּפִינּ (incorr. דְּסַגְפִיםֿ). Ib. 15. Targ. I Chr. XVII, 9 סַגְּפִינּנּ ed. Lag. (oth. ed. סַגְּפִינּנּ); Targ. Job XXX, 11 סַגֵּפוּ (ed. Lag. סגפּיני, read סַגְּפוּנִי); a. fr.—Part. pass. מְסַגַּף; f. מְסַגְּפָא Targ. Is. LVIII, 10.

Ithpa. אִסְתַּגַּף, **Ithpe.** אִסְתַּגֵּף *to be afflicted, reduced; to suffer.* Targ. Ps. CII, 24. Ib. CVII, 17; a. fr.

סְגַר (b. h.) *to bar, bolt; to lock up, close.* Snh. 38ᵃ (ref. to מסגר, II Kings XXIV, 16) כיון שסוגרין חלכה וכ׳ after they had closed the discussion about a law (declared it obscure), there was none to open again; Gitt. 88ᵃ; Sifré Deut. 321 אחר שפותח אין סוגר after he has opened (explained), none can close (raise objection). Tanḥ. Sh'mini 9 עבר על כל בתי .... אותם he passed over all synagogues and schools and closed them. Mekh. B'shall., s. 3 הים סוגר והשונא רודף וכ׳ the sea forming a bar, and the enemy pursuing &c.; Ex. R. s. 21 (not סגר). Mekh. Yithro, Amal., s. 1 שודיהא סוֹגֶרֶת ומסגרות וכ׳ ... formerly no slave could flee from Egypt, for it was shut up and barred (Josh. VI, 1); a. fr.—Cant. R. to III, 10 (expl. וזהב סגור) שוׁדירא סוגר בעד כל וכ׳ it locked up the shops of all workers in gold (ruined their trade); Y. Yoma IV, 41ᵈ top מכסית (corr. acc.); Num. R. s. 12 (not סגרו); Ex. R. s. 35 שודירא סוגר כל וכ׳ (corr. acc.).

Nif. נִסְגַּר *to be locked up.* Yoma 45ᵃ כל הדהנויות נִסְגָּרוֹת all (gold) shops were closed (their business ruined, v. supra); a. e.

Hif. הִסְגִּיר *to lock up; to bind over, hand over, deliver.* Sifré Deut. 322 בקשו ישראל לבריוח ... וּדיר מַסְגִּירִים אוֹתָם when the Israelites attempted to flee northward, they blocked their way. Ib. 323 (ref. to Deut. XXXII, 30) אינכי מַסְגִּיר אתכם פ״ר עצמי וכ׳ I shall not deliver you (into the hands of the enemy) directly, but through others (who will betray you). Ib. ומַסְגִּירֵנִי מיד תובכיני מיד I sell and immediately deliver you. Tanḥ. Sh'mini l. c. (ref. to המסגר, v. supra) שוֹכֵן מַסְגִּירִין לכל האומות all nations go before them into enclosures and flee, for they cause all nations to lock themselves up; a. fr.—Esp. *to lock up the leper* pending the priest's observation (Lev. XIII, 4, a. e.). Neg. V, 1; a. fr.—Part. pass. מֻסְגָּר a leper under trial, opp. מוחלט (v. חָלַט I). Meg. I, 7; a. fr.

Pu. סֻגַּר *to be closed, locked.* Part. מְסֻגָּר, f. מְסֻגֶּרֶת, v. supra.

סְגַר **ch.** same. Targ. Job XXXVIII, 8 Var. Ms. (ed. אגף). Targ. Y. Deut. XXI, 5.—Part. pass. סְגִיר, סְגִירָא, a) *fenced in, barred.* Targ. Cant. I, 9.—b) *leprous,* v. סְגִיר.

Af. אַסְגַּר, אַסְגִּיר same. Targ. Lev. XIII, 4. Ib. XIV, 38; a. fr.

Ithpa. אִסְתַּגַּר, **Ithpe.** אִסְתַּגַר 1) *to be locked up, closed.* Targ. Y. Gen. VIII, 2 (h. text וַיִּסָּכְרוּ). Targ. O. Num. XII, 14; a. fr.—Trnsf. *to be engrossed with; to be bewildered,* v. אִסְתַּגַּר.—2) (v. סְגִיר) *to become leprous.* Targ. II Chr. XXVI, 22.

סַגֵּר or סֶגֶר m. (preced.) *lock, bolt.* Tanḥ. Hayé 3 ונעל הסֶגֶר לפניהּ and he shut the lock before her [perh. סָגוֹר].

סַגְרְגַר, Targ. Ps. I, 3 Var. corrupt of מְגַרְגַּר, v. גְּרַר.

סִגְרוֹן v. סִימָרוֹן.

סַגְרְיוֹת v. אַכְסַנְיָרִיוֹן.

סַגְרִיס v. זַנְהִים.

סַגְרִיר m. (b. h.; *Saf.* of גְּרַר II, cmp. Jer. XXX, 23) *severe rain storm.* Y. Meg. I, 71ᵈ; Gen. R. s. 13 מטשטם וּרא ביום ס׳ וכ׳ it happened on a stormy day, when the teachers did not come to school &c. Y. Ḥag. II, 77ᵈ bot.; Y. Snh. VI, 23ᶜ bot. Yeb. 63ᵇ ס׳ ביום ... קשה a bad wife is as hard to bear as a stormy day.

סַגְרִירָא **ch.** same. Targ. Prov. XXVII, 15.

סַד m. (b. h.; סדד *to join;* Arab. *sadda, to obstruct, block) block, torturing stock.—Pl.* סָדִין. Tosef. Ab. Zar. II, 4 לא ס׳ וכ׳ (ed. Zuck. רהסן), v. כֶּבֶל.

סַדָּא **ch.** same. Pes. 28ᵃ (prov.) סַדָּאה בסהיה יתיב וכ׳ Ms. M. 2 (ed. סַדָּנָא בסַדָּנָיה, not בסהיר; early eds. נגרא) when the maker of the stocks (the carpenter) sits in his own stocks, he is paid &c., v. הַיְּל; Yalk. Ex. 201 סדנא בסהריה.

סַדָּאה m. (preced.) *carpenter,* v. preced.

סָדַח v. סָדַח.

סַדָּה *raft,* v. אַסְדָּא.

סְדוֹם (b. h.) pr. n. pl. *Sodom,* one of the cities in the plain of Jordan destroyed for their wickedness. Snh. X, 3 (108ᵃ) (ref. to Ps. I, 5) ס׳ אנשי אלו this alludes to the men of S. Ib. 109ᵇ וכ׳ בס׳ ... ארבעה four judges lived in S. &c., v. וְדַיְמָי; a. fr.—ס׳ סְדַת *Sodomitic rule, unfairness, selfishness.* Ab. V, 10 'mine is mine, and thine is thine', וו דיא מ׳ ס׳ that is a Sodomitic principle (justice without charity). B. Bath. 12ᵇ כופין על מ׳ ס׳ the law may use force against unfairness (where one claims a privilege which causes the neighbor no loss); a. fr.—Ib. 114ᵇ בס׳ יוסף .. הלכתא Ar. (ed. בסהורה) the law follows R. Joseph's opinion as to using force against unfairness.—*the Lake of Sodom* (usu. ימא דסדום, v. מֶלַח) רמא דס׳. Sabb. 108ᵇ מֶבַע I; a. e.

סְדוֹמִי, סְדוֹמָי m. (preced.) *Sodomite.* Gen. R. s. 41 כשאדם רע קורין אותו ס׳ when a man is bad, they call him

a Sodomite; Tosef. Sabb. VII (VIII), 23. Ib. 24; a. fr.—
Pl. סוֹדְמִים, סוֹדְמִין, סוֹדְמִיתָא, סוֹדְ׳. Gen. R. s. 26; Yalk. ib.
44; a. fr.—Y. B. Bath. II, 13ᶜ top סדומין כוחל a wall of the
Sodomites', i. e. a wall which may not have windows
looking into the adjoining lot.

סָדוּרָא, סָדוּר, סְדוּק, v. sub סידי.

סָדְיָא f. (v. סָד a. אִיסְדְרָא) *the head-board of a couch,
head-side.* Keth. 61ᵃ ס׳ אבי by the head-side.—Esp.
ס׳ בֵּי ס׳ *pillow, bolster.* Ber. 56ᵃ. Sabb. 118ᵇ; a. e.—*Pl.*
סָדְיָיתָא. Ib. 124ᵇ חגוהו בי ס׳ Ar. (ed. סדייותא; Ms.
M. מסדייתא, read: בי סָדְיָיתָא, v. Rabb. D. S. a. l. note).—
[Hebr. pl. סְדִיּוֹת. Y'lamd. to Gen. XXVIII, 10, quot. in Ar.
מסדיות, read: ס׳ בי cushions.]

סְדִידִין, Tosef. Kidd. V, 14 Var., v. סָדָד.

סְדִירִין, Koh. R. to V, 8, v. סָדֵן ch.

סָדִין m. (b.h.) *sheet,* usually of fine linen (cmp. σινδών;
v. Sm. Ant. s. v. Pallium). Yoma III, 4 ובי׳ של ס׳ פרשו
they spread a sheet of linen (for the high priest to walk
on) between &c. Y. Kil. IX, 32ᵇ top בס׳ אחד נקבר
רבי Rabbi was buried in one linen shroud (without any
other garments); Y. Keth. I, 35ᵃ top. Y. Yeb.I, 2ᵇ; Gen.
R. s. 85 ס׳ דרך each wrapped in a sheet (preventing
direct contact). Men. 37ᵇ, a. e. ס׳ בציצית a linen cloak
with woollen show-fringes; a. fr.—*Pl.* סְדִינִין,סְדִינִים. Nidd.
61ᵃ. Kel. XXIV, 13 ס׳ שלשה there are three classes
of sheets with regard to Levitical purity. Tosef. ib. B.
Mets. I, 14 לצורות ס׳ canvas sheets for paintings; ס׳
לאוהלים sheets for awnings. Tosef. Bets. II, 13 היו ס׳
פרוסין sheets (covering the floor of the dining room) were
spread; Bab. ib. 22ᵇ; Y. ib. II, 61ᶜ bot.; a. fr.

סָדִינָא ch. 1) same. Targ. Ps. CIV, 2 (h. text שלמה).—
Men. 40ᵇ לסְדִינֵיה ... שרא R. Z. untied the show-fringes
of his linen sheet. Ib. 41ᵃ מיכסי ס׳ he was wrapped in
a linen sheet (without show-fringes). Ib. בקייטא ס׳ וכי you
wear a linen sheet in the summer, and a sarb'la in the
winter (without show-fringes), what is to become of the
law &c.?; a. fr.—*Pl.* סְדִינַיָא. Targ. Lam. II, 20;
22.—Y. Sabb. VI, 8ᵇ bot. (interpret. סדינים. Is. III, 23).—
*2) (comp. סְדָנָא) *a litter.* Y. Bets. I, 60ᶜ bot. טיסעני חורי׳
וכי ס׳ allowed Bar G., the physician, to be carried in a
litter to visit the sick on the Sabbath.

סְדִיק, v. סדק.

סְדִיקָא, v. סדקא.

סָדֵן m. (v. סָד) *block.* Ex. R. s. 1 (ref. to Ex. I, 16) אין
ס׳ (gloss: קשוה דבר שדוא) *obhnayim* means a
block (which means a hard object); וכי׳ יוצר מה ... as
the potter sits with one leg on each side of
the block (mould); Sot. 11ᵇ. Gen. R. s. 10, end באמצע
חס׳ על ... שדוא as one striking with the hammer on
the block (anvil); Sabb. XII, 1. Snh. VII, 3 על ... מניחין
הס׳ they put his head on the (executioner's) block; a. fr.—
Esp. ס׳ של שקמה (or sub. שקמה) *the trunk of the sycamore

tree.* Kil. I, 8 של ס׳ בתוך ... אין you must not plant
vegetables in a trunk &c. B. Bath. IV, 9; a. fr.—Pesik. R.
s. 1 (ref. to Is. LXV, 22) [read: ושכותה׳ וכי׳] זה עץ חס׳ that
means the wood of the sycamore trunk, which endures
in the ground for six hundred years; (Gen. R. s. 12 כשקמה
וחוו); a. e.— *Pl.* סָדָנִים. Ib. s. 42 (expl. חשדים עצמן, Gen.
XIV, 3) שחוא מגדל which produces sycamore trees.

סָדְנָא I,סַדְנָא, סָדָן ch. 1) same. Targ.Jer.XVIII,3
(h. text אבנים).—Hull. 16ᵃ דפתורא ס׳ Ar. (ed. סרטא) the
potter's block (wheel turned by hand); ס׳ דמיא wheel
turned by water. Pes. 94ᵇ דידחייא ס׳ כי Ms. M. 2 a. Ar.
(ed. כמבוינא) like the movement of the block of the mill
(millstone, the pivot remaining stationary, v. נוצעינא). Ib.
28ᵃ, v. סָרָא. Kidd. 27ᵇ דארעא חד דוא ס׳ the land (although
consisting of disconnected fields) is one block (by taking
symbolical possession of one field, you take possession of
the whole complex contracted for); B. Kam. 12ᵇ (Ms. M.
פרשא).—Lev. R. s. 22 ס׳ חד בית וחות there was in the
garden one sycamore trunk; Koh. R. to V, 8 סדירין (a. otherwise corrupted; corr. acc.).—[Pes. 113ᵃ בי סדעא Ar., v.
סַדְנָא.]—2) (perh. an adaptation of Latin essedum) *travelling carriage.—Pl.* סָדָנַיָא, סַדָנֵי, סָדְנֵי. Targ. Y. Gen. XLV,
19; 21; 27 (ed. Amst. a. oth. ס׳, with ר).

סָדָנָא II m. *block-maker, carpenter.* Pes. 28ᵃ, v. סַדְאָה
a. סָרָא.

סְדָסִים, Sifré Deut. 234, v. בְּרָסִין.

סָדַק (Saf. of דק) *to cleave, tear apart.* Part. pass. סָדוּק;
f. סְדוּקָה; *pl.* סְדוּקוֹת, סְדוּקִין. Hull. 59ᵃ פרסיותיו אם
ס׳ if its hoofs are cloven. Cant. R. to VII, 3 חטה מה
וכי׳ as the wheat grain is split (has an incision) &c. Nidd.
25ᵇ; a. e.

Pi. סִיּדֵק 1) same. Cant. R. to III,3 סִרְדְּקָה כדג he split
it as a fish is split; Gen. R. s. 77; Yalk. ib. 132 (corr.
acc.).—2) *to chip, chisel* (the surface of a stone). Cant. R.
to I, 1 וכי׳ וסותה וסידקה (ed. Wil. וסירקה, corr. acc.) he
carved and chiselled and polished it; Yalk. Kings 182
וסירקה וסרקה; Yalk. Prov. 960 וסירקה (corr.acc.); (Koh. R.
introd. וסירקה וסרחה ושבבה).

Nif. נִסְדַק 1) *to be split, cut into.* Bekh. VI, 1 נִסְדְּקָה if
there is a slit in the ear of the first-born animal, contrad.
to נפגמה; a. e.—2) *to be chipped off;* trnsf. (comp. פָּסַל) *to
become unfit for use, to be abrogated.* B. Kam. IX, 2 גזל
וכי׳ מטבע if a man stole a coin and it became 'chipped';
expl. ib. 97ᵃ ל׳ מטמע chipped in its literal sense, i. e. the
stamp was chipped off; [anoth. opin.] נמי מלכות מסלתו
ס׳ if the government abrogated it, it is the same as
chipped off; Y. ib. IX, beg. 6ᵈ.

סָדַק, סָדֵיק ch. same. Targ. I Kings XI, 30 סָדֵיקְתָה (not
סִרֵיקא, ed. Lag. סָרְקָה; h. text קירע). Targ. II Kings II, 12.—
Part. pass. סְדִיקָא; f. סְדִיקָא; *pl.* סְדִיקִין, סָדִיקִין *clovens.* Targ.
Lev. XI, 7. Ib. 3. Ib. 4 מַסְדְּיקֵי (O. ed. Vien. ׳סדי Af.). Targ.
Y. Deut. XIV, 7; a. fr.

Af. אָסְדֵיק *to have a cloven hoof.* Targ. Lev. XI, 5 sq.
ed. Vien. (ed. Berl. מסדיק). Ib. 4, v. supra. Targ. O. Deut.
XIV, 7 (ed. Berl. מַסְדְּיקֵי).

Pa. סַדֵּיק *to split.* Targ. Ps. LX, 4 סַדֵּיקוּ (some ed. 'סְלֵק; ed. Lag. סרדק; corr. acc.; h. text פצמתּ).

סְדַק m. (preced.) 1) *split, slit.* Bekh. 37ᵇ הוּם כל שׁחוּא a slit in the ear disqualifies, even if it be of the minutest size. Koh. R. to I, 8 כמכני סִידקין שׁל פתחא like looking through the crack of a door; a. e.—*Pl.* סְדָקִין, סְדָקִים. Pes. 8ᵃ לחורין סִידוּק שׁנתרבבו (48ᵇ) III, 5 .Ib. וּלם into holes and fissures. Ib. III, 5 (48ᵇ) סִידוּק שׁנתרבבו סִדְקָיו וכ' (Bab. ed. סדקין) dough is called *sidduk,* when its cracks run into one another. Ib. 48ᵇ אין לך כל סדק וסדק וכ' for every crack on the surface there are several inside. Ib. III, 2 סְדְקֵי עריבת (Bab. ed. 45ᵃ סִרדְקי) the cracks in the kneading trough; a. fr.— 2) *a strip* of a sheet. Tosef. Kil. V, 22 ed. Zuck., v. סֶרֶט II.

סִידְקָא, סִדְקָא ch. same, *split, slit; rent.* Targ. Y. Deut. XIV, 6.—*Pl.* סִרי, סִדְקִין. 1 Kings XI, 30. Targ. II Kings II, 12 (ed. Wil. סְדָרִיקִין); a. e.

סֶדְקָארִים, read: סִרִידְקָארִיוּם m. (sericarius, sub. textor) *silk-weaver.* Cant. R. to VIII, 11. V. סִילִיקְראִית.

סִדְקִי, סֻדְקִית, v. sub סִיד.

סֵדֶר (Saf. of הדר) *to arrange, order* (corresp. to b. h. עריך). Pes. 54ᵃ סוֹדְרָן על חבוֹם he pronounces them (the benedictions) in successive order over the cup. Yoma 45ᵇ top שׁסוֹדרין ע"ג המזבח that he must place them in order on the altar; וסודרין ... כל הכבש that he must arrange them on the bridge or on the rim of the altar, until a large pile (of wood) is formed, when he must put them in order (on the altar); Tam. II, 1; a. fr.—Part. pass. סָדוּר; f. סְדוּרָה &c. Taan. 8ᵃ בשׁביל משׁונה שׁאינו סדורה עליו כל' it is because his learning is not properly systematised in his mind. Ber. 57ᵇ עונותיו ס' לו כל' his sins are arranged before him; מאר ס"ס ליטבּיחל what does this mean? It means that they are arranged (ready) to be forgiven; Yoma 88ᵃ. B. Bath. 69ᵃ אבנים הם' לגדר stones arranged for erecting a fence, contrad. to צבורות piled up (v. סָוַר; a. fr.

Pi. סִידֵּר 1) same Tam. II, 3 לְסַדֵּר אשׁ המערכה to arrange the pyre, v. בְּצֵצְבָה. Num. s. 4 כיצד מְסַדְּרִין לחם וכ' how did they arrange the showbread; ib. also מְסָדְירִים, מְסָדִירִין (*Hif.*); a. fr.—שׁבח ס' (comp. עריך, Ps. V, 4, a. e.) *to offer praise.* Ab. Zar. 7ᵇ; Ber. 32ᵃ לעולם יְסַדֵּר אדם וכ' one should always offer praise to the Lord first, and then pray (for what he needs). Ib. 34ᵃ ראשׁונות דומה לעבד שׁמְסַדֵּר וכ' in the first three benedictions of the T'fillah one is like a servant that offers praise to his master; a. fr.—Part. pass. מְסֻדָּר Men. 95ᵃ בׁמ when everything in the Tabernacle was arranged, opp. בׁמסולק when arrangements for moving were being made.— 2) (corresp. to הׁעריך, Lev. XXVII, 8) *to assess a person's value* with reference to the vower's ability to pay, whence: *to exempt from seizure* (bed, tools &c.; v. Arakh. VI, 3, sq.). B. Mets. 113ᵇ כדרך שׁמסדרין בערכין כך מסדרין בבעל חוב as well as we allow an exemption from seizure in cases of vows, so we allow it in cases of debt; [Rashi quotes a Var. מְשׁרדרין, v. שָׁרַד]. Ned. 65ᵇ שׁמעת מינה אין מסדרין וכ' (Var. מְשׁרְירִין) from this you may deduce that no exemption

is granted the debtor; B. Mets. 114ᵃ מדא שׁיקְסַּרדrig וכ' is a debtor allowed an exemption? Y. B. Kam. IX, 7ᵃ top על מנת שׁלא לסדר מה וכ' with the condition that what my wife or my child wears is not to be exempted from seizure. Ib. אין מסדרין לו באותו החפץ this special object is not exempted; a. e.

Hif. הׁסְדיר *to arrange, establish the order of.* Num. R. l. c., v. supra. Ber. 28ᵇ; Meg. 17ᵇ ח' ... על חסדר וכ' arranged the eighteen benedictions before Rabbi in the order in which they are to be recited. Sifra Tsav, Mill. כשׁם שׁח' וכ' as Moses arranged the service of the Tabernacle, so he arranged &c.; a. e.

סְדַר ch. same. Targ. Y. II Ex. XL, 23 (Y. I a. O. סַדַּר, some ed. סְדַר). Targ. Y. ib. XII, 39; a. e.—Part. pass. סְדִיר; f. סְדִירָא Targ. Ps. VII, 13 *ranged.*

Pa. סַדֵּר 1) same. Targ. Gen. XXII, 9 (Y. ed. Vien. סָדַר). Ib. XIV, 8 (O. ed. Amst. סְדַר). Targ. Job XIII, 18 (ed. Wil. סְדַר); a. fr.—Targ. Ps. V, 4 (v. preced.).—Part. pass. מְסַדֵּר Targ. Y. Lev. XXIV, 6 (not מְסָדֵר). Targ. Y. Ex. XXXIX, 18; 37.—Ber. 13ᵇ תחם נביא הוא דקא מְסַדֵּר לשׁבחיה וכ' there (Neh. IX, 7 where Abram is used instead of Abraham) the prophet praises the Lord by referring to the past. Yoma 38ᵇ דׁתוה מְסַדֵּר אגדתא קׁמיה who reviewed before him the homiletic sayings according to a certain system; a. fr.— Y. Ab. Zar. V, 44ᵈ נקרים מְסַדֵּר לאילין וכ' let us get up early and set in order those thorn-bushes (meaning, let us kill those men).—Shebu. 30ᵇ דכותהו כמאן דמְסַדֵּר דיניה Ms. M. (ed. דׁסֵדֵר ליה לדיניה) he has the appearance of one whose case has been prearranged (with the judge; ed.: of one who has prearranged his case).— 2) *to allow exemption from seizure* (v. preced.). B. Mets. 113ᵇ סָהדי מְסַדְּרינן ליה וכ' השׁתא since we order his pledge (which consists of necessaries) to be sold for his debt, how can we allow him an exemption (so as to leave him a certain amount from the money realized by the sale)?

Ithpa. אׁסְתְּדֵּר *to be arranged,* (of prayers) *to be offered.* Targ. Job XXXVI, 19.

סֵדָר, v. סֵדֶר.

סֵדֶר m. (b. h. סֵדֶר) *pl.*; סְדָרִים, *row, pile, arrangement, order, succession.* Num. R. s. 4 ו' חלות כל זה וכ' six cakes in one pile and six in the other. Yoma V, 7 כל .. האמורין על הם וכ' as to all the acts for the Day of Atonement here told in their consecutive order, if he advanced (changed the order) &c. Sifra Tsav, Mill. הסדיר את הקרבנות סׁדרין the text arranges the sacrificial functions in their proper succession. Yoma 73ᵃ sq. דׁוד שׁאל שׁלא כׁם David did not put his questions (I Sam. XXIII, 11) in their natural order. Meg. III, 4 לׁמכירן the regular reading (interrupted during the four distinguished Sabbaths, v. פָּרָשָׁה) is resumed. Ib. 30ᵇ לׁם פׁרסיות היא חׁוׁר the regular order of the Pentateuch sections is resumed; לׁם הׁפטרות וכ' the regular order of Haftaroth is resumed; a. v. fr.—זׁרעים ס' the Order of Seeds, the first Order of the Mishnah; מׁועד ס' the Order of Festivals, the second Order of the Mishnah &c. Sabb. 31ᵃ; a. fr.—Keth. 106ᵃ אׁלידתו v. (ר) ס', אׁלִידְתוּ.—Esth. R. to

I, 9 ראש חס׳ as the first words of a pericope (Lev. R. s. 3 ראש סדרא).—*Pl.* סְדָרִים, constr. סִדְרֵי, —.סד׳ סדרי —.משנה, v. מִשְׁנָה.—Keth. 103ᵇ ס׳ חכמה orders (rules) of wisdom; ס׳ נשיאות rules for the conduct of the Nasi's office. Sabb. 53ᵇ ס׳ בראשית the order of nature; a. fr.—Esp. *regular homilies on the weekly portion.* Sot. 49ᵃ (ref. to Job X, 22) אם יש סדרים תופיע וכ׳ but if regular homilies are held, it (the earth) will come forth bright out of the dark.

סִדְרָא, סִדְרָה, סִ׳ ch., constr. סְדַר a. סְדָר, same, 1) *row, order.* Targ. Ex. XXVIII, 17, sq. (h. text טור). Targ. O. Lev. XXIII, 44 (Y. סידורי); a. fr.—*Pl.* סִדְרִין, סִדְרַיָּא, סִדְרֵי, סד׳. Targ. Ex. l. c. (Y. ed. Vien. סְדָ׳). Targ. O. Lev. XXIV, 6, sq. (Y. סידורי׳).—Targ. Y. Deut. V, 28 ס׳ דלעיל the upper ranks (angels). Targ. Y. Gen. XIV, 8 ס׳ קרבא battle-lines. Targ. II Esth. III, 8 בנו סדרוי (ed. Vien. בנו סדרי; ed. Lag. בניסדרוי, corr. acc.) when among his troops; a. fr.—2) *order* or *section* of the Scriptures, *the portion of the Pentateuch* to be read at public service on Sabbaths &c.; in gen. *Scripture lesson.* Sabb. 116ᵇ מפסקי ס׳ בכתובים (not דכת׳) they closed the reading from the Pentateuch with a reading from the Hagiographa (v. הַפְטָרָה). Yoma 87ᵃ bot. חוה פסיק ס׳ וכ׳ was reading the Haftarah; a. fr.—Sot. 49ᵃ קדושא דס׳, v. קְדוּשָּׁא.—3) *order* or *part of the Mishnah.* Keth. 103ᵇ אתני סִדְרָךְ לחברך teach thy fellow student the Order which thou hast learned; a. e.—*Pl.* as ab. Ib. [read:] מתנינא שיתא סדרי לשיתא ינוקי סדרא לכל חד וחד I taught six boys the six Orders of the Mishnah, one Order to each; a. e.—4) *colonnade*, esp. *the hall of studies* (cmp. אַכְסַדְרָא). Y. Sabb. VII, 8ᵃ מן ס׳ רובא וכ׳ from the large colonnade to the store of &c.; Y. Snh. X, 28ᵃ bot. Y. Ber. III, 6ᵇ top כד הוו מסקין ליה לס׳ when they were carrying him to the hall; a. fr.—[סִדְרָא, סְדָרָא *net*, v. סְדָרָא.]

סדרונגיא, v. סְרוּנְגַיָּא.

סַדְרוּתָא, v. סְרְהוּתָא.

סדריוט, v. סְרָיוֹט.

סַדְרִיתָא, v. סְרִיתָא.

סַדְרָן, סוֹדְרָן m. (סֶדֶר) *one who arranges traditions systematically, systematic scholar*, opp. פילפלן dialectician. Y. Hor. III, 48ᶜ top חסר׳ (Bab. ed. חסד׳). Midr. Till. to Ps. LXXXVII (ref. to II Kings XX, 20) 'he brought the water (of the Law) into the city', שהוא סד׳ because he (Ezekiah) was a collector, v. next w.

סַדְרָן, סַדְרָנָא, סוֹד׳ ch. same. Midr. Till. to Ps. LXXXVII (v. preced.) חמי ס׳ טב וכ׳ when he (Ezekiah) saw a good systematiser, he made him come (to Jerusalem); Yalk. ib. 837 סודר. Pes. 105ᵇ גמרנא וס׳ אנא (v. Rabb. D. S. a. l. note 400) I am a teacher and systematiser of traditions.

סָהַד (v. next w.) *to be witness.*

Pi. סִיהֵד *to provide witnesses for.* Tosef. Gitt. VIII (VI), 8 הנותן גט לאשתו ולא סִיהֲדוֹ (ed. Zuck. שִׂהֲדוֹ) if a man gives his wife a letter of divorce without witnesses.

סְהֵד, סְהִיד (v. עֵד, a. יְדַה; Sam. סעד, סהד, v. Sam. Pent. Gen. XXXI, 52; cmp. also עֵד=סעד ib. VII, 16; for interch. of ע a. ה a. ח, v. letters ה a. ו) *to be sure, be present; to witness.*

Af. אַסְהֵד, אַסְהִיד (corresp. to b. h. הֵעִיד) 1) *to testify.* Targ. O. Ex. XX, 13; a. fr.—Keth. 21ᵃ א׳ אתהימנות v. הֵימָנוּתָא. Ib. לא צריך אירהו לאַסְהֲדֵי וכ׳ he would not need to identify his own signature; ואזל אירהו ותאי ומַסְהֲדֵי וכ׳ (or וּמְסַהֲדֵי *Pa.*) and thus he and the other man might identify the signature of that man (the deceased); a. v. fr.—2) *to call to witness; to give warning.* Targ. Deut. IV, 26. Targ. Ps. LXXXI, 9. Targ. II Chr. XXXIII, 10; a. fr.

Pa. סַהֵד, שַׂהֵד same, 1) *to testify.* Targ. Y. Ex. XX, 13; a. e.—Keth. 21ᵃ מְסַהֲדֵי, v. supra. Y. Snh. I, 18ᵇ top איתא שַׂהֵד עלי come, testify in my behalf. Y. Shebu. VI, end, 37ᵇ כארנש ... דלא יְשַׂהֲדוּן like one that ties up the mouth of witnesses that they may not testify; a. fr.—2) *to warn.* Targ. Y. Gen. XLIII, 3 מְסַהֲדָא אַסְהִיד; a. e.

Ittaf. אִיתַּסְהַד *warning has been given.* Targ. Ex. XXI, 29.

סָהֵד, v. סָהִיד.

שָׂ׳, סָ׳, סָהֲדָה, סָהֲדָא m. (preced.) 1) *witness.* Targ. O. Deut. XIX, 18. Targ. Prov. XII, 19; a. fr.—B. Bath. 33ᵇ. Sabb. 65ᵇ מטרא .. ס׳ רבה פרת (the rise of) the Euphrates is a weighty witness (indication) that it rained in Palestine; a. fr.—*Pl.* סָהֲדִין, סָהֲדַיָּא, סָהֲדֵי, שָׂ׳. Targ. Ex. XXII, 12. Targ. O. ib. 2; a. fr.—B. Bath. l. c. Kidd. 65ᵇ לא איברו ס׳ אלא לשקרי witnesses are created only for liars, i. e. the institution of witnesses is not intended to legalise an act, but only as a guard against faithless persons who might deny the transaction. Y. Shebu. VI, end, 37ᵇ פומהון דש׳, v. preced. art. Ib. ייתי עלוי ש׳ let him produce witnesses to confirm it. Y. Snh. III, end, 21ᵈ וקבלון לש׳ וכ׳ and they received (heard) the witnesses in the absence of &c.; a. fr.—Ber. 17ᵇ, a. fr. אנן ס׳ we know certainly.—Fem. סָהֲדָא. Targ. O. Gen. XXXI, 52.—V. סָהִיד.—2) *pl.* סָהֲדִין, constr. סָהֲדֵי *testimony.* Targ. Y. Ex. XX, 13. Targ. Y. Deut. XIX, 18 סהדין שקרא; a. e.; v. next w.

סָהֲדוּ, סָהֲדוּתָא, שָׂ׳ f. (preced.) *testimony, evidence; warning.* Targ. Deut. V, 17. Targ. Is. VIII, 20; a. fr.—Y. Snh. III, end, 21ᵈ קביל .. ס׳ דלא באפוי וכ׳ R. E. heard evidence in the absence of the party; a. fr.—ידע בס׳ to know evidence, to have something to testify to. Macc. 5ᵇ; a. fr. Y. Snh. I, 18ᵇ top ידע ש׳; a. fr.—*Pl.* סָהֲדְוָון, סָהֲדָן, סָהֲדָ׳, סָהֲדֵי; constr. סָהֲדְוָות. Targ. Jer. XVIII, 18 סהדון (ed. Lag. סָהֲדִין, v. preced.). Targ. Y. Deut. XXII, 14 (not דוון ...) *evidence of virginity.* Targ. Ps. CXIX, 14; a. fr.

סְהֵיד, v. סְהֵד.

סָהִיד, סָהֵד m. (part. of preced.) *witness.* Targ. Prov. XII, 17 סָהֵד ed. Wil. (ed. Lag. סהדא). Targ. O. Deut. XIX, 15; 18; a. fr.—Fem. סָהִידָא. Targ. Y. Gen. XXXI, 52.—*Pl.*, v סָהֲדָא.

סְהִידְוָון, סָהֲדָן, סְהִידְוָותָא, סָהֲדוּ, v. סָהֲדוּ.

סַחַר c. (b. h.; cmp. סחר) 1) *an enclosed place*, esp. *the enclosure for cattle* near a dwelling; *stable*. Erub. II, 3 (18[a]; Mish. a. Ms. M. everywhere סְהַר). Ib. 22[a]; Y. ib. IV, 21[d] bot.; Tosef. ib. III (II), 9. Tosef. Sabb. X (XI), 1. Shebi. III, 4 עושה ס׳ וכ׳ may put up (in the field) an enclosure covering an area of &c.; Tosef. ib. II, 15. Ib. 16 שהר; a. fr.—Tanh. Ki Thissa 2 (play on הסהר, Cant. VII, 3) הס׳ שדומה לסוחר וכ׳ (the meeting place of the Sanhedrin is called) *hassahar*, because it resembles a merchant's store.—2) (cmp. next w.) *moon*. Ib. ed. Bub. 1 אגן הס׳ כחצי הירח *ăgan hassahar* means, 'like a half-moon' (the semicircular seats of the Sanhedrin), v. פַּתְרוֹן I.—*Pl.* סְהָרִים, סַהֲרִין. Tosef. Shebi. II, 19; Y. ib. III, 34[c] bot. סידורין (corr. acc.).—Tosef. Dem. VI, 11 זה (ש) הביא שַׂהֲרֵי שבלים וכ׳ if one brought (into the partnership) stores of ears of his own crop &c.; a. e.

סַהֲרָה, סַהֲרָא m. ch. (זהר=סחר) *light*, esp. *moonlight*. Cant. R. to VII, 3, v. זִהֲרָא I. Ber. 53[a] דאיכא ס׳ (Ms. F. סידורא) when there is moonshine.—V. סִיהֲרָא.

סַהֲרוֹן m., *pl.* סַהֲרוֹנִים (b. h. שַׂהֲרֹנִים; preced.; cmp. זְהוֹרִית) *crimson* (or *saffron*) *colored ribbons*. Y. Sot. IX, 24[c] top וסַהֲרוֹנֵי זהב תלויין בהן with gold-embroidered ribbons hanging thereon (Tosef. ib. XV, 9 וזהוריות מוזהבות); [oth. opin.: *moon-shaped* ornaments of gold].

סַהֲרָנָא, *pl.* סַהֲרָנַיָּא ch. same. Targ. Jud. VIII, 26 (Rashi: שנקיא as Targ. ib. 21).

סוֹא, v. סִיר.

סוֹאֲבָא m. (=מְסוֹאֲבָא; סְאַב) *unclean*. Targ. Y. II Deut. XXVI, 14 בס׳ while unclean.

סוֹאֲבוּתָא f. (preced.) *uncleanness*. Targ. Y. Gen. XXXV, 2. Targ. Lam. I, 9; a. e.

סוֹאַבְתָּא, v. סְאוֹבְתָּא.

סַוָּור, סְוָואר, סָוָואר m. (dial. for צֵבֶר=צְוָאר; סָיִר; v. Maim. to Ohol. III, 7 ed. Dehr.) *a pile of joists, frame*. Ohol. III, 7 ס׳ של קורות (ed. Dehr. צואר, in comment. צִוּוּר, Var. צִבֵּר); Succ. 20[b] (Ms. M. סוואר); Y. Sabb. IV, 7[a] top צבר. Bets. 31[b] אין מבקעין עצים לא מן הס׳ וכ׳ we must not chop (on the Holy Day, for immediate use) wood from a pile of joists (intended for building purposes), v. מוּכָן.—Tosef. Kel. B. Mets. V, 4 ס׳ של נחתומין חפרוס וכ׳ (R. S. to Kel. XV, 2 סרוד) the baker's frame when it is plain (without rims) is unclean, because dough is cut and carried to the stove on it.—V. סָוִיר.

סוֹב (sec. r. of סבב), *Pa.* סַיֵּיב [*to go all around*,] *to finish up, trim*. Gen. R. s. 78 (a proverbial expression) שיירצת סַיֵּיבְתְּ hast thou finished? hast thou trimmed (so as to be entitled to wages)?; Yalk. ib. 133 סיירת.

סוֹב, *pl.* סוֹבִין, v. סוּבִין.

סוֹבֵב m. (סָבַב) *ring, hoop*. Kel. XI, 3, a. e. ס׳ של גלגל the iron hoop of a wheel.—Esp. הס׳ *the Sobeb*, a sort of gallery around the altar for the priest to walk on. Midd. III, 1 זה הס׳ there (at five cubits from the bottom) the Sobeb was attached. Zeb. V, 3; a. fr.

סוֹבְבָא, סוֹבִיבָא ch. same. Targ. O. Ex. XXVII, 5 סוֹבַ׳ (ed. Berl. סוֹבֵי׳, ed. Vien. סוֹבָבֵי, *pl.*; Y. סובבי; h. text כרכב). Ib. XXXVIII, 4 סוֹבָבֵיהּ (ed. Berl. סיבי׳; Y. סוֹבְבֵ׳).

סוֹבִייה, v. סוֹבְיָיה.

סוֹבִין m. pl.=סוֹבְבִין (סָבַב) *galleries*. Tosef. Kel. B. Mets. II, 8 [read:] הס׳ והסטיוין שלהן (v. סְטָיו) the galleries and colonnades on turrets (v. אַקְוּבְּי).

סוּבִּין m. pl. (preced.; cmp. חֲרִירָאָה) *flour of the second course, bran-flour* (differ. fr. מוּרְסָן). Keth. 112[a]; Y. Sot. I, 17[b], a. e.—B. Bath. 98[b] (from Ben Sira) הכל ... קל מס׳ וקל מס׳ וכ׳ I have weighed everything ..., and found nothing lighter than bran, but lighter (in mind) than bran is &c.; a. fr.—Sing. סוּב, with suffix סוּבָּן. Hall. II, 6. Sabb. VII, 4 (76[b]).

סוֹבֶךְ m. (סְבַךְ) [*thicket*,] *the fleshy part of the leg, calf*. Hull. X, 4. Y. Yeb. XII, 12[c] bot.; Tosef. Yad. II, 1 ברגל עד הס׳ he must wash his feet up to where the calf begins.

סוּבַּלְתָּא, v. שׁוּבַּלְתָּא.

סוּבְנִי, v. סִבְנִי.

סוּבְעָא m. (סְבַע) *plenty*. Targ. Ps. XVI, 11. [סוּבְעָא, v. סְבָעָא.]

סוֹבְרָא m. (סְבַר II) *carrying*. Y. Taan. IV, 68[b] ס׳ דקיסא טרד (not סוכרא) the carrying of wood kept them busy.—[Hull. 18[b] מסוברא, v. סְבָרָא II.]

סוּבְרוּתָא, סוּבָּרָה, סוּבָּרָא, סוֹבְרָא, v. סְבָרָא a. סַבָּרוּתָא.

סוּבְרִיקִין, v. סְפַרְקִין.

סוּבְתָּא, סוּבְתָּא, v. סְאוֹבְתָּא.

סוּג I (b. h.) [*to cut off, separate*,] *to fence in, mark off*. Y. Ab. Zar. IV, 43[c], sq. כל שהוא סג וכ׳ any stone that is put up to mark the sea-shore or the roads. Y. M. Kat. I, 80[c] פירצה שהיא סָגָה וכ׳ a fence which, though broken, still bars the ground behind it (from falling out); Y. Shebi. III, end, 34[d]; a. e.—Trnsf. (v. סְיָג a. גָּדַר) *to guard against trespassing a law, to make a prohibition more restrictive; to exaggerate*. Ab. d'R. N. ch. I סייג שסג ... לדבריו (v. ed. Schechter) the guard which Adam set to his words (by adding the prohibition to touch the tree of knowledge). Ib. אם סג אדם לדבריו וכ׳ if a person exaggerates his words, he cannot abide by them.

Pi. סַיֵּיג *to fence in*. Part. pass. מְסוּיָּיג. Koh. R. to V, 14 והיתה סס׳ וכ׳ it (the vineyard) was fenced in on all sides.

Hif. הֵסִיג (with גְּבוּל) *to remove the landmark*. Sabb. 85[a] (ref. to Deut. XIX, 14) לא תַסִּיג ... גבול do not remove the landmark which those before thee (the Canaanites) have set.

סוג ch. same. Targ. II Esth. III, 3 סַג יתירה (not סגיתירה).—Part. סָיֵיג, סַיג. Targ. Hos. II, 8 כמא דסַיְגִין (missing in ed. Lag.).—Y. M. Kat. III, 83[c] top יְסוּג תורעתך may the Lord fence in thy breach (guard thee from further trouble); Gen. R. s. 100. Y. Kidd. I, end, 61[d]; Y. Shebu II, end, 33[c], a. e. סָיְיגִין סייגה ותרעין וכ׳ a fence is fenced around, and a breach broken into, i. e. the good are assisted by Providence in their good work, and the bad in their evil ways; וכיני סייגין וכ׳ (not ובני) but is it right that the fence &c.?; Yalk. Prov. 935 סגייר סוגיירא (corr. acc.).

סוג II m. (preced.) [*partition,*] *a large chest* or *basket* with partitions for various kinds of provision. Dem. V, 6 אפי׳ מאותו הס׳ וכ׳ even if he buys the second time from the same chest and of the same kind (quality). Y. B. Kam. II, 3[a] ס׳ שנתון וכ׳ a dealer's chest which stands at the entrance of the shop; a. e.—*Pl.* סוּגִים, סוּגִין. Kel. XVI, 3 הס׳ הגדולים (R. S. a. l. Var. סוֹאִין; Tosef. ib. B. Mets. V, 3; 13 הסאין, v. סוֹי) the large provision chests; Sifra Sh'mini ch. VII, Par. 6 סיגים (corr. acc.). Y. Sabb. XVII, 16[a] bot.; a. e.—[In later philosophical literature: סוּג *class, species.*—[Midr. Till. to Ps. CXIX, 119 עושה סוגים, v. סִיג I.]

סוּגָא I m. *Suga,* name of *a bird.* Ḥull. 62[b].

***סוּגָא II** pr. n. m. *Suga.* B. Bath. 90[b] Ms. M. (ed. פוגא; v. Rabb. D. S. a. l. note).

סוּגְאָה, סוּגְאֵי, v. סוּגֵי.

סוּגָה f. (סוג) *fence, enclosure.* Snh. 37[a] (ref. to Cant. VII, 3) אפי׳ בס׳ של שושנים וכ׳ even in a fence of lilies they will make no breach (they will not trespass a law however slightly guarded). Ib. (second time) בס׳ בשושנים ed. (Ms. M. של ש׳; v. Rabb. D. S. a. l. note).

סוּגְגוּן, סוּגְגוּ *much, very,* v. סַגִּי I.

סוּגֵי, סוּגְאֵי, סוּגְאָה, סוּגְיָא I m. (סְגֵי I) *multitude, largeness.* Targ. Prov. VII, 21 סוגי Ms. (ed. סוגיא). Ib. V, 23 סוגאי (Ms. סוגיא). Targ. Ps. LXIX, 14 Ms. (ed. סגיעי); a. fr.—V. סוּגְעָא.—Lam. R. to I, 1 (שרתי) סוּגֵיהוֹן בישין their masses are bad; Gen. R. s. 50 סוּגְיָיה בישין the masses of the place are bad; Yalk. ib. 84 סוּגְיָא. Y. Ab. Zar. I, 39[c] סוגיירה שמריין (not סי׳; prob. to be read רומיין) most of the garrison are Samaritans (Romans).

סוּגְיָא, סוּגְיְיא II m. (סְגֵי II) 1) *walk.* Sabb. 66[b] top לתרוצי ס׳ הוא דעביד Ms. M. it (the cane) serves merely to direct the walk (not as a support).—2) (cmp. הֲלָכָה) *study, lesson, subject; practice, usage.* Num. R. s. 12; Lam. R. to I, 3, v. בְּזַז I, a. גְּזַז. Snh. 6[a] סוּגְיָין דעלמא (Ms. M. ס׳ דשמעתתא בעלמא) the general practice (as regards that subject).—[Yalk. Prov. 935 סגייר סוגיירא, v. סוּג ch.—Koh. R. to V, 8 סוּגְיָא, v. סִיגָא.]

סוּגְיָינָא m., *pl.* סוּגְיָינֵי (סְגִי I, cmp. סַנְסִינּוֹת) *twigs.* Erub. 29[b] ס׳ דערבתא (some ed. סַנְסִינֵי; Ms. M. סיגייתני, corr. acc.; Ms. O. סַבְּכֵי) twigs of a willow.

סוּגְנֵי m. pl., with suffix סוּגְנוֹי (סְגִי I, v. סוגגון, סוגגו) *plenty of it.* Targ. Y. Gen. XXVII, 28.

סוּגְעָא, סוּגְעָה m. (סְגָא) *plenty, largeness;* (adv.) *much, frequently.* Targ. Job XXXI, 25. Targ. Prov. X, 19 (ed. Lag. סוּגְאָה).—Targ. Ps. LI, 4. Targ. I Chr. XXII, 8; a. fr.—*Pl.* סוּגְעֵי. Targ. Ps. XXXIII, 16 Ms. (ed. סַגִּיאֵי). Ib. 17 (ed. סגעי; some ed. סַגִּיעֵי); a. fr.

סוּגְעָתָא f. same. Constr. סוּגְעַת (adv.) *enough.* Targ. Ps. CXXIII, 4 (h. text רַבַּת).

סוּגַר m. (b. h.; סָגַר) *collar* or *muzzle.* Sabb. 51[b]. Y. ib. V, end, 7[c]; Y. Bets. II, end, 61[d], v. חָכָה.

סוֹד m. (b. h.; cmp. סַד a. יָסַד) 1) *foundation.* Snh. 92[b] סוֹדוֹ (Tanḥ. Noah 10 יסודו), v. מָקָק.—Trnsf. *principle.* R. Hash. 20[b] ס׳ העיבור the Principle of Intercalation (title of a book). Ex. R. s. 15 ס׳ הלבנה the principle of the lunar calendar.—2) *intimate union, circle, council.* Y. R. Hash. II, 58[b] (ref. to Ez. XIII, 9) זהו ס׳ העיבור that means the council (of the Sanhedrin) for intercalation; Keth. 112[a]; Y. Snh. I, 18[c] bot. זה עיבור (corr. acc.).—3) *deliberation, counsel.* Erub. 65[a] (ref. to the numerical value of יַיִן and סוֹד) נכנס יין יצא ס׳ where the wine enters, counsel leaves; Snh. 38[a]; Num. R. s. 10; s. 11. Ib. יצא יין נכנס ס׳ when the wine has left (where there is abstinence), deliberation enters. Ib. (ref. to Prov. III, 32) ... הוא נוזר זוכה לס׳ החכמה he is abstinent ..., therefore he is granted the counsel of divine wisdom. Ib. אנשי סוֹדוֹ the men of his (God's) counsel, i.e. his friends. Pes. 113[a] (play on סוֹדְנָא) סוֹד נאה וכ׳ (beer-brewing is) a profitable device and a charity (requiring a very small capital); a. e.—4) *secret.* Ib. 49[b] אין מגלין להן ס׳ we must not entrust a secret to them. Ḥag. 14[a] הקב״ה מגלה להם ס׳ וכ׳ the Lord shall reveal a secret (solve mysteries) to them in the hereafter. Yeb. 63[b] (fr. Ben Sira) גַּלֵּה ס׳ וכ׳ reveal a secret to one out of thousand; a. e.

סוּד [cmp. זוּד, *to boil,* fr. which סִיד *lime;* denom. סוּד or סִיד (b. h. שִׂיד),] *to plaster, whitewash.* Sot. VII, 5 סְדוּהוּ בסיד they whitewashed it (the altar) with lime. Ib. 35[b]. Tosef. Sot. XV, 9 שלא יָסוּד אדם וכ׳ that a person must not plaster his rooms &c. Tosef. B. Bath. II, 17; B. Bath. 60[b] סָד אדם וכ׳ a man may plaster all his rooms &c.; a. e.—Esp. *to paint the skin* with a depilatory (of lime or orpiment). Sabb. VIII, 4 כדי לָסוּד וכ׳ as much as may be required for painting a little girl; ib. 80[b] כדי לסוד אצבע וכ׳ to paint the little finger &c.; Tosef. ib. VIII (IX), 20; a. e.

Pi. סַיֵּיד *to cover with plaster.* Tosef. Sot. VIII, 7 וְסִיְּידוּהוּ, v. סִיד. Ab. Zar. III, 7; a. fr.—Part. pass. מְסוּיָּיד; f. מְסוּיֶּידֶת. Tosef. B. Bath. l. c.; B. Bath. l. c.; a. e.—[Incorr. סייד in some ed.]

סוּד ch. same. Targ. Am. II, 1. Targ. O. Deut. XXVII, 2 תְּסוּד (some ed. תְּסִיד).

סוּדְמִי, v. סְדוֹמִי.

סוּדְנָא m. (v. סוֹד h.) *brewer;* [oth. opin. סוּדְנָא *beer*]. Pes. 113[a] לבי ס׳ (Ar. סרי) to the brewery, v. חֲלוּז. Ib. מאי ס׳ why is the brewer (beer) called ס׳?; v. סוֹד.

סוּדָנִי I m. (preced.) *brewer.* Ber. 44[b]; Men. 71[a];

Nidd. 12ᵇ top (applied to R. Papa, the brewer). [Other opinion: 'ס (denom. of סוד) *wise man*.]

סוּדָנִי II m. *Sidonian*.—*Pl.* סוּדָנִיִּים. Tosef. Kel. B. Bath. VII, 10 ed. Zuck. (Var. צִידֹנִים; R. S. to Kel. XXX, 3 צִידוֹנִים).

סוּדָר (mostly pl. form סוּדָרִין) f. (סָדַר; cmp. הדר II) *scarf wound around the head and hanging down over the neck, turban*. Sabb. 120ᵃ וסודר שבצואריו and a scarf hanging down over his neck (v. Rashi); Y. ib. XVI, end, 15ᵈ וסודרין שעל זרועותיו (not וסד׳) hanging down over his arms. Succ. 51ᵇ והסודרין בידו.. חזן and the superintendent of the synagogue stood there with a scarf (as a flag) in his hand; ומניף בסודר; Tosef. ib. IV, 6 בסודרין; Y. ib. V, 55ᵇ top בסודרין, v. נוּף; Snh. VI, 1. Ib. VII, 2 (52ᵇ) ונותנין סודר קשה לתוך הרכה (Y. ed. סודרין) they put a twisted scarf of coarse material within a soft one and wound it around his neck; a. fr.—[Lat. *sudarium* is a phonetic coincidence with our w., from which it differs in meaning.]

סוּדְרָא, סוֹדְרָא ch. same. Targ. Ruth III, 15 (h. text מטפחת). Targ. Y. Ex. XXXIV, 33, sq. (h. text מסוה). Targ. Y. Lev. XX, 10 שינוק ס׳ וכ׳ strangulation with a twisted scarf &c. (v. Snh. VII, 2 quot. in preced.); Targ. Y. Ex. XXI, 15; a. fr.—Ab. Zar. 4ᵃ רמו ליה ס׳ וכ׳ they twisted a scarf around his neck and tortured him. Ber. 51ᵃ (expl. עיטוף) פריס ס׳ וכ׳ spread the scarf over his head; a. e.—Esp. *turban*. Pes. 111ᵇ סודריה דמר כי וכ׳ your turban looks like that of a scholar, yet I am sure you do not know the benediction (on putting it on: עוטר ישראל בתפארה). Sabb. 77ᵇ (playful etymology) סוּדְרָא סוֹד ה׳ לִירֵאָיו 'the secret of the Lord is revealed to those that fear him' (the turban being the scholar's apparel); a. e.

סוּדְרִין, v. סוּדָר.—[Yalk. Prov. 947 מעלים לו ס׳, v. סָלְרִין.]

סוֹדְרָן, v. סַדְרָן.

סְוָואר, v. סַוָּאר.

סוודא, v. סוּתָא.

סוודיר, v. סַחְיָיא.

סְוָון, v. סִיָן.

סְוָוס m. name of a *bitter herb*. Pes. 39ᵃ ס׳ וסורא Ms. M. (ed. עסוס וטורא; Ms. O. סְוָאס; v. Rabb. D. S. a. l. note).

סְוַוסְטֵר, v. סְבַסְטֵר.

סוּוסְרִיתָא, v. סְרִיסָא.

סְוָור, v. סָאַר.

סְוָורִיקִין, v. סְפַרְקִין.

סוּחַ, שׂוּחַ (b. h. שׂוּחַ) [*to think*,] *to talk; to tell*. Shebu. VIII, 3; 6 איני יודע מה אתה סָח (Y. ed. שָׂח) I do not know what you are talking about. Ber. 51ᵃ סח לי told me. Sot. 44ᵇ שח בין תפילה וכ׳ if one talks between putting on the T'fillin of the arm and of the head; Men. 36ᵃ סח; a. fr.—Hull. 27ᵃ, v. חָבָא I.—[Yalk. Ps. 755, read: שָׂח, v. שוחה.]

Hif. הֵסִיחַ, הֵשִׂיחַ same. Ber. 51ᵇ אין מְסִיחִין על כוס וכ׳ you must not converse while holding up the cup of benediction. Sabb. 13ᵇ והיתה מְסִיחָה וכ׳ and she told (me) all that happened to her. Y. Gitt. IX, end, 50ᵈ מש׳, בְסִיחִין, v. סִיחָה. Pesik. R. s. 31 עומד ומֵסִיחַ וכ׳ (the text, Is. XLIX, 8 sq.) stands and speaks (is a standing prophecy) of the king Messiah. Deut. R. s. 1 מי אתה מסיח עמי וכ׳ who art thou that art talking to me &c.?—Gen. R. s. 13, beg. (ref. to שיח, Gen. II, 5) כל... כאילו מְשִׂיחִין אלו וכ׳ all trees speak to one another as it were; מש׳ עם הבריות speak to men; Yalk. ib. 20. Ex. R. s. 1 לְהָשִׂיחַ עלינו to talk against us. Tanh. T'rum. 9; Yalk. Mal. 587, v. קָבַע I; a. fr.—מסיח לפי תומו, v. תּוֹם.—Yoma 75ᵃ (ref. to ישחנה, Prov. XII, 25) חד אמר יְשִׂחֶנָּה מדעתו וחד אמר יְשִׂיחֶנָּה לאחרים one says, let him dismiss it (fr. נָסַח = נְסַח; Ms. M. 2 יַשִׂיחֶנָּה) from his mind; the other says, let him speak it out to others; Sot. 42ᵇ; Snh. 100ᵇ; Yalk. Prov. 950; v. נָסַח.

סוּחַ ch. same. Hag. 5ᵇ שמעיה דסָח וכ׳ heard him talk and laugh.—Part. סָיַיח. Lev. R. s. 26 גחין וס׳ יתה bending down and talking to her (rebuking her in a persuasive way; prob. to be read: ומפייס).

Af. אַסִּיחַ, אַשִׂיחַ same. Targ. Job VII, 11. Targ. Y. I Num. XXI, 27 (not מַשִׂיחַ). Ib. 28 (not מְשִׂיחִין); a. e.—[Targ. Prov. VIII, 15 אנא משיחין ed. Lag. (ed. Wil. מְשַׁחָא), fr. מְשַׁח I.]

סוּחָא m. (נְסַח; cmp. b. h. סוחה, a. סְחִיתָא) *that which is thrown out, dirt, disgusting matter*. Targ. Prov. XXIII, 29 ed. Compl. (ed. Lag. סודא, Var. סַיְרָא; ed. Wil. שׂוּחָא; h. text שִׂיחַ).

סוּחִיתָא, v. סְחִיתָא.

סוּחֵר m. (b. h. סֹחֵר; סְחַר) 1) *traveller, beggar*. Snh. 107ᵃ דומה לס׳ כותי like a Samaritan beggar (v. Midr. Till. to Ps. XIX, end, a. Lev. R. s. 5; Rashi: a Samaritan *peddler* that offers his goods by degrees, from the worse to the better).—2) *travelling merchant*, in gen. *merchant*. Tanh. Ki Thissa 2, v. סְחַר; a. e.—*Pl.* סוֹחֲרִים, סוֹחֲרִין. Gen. R. s. 84 אחיו.. לס׳ וס׳ וכ׳ his brothers sold him (Joseph) to the Ishmaelites, the Ishmaelites to the merchants, and the merchants to the Midianites &c. Shek. VII, 2 סוֹחֲרֵי בהמה cattle merchants (in Jerusalem); a. fr.

סוּחְתָא, v. סְחִיתָא.

סוּט, (יָסַט) (b. h. שׂוּט) *to move about, be unsteady*, v. סָטָה.

Hif. הֵסִיט, הִסִּיט *to shake; to swing* (v. הֵיסֵט), contrad. to נגע to touch directly. Zab. V, 1 המסיט את הזב או שהזב מְסִיטוֹ he who moves a *zab* (v. זָב) (by shaking the board on which he stands) or whom the *zab* moves. Hull. 124ᵇ והֱסִיטָן and shook them; a. fr.—[Ex. R. s. 23; Lev. R. s. 11; ib. s. 16 חסיטן, read חטיטן, v. חטט h.]

Nif. נִיסּוֹט *to be shaken, moved*. Tosef. Zab. IV, 6 אם היו נִיסּוֹטִין if they moved (on account of his rapping, and did not merely vibrate). Tosef. Toh. X, 8 [read:] ובלבד

שלא יהו נירסוטין וכ׳ provided they are not shaken up by the vibrations of the partition.

סוּט (יְסַט) ch. same, 1) *to be unsteady, go astray.* Targ. Koh. II, 15 (ed. Lag. סָטָא).—Snh. 67ᵃ (missing in some ed.) סָטַת, v. סִטְרָא.—2) *to move, swing.* Targ. Lam. II, 8 סָאט (h. text נטה).

Af. אַסֵּיט, אוֹסֵיט *to shake.* Targ. Y. Lev. XV, 10; a. e.

Ithpe. אִיסְתְּוִיט, 'אִיסְט *to become wild* (cmp. שָׂטָה); *to shy.* Ned. 41ᵃ אִיסְתּוִיט ed. (Ar. אִיסְטוּיט, אִיסְטְרוּט, cler. error ויס . . .).

סוּטְרָא, v. סִטְרָא.

סוֹטָה f. (סָטָה) *faithless wife, a woman suspected of faithlessness,* to whom the law, Num. V, 12-31, applies; *Sotah.* Sot. 2ᵃ, a. e. פרשת ס׳ the chapter concerning the Sotah (Num. l. c.). Ib. כל הרואה ס׳ בקילקולה וכ׳ whoever sees a Sotah in her disgrace, will vow abstinence from wine. Yeb. 85ᵇ ס׳ ודאי a convicted adulteress. Ib. מחזיר ספק סוֹטָתוֹ as to taking back his wife suspected of adultery; a. fr.—Y. Keth. VII, 31ᶜ אין סוֹטָה היא וכ׳ if she is declared a Sotah, let her get out without dowry, and if she is not &c.—*Pl.* סוֹטוֹת. Sot. I, 5 ששם משקין את הס׳ there (in the Nicanor gate) they made the suspected women drink (the bitter water). Ib. 8ᵃ אין משקין שתי ס׳ כאחת two suspects must not be made to drink at the same time; a. fr.—*Sotah,* a treatise, of the Order of Nashim, of Mishnah, Talmud Babli a. Y'rushalmi, a. Tosefta.

סוּטְנָא, v. סָטָן II.

סוּטנחוֹן, Targ. Is. XXI, 8 ed. Lag., v. סִיטוֹנָא.

סוּטַר* pr. n. m. *Sutar.* Y. Ber. I, 2ᶜ top (for which Yalk. Ez. 340: סִיסְרְטָאִי).

סוּטְרָא, סו׳ m. (Saf. of נטר, cmp. סְנַטַּר) [*that which is reserved,* cmp. נְטוֹרָא] *reward, wages.* Targ. Y. Ex. XXII, 30 בסוּטְרֵיה as his reward (for not barking at the Israelites, v. Ex. R. s. 31). Targ. Y. Lev. XIX, 13. Targ. Y. Deut. XXIV, 14, sq. Targ. Job XIV, 6. Ib. VII, 2 'סָט.

סוּר m. (נשא=נסא; cmp. שׂוֹא, Ps. LXXXIX, 10) [*load,*] *large basket.* B. Kam. 20ᵃ ס׳ מקצתו וכ׳ (quot. by R. H. G. to Kel. XVI, 3; ed. מַשּׂוֹי).—*Pl.* סוּאִים, סוּאִין. Kel. XVI, 3 R. H. G., a. R. S. a. l. Var. (ed. סגים); Tosef. ib. B. Mets. V, 1; 13 (quot. by R. S. l. c.; ed. Zuck. חסאין, read: וְהַסּוּאִין), v. סוג II.

סְוַר* (cmp. Syr. סוא a: סוח cupio, P. Sm. 2540; 2546, a. זוח I) *to be bright, cheer up.* Keth. 62ᵇ דל עינה . . ס׳ לבה וכ׳ he lifted up her eye (attracted her attention), she saw him, her heart was overjoyed, her spirit fled (she fainted).

Af. אַסְוַר *to look up with joy.* Ib. 60ᵃ הוה קא מַסְוַר לאפה (not חזה) the child looked up to her with joy (showing that he recognised his mother).

סְוִירָא* m. (סאר, cmp. Syr. סורא mucus nasi, P. Sm. 2584) *nasty secretion, vomit.* Targ. Prov. XXIII, 29 some ed. (Ms. Var. סִירָא; ed. Lag. סוודא, read סְוָירָא), v. סִירָא.

סוּךְ (b. h.; cmp. נָסַךְ) *to pour (oil), to anoint; to oil.* Dem. I, 3 שמן לָסוּךְ בו וכ׳ oil for vessels. Ib. 4 שהגרדי סָךְ וכ׳ with which the weaver oils his fingers. Sabb. VIII, 1 כדי לסוך אבר קטן as much as required to rub one small limb. Tosef. Ter. X, 10 לא יָסוּךְ כהן שמן וכ׳ a priest must not pour oil of T'rumah on a marble plate &c. Ib. 11 ואין סָכִין בו מנעל וכ׳ nor must you use it for oiling a shoe &c. Shebi. II, 5 סָכִין את הפגים וכ׳ you may pour oil on green figs and pierce them (to accelerate ripening); a. fr.—Part. pass. סוּךְ; f. סוּכָה; *pl.* סוּכִים, סוּכִין; סוּכוֹת. Y. Bicc. I, 63ᵈ bot. תאנים ס׳ וכ׳ figs which have been oiled and pierced.

Hif. הֵסִיךְ same. Yalk. Ex. 165 הסלע . . . מֵסִיךְ . . כחיה שהיא מְסֶכֶת את בנה (not ממסכת) the rock by their side anointed them with oil like a confined woman that anoints her child; Pirkê d'R. El. ch. XLII מניקה . . מניק (corr. acc.).

Nif. נִיסַּךְ *to be oiled, perfumed.* Tosef. Ter. X, 10 אין הזר . . . אע״פ שה׳ מבנו the non-priest need not hesitate to rub it (on the priest's body), although he himself (his hand) is perfumed thereby.—[*Nithpol.* נִסְתּוֹכֵךְ, v. סָכַךְ II.]

סוּךְ ch. same. Targ. Ruth III, 3. Targ. O. Deut. XXVIII, 40 תְסוּךְ (some ed. תְּסִיךְ; ed. Berl. תְשׁוּךְ).

Ithpe. אִתְּסַךְ *to be poured., rubbed.* Targ. O. Ex. XXX, 32 ed. Berl. (ed. Vien. יִתְנַסַּךְ).

סוֹךְ (שׂוֹךְ) m. (b. h. שׂוֹךְ; סוך=סבך) *bough, bush.* B. Kam. X, 2 (114ᵃ) לא יקוץ את סוכו וכ׳ (some ed. 'שׂ; Y. ed. חסוכה; v. Rabb. D. S. a. l. note 100) he must not cut off the bough of his neighbor's tree &c. Y. Keth. II, end, 27ᵃ בשׂוֹכוֹ when the bees have settled on his neighbor's bough (or bush); a. e.—*Pl.* סוֹכִים, constr. סוֹכֵי. Succ. 13ᵇ; Tosef. Maasr. III, 5 ס׳ תאנים boughs of fig trees. Erub. 101ᵃ ס׳ קוצים וכ׳ boughs of thorn-bushes and bundles of twigs of which one made a movable hedge before a breach; Tosef. ib. XI (VIII), 11, חבילי וסיכה של קוצים ed. Zuck. (Var. סוכה); v. סוֹכָה.

סוֹכָא ch. same. Targ. II Sam. XVIII, 9 (h. text שׂוֹבֶךְ). Targ. Jud. IX, 49. Targ. Is. XVII, 6 (ed. Lag. a. oth. סוֹכַה); a. e.—V. סוֹכְתָא.

סוּכָּא, pl. סוּכַּיָּיא, v. סֻכָּא.

סוֹכָה, שׂ׳ (b. h. שׂוֹכָה)=סוֹךְ. Makhsh. I, 3. Y. Sabb. XV, end, 15ᵇ. B. Mets. 105ᵇ, v. חָזִיז II. Pesik. R. s. 15 מס׳ לס׳ from bush to bush; Cant. R. to II, 9; Yalk. ib. 986. Ab. d'R. N. ch. XXXIX קוצו ס׳ זו וכ׳ cut this limb off the tree. Pesik. R. s. 10, beg. הס׳ הזו של קוצים (not הזה) this thorn-bush. Tosef. Erub. XI (VIII), 11 (not סיכה), v. סוֹךְ. Lam. R. to V, 13 בס׳ אחת, v. חָזִיז; a. e.—*Pl.* סוֹכוֹת. Y. Bets. IV, 62ᶜ top ס׳ תאנים, v. סוֹךְ.

סֻכָּה, סוּכָּה f. (b. h.; סָכַךְ) *cover* of twigs; *booth*; esp. *Succah, the booth* covered with twigs &c. *for the seven days of Succoth.* Maasr. III, 7 סוּכַּת גינוסר the lodge of Genezareth gardens (inhabited during vintage); ס׳ הדוצרים

the potter's hut (the outer compartment serving as a workshop, the inner as a dwelling); סֻכַּת החג the festive booth. Num. R. s. 4 (ref. to יֻסַּךְ, Ex. XXV, 29) שהיו מעמידין .. כמין ס׳ they put the bread up in the shape of a hut; שכל חלה ...ס׳ וכ׳ each cake forming a roof over that below (tubes being placed between them to allow the air to strike). Succ. I, 1 ס׳ שהיא גבוהה וכ׳ a Succah which is higher than twenty cubits is unfit for ritual use. Ib. 2 העושה סוכתו וכ׳ he who put up his Succah under a tree; a. v. fr.—*Pl.* סֻכּוֹת, סוכות. Ib. 8b שתי ס׳ של יוצריים the two combined huts of the potters, v. supra; a. fr.—*Succah*, name of a treatise, of the Order of Mo'ed, of the Mishnah, Talmud Babli a. Y'rushalmi, a. Tosefta.

סוֹכוֹ (b. h. שׂוֹכֹה a. שׂוֹכוֹ) pr. n. pl. *Soco, Sokho*, name of two towns in Judaea. Ab. I, 3, v. אַנְטִיגְנוֹס.

סוכות (סכות), ס׳ בְּנוֹת (b. h.) *Succoth B'noth*, name of an idol. Snh. 63b ס׳ ב׳ ... תרנגולת Succoth B'noth (covering the young) ... is a hen; Y. Ab. Zar. III, 42c sq. תרנגולתא ופרחיה a hen and her chickens.

סוּכִי, Tosef. Succ. III, 6, v. סָחוּ.

סוֹכָיָא, סוֹכָיָיה m. (סוכו) *of Sokho*. Y. Yoma VIII, 45b bot. לוי ס׳; Y. Erub. X, 26a bot. סוכיא (not ס׳׳); ib. 26c bot. סוכייה (corr. acc.); Y. Pes. VI, 33b ר׳ סוכיה (read: לוי סוכ׳); Y. Shebu. I, 33b לוי שובדא (read: שׂוֹכְיָא).

סוּכְלָא, v. סִכְלָא.

סוּכְלְתָן, סוּכְלְתָנָא, ש׳ m. (סְכַל I) *intelligent; intelligent person*. Targ. Prov. I, 5. Ib. X, 5. Ib. 19 ש׳; a. fr.—*Pl.* סוּכְלְתָנִין. Targ. Deut. I, 13. Targ. Is. XXIX, 14; a. fr.—[Targ. Prov. XXI, 11, v. next w.]

סוּכְלְתָנוּ, סוּכְלְתָנוּתָא f. (preced.) 1) *intelligence, intellect*. Targ. Ex. XXXI, 3. Targ. Is. XXIX, 14; a. fr.—2) *reasoning*. Targ. Prov. XXI, 11 בסוּכְלְתָנוּתֵיהּ דחכימא (Ms. בסוכלתנוד, some ed. בסוכלתנוה, corr. acc.) when the wise man is reasoned with.

סוֹכֵר, עֵין ס׳ pr. n. pl. *'En Sokher*. Sot. 49b בקעת ע׳ ס׳ the valley of 'E. S.—Y. Shek. V, 48d; Men. 64b, v. next w.

סוּכְרָא m. (סְכַר) 1) *bolt*. Targ. Prov. XVIII, 19.—Y. Shek. V, 48d (of a mute man that wanted to point out the place 'En Sokher, v. preced.) והוה יהיב ... וחדיה על ס׳ he put one hand on his eye and the other on a bolt; Men. 64b סיכ׳ (corr. acc.; v. Rabb. D. S. a. l. note 5); Yalk. Ezra 1067.—2) ס׳ דנהרא *dam, lock*. Y. Bets. III, 62a top ס׳ דנהרא שרו it is permitted to catch fish (on a Holy Day) which are kept in the lock of a river, v. דעמים; Y. Sabb. III, 14a bot. סבריא (corr. acc., or סִכְּרָא).—[Y. Taan. IV, 68b ס׳ דקיסא, v. סוּבְרָא.

סוּכְּתָא f. ch. = h. סוּכָּה. Targ. Jud. IX, 48.

סוּל m. (v. סִילוֹן I) *thorn, a wooden prick*. Y. Kidd. I, 59d top (ref. to Deut. XV, 17) מניין אפי׳ בס׳ וכ׳ whence do you prove that you may also use a prick, a thorn &c.?; Bekh. 37b; Shebu. 4b; a. e.—*Pl.* סוּלִין, סוּלִּים. Num. R. s. 3, beg. כזה התמר .. עושה ס׳ as the palm bears dates ... and also pricks (v. נוֹבְלֶת); Midr. Till. to Ps. XCII, 13 סילין; ed. Bub. סילון (corr. acc.). Y. Ab. Zar. III, 42c bot. והסולים (ed. Krot. והסלים, corr. acc.), v. סָמַל.

סוּל ch. same. Targ. Y. Num. XIX, 2.—*Pl.* סוּלַיָּא. Targ. Ps. CXIX, 119 (ed. Lag. פסוליא; h. text סִגִים).

סוּל, *Pol.* סוֹלֵל, v. סָלַל I.

סוּלָא* pr. n. pl. *Sulla*. Cant. R. to II, 17 (ref. to בתר ib.) כד חסב מלכותא בתר ס׳ when the (Roman) government will receive the payment for the massacre of S.

סוּלָאנָא m. (סְלֵי) *offal, dross*. Targ. Prov. XXV, 4 (some ed. סוּלְאָנָא; h. text סִיגִים; v. סוּל ch.).

סוּלְגִּיתָא, סַל׳ f. *bread-basket* (?). Gen. R. s. 65 לא דמי האי דחמי ס׳ וכ׳ you cannot compare him who sees an empty basket and is hungry, to him who sees it filled and is satisfied (even without eating); Koh. R. to V, 10 סַלְגִּיתֵיהּ his basket; Yalk. Gen. 114; Yalk. Koh. 972 סולג׳ (?).

סוליים, read:

סוֹלְיָים m. (*solea*, accus. *pl.*) *sole, slipper* without heels. Yeb. 103b, a. e. Ar., v. כְּסוּלְיָים. Kel. XXVI, 4 (not סוליים). Y. Sabb. I, 3c top (ref. to Ps. CXI, 10, a. Prov. XXII, 4) מה ... עשת ענוה עקב לסוּלְיָיסָהּ that (fear of the Lord) which Wisdom makes the crown of her head, Humility makes the imprint of her shoe; Yalk. Prov. 960 עשתה ענוה סוליית לרגלה (corr. acc.) Humility makes the shoe of her foot.—Hebr. adapt.: סוֹלִית (as if from סָלַל II). Tanh. B'resh. 1 סוֹלִיתָהּ ענוה וכ׳ the Law,—her shoe (footprint) is humility, her crown, fear.

סוֹלְיָים ch. same. Y. Taan. I, 64c bot. לביש סוֹלְיָיסֵיהּ wearing his slippers; Y. Yoma VIII, 44d bot. סוֹלְיָסָהּ.

סוֹלִית, סוֹלִיס, סוליית, v. preced. h. a. ch.

סוּלָּם m. (b. h. סֻלָּם; סָלַל II) 1) *ascent, ladder*. B. Bath. III, 6, v. בְּצָרִי II. Gen. R. s. 68 בו עולים ויורדים בס׳ *bo* (Gen. XXVIII, 12), that is, they went up and down the ladder. Ib. סֻלָּם זה סיני *sullam* (whose numerical value is 110) is Sinai; a. fr.—סוּלָּמָהּ של צור *the Ladder of Tyre* (Scala Tyriorum), a promontory south of Tyre. Y. Ab. Zar. I, 40a bot.; a. e.—*Pl.* סוּלָּמוֹת. Gen. R. l. c. הקב״ה יושב ועושה ס׳ וכ׳ the Lord makes ladders, causing one to go down, the other to rise (on the social scale). Sabb. 26a מס׳ של צור וכ׳ from the Promontory of Tyre (along the sea-coast) to Haifa. Ruth R. to IV, 21 (play on שַׂלְמוֹן) עד כאן עשו ס׳ לנשיאים וכ׳ thus far they made ladders for princes (the genealogical tree of chiefs), from now (Salmon) they made ladders for kings; a. fr.—2) *a yoke* in the shape of a ladder, put on the ass to prevent him from scratching a sore. Sabb. V, 4 (54b), v. לוֹיָא.—3) a sort of *hem, chain-stitch*. Y. M. Kat. III, 83d, v. קָפַשׁ.—*Pl.* as ab. Bab. ib. 26b הקורע ... מתוך ס׳ he who rends his garment (in mourning) where it has been mended with chain-stitches after a previous rent.

סוּלְמָא, סוּלָּמָא ch. same, *ladder*. Targ. Gen. XXVII, 12. (O. ed. Vien. סֻלְמָא; oth. ed. סוּל׳).—Y. R. Hash. II, 58ª, v. חֲסַךְ. Y. M. Kat. I, end, 81ª איתבר עוקא דסוּלָמֵיה a round of his ladder broke; a. e.—Succ. 53ᵇ ס׳ דפרת (Rashi סוּלָמֵי pl.; Ms. M. 2 סולמות) the upper part (the source) of the Euphrates.—*Pl.* סוּלָמַיָּא, סוּלָמַיָּה, סוּלָמֵי. Targ. I Chr. II, 54 (v. Taan. 28ª).—Y. B. Kam. IV, 4ᵇ לא מטון לס׳ דצור וכ׳ they (the Roman delegates) had not yet arrived at the promontory of Tyre (v. preced.), when they had forgotten everything. Bekh. 55ᵇ ס׳ דפרת, v. supra.

סוּלְעֲמוּתָא, v. סַלְעֲמִיתָא.

סוּלְפִירִין, סוּלְפִירִים, v. סַלְפִּירִנְגָּס.

סוּלְקוֹס, v. סְלֶוְקוֹס.

סוּלֶת, סוּלַת, סוּלְתָּא, v. סֹלֶת, סֹלֶת.

סוּלְתָא, Lam. R. to I, 15 Ar. ed. Koh., v. סַלוּתָא.

סוּלְתִי, Sabb. 150ᵇ, v. סִילְתָא.

סוּלְתִין, Tosef. Kel. B. Mets. V, 5 ed. Zuck., v. סֹלֶת.

סוּלְתָּנִית, (סוּלְתָּנוּת) f. (denom. of סוֹלֶת) [*fish fried with flour*,] *a small fish* believed to grow scales on reaching a certain age (cmp. אַסְפָּיָין). Hull. 66ª; Ab. Zar. 39ª אין לו... כגון הס׳ וכ׳ one that has no scales now but will grow them after a time, as, for instance, the *sultanith* &c. Ib., expl. חִילֶק I. (Ar. סַלְתָּ׳).

סוּלְתָּנִיתָא ch. same. Y. Ab. Zar. II, 42ª (expl. חילק) רב אמר ס׳ (Ar. סַלְתָּ׳).

סוּם I (v. שׂוּם) *to attach, place; to tie together*. Tosef. Shebi. I, 11 אין סָמִין את הגפנים וכ׳ Var. ed. Zuck. (text: אֵין סכין; oth. ed. אין סכין) you must not bind the grape-vines in the Sabbatical year.

Pi. סַיֵּים 1) same. Cant. R. to VII, 1 (ref. to שולמית ib., a. Num. VI, 26) אומה שמְסַיְּימִים לה שלום וכ׳ a nation to which peace is assigned every day; (Gen. R. s. 66 שהכהנים מְשִׂימִין לה שלום וכ׳).—2) *to mark, name* (cmp. שׁוּם, שֵׁם); *to distinguish*. Y. Peah VII, beg. 20ª הדקל מְסַיְּימוֹ the neighboring palm-tree serves as a mark for it (that the owner did not forget it); זה מְסַיֵּים וכ׳ they mark each other (cmp. Mish. ib. 1 שיש לו שם). Deut. R. s. 7 סַיְּימֵנִי בתוך המדינה וכ׳ give me some distinction in the country, (by which to show) that I am thy son. Y. Ber. V, end, 9ᵈ וסַיְּימוּ באותה וכ׳ and they noted (the time when he said it), at that very time he (the patient) asked for food. Y. Meg. I, 71ᵈ וסיימו אותן חכמים וכ׳ the scholars noted them (took their names &c., in order to be able to observe their career), and all of them turned out great men; Gen. R. s. 1. Y. Dem. V, 24ᶜ bot. ומְסַיֵּים... סַיַּימְתִּי and he makes a mark (on the pile), and says to the priest, so far I have marked (as tithe); a. fr.—[Gen. R. s. 42 end ומסיים את עצמך, v. סוּף II.]—Part. pass. מְסוּיָּים, מְסוּיָּים; f. מְסוּיֶּימֶת &c. Y. Peah l. c. היה מס׳ בדעתו if it (the olive or the sheaf left behind) was noted in his mind (so that he could identify it), כאילו הוא מס׳ it is to be considered as if it were marked (by a special name, locality &c.). B. Bath. 54ª שדה המס׳ במצריה a field definable by its boundaries. Y. Yeb. XV, 15ª אדם מס׳ a well-known man. Y. Shek. I, 46ᵇ top דבר המס׳ an object which bears the name of its owner. Gen. R. s. 44 מה איים הללו מס׳ בים וכ׳ as the islands are distinguishable in the sea, so were Abraham and Shem distinguished in the world; a. fr.—3) *to tie up; to finish, wind up*, opp. פתח. Arakh. 10ᵇ פתח בחליל ומסיים באבוב the Mishnah begins with *ḥalil* and ends with *abbub!* Ber. 10ª פתח בה באשרי וס׳ באשרי he began it (the psalm) with *ashré* and closed it with *ashré*; a. fr.—Part. pass. as ab. Y. Bets. I, beg. 60ª בהמה יולדת לחדשים מס׳ every animal gives birth after a certain number of complete months, opp. למקוטעין counting a fraction of the last month as a whole month.

Nithpa. נִסְתַּיֵּים 1) *to be marked, defined*. Y. Ter. III, 42ᵇ top מקום שנִסְתַּיְּימָה וכ׳ where the T'rumah of one pile was marked, there (in the corresponding place) the T'rumah of the other pile was meant to be dedicated. Y. Shebi. VIII, 38ª זה שהוא.. ונסתיימה לו וכ׳ if one used a basket for measuring and after using it two or three times knew exactly how much it contained; a. e.—2) *to be finished, concluded*. B. Bath. 125ᵇ דבר זה נפתח בגדולים ונ׳ וכ׳ this subject was opened by great men and has been concluded by small men.

סוּם, סִים ch. same. Targ. O. Lev. XIX, 14 תְּסִים ed. Berl. (oth. ed. תְּשִׂים); a. e.—Part. סָאֵם, סָאִים, סַיִּים, סָיֵם. Targ. Prov. VI, 27. Ib. XXVI, 24. Ib. XI, 15.—V. שׂוּם.— Gitt. 56ᵇ הוה סיים חד וכ׳ he had tied (put on) one shoe. Taan. 22ª הוה סיים וכ׳ used to wear black shoes; a. e.

Pa. סַיֵּים 1) same, esp. *to put on shoes* (cmp. Ez. XXIV, 17). Gitt. l. c. בעא לְסַיּוּמָא וכ׳ he wanted to put on the other shoe. Taan. 12ᵇ דמְסַיְּימֵי מסנייהו וכ׳ that they wear their shoes and come to the fast-meeting. Ib. כי מסיימי וכ׳, v. אַפַּנְתָּא; a. e.—2) *to mark, define*. Y. Sabb. VI, 8ᶜ bot. סַיְּימוּן וכן וכ׳ they marked (the time), and so it was.— Part. pass. מְסַיַּים. B. Bath. 100ª דמְסַיְּימָן מחיצתא when the partitions are distinctly defined; a. e.—3) *to finish*. Targ. Y. Gen. XLIV, 18 Tosefta (ed. מחסיל).—Meg. 25ª סַיֵּימְתִּינְהוּ לשבחיה וכ׳ hast thou exhausted all the praises of the Lord? Ber. 12ª פתח.. דשכרא וס׳ בדחמרא he began the benediction under the impression that it was beer, and closed with the benediction over wine. Ib. 17ª כי הוה מְסַיֵּים צלותיה וכ׳ when he closed his prayer, he said &c. B. Mets. 76ᵇ סַיְּימוּהָ קמיה they cited it (the Boraitha) before him to the end; a. fr.—Part. pass. as ab. Cant. R. to I, 11 מְסַיְּמָה, v. חָתַם.—[Targ. Y. I Deut. VIII, 9 מסימין, v. חֲסַם.]

Ithpa. אִסְתַּיֵּים 1) *to be marked, named*. Ab. Zar. 16ᵇ, a. e. מינאי ומינך תִּסְתַּיֵּים שמעתתא this tradition will be named from myself and from thee.—2) *to be concluded, proved*. Sabb. 31ᵇ תסתיים דר׳ וכ׳ it can be conclusively proved that it was R. .. who said &c.; תסתיים it is proved.

סוּם II (or סָמַם) (preced.) [*to tie up the eye*,] *to blind; to be blind*.—V. סמי, סַמְיָא I.

Nif. נִסּוֹם, נָסוֹם *to be blinded.* Taan. 21ª עיני.. יִסּוֹמוּ (or יִסּוֹמוּ) may my eyes.. become blind.—V. סָמָא.

סום ch. same; *Pa.* סַיֵּים *to blind.* Targ. Cant. V, 7.—V. סְמִי.

סוּמָא I m. (preced.) *blind, blind man.* Ḥag. I, 1. Ib. 2ª ס׳ באחת מעיניו blind in one eye. Taan. 21ª ס׳ משתי עיניו blind in both eyes. Ex. R. s. 36 פקח וס׳ שהיו וכ׳ a seeing and a blind man that were walking &c. B. Bath. 12ᵇ; Nidd. 20ᵇ כס׳ בארובה, v. אֲרוּבָּה; a. fr.—*Pl.* סוּמִים, סוּמִין. Gen. R. s. 53 בשעה ... הרבה ס׳ נתפתחו when Sarah was remembered, many childless women were remembered with her, ... many blind persons had their eyes opened. Ib. (ref. to Gen. XXI, 19) הכל בחזקת ס׳ עד וכ׳ all men are to be considered as blind, until the Lord opens their eyes. Snh. 34ᵇ שלא בס׳ cannot be performed by blind persons; a. fr.—*Fem.* סוּמָה, סוּמָא. Keth. 17ª הרי.. או ס׳ suppose the bride is lame or blind. Y. Sot. II, end, 18ᵇ הוא סומא היא ס׳ whether he (the husband) be blind, or she, (the law is the same). Ḥull. 139ᵇ; a. fr.—[Ch. סוּמָא. v. סַמְיָא.]

סוּמָא II f. ch. (סום I, cmp. שׁוּמָא) *mark, spot.* Targ. Y. Lev. XIII, 10. Targ. Y. II ib. 2 some ed. (oth. שׁוּמָא). [Targ. O. Num. XXXII, 3 quot. as. Var. by Levita: ס׳ דבית קבורתא וכ׳ (or סִימָא) the mark of the burial place of Moses, h. text שבם ונבו; ed. Amst. and oth. סיעת בית וכ׳; Y. I שירן ובית וכ׳. The entire passage came into Targ. O. by mistake; v. Berl. Mass. p. 60.]

סומבק, v. סִיבַק.

סוּמָה I, v. סוּמָא I.

סוּמָה II pr. n. m. *Sumah.* Num. R. s. 14 ס׳ בר כתבה.

סומוקן, v. סוּמַק.

סומוקריי, v. סְמוֹקְרַיי.

סוֹמֶךְ m. (סָמַךְ) *the pin for attaching the pole to the wagon,* Maim.; [*the ring* (ס) *suspended from the yoke and pulled over the front end of the pole,* R. Hai G. a. Ar.) Kel. XIV, 4.

סוּמְכָא m. (סְמַךְ) *thickness.* Targ. I Kings VII, 26; a. fr.—Ḥull. 55ᵇ בסוּמְכֵיה on the thick part of the milt, opp. קִילְשָׁא. Sabb. 98ª ס׳ דקרש the thickness of each board. Succ. 53ᵇ ס׳ דארעא the thickness of the rind of the earth (beneath which there is water); a. e.

סוּמְכַי, סוּמְכְוָתָא, סוּמְכְוָון f. pl. (סְמַךְ) 1) *approaches* (cmp. Ez. XXIV, 2), *works and troops of siege, forts.* Targ. Ez. XVII, 23. Ib. XXIX, 7 בית ס׳ *fortification.* Ib. XXIV, 5; a. e.—2) *auxiliaries.* Targ. I Kings X, 15; Targ. Jer. XXV, 20, a. e. (h. text הערב). Targ. Nah. III, 9 סוּמְכְוָותִיךְ ed. Lag. (oth. ed. סוּמְכְתָךְ; h. text עצמה).

סוּמְכוֹס pr. n. m. *Sumkhos* (*Symmachos*), a Tannai, pupil of R. Meïr. Erub. 13ᵇ. Ib. III, 1. B. Bath. 73ª; a. fr.—(V. Fr. Darkhé. p. 198.)

סוּמְכְתָא, סוּמְכוּתָא, v. סוּמְכְוָון.

סוּמָנָא m. (סום I; v. סִימָנָא) *mark, balk.*—*Pl.* סוּמָנִין. Targ. Is. XXVIII, 25 (h. text נסמן).

סוּמְפּוֹנְיָה, סוּמְפַּנְ׳, v. סִימְפּוֹנְיָא.

סוּמַק *to be red,* v. סְמַק.

סוּמַק, סוּמְקָא, סוּמַ׳ I m. (=סמק, Saf. of עמק; cmp. עָמוֹק) [*dark,*] *red.* Targ. O. Lev. XIII, 30 (h. text צהב). Targ. O. Gen. XXV, 30 ed. Berl. (v. סִימוּקָא). Targ. Y. Lev. XIII, 24 סוּמַקְתָּא (ed. Amst. סוּמ׳) *red spot;* a. e.—Pes. 25ᵇ, a. e. מאי חזית דדמא דידך ס׳ טפי וכ׳ what reason hast thou to assume that thy blood is redder? may be thy neighbor's blood is redder, i. e. you dare not save your life at the expense of your fellowman's life. Sabb. 134ª האי ינוקא דס׳ an infant that looks red. Gitt. 67ᵇ בישרא ס׳ red meat. B. Mets. 58ᵇ, v. חִיוָּר; a. fr.—Yeb. 64ᵇ יצחק סומקא surname of R. Isaac ben Joseph.—*Pl.* סוּמָקִין, סוּמְקִין, סוּמְקֵי, סוּמ׳. Targ. II Kings III, 22; a. e.—Y. Snh. I, 18ᶜ bot.; Y. R. Hash. II, 58ᵇ top (not סומוקן). Ḥull. 93ᵇ ס׳ שורייקי red veins. Sabb. 147ª חיורי וס׳ white or red garments; a. fr.—*Fem.* סוּמַקְתָּא, סוּמְקָא. Targ. Y. Num. XIX, 2.—Ḥull. 46ᵇ, v. אֲחוּנָא.

סוּמְקָא II m. (preced.) 1) *milt.*—*Pl.* סוּמְקֵי. Gitt. 69ª.—2) *inflammation of the eye.* Y. Ab. Zar. II, 40ᵈ top; Y. Sabb. XIV, 14ᵈ top, v. סַבְּנָה.

סוּמְקִי pr. n. *Sumki,* a fictitious name in a charm formula. Gitt. 69ª.

סומקינו, Pesik. R. s. 29-30 beg., read וּמַקְרִיבוֹ.

סוּמְקָנוּתָא f. (סוּמַק) *redness.* Targ. Prov. XXIII, 29 סוּמְקָנוּת עֵינוֹ (ed. Lag. יורים קנצין, corr. acc., v. יורים).

סוּמַקְתָּא, v. סוּמַק.

סוּמַקְתָּא, סוּמַ׳ pr. n. חקל ס׳ *Red-Field.* Y. Snh. II, 20ᵇ bot.; a. e., v. חֲקַל II.

סוּמָקְתָּי m. (preced. wds.) *red-painter.* B. Bath. 84ª האי שמשא ס׳ הוא the sun paints red.

סון, *Hithpol.* הִסְתּוֹנֵן, v. סְנַן.

סונבא, Pesik. R. s. 29-30 (Var. שינבא) quid?—perh. סִקְבָא (v. סְקַב) *contusion.*

סונדוקרוס, v. סִנְקְתֶּדְרוֹס.

סונטימוס, v. סִינְטוֹמוֹס.

סונטמא, Lev. R. s. 12, quot. in Ar., quid?—perh. סִיפוֹנָא (σίφων) *tube?*

סוּרִיָא f. (v. סַנְיָא II) *evil habit,* (by way of angry antiphrasis) *practice, virtue.* Gen. R. s. 50 אוף הדא ס׳ בישא וכ׳ (Ar. ed. Koh. סניתא) wilt thou introduce also this bad practice (another of your noble virtues)?; Yalk. ib. 84 הדין סוריתא (corr. acc.). [Ar. refers to συνήθεια.]

סוּנְקַתֶּדְרוֹס, סוּנְקְלִיטִיקוֹס, סוּנְקְלִיטוֹס, v. sub סִנְק.

סוּס *to be bright, glad*, v. שׂוּשׂ.

סוּס m. (b. h.; v. Nöld. Mand. Gr. p. 147) *horse*. Pes. 113^b. Succ. 26^b שינת הס׳ the (short) sleep of the horse, v. נְשִׁמָא. Cant. R. to VIII, 9 אם ראית ס׳ פרסי וכ׳ when thou seest the Persian horse (Parthian cavalry) tied &c. Snh. II, 5 על סוּסוֹ on the king's horse; a. fr.—[Gen. R. s. 95, end הס׳ לקבלי (read: לקבלך) the horse is before thee (has been surrendered), v. בּוּצְלָא.]—*Pl.* סוּסִים, סוּסִין. Snh. II, 4. Ib. 21^b ס׳ הבבלנין, v. בַּבְלָן; a. fr.—Cant. R. to I, 9 ס׳ נקבות mares.—*Fem.* סוּסָה. Ib. Pirké d'R. El. ch. XLII; סוּסְיָא.—*Pl.* סוּסְיוֹת. Ex. R. s. 23, end ס׳ נקבות, v. supra.

סוּסָא ch. same, v. סוּסְיָא.

סוּסְבִּיל m. a species of *locusts*. Ab. Zar. 37^a, expl. איל קמצא.

סוּסָה, v. סוּס.

סוּסְיָא I b. h., *she-horse*, v. סוּס.

סוּסְיָא c. ch.=h. סוּס. Targ. Ps. XXXII, 9 (Ms. סוּסָא). Ib. XXXIII, 17 סוסא. Targ. O. Ex. XV, 1; a. fr.—Ḥag. 9^b, v. בַּרְזָא II. Snh. 105^b מ״ט לא רכבת (א) ס׳ why didst thou not come riding on horseback?; a. fr.—[Ab. Zar. 4^a דאית ליה ס׳, v. סִיסְיָא.]—*Pl.* סוּסְוָן, סוּסָוָתָא, סוּסָוָן, סוּסִין׳. Targ. Y. Ex. XV, 1. Targ. Gen. XLIX, 17. Targ. Is. XXX, 16 סוסוון ed. Lag. (ed. Wil. סוסותא; some ed. סוּסָוָתָן *our horses*). Targ. Ex. XIV, 23 סוּסַוַת constr.; a. fr.—Cant. R. to I, 9 (ref. to סוסיך Hab. III, 8) [read:] סוסוון סגיין 'horses' in the plural.

***סוּסְיָא** II m. (b. h. סוס or סיס) *swallow*. Targ. Is. XXXVIII, 14 כס׳ דאחיד (h. text כסוס עגור).—[Targ. Jer. VIII, 7 (h. text סיס ועגור) כורכיא וסנוניתא,—from which it would appear that our w. is meant for *horse*.]

סוּסִיתָה, סוּסִיתָא pr. n. pl. *Susitha (Hippos); district of Hippos* (Hippene, Jos. Bell. Jud. III, 3, 1). Tosef. Ohol. XVIII, 4 (gentile towns in Palestine) כגון ס׳ וחבירותיה (Var. סִיסִית) like S. and her sister towns. Tosef. Shebi. IV, 10 תחום סוסיתה Var. ed. Zuck. (ed. ציצית, ציציתה) the district of S.; Y. Dem. II, 22^d top ס׳. Y. Shebi. VI, 36^c bot. ארץ טוב זו ס׳ 'the land of Tob' (Jud. XI, 3) that is the district of S. Ib. VIII, 38^a מן ס׳ לטבריא from S. to Tiberias. Gen. R. s. 31; s. 32 כמן טבריא לסוסיתא (ed. Leipz. לסיסטא; corr. acc.) as the distance (on the Lake of Tiberias) from T. to S. Lev. R. s. 23 כגון.. ס׳ לט׳ as hostile as S. to T.; Cant. R. to II, 2 סוסיתן (corr. acc.); Lam. R. to I, 17; a. e.

***סוּסְכִּינְתָּא** f. (=סכסכ׳; cmp. סִיכָּא I a. סַכִּין) *a cutting pain in the bladder, stone*. Yeb. 64^b (Ar. סטגנייתא).

סוּסְרִיתָא, v. סִרְסְיָא.

סוּסְרְנָא m. (σισύρνα) *a garment made of goat-skin with the hair on*.—*Pl.* סוּסְרְנַיָּיה. Y. Ned. VII, end, 40^c כגון אילין ס׳ (not סוסרנה) like those garments made of goat-skins (the hair of which is not used for clothing).—V. סִיסְרְנוֹן.

סוּסתא, v. סוּסִיתָא.

סוּעַ, v. סִיעַ. [Targ. O. Lev. XIV, 42 ויסוע some ed., v. שׁוּעַ ch.]

סוֹעָד m., v. סָעַד.

סוֹעֲרָה, סוֹעֲרָא, v. סְעוֹרָא.

סוֹעֲרָה f. (b. h.;=מסוערה, v. סָעַר II) *storm-beaten, restless*. Pesik. R. s. 32; Yalk. Is. 339 ס׳ מיסערתא וכ׳ *so'ărah* (Is. LIV, 11) means *stirred up*, for the nations have stirred her (Israel) up (with ref. to Ps. CXXXVII, 7). [Pesik. R. l. c. ס׳ מן חמצית, read, with Yalk. l. c., עֲנִיָּיה.]

סוֹעֲרָן, v. סְעוֹרְנָא.

סוּף I m. (b. h.; v. סוּף II) *reed, bulrush*.—ים ס׳ *the sea of Suf* (Red Sea). Sot. 12^a sq. (ref. to בסוף, Ex. II, 3) ר״א אומר ים ס׳ וכ׳ R. E. says, that means the sea; R. S. says, it means *ăgam* (v. אֲגַם II, 2); Ex. R. s. 1. Ib. s. 22 קריעת ים ס׳ the splitting of the Red Sea (for the passage of the Israelites); Y. Ber. I, 3^d bot.; a. fr.

סוּף ch. same, only with יַם, יַמָּא. Targ. Ex. XIII, 18. Targ. Jon. II, 6; a. fr.

סוּף II (b. h.) *to cut; to be cut off; to end*. Tanḥ. B'resh. 12 וסָפַת הטובים וכ׳ and destroys the good and the bad.

Pi. סִיֵּיף *to cut, diminish; to exterminate* (corresp. to b. h. כִּלָּה). Gen. R. s. 100 מי יכול לסַיֵּיף וכ׳ who can annihilate the dust? ... the beasts of the field? &c. Ib. s. 42 מה אתה חילך ומְסַיֵּיף את עצמך וכ׳ Var. in Yalk. ib. 73 for מסרס (ed. מסיים) why wilt thou reduce (weaken) thyself among thy enemies? (v. Tanḥ. Vayera 3).—*Part. pass.* מְסוּיָּיף (denom. of סוֹף); f. *pl.* מְסוּיָּיפוֹת *left to the end, ripening late*; opp. בְּכוּרָה, בָּכִּיר. Y. Dem. I, beg. 21^c חבכירות והכס׳ (Tosef. ib. I, 3 חבכורות והסייפות). Y. Shebi. IV, end, 35^c; a. fr.

Nithpa. נִסְתַּיֵּיף *to be late in ripening, to be left on the tree beyond cutting time*. Y. Dem. I, beg., 21^c נִסְתַּיְּיפוּ וכ׳, v. סוֹף a. סוֹפֵת.

סוּף ch. same, 1) *to finish; to destroy*. Targ. Y. II Num. XXXIII, 52 תְּסוּפוּן (Y. I תְּסָפוּן a. תְּסַיְּיפוּן). Targ. Lam. IV, 11; a. e.—2) *to cease*. Targ. Is. XIV, 4. Targ. Lev. XXVI, 20. Targ. Prov. II, 22; a. fr.—Part. סַיֵּיף. Ib. XI, 31; a. e.—Koh. R. to X, 15 מבינר.. סָפַת וכ׳ between the two (disputing) that unfortunate woman (Jephthah's daughter) perished; Lev. R. s. 37, end בין דין לדין ספת וכ׳ (some ed. נספת, corr. acc.).

Pa. סַיֵּיף *to finish; to consume, ruin*. Targ. Y. Gen. XLIV, 12 Ar. (ed. פסק). Targ. Y. Lev. XIX, 9. Ib. XXVI, 16; a. e.—Part. pass. מְסַיַּיף. Targ. I Kings XIV, 10.—Yalk. Gen. 133 סַיֵּיפַת, v. סוּב.

Af. אַסֵּיף, אָסֵיף same. Targ. O. Deut. XXXII, 22 (ed. Berl. אַסִּ׳; ed. Vien. אָסֵ׳; h. text אכלת). Ib. 23 (h. text אספה). Targ. Zeph. I, 3; a. fr.

סוֹף m. (b. h.; preced.) 1) *end.* Yeb. XVI, 4 (121^a) מים.. שאין לחם ס׳ waters without end (the shores of which you cannot see from all sides). Ned. 62^a וס׳ הכבוד לבא and honor will finally come of itself. Gen. R. s. 71, beg. (ref. to Ps. LXIX, 34) לא ראשו.. סופו ולא סופו ראשו the first clause of this verse does not correspond (in syntactical construction) to its final clause &c. Sifra K'dosh. ch. III, Par. 2 אם גנבת סופך לכחש וכ׳ if thou stealest, thou wilt finally deny &c. Kidd. 31^a מס׳ דברך, v. נבר. Meg. 7^a בתחלה קבעוה בשושן ולבסוף וכ׳ at first they established it (the festival of Purim) in Shushan, and then for the whole (Jewish) world; a. v. fr.—לא ס׳ דבר אלא... this is not the end of it ...., but. Gen. R. s. 38 (ref. to Prov. XVII, 13) לא ס׳ ר׳ משיב וכ׳ after all, not only he who requites evil for good, but even he who requites evil for evil &c. Y. Shebi. III, end, 34^d; a. fr.—2) *remnant*, esp. *pl.* סופין *fruit remaining on the tree after harvest time, late fruit.* Y. Yeb. XII, 12^d bot. קידש בגופו של ס׳ (prob. to be read בנופו) if one betrothed a woman, giving as a consideration a branch of a tree of his containing remainders (mostly worthless). Pes. 6^b סופי... ומשמר וכ׳ if there are in a man's field late figs, but he watches his field for the sake of the grapes; v. סופת.—[Tosef. Kel. B. Mets. II, 8 סופין ed. Zolk., read: סובין.]

סוֹפָא, סוֹף ch. same. Targ. Job XXVIII, 3; a. fr.—Y. Snh. X, 29^a bot. ידתא סופיה וכ׳, v. חנק. Ab. Zar. 41^a מעיקרא... ולבס׳ וכ׳ at first ..., but finally &c.; a. fr.

סוּפְגָּנִין, סוּפְגָּנִים m. pl. (ספוג) *cakes made of spongy dough*, a sort of *crackers.* Ḥall. I, 4, expl. Y. ib. 57^d טריקבא. Ḥall. l. c. 5 תחלתה עיסה וסופה ס׳ if his first intention was to make regular dough (for bread), and then it was changed for crackers. Y. l. c. ס׳ שנעשו באור crackers baked over fire, opp. בחמה baked in the sun. Kel. V, 8; a. fr.

סוּפְדָא, v. ספדא.

סופיינוס, Y. Ber. IX, 13^a bot. מן דס׳; Yalk. Joel 537 מן דסופיינוס אנא, read דאספסיינוס, I am a follower of Vespasian; cmp. אספסיאני.

סוֹפִינָא, סו׳ m. (v. סוף) *metal spike at the butt-end of the spear* (v. Sm. Ant. s. v. Hasta). Targ. II Sam. XXI, 16 (h. text קין).—**Pl.* (in Hebr. dict.) סופיני. Tosef. Kel. B. Mets. V, 6 תלוי זיני וס׳ ed. Zolk. (ed. Zuck. ספטני) the handles of weapons and spikes.

סוֹפִיסְטִיס, ...טָה, סוֹפִיסְטָא m. (σοφίστης, sophista) *sophist*, teacher of grammar, rhetoric, mathematics &c., esp. *arithmetician.* Y. Shebi. IX, 38^d bot. Pesik. R. s. 21 עד מקום שאין ס׳ יכול לחשוב (not טוס ...; some ed. טופ׳, corr. acc.) up to where no arithmetician can count; Pesik. Baḳod., p. 107^b עד מקום שהספיטס וכ׳ (corr. acc.).—*Pl.* סופיסטין. Targ. I Chr. XII, 32.

סוֹפֵיק, v. ספק II, a. סיפוק ch.

סוּפְלֵי m. pl. (ספל, v. ספל) *scrapings*, esp. [*scraped*] *date-stones* used as *fodder* (eventually as fuel). Bets. 21^b. B. Bath. 11^a פירא דס׳ a pit where offal is deposited for fodder. Gitt. 69^b bot. מיא דס׳ water in which date-stones have been soaked; a. e.—[Tosef. Sabb. XV (XVI), 3 סופלי של שמן, v. ספל.]

סופלני, v. סיפלני.

סוּפְנֵי, pr. n. ימא דס׳, ימה של ס׳ *Lake of Sof'ne.* Tosef. B. Kam. VIII, 18; Targ. Y. I Deut. XXXIII, 23 (h. text ים); v. סיבכיי.

סוֹפַפְתָּה pr. n. pl. (?) *Sofafta.* Y. Snh. II, 20^a bot. שמואל דס׳; (Y. Ber. III, 6^b שמעון דתוספת׳).

סוּפֵק, v. ספק II.

סוּפְקָא m. (ספק II, cmp. איספקא) *large wine vessel.* Yalk. Esth. 1048 the Persians had a large goblet ... ומתקרי ס׳ quot. in Levy Talm. Dict. (ed. Frf. a. oth. והוא נקרא פוסקא) which was called *Sufḳa*; (Targ. II Esth. I, 8 פיתקא).

סוּפְקָנָא m. (preced.) *sufficiency.* Targ. Prov. XXVII, 27. Ib. XXV, 16 סופקנך (not הופ׳).

סוֹפֵר m. (b. h.; ספר) 1) *scribe, writer of documents, copyist* of prayers &c. Gitt. VIII, 8 כתב ס׳ גט וכ׳ if the scribe wrote the letter of divorce for the husband and a receipt for the wife &c. Keth. 51^a, a. e. טעות ס׳, v. אחריות. B. Bath. 21^b ס׳ מתא (Ms. M. ספר) town-scribe (libellarius); B. Mets. 109^b top ספר; B. Bath. 21^a ס׳ מתא (some ed. ספר), v. Tosaf. a. l.; (Rashi: *principal of a town-school keeping assistants*, v. infra); a. fr.—2) *a scholarly man*, opp. בור illiterate. Ber. 45^b אחד ס׳ וכ׳ if one is a scholar (knowing the prayers) and the other illiterate.—3) *school teacher, primary teacher.* B. Bath. l. c. ס׳ יהודי a Jewish teacher; ס׳ ארמאי a teacher of secular branches (oth. opin.: a gentile teacher). Ib. ס׳ מתא, v. supra. Tosef. Meg. IV (III), 38 והס׳ מלמד כדרכו but the Bible teacher teaches (these passages) in his usual way; a. fr.—*Pl.* סופרין, סופרים. Gitt. 24^b ס׳ העשויין וכ׳, v. למד. Y. Ḥag. I, 76^c, a. e. ס׳ ומשנים, v. משנים. Ber. l. c. בששניהם ס׳ when both of them are scholarly men (knowing the prayers); a. fr.—Kidd. IV, 13 לא ילמד ס׳ must not be a teacher of primary schools.—מסכת ס׳ *the Treatise Sof'rim*, one of the small treatises attached to the Talmud, containing rules for writing Torah copies; (in Septem Libri &c., ed Kirchheim: מסכת ספר תורה).—Esp. *Sofer, pl. Sof'rim*, title of the scholars of the ante-Tannaic period, beginning with Ezra (v. Ezra VII, 11). Y. Shek. V, beg. 48^c. Kidd. 30^a לפיכך ... ס׳ שהיו סופרים וכ׳ the early scholars were called Sof'rim, because they counted all the letters in the Torah; a. fr.—דברי ס׳ *enactments or interpretations* dating from the Soferic period. Yeb. II, 4 מד׳ ס׳ belonging to the prohibitions ascribed to the Sof'rim. Snh. XI, 3 חומר בד׳ ס׳ וכ׳ disregard of Soferic enactments is more strictly dealt with &c., v. חומר I. Ib. 88^b דבר שעיקרו.. מד׳ ס׳ a law which is founded on the Torah, but the interpretation of which dates from the Soferic period. Tosef. Kidd. V, 21; a. fr.—תקון ס׳, v. תיקון.

סוֹפְרָא, v. סָפַר.

סוֹפֶת f. (v. סוֹף) *late fruit.* Tosef. Maasr. III, 12 ס׳ תאנים וכ׳ (ed. Zuck. אסיפת) if there are figs left on the tree, but he guards his field &c.; v סוֹף.

סוֹפְתְּקָא, v. סִיפְתְּקָא.

סוֹקְווֹסִין, v. סִיקוֹסִים II.

סוּר I (b. h.) 1) *to go around; to turn*; with ל *to turn to, follow*; with מן, מ־, *to turn away*; in gen. [*to turn from the right path,*] *to go astray; to degenerate.* Snh. 21[b] (ref. to Deut. XVII, 17) אני ארבה ולא אָסוּר I (Solomon) will take many wives and yet not go astray. Ber. 19[b], a. fr. לאו דלא תָסוּר the prohibition inplied in the words, 'thou shalt not deviate' (from the decisions of the courts, the interpretations of the Rabbis, Deut. XVII, 11); a. fr.—2) *to pass away, cease.* Num. R. s. 9 (ref. to Am. VI, 7) אותה שעה תָסוּר שמחת הסרוחים at that time shall the joy of the (corrupt) banqueters cease; a. e.

Hif. הֵסִיר 1) *to remove, take off.* Num. R. s. 14 (play on סיר, Ps. LX, 10) וַהֲסִרוֹתִי הצרעת מעליו and I removed the leprosy from him; שהסרותי אותו מן הטביעה whom I removed (saved) from drowning, v. טְבִיעָה I; Num. R. s. 12 הָסֵר הטומאה וכ׳ remove the uncleanness out of thy house; a. e.—2) *to cause to deviate, to corrupt.* Snh. II, 4 (ref. to Deut. XVII, 17) ובלבד שלא יהו מְסִירוֹת את לבו provided they (the wives) do not corrupt his heart; אפי׳ אחת וּמְסִירָה וכ׳ even one wife, if she might corrupt his heart, he must not marry. Kidd. 68[b] (ref. to Deut. VII, 4) לרבות כל הַמְּסִירִים this is to intimate the extension of the prohibition of intermarriage to all nations that might lead astray; Yeb. 23[a]; Ab. Zar. 36[b] הַמְּסִירוֹת.

Hof. הוּסַר *to be removed.* Macc. 5[a] (ref. to סרה Deut. XIX, 16) עד שתּוּסַר גופה של עדות Ar. s. v. זמם (ed. שתסרה) until the testimony itself has been removed (an alibi has been proved).

סוּר ch. same, 1) *to turn*, esp. ס׳ סכינא (v. Hull. 17[b], quot. s. v. מְאַפְּרָא) *to turn the slaughtering knife on all sides, to examine.* Erub. 63[a] רבינא סַר סכינא וכ׳ R. examined the slaughterer's knife (assumed the rabbinical function of superintending the slaughtering) in Babylonia. Hull. 18[a] דלא סר וכ׳ who failed to examine his knife before an authorised scholar.—2) *to go around, visit, superintend*, esp. ס׳ ניכסיה (or ארעיה) *to superintend one's estate, examine, watch laborers* &c.—Part. סָיֵיר. Ib. 105[a] מאן דסייר ניכסיה וכ׳ (Ar. סָאֵיר) he who goes around examining his property every day. Ib. אבא הוה ס׳... ואנא לא סָיַירְנָא וכ׳ my father used to examine his estate twice a day, but I do it only once a day.

Pa. סַיֵּיר same. B. Mets. 76[b], sq. [read:] סַיְּירָהּ לארעיה וכ׳ (v. Rabb. D. S. a. l. note) he visited his fields &c. Gitt. 38[b] דמְסַיְּירֵי וכ׳ Rashi (ed. דסָיְירֵי) those who examine their property on the Sabbath; a. e.—V. סְטַר I.

סוּר II (b. h.) pr. n. שער הס׳ *the gate of Sur*, name of a Temple gate. Y. Erub. V, 22[c].

***סָ־ר** (cmp. צבר, v. סָוָאר) *to pile, arrange.*—Part. pass. סָיוּר; f. סוּרָה; *pl.* סְוּרוֹת. Tosef. B. Bath. III, 6 .. העצים והאבנים ס׳ וכ׳ ed. Zuck. (Var. סוררות, some ed. סוירות, corr. acc.) wood or stones piled up whether for his untilled field (for building) or for his fence; v. סָדַר a. צָבַר.

סוֹר m. (=סאור, v. סְיאוּר) *fermentation, froth, leaven*; trnsf. (cmp. שְׂאוֹר, עִיסָה a. חָמֵץ) *germ, original nature, character.* Snh. 92[b] סוֹרוֹ his haughty nature; [oth. opin.: its (the kiln's) froth], v. מְקַק a. מָרַק. Kidd. 82[a] כל שעסקיו ... סורו רע he who has a business which brings him in contact with women, has bad leaven in him (or else he would not have chosen such a trade). Hor. 13[a] מפני שסוֹרָן רע because they (the mice) are of a mischievous nature. B. Mets. 59[b] the Torah cautions repeatedly against ill-treating the proselyte (גֵּר), מפני שסורו רע because his original character is bad (into which ill treatment might cause him to relapse). Kidd. 17[b] שמא יחזור לסורו lest he (the proselyte) relapse &c., v. קִילְקוּל. Gen. R. s. 70 הויה חוזר לסורו he (Aquila) might have gone back to his evil ways (to heathenism); v. סְיאוּר. Ib. s. 74, end (expl. למקומו, Gen. XXXII, 1) לסורו to his evil manners (sensual pleasures). Cant. R. to II, 5; a. e.—*Pl.* סוֹרִים *degenerate, bad people.* Num. R. s. 3 אפי׳ סוֹרֵיהֶן וכ׳ even the bad among them are charitable; (Midr. Till. to Ps. XCII בּוֹרִים שבהם).

סוֹרָא I (or **סֻרְיָא**) m. name of *a bitter herb.* Pes. 39[a], v. סְוִיס.

סוּרָא II pr. n. pl. *Sura*, 1) a town in Southern Babylonia between the canals, seat of the college founded by Rab. Erub. 8[a]. B. Mets. 67[b], a. e. משבנתא דס׳, v. מַשְׁכַּנְתָּא. B. Bath. 89[a] רב יהודה מס׳; a. fr.—2) ס׳ דפרת *Sura on the Euphrates* (*Soura-Soura*, mod. Surie). M. Kat. 24[b] (v. Neub. Géogr. p. 343, sq.).—[Y. Shebi. VI, 36[d] בסורא, read: כסּוּרְיָא.—Midr. Till. to Ps. XII מס׳ ... למזבן ed. Bub. (oth. ed. מסורתא), prob. to be read: מסּוּרְיָא.]

סוּרָאָה m. (preced.) *of Sura.* Keth. 39[b] בת אבא ס׳ the daughter of Abba of Sura (wife of R. Papa). Ib. 52[b]; a. e.

סוּרְבָּנָא, סוּרְבְנָא, v. סַרְבָּנָא.

סוֹרֶג m. (סָרַג) *lattice-work, Soreg*, name of one of the approaches of the Temple fortification. Midd. II, 3; Yoma 16[a].

סוּרְהֲבָן m. (סַרְהֵב) *rebellious.* Targ. Y. Deut. XXI, 18; 20.—*Pl. fem.* סַרְהֲבָנִין. Targ. Y. Gen. XXVI, 35 (ed. Vien. a. oth. סַרְהֲבִינִין, corr. acc.; Ar. סַרְבָּנִין, v. סַרְבָּנִיתָא).

סוּרְהַבְנוּתָא f. (preced.) *rebelliousness.* Targ. Y. Deut. XXXI, 27.

סוּרְחָא m. (סְרַח II) *overhanging part.* Targ. O. Ex. XXVI, 12 (some ed. סְרִי, סְרִ׳).

סוּרְחָן m. (סָרַח III) *corruption, sin, offense.* Yoma 86[b] יכתוב סוּרְחָנִי let my sin be recorded; Yalk. Ps. 718 סִרְחָנִי. Tanh. Ki Thissa 22 מה סרחני what is my sin?; a. e.—V. סֵרָחוֹן.

סורחנא, סורחן ch. same. Targ. Gen. XXXI, 36. Targ. Job XXXIV, 37; a. fr.—Lev. R. s. 27; a. e.—*Pl.* סורחנין, סורחניא. Targ. Job II, 1 ed. Lag. (oth. ed. סיר׳, סר׳).—Cant. R. to V, 16.

סורחנותא, סורחנתא f. same. Targ. Job XXII, 29 Ms. (ed. סורחנא). Ib. XXXVI, 14 Ms. (Var. Ms. a. ed. טלותה). Targ. Y. Lev. X, 17 סרחת. Targ. Y. Deut. IX, 21 סורחנתך; a. e.

סוריא pr. n. (Συρία) *Syria*, name of several districts situated north-east of Palestine (v. Neub. Géogr. p. 292), sharing in many respects the sanctity of the Holy Land. Ab. Zar. I, 5 ובס׳ וכ׳ but in Syria &c., contrad. to א״י (Palestine) and to חוצה לארץ (v. ארץ). Hall. IV, 11. Shebi. VI, 2; 5, sq. Ohol. XVIII, 7; a. fr.

סוריאל pr. n. *Suriel*, name of an angel. Ber. 51[a] (v. Rabb. D. S. a. l. note 100).

סוריאתא, v. סירתא.

סוריבמין, v. סוריסטין.

סוריגא, סוריגה m. ch.=h. סורג. Meg. Taan. ch. VIII איסתתר ס׳ the Soreg was broken up (v. Graetz Gesch. d. Jud. III[2], p. 420).

סורייקא, סוריקא, v. שורייקא.

סוריסטין (Συριστί) *in the Syrian language*; מישמע ס׳ (ἐπίστασθαι Σ.) to understand Syrian. Y. Ned. X, 42[a] bot. (not סוריב׳).

סוריקא, v. סורייקא.

סורכייתא, Targ. Y. Gen. XXX, 38, ed. Amst., read: מורכיותא.

סורמקי pr. n. m. *Surmaki* (cmp. סומקי). Yoma 10[a] (Ms. M. סיר׳, v. Rabb. D. S. a. l. note).

סורס m. *Sores* (?), name of a plant (?). Y. Ned. IV, 38[d] top מי ס׳ וכ׳ a solution of S. &c., a spiced drink (perh. סורא?).

סורסי m. (סרס) 1) (cmp. meanings of ἀπόκοπος a. ἀποκοπή) [*castrated*,] לשון ס׳ *aphæresis, dropping of a radical letter*. Mekh. Bo, s. 3; Pes. 61[a]; Y. ib. V, 32[a] bot. expl. תכסו (Ex. XII, 4)=תנכסו, v. כסס. Ex. R. s. 42, end לשון סרדיוטין (corr. acc.), v. משפחה III.—2) (a contemptuous perversion of סוריי) לשון ס׳ *Syrian*, in gen. *Aramæan language*. Sot. 49[b]; B. Kam. 82[b] sq. בא״י ל׳ ס׳ למה וכ׳ what has the Syrian tongue to do in Palestine? Speak either Hebrew or Greek. Y. Sot. VII, 21[c] top לא יהא ל׳ ס׳ קל וכ׳ do not despise the Syrian language, for it is employed in the Torah (Gen. XXXI, 47) &c.; Gen. R. s. 74 פרסי (corr. acc.); Yalk. Gen. 130 פרסי (corr. acc.); (Yalk. Jer. 286; Yalk. Dan. 1060 ארמי). Y. Sot. l. c.; Y. Meg. I, 71[b] bot., v. אילייא; Esth. R. to I, 22 פרסי (corr. acc.).—*Pl.* סורסין *Syrian cakes*. Y. Pes. II, 29[b] bot.; v. סריקין.

סורקין, Tosef. Kel. B. Bath. V, 11 ed. Zuck., v. סירייקון.

סורתא, Midr. Till. to Ps. XII, v. סורא II.

סות* or **סות** f. (b. h.; סות, v. מסוה) *dress, cloak*. Kel. XVI, 7 עושה ס׳ ed. Dehr. (oth. ed. סותות or סותות *pl.*), v. אמום. [Var. in Mish. ed. סיאגום, prob. meant for סאגום =סגוס, as a gloss to our w.; R. S. to Kel. l. c. שיאגות, Var. סבאות; Hai G. סאיכות, Var. סיאות.]

סות or **סית**, *Hif.* הסית, v. יסת.

סותה f. (homilet. etymology fr. יסת) *being misled, error*. Tanh. Vayhi 10 (ref. to סותה, Gen. XLIX, 11) אין ס׳ אלא טעות וכ׳ (not סיתו) *suthah* means error, as we read כי יסיתך (Deut. XIII, 7): when an error in law is committed, it shall be washed clean in his (Judah's) borders (by the Sanhedrin); cmp. Gen. R. s. 98, quot. s. v. חור.

סותורייתא, v. סיתורייתא.

סחא, סחה, v. סחי.

סחו f. (b. h. שחו; סחה) *swimming*. Tosef. Succ. III, 6 אבל יעבירנה בס׳ Var. ed. Zuck. (anoth. Var. סחוי; ed. Zuck. סובי, corr. acc.) but one may be able to cross it by swimming.

סחוא ch. same. Targ. Ez. XLVII, 5.

סחוי, v. סחו.

סחוס, with art. הס׳, contract. of החסחוס, v. חסחוס.

סחור m. (סחר) *surrounding*; ס׳ ס׳ *all around*. Targ. O. Num. I, 53; a. fr. (v. חזור).—Sabb. 13[a], a. fr. ס׳ ס׳ לכרמא וכ׳, v. נזירא I.

סחורא, סחורתא f. (preced.) 1) *going around, circuit* (cmp. סחר I ch.). Targ. Jer. XIV, 18.—2) *circulation, exchange*. Targ. O. Gen. XXIII, 16 מתקבל ס׳ received as exchange.—3) *trade, traffic; goods*. Ib. XXXIV, 10. Ib. 21 (ed. Berl. סחורתא).—Lam. R. to I, 1 רבתי (חד מאת 8) אי... בהדא ס׳ וכ׳ if I come to you with this ware (shoes), wilt thou sell it for me? Ib. זבין ס׳ דסנדליא he bought an assortment of shoes.

סחורה f. h. (b. h.) same, *traffic; goods*. Pesik. R. s. 10 (play on סחר, Cant. VII, 3) בשעה... הס׳ והשכר היו בעולם when they (the Sanhedrin) were in session, there were traffic and profit in the world. Ab. II, 5 לא כל המרבה בס׳ מחכים not every one that has a large trade obtains wisdom. B. Mets. III, 2 כיצד הלה עושה ס׳ וכ׳ how (can this be)? Shall this man traffic with his neighbor's cow? Sifré Num. 23 שומע אני מסחורתו ומרפואתו I might understand, that the Nazarite must abstain from trading in wine or using it as external medicine; Num. R. s. 10. Ab. VI במיעוט ס׳ by contentment with small business; a. fr.

סחורתא, סחורתא, v. סחורא.

סחותא, v. סחיתא.—[Y. Shek. VI, 50[a] top, Bab. ed. Ms. M. סחותא, read: סחוונא, v. סחייא.]

סָחַט (b. h. שָׂחַט) *to press out, wring, cause to flow.* Sabb. XXII, 1 אין סוֹחֲטִין וכ׳ you must not press fruits (on the Sabbath) for the sake of the juice. Ib. 144ᵇ הוו סוחטין ברימונים they squeezed pomegranates. Y. ib. X, 10ᶜ top הסוֹחֵט והמכבס מלאכה וכ׳ wringing clothes and washing are in the same category of labor. Bets. 3ᵃ שמא יִסְחוֹט lest he may squeeze (fruit); a. fr.—Hull. 27ᵃ א״ת וְשָׁחַט אלא וְסָחַט וכ׳ read not (Lev. I, 5) *v'shaḥaṭ* (and he shall cut), but *v'saḥaṭ* (and he shall get the blood out) &c., v. חָטָא I.

סְחַט ch. same, *to absorb.* B. Mets. 114ᵇ ס׳ גלימא ריחא his cloak had absorbed the scent (of Paradise; Ms. F. סַחְטֵיה לגלימיה he wrung his cloak out; v. Rabb. D. S. a. l. note 60); Yalk. Lev. 675 ס׳ גלימיה ריחה.

סְחָא, סְחֵי 1) (b. h. שָׂחָה) *to swim.* Part. סָחֵי; f. סַחְיָא. Targ. Y. Gen. VII, 18.—Y. Sabb. VII, 10ᵃ bot. הוּתְךָ דסָ׳ וכ׳ swimming (on the Sabbath).—2) (=h. סָחָה, v. Ez. XXVI, 4) [*to scrape, sweep,*] *to wash, bathe.* Targ. Lev. XIV, 8; a. fr.—Y. l. c. עאל מִיסְחֵי וכ׳ went bathing with &c. Bab. ib. 141ᵃ מאן דסָחֵי במיא וכ׳ he who bathes in the river &c. Y. Pes. X, beg. 37ᵇ סְחָה וצחא had taken a bath and was thirsty. Y. Ter. VII, end, 46ᶜ סְחוֹן וכ׳ take ye a bath, for your Creator will help you &c. Ib. עד דאינון סַחְיָין until they shall have taken a bath. Ruth R. to II, 19 נחתון מִסְחֵי וכ׳ (not מסחו) they went down to bathe &c.; a. fr.

Pa. אַסְחֵי *to wash, cleanse, bathe.* Targ. Job IX, 30 (Ms. אשתזיג, v. שְׁזַג). Targ. Lev. XIV, 9 (not וִיסְחֵי); a. fr.—Ruth R. l. c. כי קדמין מְסַחְיָין יתיה (or מְסַחְיִן) when they were washing his body. Lev. R. s. 28 עאל אַסְחֵיה (not אסחי) he went in and scoured him (Mordecai); a. e.

סְחִיטָה f. (סָחַט) *pressing, wringing.* Sabb. 144ᵃ בני ס׳ fruits designated to be pressed (for the juice). Y. ib. VII, 10ᶜ top הצבעים .. עושים ס׳ מלאכה וכ׳ the dyers in Jerusalem made the wringing (of dyed clothes) a special work; a. e.

סַחְיָיא or **סַיְיחָא** m. (סְחֵי or סוּחַ) *swimmer.* Yoma 77ᵇ שכן קורין לשייטא סיי׳ ed. (Ms. M. שַׁיָּיחָה; Ms. M. 2 סַחְוָא; Ar. סוודי) for the swimmer is called *s.*; Yalk. Ez. 381 שַׁחְיָיא; Y. Shek. VI, 50ᵃ top שַׁחְיָינָא (Bab. ed. שַׁחֲוָנָא; Ms. M. סחותא, read: סַחְיָינָא).

סחינין, Y. Dem. I, 22ᵃ, read: מְחִינִין.

סְחִיפָא m. (סְחַף II) *an inverted vessel,* opp. זְקִיפָא. Pes. 40ᵃ ס׳ שרי (ed. סחיפה; Ms. M. סִיחְפָא) if the grain is roasted in an inverted vessel &c., v. זְקִיפָא I.

סָחוּתָא, סְחִיתָא f. (סְחֵי 2)=b. h. סְחִי, *sweepings, refuse.* Targ. Zeph. I, 17 (ed. Wil. ס׳; Ar. סִיחֲתָא). Targ. Is. V, 25 (Regia סוחי׳; some ed. סִיחָ׳; h. text סוחה).—Sabb. 121ᵇ הוה שדי ס׳ Ar. (ed. רוקא) threw refuse (disgusting matter, cmp. סַחְוָא, before the Resh G'lutha). Y. M. Kat. II, 81ᵈ top והמת הדא איתא ס׳ דביתא וכ׳ (not והמת) a woman swept the refuse out of the house and threw it &c. Lam. R. to I, 15, v. כְּאַתָּא II.

סחן, Y. Snh. X, 29ᵇ top אסחין, v. חָסַן I.

סָחַף (b. h.; cmp. חָפַף II) *to rub, sweep.* Pirkê d'R. El. ch. XIV בעצבון .. סוֹחֵף במעיו על הארץ in the pain of its growth, it (the serpent) shall sweep along (drag itself) with its belly on the ground.—*Part. pass.* סָחוּף, *pl.* סְחוּפִין, סְחוּפִים *swept away, driven about.* Tanḥ. P'kudê 3 like a dog שהוא ס׳ וכ׳ (some ed. חשוף, חצוף) that is pushed this way and that way. Yeb. 47ᵃ דוויים דחופים ס׳ ומטורפין broken down, pushed about, swept (from place to place) and tossed about; [Rashi: *covered* in mourning, v. חָפָה a. חָפַף I]. Yalk. Ps. 735, v. סָבַךְ.

Nithpa. נִסְתַּחֵף *to be swept, be inundated, ruined by a flood.* Keth. I, 6 (12ᵇ) נִסְתַּחֲפָה שדך (Y. a. Bab. ed. שדהו, euphemism) thy field has been ruined, i. e. it is thy misfortune, and I cannot be made to suffer for it. Ib. 2ᵃ נ׳ שדהו it is thy misfortune (that I was taken sick). Ib. VII, 8 האב ... ונ׳ שדהו the father has to bring evidence that these blemishes arose while she was betrothed and therefore it was his (the husband's) misfortune; a. e.

Nif. נִסְחַף *to be swept away, struck down*; (homilet. =נספח) *to be smitten with leprosy* (v. סַפַּחַת). Tanḥ. Thazr. 11; Yalk. Kings 229; Zech. 586 (interpret. נסחף, Jer. XLVI, 15); Yalk. Lev. 555.

סְחַף I ch. same, *to sweep away; to reject, despise.* Targ. Prov. III, 34. Ib. X, 3 (h. text יהדף).—*Part.* pass. סְחִיף *hurried.* Targ. Esth. VIII, 14 (h. text דחוף).

Ithpe. אִסְתְּחֵף *to be swept away; to be inundated, ruined.* Targ. Prov. XIV, 32 (h. text ידחה). Targ. Y. I Gen. XLIX, 4.

סְחַף II (v. חפף I) *to put on as a cover, to tilt over, invert.* Snh. 104ᵃ אוכלא (אובלא) .. ס׳ ארישיה he inverted a fuller's trough over his head. Ned. 51ᵃ וסַחְפֵיה על רישיה and tilted it over &c. Sabb. 110ᵃ ולִיסְחוֹף דיקולא ארישיה (Ms. M. incorr. וליחטוף) and let him put a basket over his head. Ib. 121ᵇ. Hull. 8ᵇ לא ליס׳ ... בפלי וכ׳ one must not cover up meat with groins; a. e.—Part. pass. סְחִיף; f. סְחִיפָא. Ab. Zar. 51ᵇ, v. מְשִׁירְקָא. Hag. 15ᵃ כתרי כסי דסְחִיפֵי אהדדי (Rashi דסחופין, read: דסחי׳) like two cups inverted one over the other.—V. סְחִיפָא.

סָחַק, v. שָׁחַק.

סָחַר (b. h.) *to go around; esp. to travel as a merchant.*—[Num. R. s. 13 אינה סוחרת, read, as Yalk. Lev. 554, a. Yalk. Prov. 959 סוֹחַתַת, v. סָרַח III.]—Denom. סוֹחֵר.

סְחַר ch. same, 1) *to go around, turn* (corresp. to h. סָבַב). Targ. Koh. XII, 5. Targ. Cant. III, 2 (ed. Vien. *Af.*); a. fr. (V. *Af.*).—2) *to trade.* Gen. R. s. 52 אזלת .. סְחַרְת בה וכ׳ thou wentest to Egypt and tradedst with her (Sarah), thou hast come here and tradest with her.

Pa. סַחַר *to go around.* Targ. Koh. l. c. Targ. Lam. I, 6.

Af. אַסְחַר 1) *to surround, enclose.* Targ. Josh. VI, 3; 11; 14 (interch. with Pe.); a. fr.—2) *to go about.* Targ. II Chr. XVII, 9.—3) *to lead about, to move.* Targ. O. Ex. XIII, 18. Targ. I Sam. V, 8; a. fr.—4) (cmp. סָבַב *Hif.*) *to recline around the table, to dine.* Targ. Ex. XXXII, 6. Targ. I Sam. XX, 5; a. fr.

Ithpa. אִסְתַּחַר, *Ithpe.* אִסְתְּחַר 1) *to turn around, turn to* or *from, to be carried around.* Targ. O. Gen. XLII, 24. Targ. O. Ex. X, 10 (v. Berl. Targ. O. II, p. 22). Targ. O. Num. XXXIV, 4, sq. (some ed. *Pe.*, others *Af.*). Targ. I Sam. V, 8; a. fr.—2) *to be seated at the table.* Targ. Ps. I, 1. Targ. Gen. XXVII, 19.

סַחַר m. *enclosure*, v. סְחַר.

סַחֲרוֹנֵי, v. סַחֲרָנֵי.

סַחֲרָן m. (סְחַר) *travelling merchant.*—*Pl.* סַחֲרָנִים, סַחֲרָנִין. Erub. 55ᵃ; Yalk. Deut. 940.

סַחֲרָנוּתָא, סְחָ׳ f. (סְחַר) *surrounding*; constr. סַחֲרָנוּת (adv.) *in the neighborhood of, round about.* Targ. O. Ex. VII, 24. Targ. Ez. XXXII, 22, sq. (some ed. סַחֲרְתְּהוֹן).

סַחֲרוֹנֵי, סַחֲרָנֵי m. pl. constr. (preced.) *neighborhood, neighbors of.* Targ. Jer. XLVIII, 17. Ib. XXXIII, 13; a. fr.—Sabb. 152ᵃ סחרוני גלידן (Ms. M. סַחֲרָנִיתִי; Ms. O. סַחֲרוֹנוֹתִי), v. גְּלַד.

סַחֲרְתָּא f. *neighborhood*, v. סַחֲרָנוּתָא.—[Tosef. Shebi. IV, 11, v. מְחַרְתָּא.]

סֵט m. (סוּט; cmp. חֲשֵׁט, a. the phrase נטה יד) 1) *handle, that part of a handle which is indispensable in using the tool.* Tosef. Mikv. VI (VII), 21 מִסֵּטָּה ולחוץ beyond the indispensable part of the handle, מס׳ ולפנים within that part.—2) *swinging the forefinger*, v. סִיט.

סְטָא, v. סְטֵי.

סַטְדָּא, (סוֹטְ׳) pr. n. (prob. of Greek origin, cmp. pr. n. Στάδιεύς) *Saṭda*; בן ס׳ son of S., surname of Jesus of Nazareth. Sabb. 104ᵇ; Tosef. ib. XI (XII), 15; Y. ib. XII, end, 13ᵈ והלא בן ס׳ לא הביא וכ׳ but did not Ben S. bring sorcery from Egypt only in this way (by making incisions in his flesh)? Y. Snh. VII, 25ᵈ top כך עשו לבן סוט׳ וכ׳ so they did to Ben S. in Lydda, when they made two scholars lie in wait for him &c.; Y. Yeb. XVI, 15ᵈ bot. Sabb. l. c. (in editions not controlled by censors, v. Rabb. D. S. a. l.) בעל ס׳ בועל וכ׳ her husband's name was S., her lover's, Pandera; (refuted and changed) אמו ס׳ וכ׳ his mother's name was S.... סְטַת דא וכ׳ this one deserted her husband; Snh. 67ᵃ סְטַת דא וכ׳ (v. Rabb. D. S. a. l. note).

סְטוּמְתָא, v. סִיטוּמְתָא.

סְטוּתָא f. (סְטֵי) *aberration, madness.* Targ. Koh. II, 15 (ed. Vien. סטו׳).

סַטְטְיוֹנָר m. (stationarius) *station-master, police officer.* Gen. R. s. 26 הקב״ה עושה... ס׳ שלהם the Lord will make the angel of death their (the nations') officer (in the place of tyrants like Pharaoh &c.); ['Rashi': מיטוטר, v. מִיטְטוֹר;] Yalk. Is. 295 אִסְטַטְיוֹ׳. Ex. R. s. 51 ס׳ בראתיך וכ׳ I have created thee (the angel of death) a *stationarius* for &c.—*Pl.* סַטַטְיוֹנָרִין, אִסְטַ׳, אִיסְטַ׳. Cant. R. to VII, 1 (not רין...), v. אִיסְטַטְיוֹן.

סטיטירין, סטטירין, v. לִיסְטֵירִין.

סְטָה, סטי (b. h. שָׂטָה; v. נָטָה) *to deviate, to turn to* or *from.* Koh. R. to I, 16 הלב סוֹטֶה the heart deviates (turns to evil).—Esp. (of woman) *to be faithless.* Y. Sot. II, 18ᵇ top; Y. Kidd. I, 60ᵈ אמן שלא סָטִיתִי ארוסה וכ׳ 'Amen', that I have not been faithless as a betrothed, as a married woman &c.—V. סוֹטָה.

סְטָא, סְטֵי ch. 1) same (corresp. to b. h. נָטָה). Targ. Gen. XXXVIII, 1; 16 (h. text ויט); a. fr.—Esp. *to deviate from the right path, to go astray; to be faithless.* Targ. Num. V, 12 (h. text תשטה); a. fr.—Sabb. 104ᵇ סַטְיַת; Snh. 67ᵃ סְטַת, v. סַטְדָּא.—2) (of the mind) *to wander, be mad* (cmp. h. שָׁטָה). Targ. Koh. II, 15 סטא ed. Lag. (ed. Vien. סַט, v. סוּט).—*Part.* סָטֵי; f. סָטְיָא; *pl.* סָטְיָין, סָטַיִן a) (of the mind) *distracted.* Targ. I Kings XXI, 5 (h. text סרה).—b) *inclining.* Targ. Y. Ex. XXIII, 2 (h. text לנטות).—c) *deviating from the right path, rebellious.* Targ. O. Deut. XXI, 18; 20 (h. text סורר). Targ. Jer. V, 23. Targ. Ps. CI, 3 Ms. (ed. שָׂטִין, ed. Wil. שָׂ׳). Ib. CXXV, 5; a. fr.

Af. אַסְטֵי 1) *to turn (one's own way), to deviate.* Targ. Prov. XIV, 27 (h. text סור).—2) *to turn, direct.* Targ. O. Num. XXII, 23 (h. text להטות); a. fr.—Esp. א׳ דינא *to divert justice; to oppress.* Targ. Is. XXIX, 21; a. fr.—V. מַסְטֵי.

סַטְיָא f. (preced.) *deviation, revolt.* Targ. Deut. XIX, 16 (h. text סָרָה). Ib. XIII, 6; a. fr.

סְטִיבָס m. (στιβάς) *straw-mattress.* Tosef. Sabb. XIII (XIV), 15 לווחין של יסטיבס (Var. סקיבס, יסטבס) the boards on which the straw rests; Y. ib. XII, beg. 13ᶜ ספינה (corr. acc.); Bab. ib. 47ᵃ סקיבס (Ms. M. סקבין; Ms. O. סקיבוס; v. Rabb. D. S. a. l. note). Tosef. Kel. B. Mets. VIII, 4 סטיבס (corr. acc.; R. S. to Kel. XVIII, 3 סקבס). [The phonetic corrupt. of ט into ק in the Babylonian Talmud has been reimported as Variant into Tosefta.—For the phonetic relationship between *t* and *k*, cmp. Lidd.-Scott. Gr. Dict. sub lit. K.]

סְטֵיו m. = אִיסְטֵיו, *colonnade.* Y. Succ. V, 55ᵃ bot.; Y. Taan. III. 66ᵈ bot. אסטיו לפנים מס׳ a colonnade within a colonnade; Pes. 13ᵇ ס׳ כפול = ס׳ לפנים מס׳; ib. 52ᵇ; Succ. 45ᵃ; Tosef. ib. IV, 6. Tosef. Sabb. X (XI), 1 דרך ס׳ וכ׳ through a colonnade into the street. Tosef. M. Kat. II, 13 חנות פתוחה לס׳ a shop having an entrance from a colonnade; a. e.—*Pl.* סְטֵיוִין. Tosef. Kel. B. Mets. II, 8 והסיטיון ed. Zuck. (ed. Zolk. והסטיין, corr. acc.), v. סוֹבִין.—V. אִיסְטֵיב, אִיסְטְבָא.

סְטָיו m. *mosaic pavement.* Targ. Esth. I, 6 (h. רצפה). Targ. Y. Lev. XXVI, 1 סַטְיו.

סטיטירין, v. סטטירין.

סטיין, v. סְטֵיו.

סְטֵים, v. סְטַם.

סְטִיס, סטים, v. אִיסְטְטִיס.

CPSIA information can be obtained
at www.ICGtesting.com
Printed in the USA
BVHW01s2006270118
506493BV00004B/132/P

9 781376 199154